THE URBAN TRANSPORTATION PROBLEM

THE URBAN TRANSPORTATION PROBLEM

J. R. Meyer, J. F. Kain, M. Wohl

Harvard University Press, Cambridge, Massachusetts

Fifth Printing, 1972

Distributed in Great Britain by Oxford University Press, London

Library of Congress Catalog Card Number 65–13848

Printed in the United States of America

Preface

Urban transportation, for a complex set of reasons, has become a major concern of American life and public policy in the mid-twentieth century. It is perhaps an example *par excellence* of the type of problem given priority by a society which has solved many of its more basic economic problems, such as achieving a high general standard of living and eliminating its more obvious or pressing problems of unemployment and poverty. Whatever the cause, it has become increasingly fashionable within the United States to say that "an urban transportation problem" exists and to explore a variety of ways, some quite exotic, to alleviate or eliminate this "problem." It is the purpose of this study, by integrating many diverse but relevant pieces of information, to help focus and expedite more cogent discussions of urban transportation alternatives. In broadest context, an integrated set of data is presented on the forces that affect the demand for and supply of urban transportation services in order to provide a more rational context for decision-making on these problems. The underlying premises are that it should be possible to identify, with reasonable agreement, basic economic and technological forces that are affecting our urban areas and that if this is accomplished it will then be possible to focus discussion on appropriate goals or criteria in setting urban transportation policies. Debate on appropriate goals or criteria in a context of reasonable agreement about basic economic and technological forces should improve decision-making in this area significantly.

This book is one report of many developed as part of a RAND Corporation study of urban transportation problems which started in the summer of 1960. It should be immediately emphasized that this particular study is heavily indebted to the other RAND urban transportation reports for much of its evidence, data, and analyses. Citations of the contributions of these different reports are to be found throughout the text.

The RAND urban transportation study was largely financed by a grant made by the Ford Foundation to The RAND Corporation to undertake an exploratory study of urban transportation. The RAND Corporation has also used its own funds to provide supplementary support needed to bring certain aspects of the program to a conclusion. A primary motivation, to both the Ford Foundation and The RAND Corporation, in undertaking the study was a common concern that in spite of a number of very good studies under way on the particular problems of some of our major metropolitan areas, no one was taking a comprehensive or overall look at the urban transportation problem. It was also believed that RAND was uniquely situated to bring to focus a specialized competence in systems analysis and, in particular, to integrate the skills and disciplines of both social scientists and engineers for the analysis of such problems. The emphasis throughout the RAND study, moreover, was upon the adoption of a longer-range point of view than seemed possible for governmental or industrial units which necessarily must be concerned with immediate operating and policy problems.

In short, the emphasis has been upon the study of basic issues rather than an attempt to solve the particular problems of specific urban areas. That is, the study does not focus directly on whether or not the Bay Area Transportation System for San Francisco is reasonable or on the problems of a National Capital Transportation Agency for Washington D.C. or, for that matter, on the urban transportation problems of any other specific metropolitan area. The assumption was that conclusions or policy prescriptions for these and other cities depend heavily on identification of the underlying forces conditioning the growth and development patterns of all metropolitan areas and that these forces needed exploration and study. Four areas were identified by the RAND group for particularly intensive study: (1) changes in the technology of urban transportation; (2) the changing pattern of land use within our metropolitan areas; (3) trip-making behavior, including the choice of mode; and (4) governmental policy affecting land use and transportation requirements.

It is our belief that the RAND study, as represented by this book and other reports, has made at least some contribution to a better understanding in all of these problem areas. The long-run aim is to achieve a better understanding of urban change and the role transportation plays in this process. While it is our belief that this book has contributed in this regard, much more work is needed before we can feel completely confident when making important decisions in the urban transportation field.

The ultimate goal is to improve urban living, not to eliminate congestion, or maintain investments in real estate or transportation facilities as such. Urban transportation investments use resources that alternatively could be used for educational, health, recreational, or other purposes. It is, therefore, important that we bring all our wisdom together in making these and related decisions.

* * * *

One final note is in order on the question that invariably occurs when a book has been jointly authored: this is, who wrote what. This question can be answered in this particular case only in very sketchy or broad outline for the simple reason that it is not too great an exaggeration to say that virtually every page in this book has in some way or another been affected by the work of each of the three authors. With this qualification in mind, however, it can be asserted that the broad areas of responsibility of each of the three were as follows: Meyer was primarily concerned with establishing the conceptual framework, that is, the hypotheses, and assumed special responsibilities for some of the cost analyses; Wohl was primarily concerned with matters of costing and technology; Kain had the initial responsibility for the empirical materials on basic population, housing, and employment trends. To a rough approximation, therefore, it could be said that the first three chapters were jointly authored by Kain and Meyer; the next four chapters, 4 through 7, represent a rather complete collaboration by all of the authors; chapters 8 through 12, dealing primarily with matters of costing and technology, were drafted by Wohl and Meyer, with Kain contributing importantly to certain specific sections; and the final two chapters were written by Meyer with the aid of the other two authors. Wohl and Meyer shared responsibility for preparation of the appendixes.

Charles Zwick

Member of the Research Council
and Director of the Urban
Transportation Study

The RAND Corporation
Santa Monica, California

Acknowledgments

Needless to say, with an undertaking that has extended over as long a time period as this, and has involved as many complex issues, the debts of the authors to others are quite extensive. In the first instance, much help was derived from the published and unpublished reports of others at RAND who were involved in the urban transportation study. These same people, and colleagues elsewhere, have freely given their time and help in reviewing and analyzing various parts or even the entirety of the manuscript. In this connection we would like to thank A. Scheffer Lang, Charles Warden, Richard Soberman, Edward Tennyson, Thomas Deen, Brian Martin, George Hoffman, Richard Haase, Edward Hearle, John Niedercorn, Ira Lowry, and Anthony Pascal. Very special thanks are due to Pascal, Lowry, and Hearle not only for reading part of the manuscript once but for reading the entire manuscript at two or three different stages of development. Similarly, we were greatly helped in assembling data by the generous assistance of Douglas Carroll, Albert Mayer, and Sue Smock.

Our thanks are also due to a veritable battery of RAND and Harvard secretaries who have borne the burden of typing and correcting this manuscript in its many different forms. In some cases, too, their help has extended well beyond routine duties to aid in coordinating tables, citations, and all of the other details required to put a book in publishable form. In this regard, our debts are particularly extensive to Miss Jean Scully, Mrs. Marina Ochoa, and Miss Claire Gilbert.

Professor Meyer owes a special debt of gratitude to the Ford Foundation for a Faculty Research Fellowship that gave him the time to do much of his portion of the drafting of the manuscript. Similarly, Professor Kain wishes to acknowledge the cooperation of officials at the U.S. Air Force Academy; they made it possible for him to continue the drafting of the manuscript while assigned there. Special thanks in this regard are due to Col. Wayne A. Yeoman, Chairman, Department of Economics, Air Force Academy.

Contents

Tables

Figures

Chapter 1 | A Problem in Search of a Solution

There is no doubt that Americans are becoming an urban people, with the consequence that urban problems, especially of transportation, have received considerable popular attention in recent years. Articles on these matters abound in both learned and popular journals. Attempts, thus far unsuccessful, have been made to establish a Department of Urban Affairs within the Federal Government. President Kennedy, in a major policy message to Congress, stated, "Our national welfare . . . requires the provision for good urban transportation with the proper use of private vehicles and modern mass transport to help shape, as well as serve, urban growth . . ."[1]

Alvin H. Hansen, a prominent economist with great experience in matters of public policy, in assessing the economic issues and problems of the 1960's and 1970's, has concluded:

> Inflation, I think, is not the most important of these. We may well experience an upward drift in prices in these two decades, but it is not likely to become a serious problem . . . Nor is the highly important problem of adequate aggregate demand likely to be the most important problem . . . What then is the most important economic problem which will confront the United States in the next 20 years? It is, I believe, the problem created by the sweeping increase in urbanization.[2]

Another economist, J. K. Galbraith, has expressed similar sentiments and has generalized his concern in a "Theory of Social Balance," in which he concludes that our affluent society has largely solved the problems of production and of wealth creation, but has failed signally in its allocation of final output as between "the supply of privately produced goods and

[1] President John F. Kennedy's message to Congress on transportation, April 6, 1962.

[2] Alvin H. Hansen, *Economic Issues of the 1960's* (McGraw-Hill, New York, 1960), pp. 181–182.

services and those of the State."[3] Nearly all of Galbraith's examples of underprovided, publicly produced goods are urban services: parks, playgrounds, urban highways, transit, and the like.[4]

The sheer variety of needed urban services reflects the fact that the sources of urban problems are much more complex than, let us say, a clear-cut inadequacy of transportation facilities. Many other forces are at work. The most obvious is shifting population patterns. Populations within most central cities have declined or barely remained stable within recent years while in suburbia and exurbia, populations have grown phenomenally. This outward migration has been aided and abetted by a similar migration of job opportunities, especially in retailing and in industry. Central cities have found this trend all the more damaging because the wealthy are reputedly more prone to migrate outward than the poor. Domestic problems of widespread concern, such as rising welfare rolls, prolonged unemployment among unskilled and minority groups, and racial barriers in education, housing, and public facilities, have all been more obvious, if not more acute, in urban areas.

Needless to say, the erosion of city tax bases occasioned by departure of commerce and industry has intensified urban problems; ironically, at the very time suburban growth has sapped much of the financial strength of the central cities, the rapid growth of suburbs is increasing the demands for certain urban amenities normally furnished by central cities. Archaic political institutions and boundaries further intensify these problems. In a very real sense, suburbanization often enables a portion of society to escape burdensome social responsibilities, including that of paying for certain amenities they often continue to consume.

It should therefore be immediately recognized that transportation improvements often represent an indirect attack, at best, on the more basic problems of cities. Nonetheless, it is a common belief that such improvements will help solve or ameliorate even the knottier urban problems. As President Kennedy said, urban transport is "to help shape, as well as serve urban growth." Apparently much hope is attached to the therapeutic value of urban transportation improvements because they constitute one facet of the general urban problem on which there is some possibility of action. Other basic problems are so intrinsically complex and politically explosive as to defy easy analysis or solution.

[3] John Kenneth Galbraith, *The Affluent Society* (Houghton-Mifflin, Boston, 1958, especially chap. XVIII).

[4] Several years ago when the CED asked a panel of fifty noted academicians, "What is the most important economic problem to be faced by the United States in the next twenty years?" six responded with an urban problem. (Committee for Economic Development, *Problems of United States Economic Development,* New York, 1958.)

Whether or not based on false hopes or wishful thinking, proposals now abound for improving urban transportation facilities. These plans take a variety of forms but commonly involve considerable investment in new public transit facilities, usually specialized rail rapid transit, or subsidization of existing mass transit to allow service improvements aimed at making such facilities more attractive. What are described as conservative estimates place the next decade's capital requirements for mass transportation at nearly $10 billion.[5] While of somewhat different character, serving freight as well as passenger transport needs, the costs of urban highways are indicated by the estimated $18 to $25 billion capital cost of the urban portion of the 41,000-mile Interstate System.

Capacity expansions of urban transit are usually supported by several interrelated arguments. One is that any kind of highway solution is simply too costly and that rail rapid transit, while expensive, still is cheaper and more efficient. Most new transit plans assume not only that decline in transit use will be halted, but additionally assume it will be reversed by diversion of automobile commuters to the new facilities.

A second argument is basically aesthetic. It asserts that postwar low-density urban development is attributable to private automobiles and heavy subsidization of urban highway programs; that the resultant pattern of urban development is wasteful and inherently undesirable; and that rail transit should be used as a tool in reshaping urban areas toward a more orderly and better form of urban development.

Still another argument offered in support of transit investments or subsidies involves what might be called the "vicious circle" explanation of the decline in transit ridership. That is, reductions in transit usage lead to reductions in transit service levels, and these, in turn, lead to further declines in service, and so on. According to many who adopt this "vicious circle" theory, subsidies or investments to improve transit service levels are justified because they will establish a new service-usage equilibrium at which the improved transit system will become self-sustaining or operate with only a small subsidy. Finally, at least part of the support for undertaking extensive urban transportation investments derives from a humane desire in many to do something, or anything, to help alleviate the serious problems that they believe increasingly afflict American cities.

These arguments clearly embody a number of implicit hypotheses that are susceptible to empirical testing, among them being: that urban transportation is in a "mess" which is steadily worsening, at least qualitatively; that the decline in city populations and densities is largely attributable to

[5] Institute of Public Administration, *Urban Transportation and Public Policy: Report to the Department of Commerce and the Housing and Home Finance Agency,* December 1961.

the lack of good, or at least up-to-date, mass transit facilities; that rail transit is probably cheaper than highway mass transit and certainly cheaper than private auto travel in urban areas; that people will ride transit if it is available at a decent level of service and a reasonable price (or, in the jargon of the economist, the service and price cross-elasticities of demand between transit and private auto travel are substantial); and that the type of urban transportation available is a very important factor in shaping the aesthetic character and form of a city.

A major concern of this book is to test such hypotheses empirically. Also attempted will be the formulation and testing of a series of more fundamental hypotheses about the behavior, economic and social, that shapes American cities. A statement of these hypotheses, combined with a qualitative evaluation of the underlying behavioral factors, is the principal focus of chapter 2. Chapters 3 through 7 present empirical material relevant to testing these hypotheses, as well as the hypotheses suggested by the justifications just proffered for large urban transportation investments. Chapter 3 is primarily concerned with empirically measuring the grosser dimensions of recent urban growth. Chapter 4 focuses on the supply and financing of urban transport, while chapter 5 is concerned with demand characteristics. In chapters 6 and 7 hypotheses relating to the interactions between housing and transport choices are tested, with chapter 7 emphasizing the possible effect of racial discrimination on these choices.

Throughout these first chapters the concern is with hypotheses and their testing. The assertion of the hypotheses has been largely kept separate from and antecedent to the empirical tests, following the sequence of the actual research undertaking. Because of this organization of the material, however, those unfamiliar with the field or the data often may find it helpful to read the summaries attached to the end of each chapter before reading the chapters themselves. Together, chapters 2 through 7 constitute part I of this study, "The Context of Urban Change," and are essentially concerned with describing the environment within which urban transportation systems and policies must operate.

Part II, by contrast, focuses exclusively on cost analyses; that is, the development of procedures and figures for more accurately evaluating the relative costs and efficiency of different modes available for performing urban transportation functions. Finally, in part III, "Solutions and Public Policy," the implications of these different empirical and cost findings are developed for policy formulation and planning. Part III also contains an evaluation of some alternative, newer, and somewhat less conventional technologies as means of meeting urban transportation requirements; in addition, some suggestions are made as to where research expenditures on urban transportation might be most productive. Thus, in broadest outline, this book is concerned with determining whether the hopes for reform and improvement attached to urban transportation understakings are justified; whether the most economical means are being selected to achieve stipulated objectives; and whether other, better alternatives, are available for reaching these same goals.

Before proceeding it should be noted that the primary focus is on the problem of moving *passengers* into and out of cities during the peak or rush hours, occurring mornings and afternoons of workdays. It is these movements that tax the capacity of existing urban transport facilities and create the congestion and delays that most people associate with what has come to be known, for better or worse, as "the urban transportation problem." Intracity freight movements and passenger trips at other times of the day or week can and do create important problems but these are almost always of second-order importance.

PART I | THE CONTEXT OF URBAN CHANGE

Chapter 2 | Economic Change and the City: A Qualitative Evaluation and Some Hypotheses

Information, particularly qualitative information, is by no means lacking on the basic processes that shape and condition urban growth and determine the dimensions of the urban transportation problem.[1] As is often

[1] The hypotheses and impressions presented in this chapter have been gathered from several sources. The following are among the more important and suggestive: Benjamin Chinitz, *Freight and the Metropolis* (Harvard University Press, Cambridge, Mass., 1960); William L. Garrison, *et al.* (*Studies of Highway Development and Geographic Change,* published in cooperation with the Bureau of Public Roads of the Department of Commerce and the Washington State Highway Commission [part of the University of Washington Highway Economic Series], University of Washington Press, Seattle, 1959); Harlan W. Gilmore, *Transportation and the Growth of Cities* (The Free Press, Glencoe, Ill., 1963); Charles M. Haar, *Land-Use Planning* (Little, Brown & Co., Boston, 1959); Edgar M. Hoover, *The Location of Economic Activity,* Economic Handbook Series, Seymour E. Harris, ed., McGraw-Hill, New York, 1948); Edgar M. Hoover and Raymond Vernon, *Anatomy of a Metropolis* ([part of the New York Metropolitan Region Study, Raymond Vernon, Director, Max Hall, Editorial Director], Harvard University Press, Cambridge, Mass., 1959); Edgar M. Horwood, *et al., Studies of the Central Business District and Urban Freeway Development* ([part of the University of Washington Highway Economic Studies], University of Washington Press, Seattle, 1959); Homer Hoyt, *One Hundred Years of Land Values in Chicago* (University of Chicago Press, Chicago, 1933); Walter Isard, *Location and Space-Economy* (published jointly by The Technology Press of MIT and John Wiley & Sons, New York, 1956); Richard L. Meier, *Science and Economic Development: New Patterns of Living* (published jointly by the Technology Press of MIT and John Wiley & Sons, New York, 1956); John Meyer, *et al., Economics of Competition in the Transportation Industry* (Harvard University Press, Cambridge, Mass., 1959); Robert B. Mitchell, and Chester Rapkin, *Urban Traffic: A Function of Land Use* (Columbia University Press, New York, 1954); Wilfred Owen, *Cities in the Motor Age* (The Viking Press, New York, 1959); Wilfred Owen, *The Metropolitan Transportation Problem* (The Brookings Institution, Washington, D.C., 1956); Harvey S. Perloff, ed., *Planning and the Urban Community, Essays on Urbanism and City Planning Presented before a Seminar Sponsored by the Joint Committee on Planning and Urban Development of Carnegie Institute of Technology and University of Pittsburgh* (University of Pittsburgh Press, Pittsburgh, Pa., 1961); Princeton University Conference, *Urban Development and Urban Transportation* ([Conference held April 30 and May 1, 1957], Princeton University Press, Princeton, N.J., 1957); Chester Rapkin and Wil-

true in research, demand has created its own supply and there has been a proliferation of studies on the problems and characteristics of the modern American city. Unfortunately, the results have seldom been collated or evaluated for common elements and tendencies; but certain basic patterns are discernible and widely recognized. These, in turn, are the obvious bases upon which to erect a set of working hypotheses about urban growth and transportation requirements.

Before these hypotheses are discussed, however, certain premises must be established. To begin, it is a virtual certainty that the spatial pattern of a city in a free-enterprise society is the collective result of a large number of separate business and household location decisions and transportation choices. These decisions are made in a context of and are influenced by economic, sociological, and technological circumstances, usually beyond the immediate control of the decision-maker. They are also constrained, and to some extent directed by, public policies—zoning ordinances, building codes, transportation policies, and the like. On this premise, the kind, the extent, and the importance of these different determining influences must be known if city structure and changes in it are to be understood.

Qualitative Aspects of Recent Trends in Urban Growth

Probably the most commonly noted tendency in U.S. urban growth is the decline in the relative (and often absolute) importance of the central parts of most urban areas. As noted previously, attempts to arrest this tendency account for much of the public's concern and many specific policy proposals to aid cities. The relative decline of CBD's (central business districts) and central cities[2] is attributable to several important

liam G. Grigsby, *Residential Renewal in the Urban Core,* Institute for Urban Studies (University of Pennsylvania, University of Pennsylvania Press, Philadelphia, Pa., 1960); Richard U. Ratcliff, *Urban Land Economics* (McGraw-Hill, New York, 1949); Lloyd Rodwin, *The Future Metropolis* (George Briziller, New York, 1961); Martin Segal, *Wages in the Metropolis: Their Influence on the Location of Industries in the New York Region* (vol. 4 of the New York Metropolitan Region Study, Harvard University Press, Cambridge, Mass., 1960); Ezra Solomon and Zarka Bibija, *Metropolitan Chicago: An Economic Analysis* (Graduate School of Business, University of Chicago, The Free Press, Glencoe, Ill., 1959); Raymond Vernon, *The Changing Economic Function of the Central City* (Area Development Committee of Committee for Economic Development, New York, January 1959); Raymond Vernon, *Metropolis 1985: An Interpretation of the Findings of the New York Metropolitan Region Study* (vol. 9 of the New York Metropolitan Region Study, Harvard University Press, Cambridge, Mass., 1960); and Robert C. Wood (with V. V. Almendinger), *1400 Governments: The Political Economy of the New York Metropolitan Region* (vol. 8 of the New York Metropolitan Region Study, Harvard University Press, Cambridge, Mass., 1961).

[2] CBD's are usually defined as the high-density commercial and business cores of cities. Central cities are the areas within the incorporated limits of the major cities of metropolitan areas.

technological and economic changes that make decentralization a more possible, more economic, or more desirable choice for an increasing number of household and business decision-makers.

Specifically, both recent and historical developments in transportation and communication technology have had two major impacts on city structure. First, these developments have made different parcels of land increasingly homogeneous for most manufacturing, retailing, wholesaling, residential, and other uses. Second, and in contrast to the first, recent improvements in transportation and communications have simultaneously made it increasingly possible to centralize *control* of management functions at one point in space. The first of these two effects, greater homogeneity of land, works toward decentralization *within* cities while the second, ability to centralize control activities, tends toward greater concentration in particular cities. Specifically, the first effect tends to increase the attractiveness of the outer ring of a metropolitan area as opposed to the core, while the second makes major cities, particularly major commercial, financial, and office centers, more attractive than lesser cities.

To the extent that there are compelling reasons for locating central offices or control activities in downtown areas, the new ability to centralize control functions may partially or even fully offset the effects of decentralizing influences within the city. However, as will be documented more fully in subsequent chapters, with the possible exception of the nation's commercial capital, New York, and Los Angeles, Houston, San Francisco and perhaps one or two other major regional centers, the forces creating growth in CBD's seem slight in comparison with the forces operating toward decentralization.

Increasing homogeneity of land by itself, of course, would generate *absolute* decline of the CBD only if land at the outskirts of a city were both cheaper and at the same time as good a site for activities previously located at the city core. *Relative* decentralization of cities will occur, though, even without actual relocation of existing activities, to the extent that new individuals or businesses find the outskirts technologically as good a location and cheaper than the CBD in terms of land cost (construing these broadly to include adjustment for differences in public and other services). For reasons that will be shortly elaborated, there are also important and compelling reasons why the open land at the edges of a city may be positively advantageous for many activities—and even if land costs per unit were more than at the center of the city. In general, activities that require large blocks of land almost totally free of constraints on noise or fume levels or, more importantly, a need to conform to the block pattern layout of city streets, will find peripheral locations attractive. Urban renewal can often offset these advantages of peripheral land partially, but seldom fully.

The most common cited cause of decentralization, however, has been the combined economic and technological revolution in consumption patterns since the development of the internal combustion engine. The automobile has made it technically feasible for people to live in dispersed residential locations, while rising personal incomes and mass production have made such a development economically possible. The desire, apparent particularly among younger Americans, for single-family dwellings with attached play-yards and lawns historically seems to have been both overwhelming and undeniable, at least as long as per capita incomes continued to rise. The consequence has been what some observers have called "urban sprawl," and the automobile has become one of the villains of modern city planning. In economic parlance, automobiles and suburban living space appear to be complementary superior goods (that is, consumption of one increases with increases in the consumption of the other and consumption of both goes up when per capita income increases).

The rise of suburban living has had an impact, in turn, on the location of retailing and service activities (and accompanying job opportunities) that have traditionally followed their markets. The symbol—sometimes an emotionally charged symbol—of the locational change in these activities is the suburban shopping center surrounded by parking lots for automobiles. Of course, it is really enhanced total purchasing power at the outskirts combined with mobility and flexibility afforded by private automobiles, rather than simple expansion of population, that makes development of satellite shopping areas economically feasible. Accordingly, increasing per capita incomes in suburban areas, as well as the automobile, have contributed to the relative decentralization of some retail activities. As a matter of perspective, it is well to recall that central shopping facilities have always accounted for a smaller proportion of the retailing activity in large American cities than in small ones, the implication being that commercial decentralization is an accompaniment of urban growth *per se*.

The rise of the suburban shopping center also reflects forces other than simple growth in population, auto ownership, and personal income. For one thing, it is a function of changing and improving merchandising techniques. The economies to be gained from grouping the retailing of many products at one location have long been recognized, whether the grouping is done by putting independent stores together in an arcade, or by having single ownership in the form of a supermarket or department store. Even more pertinently from the standpoint of urban transport analysis, starting anew in a suburban location often makes it possible to design retailing areas that are more compatible with modern transportation, warehousing, and distribution technologies than is possible in older downtown sectors. Technological changes of particular importance in this regard have been the replacement of horses and buggies by automobiles; of horsedrawn drays by panel, pick-up, and other small trucks; of stairs by elevators and escalators; of hired delivery by do-it-yourself; and of human labor by fork-lift trucks. Their impact on city design has been to make separation of vehicular and pedestrian traffic much more desirable, if not mandatory, than it was in an age of low vehicular speeds; to reduce the need for wide, horizontal access strips for moving local freight and, in general, the space required for local drayage; to make vertical movement of small freight packages considerably more efficient than in the past; and to decrease the need for large on-site inventories or for warehouses attached directly to the retail store. These factors, taken together with the increased use of private passenger vehicles and their accompanying need for parking space, dictate that an efficient physical layout for retailing will approximate that of a modern suburban shopping center. Indeed, it can be argued with considerable validity (but at the expense of some oversimplification) that the most serious problem of existing CBD's is that they were designed for an outdated set of technological conditions, the most serious single problem being an inadequate separation of truck, private vehicular, and pedestrian traffic.

As implied by earlier remarks about land homogenization, central-city troubles do not start and end with the relocation of residential and retailing sites. Other forces have also been at work eroding the so-called economic base of the city by reducing CBD employment in industrial and other activities. Some of the more important of these technological changes are concerned with the virtual revolution in the intercity transportation of both persons and freight.

Changes in the intercity movement of passengers have been sharply dramatized by the current economic agonies of rail passenger travel. Many who previously traveled by taking a short trip to the downtown area of their city and catching a train, now find it more convenient simply to "hop in" the family automobile and drive directly to their destinations. If they pass through the central area at all, they do so quickly and consume only the services of a downtown traffic policeman or of an urban freeway. For long trips (for example, over 500 miles), particularly business trips, the choice has increasingly been to go by air. For a number of obvious geographic, cost, and land-requirement reasons, intercity airline transportation always has tended to have its transfer point from local to intercity vehicle—the airport—located outside of and at some distance from older CBD's.

These technological developments in passenger transportation have also reduced the relative concentration of hotel, restaurant, and allied services at central-city locations. The need for hotel and restaurant services has by no means disappeared in downtown areas, but the relative proportions of such activities in central and suburban locations have been altered significantly. The growth of both auto and air travel has contributed, of course, to this decentralization of restaurants and the proliferation of motel accommodations.

The rail freight business also has been profoundly affected by recent technological changes, particularly by the development of piggyback and container shipment, whose full effects are yet to be felt. Simply described, containerization is an effort to obtain the line-haul economies of rail or water transport while retaining the flexibility and economies of truck origination and termination of shipments. The use of containers and trucks for origination and termination avoids or significantly reduces classification costs, product damage, and time losses incurred in the railway yards and on docks.

Container shipment also acts as a force for decentralization by extending the range of industries which can afford to be away from rail sidings and can depend exclusively on highway transportation for origin and termination of shipments. Industries such as steel mills and thermoelectric plants, which consume large amounts of bulky, nonsoluble raw materials, continue to be more strongly rail-oriented, though the development of bulk movement of solids in pipelines could alter even this factor in the future.

The shift to container shipment of high-value manufactured goods may be faster, moreover, than the inherent economies would dictate, as a result of price discrimination in rail rate structures. At present, carload rates normally are quoted according to "value of service," with much larger markups on the actual transportation costs attached to shipments of high-value goods than of bulk commodities. Container rates, however, are independent of the nature of the goods in the containers, and have usually been set at a level just below the line-haul cost of truck shipment. In time, as the apparent change to container shipment develops, cities can expect new land-use demands for highway-oriented warehouse and shipping facilities and some reduction in those geared to rail sidings.

Other technological and economic reasons for relocating industry at noncentral points derive from the fact that high labor costs and advancing technology have jointly contrived to make it increasingly desirable for more and more manufacturing operations to be placed on a continuous process or automatic material-handling basis. It is almost always cheaper to employ these techniques in a one-story than in a multistory plant. In fact, it is often prohibitively expensive if not almost technologically impossible to employ them in older, multistory buildings.

A one-story plant, however, requires more land per square foot of workspace than does a multistory building. Accordingly, if everything else is equal (for example, there are no compelling reasons relating to transportation or recruitment of work force for remaining in a downtown location), the introduction of these new technologies suggests a simultaneous switch to outlying areas of lower real estate values, particularly large unencumbered tracts which offer room for expansion as well.

Similarly, electronic data processing is a technological change with important implications for the location of what might be called "the bookkeeping industries," an outstanding example being an insurance company, with its need to maintain extensive files and records. Another is the check and deposit servicing performed by commercial banks. Similarly, billing and collecting give rise to a large proportion of the direct labor charges of many public utility operations. Finally, many governmental activities are large-scale record and bookkeeping activities.

The main locational impact of electronic data processing has stemmed from the reduced need of these bookkeeping industries to recruit large forces of semiskilled female clerks. In the past, central locations for these industries were often dictated by the fact that women usually had neither the income nor the incentive to justify owning automobiles; rather, they relied on public transportation. For large insurance firms, in particular, this historically has been a major reason for remaining in a downtown location. Accordingly, once electronic data processing freed insurance firms from so heavy a reliance on unskilled female labor, and the expansion of automobile ownership made it easier to recruit all types of labor at noncentral locations, many firms moved out of the central core of the city. Usually the new site has been either an area of relatively low land value just beyond the city core (what is sometimes called the "frame" of the CBD) or, more commonly, a suburban location with even lower land value and more convenient to the suburban residences of the executive, managerial, and technical personnel employed by insurance firms.

A similar but not so widespread movement to the suburbs by the bookkeeping activities of public utility and banking firms is visible. These firms have generally lagged behind the insurance companies in adapting electronic data processing to their bookkeeping needs, largely because they usually find the adaptation much more complicated. Recent technological developments, however, seem to be rapidly eliminating the remaining obstacles. A consideration still tending to retard the removal of bookkeeping activities to suburban areas has been the large investments many banking, insurance, and public utility firms have long maintained in downtown property.

Still another important technological revolution greatly influencing land uses and values in urban areas is the communications revolution now under way. Clearly, the full effects of this revolution are yet to be felt. Indeed, it is difficult at the moment even to perceive what the over-all effects might be. At least to some extent, new developments in communication technology will be offsetting—centralizing some activities and decentralizing others. Before us, though, are such intriguing and unexplored innovations as closed-circuit television, phonovision, and facsimile transmission.

At least one major impact of these innovations does seem obvious, however; a reduced need for locating all the functional activities of a given industrial firm or type of business in close proximity. Rather, it is becoming increasingly feasible to locate different functions about the city at points of maximum locational advantage. For example, such industries as women's apparel, clothing accessories, costume jewelry, and others producing specialized high-fashion goods seem to have a very real need to locate their showrooms and selling activities in reasonably central locations, thus minimizing the need for visiting buyers to travel to see the various wares. In essence, sellers in these industries strongly desire to be located in a central market so as to ensure the maximum possibility of wares being seen by important buyers. Once the marketing pattern is set, strong reasons thus exist for staying close to the central group.

Traditionally, at least in New York, these industries have also tended to perform their manufacturing functions very close to their showrooms; but with improved communications and transportation there may no longer be any great advantage in doing so. If not, showrooms may stay where they are while the manufacturing operations relocate over time at the periphery of the city or other locations with cost advantages. It also seems possible that the market place itself may move to a less central location. When most business travel is by airplane, a cluster of showrooms close to the airport would seem to be as logical as one near the rail terminal. Indeed, the recent growth of hotel and exposition facilities near big-city airports suggests that this development is already well under way.

New developments in communication technology have also exerted a decentralizing influence on other urban activities. The most dramatic example is television, which in a very real sense brings many of the entertainment—and even cultural—amenities of the central city directly into the private home. It is easy to understand why a young married couple with children hesitates to spend money for a baby sitter, parking fees, show tickets, or expenses for a trip into town to see a nightclub performance, or movie, or concert, when they can see it in their own home. To a lesser extent, television has also brought live theatre into the home. Similarly, pay television may create very large markets for even such highly specialized activities as operas, concerts, and new theatrical productions; if so, these activities would no longer require locations in the central city in order to generate enough demand to be justified economically. Such a development would be, moreover, only a continuation of well-established trends in the entertainment and theatrical field. At the turn of the century, music halls and other popular forms of entertainment could only be sustained at downtown or central theatrical locations. This was even more true for the legitimate theater. The moving picture and, more recently, television have obviously altered these circumstances. Television has created such a massive single-point-of-time market for music hall, vaudeville, and other popular entertainment that sponsors can actually be found to present such theater on a free basis (so long as they are allowed time for commercials). In short, recent developments in communication techniques have eliminated the necessity for a downtown site to produce and present theatrical entertainment. The presentation can now be made in the home or neighborhood motion picture theater, while actual production is performed at an industrial site which (because of land requirements and few transportation needs) usually is best located on a city's periphery.

A somewhat different and less predictable influence on city structure is exerted by public policy. For example, it is often argued that stricter zoning ordinances and building codes ordinarily originate at central locations, and spread slowly to suburbs and rural areas. To the extent this argument is correct, and to the extent that stricter zoning ordinances and building codes increase the cost of locating certain activities at a particular site, there is an obvious incentive for locating away from the center of the city.

Real doubts might be entertained, however, on how important this factor actually is, particularly as an influence on business location decisions. Many business organizations seem to find that conventional building codes and, to a lesser extent, zoning ordinances tend to impose standards well below the minimum that they would desire or adhere to on other grounds. Furthermore, there is some evidence that if a business finds a zoning ordinance really onerous it can often obtain an exemption from the political authorities, who usually desire to attract or keep job opportunities in their localities. On the other hand, there is a possibility that residential building, especially of a speculative or "tract" type, has been attracted to outlying areas by the prospect of more flexible zoning and building code requirements. Even in such cases, however, there are often important offsetting influences. For example, suburban areas usually have higher minimum-lot requirements than do central areas.

Another distinctly different influence possibly working toward decentralization of urban areas is commonly cited by businessmen actually making location decisions. Simply put, some of their decisions seem to have been influenced by the fact that moving to a less central location also tends to reduce or eliminate labor troubles. Built-up central locations usually have well-established unions, while suburban or rural locations may not; accordingly, a company with a serious labor union problem may find escape by moving. Also, less turnover and higher quality labor may be experienced at suburban locations.[3] How important these considerations might be is, however, difficult to assess.

As noted previously, the strongest argument favoring increased growth of central cities seems to be an argument applicable to strengthening the position of certain very large cities at the expense of lesser cities, rather than to centralization within a given urban area. Specifically, recent advances in communication, the rapidity of air travel, and the growth of electronic data processing appear to make district offices less necessary relative to regional offices, and regional offices less necessary relative to central or national offices. In short, technological progress has made greater centralization both possible and desirable in office and managerial control functions. These developments were first observed in the railroad industry as early as the 1930's, and since World War II they have become pronounced in certain other industries having geographically dispersed manufacturing and sales functions. As a result, medium-size and, particularly, large-size metropolitan areas may be adding central office functions at the expense of smaller ones. Another trend, reinforcing the development of more office activity in CBD's, is the increasing proportion of the manufacturing work force comprised of skilled, college-trained engineers and managers. That is, the central office function itself seems to be gaining at the expense of line operations, with very highly skilled man power and new capital equipment being substituted for unskilled labor.

Another development potentially favoring central cities, but probably not too extensive in importance, can be found in the retailing field. As per capita income has risen, certain highly specialized (and sometimes highly expensive) consumer wants have become more prevalent. As a rule, serving these wants is economically feasible only if a fairly large market area is served. In fact, some of these markets (for example, those for expensive European *haute couture* and works of art) are feasible only at a few locations even in a market as extensive as the total American market. Development of such markets, therefore, should benefit large cities in particular, though recent experiments with closed-circuit television marketing may somewhat offset these effects.

Some Implications and Predictions

Good hypotheses should yield some testable predictions, of course. In the present context this criterion may be applied by posing the following fundamental question: What will the city of the future resemble if the

[3] A. J. Bone and M. Wohl, "Massachusetts Route 128 Impact Study," *Highway Research Board Bulletin 227,* 1959, pp. 34–38.

technological and economic influences just described are in fact the actual determinants of city structure?

To begin, it is necessary to define the implications for the location and design of basic intercity freight transportation operations. Historically, the development and the geographic structure of cities have been heavily influenced or dominated by such considerations as the location of seaports, inland waterways, railroad terminals, and other freight-handling facilities. A major implication of the preceding analysis, however, is that there will be less and less reason in the city of the future for manufacturing and other business activities to be located near such transportation facilities. Furthermore, the facilities themselves will not be as near the centers of the cities. Indeed, there seem to be compelling reasons for the withdrawal of both transportation and manufacturing activities to lower-cost, less-encumbered sites at the edges of the cities, particularly if withdrawal would facilitate the introduction of new production techniques and the integration of rail and truck operations.

The most advantageous sites for the relocation of freight transportation activities appear to be at points of intersection between rail lines and circumferential highways already in place or planned for most major urban centers. (Without a circumferential highway, relocation would take place at sites where existing rail facilities and new urban expressways or freeways are conveniently juxtaposed, and the comments that follow would not be materially changed.) A circumferential highway, placed in the first large band of uninhabited land just beyond the city limits or built-up surburban residential area, provides an almost ideal site for the performance of truck-to-rail transfers, particularly at the point of intersection with rail facilities. Large parking lots for storing and moving containers for truck trailers, and rail sidings required to create piggyback or containerized trains, are conveniently located there.

Manufacturing and other businesses requiring transportation inputs can be expected to locate reasonably close to these new transportation facilities. *Ceteris paribus,* if the market for land rentals and leases works with reasonable efficiency, the firms locating closest to the new transportation terminals would be the ones with the largest transport requirements. Indeed, industries with very large transportation input requirements—for bulky raw materials, for example—might still be expected to require rail and water sidings. Therefore such industries may have an understandable reluctance to leave central or other locations where rail marshalling yards and industrial siding facilities are already well established. Two such industries would appear to be steel manufacturing and thermoelectric plants.

Experience and logic also suggest that locations along circumferential highways, particularly at lower-rental points some distance from rail-highway intersections, would offer excellent advantages for the bookkeeping industries. At such points, for example, the recruitment of a labor force and the maintenance of harmonious labor relations may sometimes be simpler than at more central locations. Also, a certain amount of prestige and advertising value apparently attaches to a building that is visible from the highway and placed in a well-landscaped industrial park. These industries, particularly insurance, also generate a workday traffic of agents traveling to the office from neighboring cities or towns, so that a suburban highway location can be a useful and economical compromise among disparate workday travel demands.

Some wholesaling activities, by contrast, may not move quickly to peripheral industrial areas, because wholesaling is often inextricably intertwined with the selling function. Face-to-face consultation with purchasers and others using the wholesaler's services is often required. Furthermore, the fact that some retailing will remain in the downtown area in and of itself should hold some wholesaling nearby. In general, many wholesale and warehousing functions probably will continue, as in the past, to occupy lower-value areas with rail facilities just beyond the central core; however, the railroad facilities obviously will become less important if, as expected, containerized shipping of high-value goods is increasingly emphasized.

Certain wholesale and warehousing functions oriented to servicing manufacturing industries, on the other hand, might be expected to relocate to the periphery simply to be closer to their customers. In general, such relocation should be a somewhat slower process and follow after adjustments in transportation and manufacturing.

Local consumer industries, such as bakeries, candy factories, and breweries, might also be expected to follow a mixed pattern. They will be tempted, of course, to follow their customers and retail outlets to suburban locations; and such moves will often reduce total distribution costs by eliminating the necessity to originate all shipments in congested downtown areas. On the other hand, the total trip length from factory to consumers is likely to increase with decentralization, and the face-to-face contacts needed for much of the selling in these industries will be somewhat difficult or the travel required will be more burdensome at less central locations. Accordingly, some of these industries will probably relocate into the frame of the urban core while others will move all the way out to the periphery.

The ultimate effect of these developments will be to create, in very rough approximation, a new band or perhaps many bands of manufacturing and commercial activity circumscribing the city just beyond presently built-up environs. It suggests what is often described as a "tree" or "ring" theory of city growth. In these new peripheral bands, the city of the future should have most of its light and medium manufacturing and a great deal of its transportation and bookkeeping operations. Almost by definition, the bands would usually be close to existing outlets for intercity air and auto travel. It would not be surprising, moreover, if the railroads and bus companies began relocating their passenger terminals (for whatever passenger business they retain) at points near the intersections of railroads and circumferential highways. In fact, one possible way to save something of the intercity rail passenger business might be to rationalize the operation by eliminating high-cost, highly taxed downtown rail passenger terminals. Private automobiles, parking lots, and buses might be an obvious part of a plan for connecting new suburban rail terminals to central and other city locations.

It is unlikely, however, that all railway tracks will be eliminated from the center of the city. Some will be needed to serve heavy raw-material-consuming industries, such as iron and steel, and those warehousing activities that may not move for some time to come. In many cases, moreover, it might be too difficult for the railroads to establish belt lines or circumferential rail lines to avoid the city; a simple 1- or 2-track right-of-way would then have to be maintained through the city, particularly where such natural obstacles as rivers or ravines are already bridged near the city center. Some downtown tracks will also be needed in cities where seaport or other special facilities must be served.

On balance, however, railroads should require far less downtown real estate in the future because of their reduced need for passenger terminals, passenger yards, and marshalling yards at central locations. There should be an even greater proportional reduction in transportation employment opportunities, since labor intensive yard and record-keeping activities should be more efficient at new suburban locations. Similarly, the trend toward containerized shipment should reduce the demand for longshoremen in downtown areas of seaports.

These movements toward the periphery will radically alter, of course, the central core of the city. An obvious question is, what will be left? Basically, it would seem that the city's future will depend on "control activities" requiring immediate, face-to-face communication. In particular, the city may be uniquely suited for what has been called the "central office function." This means, above all, that the city is advantageous as the site for the executive offices of business managers. These, in turn, attract legal, advertising, and financial services that cater to central office functionaries and usually are not uniquely tied to any one firm or industry. For example, one might expect a commercial bank to retain a central location for its loan, trust, and other offices requiring immediate face-to-face contact with business management, even if the more routine banking functions move outward. As a corollary, some restaurants and hotels should remain, since central offices are one of their prime sources of demand.

Many government activities, involved with bookkeeping and record-keeping, seem to be logical candidates for movement to the suburbs, but political and other considerations may keep them near central locations. (Boston is an interesting case in point, whereby the recent location plans for a new Federal office building were shifted from a noncentral to a central location on this basis. This is, of course, in contrast to some of the larger new Federal establishment locations in Washington, D.C.—such as the CIA and the National Bureau of Standards.) Furthermore, many government activities, particularly those dealing with tax collection and government-business relationships, often involve the face-to-face contact characteristics of central office operations. Most other government functions, many with very high employment potentials, such as police and fire departments, schools, and post offices, must follow population in much the same way that retailing does. Therefore, even government employment could decentralize.

As already noted, some retailing functions can be expected to remain in the central core; further, since the relative proportion of higher-income employment may increase in the core area, downtown retailing may become increasingly specialized and oriented to higher-income tastes, particularly since high-volume mass merchandising probably will continue to migrate to the suburbs. While secretaries and clerks may sustain a reasonably large popular demand for general retailing, downtown retailing will probably decline in relative if not absolute importance.

The remaining market for live entertainment also might be expected to concentrate in the central core. There may be exceptions; athletic enterprises that consume a good deal of land, for example, may be strongly motivated to move either to the suburbs or to the frame of the CBD. But live theatre and other cultural activities will probably remain in the central core. Even the need for parking space should not impede this pattern, since the demand for downtown parking space is ordinarily much lower in the evenings than in the daytime.

Stockbroking and related types of financial sales functions might also be expected to remain in central areas. Again, these are activities in which face-to-face consultation and rapid communication are usually very helpful. Accordingly, the stockbroker will tend to locate near his customers; and since higher-income groups do most of the investing, the core with its central offices is likely to remain the best location for stockbrokerage firms. On the other hand, closed-circuit television and phonovision could change these expectations.

Obviously, if these hypotheses about the future location of business and office activities are correct, a very extensive relative, if not aggregate redirection of activity is implied. Basically, relatively fewer blue-collar and lower-grade clerical employees will find work in the central core, while both the aggregate and relative proportions of higher-grade technical and managerial personnel may increase, especially in regional and national headquarter cities.

Shifts in employment opportunities for different income groups at different points in the city also can be expected to have important implications for residential location choices. Paradoxically, even slum areas around the cores of central cities may become attractive residential sites for the higher-income groups who will be increasingly employed nearby; and this attraction is likely to be greater as the city grows and commuting distances lengthen between the suburbs and core. On the other hand, the dispersion of lower-income manufacturing, transportation, and clerical workers to suburbia should continue, perhaps at an accelerated pace. These people will tend to settle near the plants in which they work. Finally, following the traditional pattern, a few very-high-income people will doubtless continue to live at or beyond the very periphery of the metropolitan area. They will include that unusually hardy breed of commuters who can stand the long daily trip into the central city, as well as the managers and technicians employed in the manufacturing, insurance, and banking service activities located around the city's periphery.

A special problem of residential site location is posed by the choice constraints usually imposed on certain minority groups. If there were no large minority groups in a city, it seems highly likely that the future residential pattern would be one of very-high-value (and probably high-rise) residences close to the city center, and a gradual tapering off in values with distance from the city center, stabilizing eventually at the point where the general mass of lower-income housing begins. This neat pattern may be made impossible, however, by the entrapment of new immigrant and minority groups in areas of high residential density just beyond redeveloped higher-income residences near the core.

The creation (or continuation) of centrally located segregated or slum areas would very likely retard higher-income residential redevelopment near the core. In particular, higher-income people with families may elect to join the long-haul commuters from the periphery, in part because of the "necessity" to rely on suburban rather than central city schools. Indeed, one might speculate that the "hardy commuter breed" is very much comprised of family-man executive types. Minority group clustering is also likely to influence the residential location decisions of secretarial and other skilled but lower-paid workers employed in the core area, generally forcing them farther out than they might otherwise choose to live.

Summary

Both early and recent improvements in transportation and communication technology have tended to create distinctly larger areas of homogeneous land use in urban areas. Superimposed on this "leveling influence," which has tended to reduce the relative attractiveness of the central city, is the further tendency of some recent technological changes, particularly in passenger transportation and those influencing the physical layout of manufacturing production, to make unencumbered open spaces, usually found only at the outskirts of a city or beyond, advantageous for certain activities. Indeed, without much question, the overwhelming impact of technological changes, recent and remote, on urban locations or structure has been to reduce densities and decentralize or disperse functions. Containerization, the jet age, telecommunications, mechanized methods of materials handling, continuous processing, do-it-yourself deliveries, automation—all these connote recent technological changes that have had a decentralizing influence on the location of urban job opportunities. The ability of Americans to afford decentralized residential locations, private yards, and automobiles as their incomes have risen has of course strengthened the trend toward urban dispersal. These decentralizing influences have been only slightly counterbalanced by other developments, particularly in the performance of managerial control functions. These underlying forces for decentralization almost surely would have been set in motion, moreover, with or without the assistance or hindrance of public policy, since they stem from fundamental changes in technology, income levels, family status, and consumer tastes.

These technological and economic developments have clear implications for the structure and organization of American cities. For example, as urban employment opportunities and residences become still more dispersed, the city center should become increasingly more specialized in office, white-collar, and service activities and less and less a locale for manufacturing, transportation, and other blue-collar jobs. The pattern will be complicated at almost every turn, though, by the very special difficulties and problems created by the often-encountered clustering of minority groups' housing possibilities. Furthermore, the rate of adjustment of urban location decisions to new technological conditions, if not the absolute character of these decisions, will always be influenced and sometimes obfuscated by the inertia of existing circumstances and commitments. Urban change, in short, tends to proceed in a slow, evolutionary fashion. The net effect is to create a complex set of urban problems in which it is sometimes difficult to identify the basic trends, let alone solutions. Still, a cogent, well-defined set of hypotheses about urban change is discernible and their testing against available data is essential to the design of better transportation policies for urban areas.

Chapter 3 | Recent Trends in Urban Location

In the preceding chapter a number of hypotheses were advanced about the changes occurring in the metropolitan distribution of population and employment; it was suggested that technological, social, and economic forces in recent decades have produced far-reaching alterations in the locational propensities of households and business firms.

In this chapter a number of these trends are empirically documented, at least in their grosser aspects. A more refined analysis would unquestionably be desirable, but the information presently at hand is not adequate for the purpose. While increased interest in the problems of urban transportation and development has led to vast improvements in the quantity and quality of data about metropolitan communities, uncertainty still afflicts efforts to specify or explain many of the trends in the spatial distribution of urban activities. Nonetheless, with the information available it is at least possible to reduce the range of uncertainty and identify those areas in which further research is most needed.

Trends in Urban Population and Employment

The best over-all view of recent patterns in urban development is obtained from population and employment data. The 1948, 1954, and 1958 Censuses of Business present data on total employment in retailing, selected services, and wholesaling for central cities and standard metropolitan statistical areas (SMSA's). Figures on total employment in manufacturing in SMSA's and central cities are available from the 1947, 1954, and 1958 Censuses of Manufacturers. Statistics for the suburban ring of metropolitan areas can be defined by subtracting central-city data from SMSA data. This geographic division of metropolitan areas is crude but it provides at least somewhat meaningful descriptions of postwar trends in urban development. Two major shortcomings of the data are the lack of more detailed information on the traits of urban development within large and heterogeneous central cities, and the lack of standardized bases, particularly areal, for comparing growth patterns.

Table 1 lists the mean annual percentage changes in population and in manufacturing, wholesaling, retailing, and selected services employment in the central cities and metropolitan rings of the 39 largest SMSA's other than New York. It is not surprising to find that metropolitan (or suburban) rings grew faster than central cities during the postwar period. The

TABLE 1

MEAN ANNUAL PERCENTAGE CHANGES IN POPULATION AND EMPLOYMENT FOR 39 CENTRAL CITIES AND METROPOLITAN RINGS

(simple, unweighted averages of individual city percentage changes)

	Central city			Metropolitan ring		
Item	1948–1954	1954–1958	1948–1958	1948–1954	1954–1958	1948–1958
Manufacturing[a]	3.0	−0.4	2.5	8.2	4.9	8.8
Wholesaling	1.8	1.8	1.9	10.4	12.4	13.8
Retailing	0.4	1.8	1.0	4.5	9.1	7.4
Services	2.8	5.7	4.4	9.3	10.9	12.3
Population	1.8	1.5	1.8	6.4	4.6	6.6

[a] Manufacturing data pertain to the years 1947–1954 and 1947–1958.

most striking items are the negative yearly rate of change (−0.4 per cent) in central-city manufacturing employment during the second period, 1954–1958, and the rapid growth of selected services employment (almost 6 per cent a year).

Unquestionably, some of the 1954–1958 decline in the manufacturing growth rate was attributable to cyclical unemployment in manufacturing in the terminal year 1958, although 1954 was also a year of mild recession. The rate of growth of manufacturing employment in urban rings during the 1954–1958 period also declined, being only about half what it was from 1948–1954. However, one indication that not all the decline in central-city growth rates is attributable to cyclical fluctuation is the fact that the ring growth rate in manufacturing declined by only 50 per cent between the first and second periods, while the central-city growth rate in the second period is only one one-hundredth of the first period. It is possible that some of this differential in ring and central-city growth rates is attributable to different cyclical characteristics of industries in the two different areas. Still, compositional disparities seem insufficient to account for all of the difference. For the entire 11-year period, 1947–1958, central-city manufacturing employment grew less than 3 per cent a year on the average, while in the ring it grew almost 9 per cent a year. Despite adverse cyclical effects, moreover, ring employment growth rates during the second period exceeded those in the first period in all categories except manufacturing.

These data, like most such data used in discussions of urban development, systematically overstate central-city growth and understate ring growth because annexations have significantly increased the size of many central cities over time. Correction of both population and employment data for annexations can be made to give at least a rough idea of what the growth within constant areas has been. The 1960 Census of Population provides the 1960 population within the central-city boundaries of 1960; data on population annexations by the 39 central cities are obtainable from the *Municipal Year Books,* 1949–1959.[1] Under the assumption that populations changed at a constant percentage rate from 1950 to 1960 in each of these areas, the population within 1950 boundaries can be estimated for 1948 (by extrapolation), 1954, and 1958. Employment data can also be at least roughly corrected for annexations by assuming that the percentage of employment annexed in each category was the same as the percentage of annexed population.[2]

Table 2 lists central-city and ring population and employment data corrected in this way for annexations. The corrected data exhibit a percentage decline in manufacturing employment during the decade in the 39 central cities. (This finding is of course subject to the same reservations mentioned above concerning cyclical effects.) During the 1954–1958 period, when central-city manufacturing employment declined al-

[1] The International City Managers' Association, *The Municipal Year Book* (1949–1959), Chicago, Ill.

[2] Formally, the annexation correction for the central city is of the form:

$$E_{50i}^{cck} = E_{Li}^{cck} - \left(\frac{P_{Li}^{cc} - P_{50i}^{cc}}{P_{Li}^{cc}}\right)(E_{Li}^{cck}),$$

where E_{50i}^{cck} is the estimated employment within 1950 central-city boundaries in the ith year ($i = 1948$, 1954, or 1958), and for the kth industry subgroup ($k =$ retailing, wholesaling, selected services, or manufacturing); E_{Li}^{cck} is the census employment of the kth industry within existing legal boundaries of the central city in the ith year; $(P_{Li}^{cc} - P_{50i}^{cc})/P_{Li}^{cc}$ is the ratio of difference of population in the legal and 1950 boundaries of the central city in the ith year to the population within central city legal boundaries in the ith year. The ring correction for the annexation is identical:

$$E_{50i}^{R} = E_{Li}^{R} + \left(\frac{P_{Li}^{cc} - P_{50i}^{cc}}{P_{Li}^{cc}}\right)(E_{Li}^{cc}),$$

except the annexation correction is added instead of substracted as for the central city from the census employment statistic. As a side condition, annexation corrections from the ring to the central city are not permitted to exceed one-half of the employment within the ring for a given employing activity.

most 2 per cent a year, ring manufacturing employment increased 7 per cent a year. For the entire period, while the corrected percentage change in central-city manufacturing employment is negative, the rate of increase for the ring is 15 per cent a year.

TABLE 2

MEAN ANNUAL PERCENTAGE CHANGES IN POPULATION AND EMPLOYMENT FOR 39 CENTRAL CITIES AND METROPOLITAN RINGS, CORRECTED FOR ANNEXATIONS (simple, unweighted averages of individual city percentage changes)

	Central city			Metropolitan ring		
Item	1948–1954	1954–1958	1948–1958	1948–1954	1954–1958	1948–1958
Manufacturing[a]	1.9	−1.7	−0.6	13.2	7.0	15.0
Wholesaling	0.9	0.2	0.7	25.4	16.8	29.4
Retailing	−0.6	0.1	−0.4	11.5	13.6	16.0
Services	1.6	3.9	2.7	18.2	16.8	24.4
Population	0.2	0.1	0.2	8.8	6.4	9.4

[a] Manufacturing data pertain to the years 1947–1954 and 1947–1958.

Under corrected data, yearly wholesaling employment in the central city has only a small percentage increase during both periods. By contrast, ring wholesaling employment increased 25 per cent a year during the first six years of the decade, and almost 17 per cent a year in the last four.

The annexation corrections also strongly affect the population growth rates. Uncorrected population data indicate an average 1.8 per cent yearly rate of increase in the central cities during the first six-year period; corrected data reduce this figure to 0.2 per cent. During the second period, rates of population increase are 1.5 per cent a year within legal boundaries and only 0.1 per cent within 1950 boundaries. The yearly rate of population growth in metropolitan rings over the decade is under 7 per cent within legal boundaries and over 9 per cent within 1950 boundaries.

Only service employment retains a healthy growth rate in the central cities using corrected data. After correction, the yearly growth rate in central-city services employment is 1.6 per cent a year in the first period, and nearly 4 per cent in the second.

Mean percentage growth rates represent but one way to examine changes in employment and population levels. If used alone, they give an incomplete and perhaps even misleading description of urban change. It is possible for an employment category to have a very high mean percentage rate of growth but an insignificant absolute change. Therefore, the mean annual absolute changes in employment and population for the 39 SMSA's included in this analysis are presented in Table 3, using the data corrected for annexations.

The importance of changes in manufacturing employment for urban development trends is evident. For the entire decade, central cities lost an average of 809 manufacturing workers a year, while rings gained 1821. (Again the caveat previously noted—that 1958 was a year of moderate recession—applies.) Retail employment changes are similar. During the decade central cities lost 285 retail employees a year, while rings gained 1427.

By, contrast, wholesaling employment in central cities did not decline over the decade 1948–1958, though it grew relatively much less than in metropolitan rings. Changes in wholesaling employment are of particular significance because the postwar locational pattern of wholesaling has been at such variance with that of the prewar period. In 1948, on the average for the 39 large SMSA's, only 12 per cent of wholesaling employment (according to 1950 central-city boundaries) was located in metropolitan rings, as opposed to an average of 37 per cent for retailing, 18 per cent for services, and 30 per cent for manufacturing employment.[3]

Perhaps the most startling aspect of Table 3 is the huge difference between the absolute population increases in central cities and rings for the decade (corrected for annexation): about 300 persons a year on the average for the central cities and 32,000 for rings. From 1948 to 1954, however, central cities annexed nearly 5000 people a year, illustrating how misleading uncorrected employment and population data can be. The

[3] New York Metropolitan Region Study findings suggest that the relocations of wholesaling employment in the New York region resembled those observed for the 39 next largest SMSA's. In *Anatomy of a Metropolis* (Harvard University Press, Cambridge, Mass., 1959), p. 83, Edgar M. Hoover and Raymond Vernon note that "between 1929 and 1954, Manhattan's share of the region's wholesale jobs fell from 76 to 59 per cent." Even more significantly, they found that Manhattan's wholesale jobs declined absolutely by 12,000 workers between 1948 and 1954—from 181,000 to 169,000. Hoover and Vernon also note that the outward shift of wholesaling was typical of each of the major types of wholesalers enumerated in the Census of Business. They do state, however (pp. 83–84):

> By and large, the outward movement was not very pronounced in those lines in which selling was a primary function, dry goods apparel and furniture being notable cases. In lines importantly engaged in the physical distribution of commodities, such as beer, wines, and spirits the decline in Manhattan's share was generally more marked.

The New York Study's survey of manufacturing plants also provides data for assessing the relative importance of rail and truck transportation in manufacturing and wholesaling. Hoover and Vernon determined that 63 per cent of the region's manufacturing plants constructed before 1920 were located on rail sidings. Of those surveyed, 50 per cent of the plants constructed between 1920 and 1945 were located on rail sidings, but only 40 per cent of those constructed between 1946 and 1956 (p. 37).

TABLE 3

MEAN ANNUAL ABSOLUTE CHANGES IN POPULATION AND EMPLOYMENT FOR 39 CENTRAL CITIES AND METROPOLITAN RINGS, CORRECTED FOR ANNEXATIONS

	Central city			Metropolitan ring		
Item	1948–1954	1954–1958	1948–1958	1948–1954	1954–1958	1948–1958
Manufacturing[a]	159	−2,502	−809	2,168	1,214	1,821
Wholesaling	86	−2	51	415	739	544
Retailing	−479	6	−285	972	2,110	1,427
Services	373	786	538	479	827	618
Population	290	308	297	29,812	34,462	31,672
Population annexations	4,180	5,532	4,721	−4,180	−5,532	−4,721

[a] Manufacturing data pertain to the years 1947–1954 and 1947–1958.

fact that annexations far outstripped absolute increases within 1950 boundaries suggests that population probably grew faster in the outer than in the inner areas of central cities, and declined in and near the cores. Rough calculations indicate that population growth in annexed areas averaged about 10 per cent a year, between 1948 and 1958, a figure about equal to the rate in metropolitan rings and far exceeding the central-city rate. Since employment increases are also more likely in newly developed areas, it is probable that employment is also growing faster on the fringes than in the cores. Therefore in many cities core employment and population are probably declining.

In fact, if Los Angeles and San Diego are deleted from the sample of 39 SMSA's, the mean absolute change in central-city population is actually negative. The rapid central-city growth of Los Angeles and San Diego is attributable to large amounts of vacant land within their central-city boundaries, which absorbed a large share of their tremendous postwar population increases. (Also, the Los Angeles central-city area is the largest in the country, followed by Oklahoma City, New York, Dallas, Chicago, New Orleans, and San Diego.)

It is also illuminating to examine the number of central cities which experienced declines in various employment categories during each period. The pervasiveness of these declines is indicated in Table 4, a tabulation of the number of declining central cities and rings in each employment and population classification. During the first period (1948–1954), retailing employment declined in 26, or two-thirds, of the central cities; manufacturing employment declined in 15 of the 39 cities during the first period and in 29 during the second (1954–1958); and wholesaling

TABLE 4

NUMBER OF CENTRAL CITY AND METROPOLITAN RINGS (OUT OF 39) HAVING EMPLOYMENT AND POPULATION DECLINES (CORRECTED FOR ANNEXATIONS)

	Central city			Metropolitan ring		
Item	1948–1954	1954–1958	1948–1958	1948–1954	1954–1958	1948–1958
Manufacturing[a]	15	29	24	6	9	4
Wholesaling	15	18	13	3	0	1
Retailing	26	17	30	4	0	0
Services	7	4	3	1	1	0
Population (legal)	17	15	16	1	2	2
Population (1950)	21	21	21	1	1	1

[a] Manufacturing data pertain to the years 1947–1954 and 1947–1958.

employment declined in 15 central cities in the first period and in 18 during the second. Only services, buoyed up by secular increases, avoided pervasive declines; service employment declined in 7 central cities in the first period and in only 4 during the second period.

The number of population declines is also large; for the entire period, 1948–1958, 21 central cities decreased in population according to 1950 boundaries, and 16 had declined according to legal boundaries.[4]

Nor did metropolitan rings escape decline entirely. The economy-wide relative decline of manufacturing, combined with especially large declines in some metropolitan areas, resulted in 6 rings experiencing reduced manufacturing employment during the first period and 9 during the second.

In sum, of the employment categories analyzed, only that of services exhibits substantial central-city growth, largely because the demand for services has grown in both absolute and relative importance in the economy as a whole and in metropolitan areas in particular for several decades. In large measure, therefore, the extent to which central-city employment in services can be expected to maintain central-city employment levels may depend on whether the secular increase in the demand for these services continues.

[4] The reader should note that the yearly absolute population increases for the two periods differ only by the differences in the rate of annexation during each of the two periods. The yearly percentage changes are obtained from 1950 and 1960 population within 1950 areas and by assuming a constant rate of change within the decade. Actually, however, there is a considerable reason to believe that central-city population increases were greater during the first period than during the second. If this is so, the yearly changes during the second period may in fact have been negative.

Relationships Between Metropolitan and Central-City Growth

It is implicit in the previous section that over-all metropolitan growth rates are highly and complexly interrelated to those of the central city and ring. It is therefore useful to compare the mean yearly percentage and absolute changes in population and employment for rapidly, moderately, and slowly growing areas. Specifically, three subgroups can be defined (for the 39 areas analyzed): the 13 SMSA's with the highest percentage rate of population growth for 1950–1960, the 13 with the second highest, and the 13 with the lowest.

In Table 5 the percentage changes in employment and population by these population growth categories are shown. Several interesting findings are observable. First, extreme regularity is displayed in the rankings by all categories. There are only three inversions in the entire table. Within every employment category and time period, the percentage rate of change of employment, in both the central city and ring, is highest for the highest population growth subgroup and second highest for the intermediate subgroup. The service employment data also bear out the earlier evaluation that the growth in central cities' service employment is largely attributable to the increasing importance of services in the economy. Percentage rates of change in services, especially those for the second period, vary much less by population growth subgroup than do those in other employment categories.

As shown in Table 6 the average annual absolute changes are similar to those for percentage changes. Service is the only central-city employment or population group for which there were increases for both the medium and lowest population growth categories for both periods. During the decade, the 13 SMSA's with the lowest growth rate lost on the average 40,000 in central-city population, 720 wholesaling jobs, almost 27,000 manufacturing jobs, and nearly 7000 retailing jobs. The only offset against these was an increase of about 5000 jobs in services. The central cities of the 13 SMSA's having intermediate rates of growth fared somewhat better. With 1950 boundaries used, their central cities in the ten years lost on the average 20,000 in population, gained only 10 wholesaling jobs, lost approximately 14,000 manufacturing jobs, lost 3500 retailing jobs, and enjoyed an increase of slightly over 4300 in service employments.

During the same 10-year period in which the central cities of the 13 slowest-growing SMSA's lost nearly 27,000 manufacturing jobs (within 1950 boundaries), their metropolitan rings gained about 13,000. Similarly, while the central-city slow growers lost about 6900 retailing jobs, their metropolitan rings had an increase of over 12,000. Wholesaling on the average declined during the 10-year period by 720 jobs in the central

TABLE 5

MEAN ANNUAL PERCENTAGE CHANGES IN EMPLOYMENT AND POPULATION (CORRECTED FOR ANNEXATIONS) FOR THE CENTRAL CITIES AND RINGS OF 39 LARGE SMSA'S, BY THE PERCENTAGE RATE OF SMSA POPULATION GROWTH FOR 1948–1958[a] AND BY INDUSTRY GROUP

Item	Central city			Metropolitan ring		
	1948–1954	1954–1958	1948–1958	1948–1954	1954–1958	1948–1958
Retailing						
Highest	0.2	0.6	0.3	19.2	20.2	25.1
Medium	−0.8	−0.1	−0.5	13.0	14.4	18.8
Lowest	−1.2	−0.1	−0.8	2.4	6.4	4.2
Services						
Highest	2.4	4.1	3.4	25.5	25.4	34.5
Medium	1.4	4.1	2.7	22.2	17.3	30.2
Lowest	1.0	3.5	2.0	7.1	7.5	7.2
Manufacturing[b]						
Highest	6.0	0.3	4.0	27.5	15.7	34.2
Medium	0.1	−1.9	0.6	9.0	3.6	8.1
Lowest	−0.4	−3.6	1.5	3.0	1.8	2.6
Wholesaling[c]						
Highest	1.2	2.0	1.5	35.4	21.8	43.7
Medium	0.5	−0.2	−0.2	33.0	16.8	33.1
Lowest	1.0	−0.3	−0.5	8.4	12.1	12.6
Population (legal boundaries)						
Highest	5.0	4.1	5.2	7.6	5.8	8.1
Medium	0.8	0.9	0.9	7.4	4.9	7.4
Lowest	−0.4	−0.5	−0.5	4.3	3.3	4.4
Population (1950 boundaries)						
Highest	1.3	1.0	1.3	12.5	9.2	14.0
Medium	−0.2	−0.2	−0.2	9.5	6.6	9.9
Lowest	−0.5	−0.6	−0.6	4.3	3.3	4.4

[a] The SMSA's in the highest population change group from 1948 to 1958 were Atlanta, Columbus, Dallas, Denver, Fort Worth, Houston, Los Angeles–Long Beach, Miami, Phoenix, San Antonio, San Diego, Tampa, and Washington, D.C.

The medium group encompassed Baltimore, Dayton, Detroit, Indianapolis, Kansas City, Louisville, Memphis, Milwaukee, Minneapolis–St. Paul, New Orleans, Oklahoma City, Oakland, and Seattle.

The SMSA's with the lowest percentage change were Akron, Boston, Buffalo, Chicago, Cincinnati, Cleveland, Jersey City, Newark, Philadelphia, Pittsburgh, Portland, Rochester, and St. Louis.

[b] Manufacturing data pertain to the years 1947–1954 and 1947–1958.

[c] Only 38 SMSA's were used in Wholesaling. The highest category in Wholesaling used only 12 of the SMSA's.

TABLE 6

MEAN ANNUAL ABSOLUTE CHANGES IN EMPLOYMENT AND POPULATION (CORRECTED FOR ANNEXATIONS) FOR THE CENTRAL CITIES AND RINGS OF 39 LARGE SMSA'S, BY THE PERCENTAGE RATE OF SMSA POPULATION GROWTH FOR 1948–1958[a] AND BY INDUSTRY GROUP

	Central city			Metropolitan ring		
Item	1948–1954	1954–1958	1948–1958	1948–1954	1954–1958	1948–1958
Retailing						
Highest	91	318	182	1,197	2,872	1,867
Medium	−446	−198	−347	898	1,628	1,190
Lowest	−1,083	−101	−690	823	1,829	1,225
Services						
Highest	587	826	682	703	1,417	989
Medium	209	771	434	304	513	387
Lowest	322	762	498	429	550	478
Manufacturing[b]						
Highest	2,332	294	1,591	2,860	2,992	2,908
Medium	−549	−2,784	−1,362	1,945	26	1,247
Lowest	−1,307	−5,015	−2,655	1,698	626	1,308
Wholesaling[c]						
Highest	245	226	237	477	1,066	713
Medium	7	−7	1	325	440	371
Lowest	18	−208	−72	447	735	562
Population (legal boundaries)						
Highest	17,000	19,000	18,000	24,000	32,000	28,000
Medium	1,000	2,000	2,000	24,000	26,000	24,000
Lowest	−5,000	−4,000	−4,000	29,000	29,000	29,000
Population (1950 boundaries						
Highest	8,000	7,000	8,000	33,000	44,000	38,000
Medium	−2,000	−2,000	−2,000	30,000	32,000	28,000
Lowest	−5,000	−4,000	−4,000	29,000	29,000	29,000

[a] See note a, Table 5.
[b] Manufacturing data pertain to the years 1947–1954 and 1947–1958.
[c] Only 38 SMSA's were used in Wholesaling. The highest category in Wholesaling used only 12 of the SMSA's.

cities of the 13 slowest-growing areas, while ring employment in wholesaling in the same 13 areas increased on the average by 5600 jobs. Also, the metropolitan rings of these 13 gained 290,000 population, while their central cities declined by 40,000. On the other hand, the increase in service employment for these 13 slowest-growing SMSA's was actually greater in the central city (nearly 5000) than in the ring (about 4800). A remarkable finding is the high average ring-population increase for the

13 fastest growing SMSA's: an average gain of 380,000 in ten years. This compares with only 80,000 for their central cities.

Employment Trends Within Central Business Districts

As repeatedly noted, one of the gravest weaknesses of the population and employment statistics presented thus far is their high degree of spatial aggregation. The central-city statistics in particular may hide very diverse growth rates in employment and population within central-city boundaries and, most importantly of all, may mask changes in the employment levels within central business districts (CBD's). The data presented thus far are also deficient in the coverage of such important CBD employment activities as office employment, finance, and the like. Unfortunately, few employment data have been collected which would permit a definite answer about changes in CBD employment levels. The fragmentary data available, however, fail to support any proposition that central-city declines in population and employment have occurred simultaneously with huge increases in CBD employment levels. The following is a 13-point summary of this fragmentary but highly suggestive information on CBD activity levels:

(1) In Detroit, the number of persons leaving the CBD during the evening peak hour by all modes of travel (including walking) averaged between 78,000 and 81,000 in the years 1944–1950, but was down to 73,000 in 1953.[5]

(2) In Dallas, despite a more than 40 per cent increase per decade in total SMSA population from 1940 to 1960, the number of people leaving the CBD during the evening peak hours increased only 14 per cent between 1946 and 1958.[6]

(3) In Los Angeles, the number of people leaving the CBD during the evening peak hour has remained stable at about 125,000 since 1941, even though SMSA population has been increasing over 50 per cent each decade.[7]

(4) In Philadelphia, SMSA population has been increasing about 15 per cent each decade since 1940, but the CBD's share of total jobs in the SMSA dropped from 41 per cent in 1950 to 39 per cent in 1956; the number of daily person-trips to the CBD has declined from 471,000 in 1947 to 373,000 in 1960, with most of the drop being concentrated in shopping and social-recreational trips. Even the daily work-trips de-

[5] Detroit City Planning Commission, *Central Business District, Land Use, Trafficways and Transit,* Detroit, 1956.

[6] Dallas, Texas, Department of City Planning, *Dallas Central District: A Master Plan Report,* Dallas, February 1961.

[7] City of Los Angeles, Department of Traffic, *Cordon Count for Downtown Los Angeles,* Los Angeles, 1955.

creased, though, dropping from 260,000 to 220,000. The peak-hour travel to the CBD remained reasonably stable from 1947 to 1960, falling only 3 per cent over those years; by contrast, travel to the CBD during the hour preceding the peak decreased 21 per cent and that during the hour following the peak decreased some 27 per cent.[8]

(5) In Houston, the number of persons entering the CBD between 7:00 a.m. and 6:00 p.m. declined from 324,000 in March and June of 1953 to 272,000 in July of 1960. During the same period, the maximum number leaving the CBD during the peak hour declined from just over 60,000 to about 52,000.[9]

(6) The San Francisco–Oakland SMSA's population rose 50 per cent between 1940 and 1950, and 24 per cent between 1950 and 1960, but the number of persons leaving the San Francisco CBD during the evening peak increased only 10 per cent between 1947 and 1959.[10]

(7) In Minneapolis, there has been a steady decline from about 110,000 people a day entering the CBD in 1947 to about 93,000 in 1960.[11]

(8) Washington, D.C., though an office and government town and therefore less likely to be sensitive to private economic forces and changes in manufacturing technology, had only a 2 per cent increase in CBD employment between 1948 and 1955; population increased more than 30 per cent in the SMSA during the same period.[12]

(9) The total number of trips to Tucson's CBD decreased from 41,500 in 1948 to 36,144 in 1960; automobile-driven trips increased from 22,280 to 23,192; bus passenger trips declined from 8250 to 3245; and other passenger trips decreased from 10,970 to 9707.[13]

[8] City of Philadelphia, Urban Traffic and Transportation Board, *Plan and Program 1955: Conclusions and Recommendations of the Board, Report of the Staff to the Board,* Philadelphia, April 1956; Philadelphia City Planning Commission, *A Comprehensive Plan for the City of Philadelphia,* Philadelphia, 1960; "Penn-Jersey Transportation Study," *PJ News,* vol. 2, no. 11, August-September 1963.

[9] Texas, State Highway Department, *Houston Central Business District Parking Survey,* conducted by Texas Highway Department, Highway Planning Survey, in cooperation with the City of Houston and the U.S. Department of Commerce, Bureau of Public Roads, Austin, Texas, 1953, p. 36; Texas, State Highway Department, *Houston Metropolitan Area Transportation Study: Origin and Destination Survey,* conducted by Texas Highway Department, Highway Planning Survey, in cooperation with the City of Houston, 1960, p. 77.

[10] City and County of San Francisco, Technical Committee of the Major Transportation Count, *Cordon Count Data, Metropolitan Traffic District,* San Francisco, July 1954 (mimeographed).

[11] Twin Cities Metropolitan Planning Commission, *Metropolitan Transportation Study,* part I, Planning Report no. 8, Minneapolis-St. Paul, August 1960.

[12] Jacob Silver, "Trends in Travel to the Central Business District by Residents of the Washington, D.C. Metropolitan Area, 1948 and 1955," *Public Roads,* vol. 29, no. 7, April 1959.

[13] *Tucson Area Transportation Study,* vol. I: *An Inventory of Existing Conditions,* Arizona Highway Department, Planning Survey Division, Tucson, 1960, p. 47.

(10) In Phoenix in 1947, 53,358 trips a day were made to the CBD from other parts of the area, and an additional 16,161 vehicle-person trips per day were made having both origin and destination within the CBD. By 1957 total trips to the CBD had decreased 33 per cent to 35,606 and intra-CBD trips had decreased 65 per cent to 5666.[14]

(11) New York City has seen a 10 per cent decline in the daily number of people entering downtown Manhattan (south of 61st Street) between 1948 and 1956, even though there was a 5 per cent increase in the number entering during the morning rush hours; between 1950 and 1958, Manhattan lost some 200,000 jobs, while during the same period the outer boroughs gained 168,111 jobs, or 15.1 per cent.[15] The New York decline represents a change in trends evident prior to this period; between 1940 and 1948, the number of persons entering lower Manhattan increased by 15 per cent.[16]

(12) A decline of CBD entrants in New York after 1948 is also supported by Francis Bello, who points out, "Despite a spectacular office building boom in Manhattan, the number of workers decreased 2 per cent from 1950 to 1955." He notes that the occupants of new Manhattan office buildings make up the headquarters staffs of national corporations, which use larger amounts of space per worker. He concludes that, "While difficult to document, it appears that the worker population has increased little, if any, in the downtown districts of most big cities."[17]

(13) For Chicago, the number of persons leaving the CBD during the evening peak hour by all modes of travel (including walking) was 225,600 in 1950 and 223,600 in 1961.[18] Similarly, the number of retail trade employees in Chicago's CBD decreased from 65,196 in 1948 to 49,458 in 1954.[19] In general, Chicago has a well-documented postwar experience of a declining movement of people into and out of its CBD that is particularly interesting. Among other things, it exemplifies how CBD employment can decline in spite of the continuance of an already well-developed public rapid transit system. Some relevant figures are shown in Table 7. It is evident that even with the expansion of express

[14] Phoenix-Maricopa County Traffic Study, *Traffic Study 1956–57,* Phoenix, 1957, p. 15.

[15] Regional Plan Association, *Hub-bound Travel in the Tri-State New York Metropolitan Region: Persons and Vehicles Entering Manhattan South of 61st Street, 1924–1960,* Bulletin no. 99, New York, December 1961; City of New York, Department of City Planning, *Employment Distribution in New York City and Its Central Business District,* New York, May 1961.

[16] Wilbur C. Hallenbeck, *American Urban Communities* (Harpers, New York, 1951).

[17] Francis Bello, "The City and the Car," in The Editors of *Fortune, The Exploding Metropolis* (Doubleday, Garden City, New York, 1958), p. 75.

[18] Chicago Transit Authority, *Traffic Trends in Downtown Chicago with Suggestions for Improvement,* Chicago, March 1960.

[19] *Ibid.*

TABLE 7

APPROXIMATE DAILY EMPLOYMENT AND NUMBER OF SHOPPERS IN THE CHICAGO CBD, 1946–1961

	Approximate employment		Approximate number of shoppers and other patrons	
Year	Number	Percentage of 1946	Number	Percentage of 1946
1946	297,050	100.0	81,228	100.0
1947	293,517	98.8	84,481	104.0
1948	297,763	100.2	72,794	89.6
1949	283,150	95.3	68,599	84.4
1950	270,020	90.9	63,134	77.7
1951	262,334	88.3	53,632	66.0
1952	271,308	91.3	59,050	72.7
1953	258,154	86.9	56,858	70.0
1954	262,224	88.3	49,146	60.5
1955	254,528	85.7	51,078	62.9
1956	265,857	89.5	51,597	63.5
1957	267,170	89.9	48,425	59.6
1958	264,681	89.1	43,589	53.7
1959	250,956	84.5	48,037	59.1
1960	243,890	82.1	45,072	55.5
1961	237,969	80.1	43,738	53.8

NOTE: Approximate employment is based on number of persons accumulated downtown between 7:00 a.m. and 9:30 a.m.

Approximate number of shoppers and other patrons are based on excess of peak accumulation of persons over the approximate employment.

highway access to the Loop, the number of people accumulating and employed in that CBD has steadily declined since the late 1940's. The number of downtown shoppers has also declined. The city's population, however, has remained stable, though Chicago SMSA population actually has risen about 20 per cent. Nonetheless, the peak accumulation of persons in the downtown area fell by almost one-sixth from 1950 to 1961 even though, as previously reported, the number of people crossing the CBD cordon in the evening peak hour has dropped only from 225,600 to 223,000. The stability of this cordon count, in the face of declining peak accumulation, expanded highway capacity, and continuance of large-scale rail transit suggests that Chicagoans are enjoying better urban transportation services today than they did a decade ago.

Many of these figures, it should be emphasized, relate to *all* people entering CBD's, regardless of purpose or transportation mode. In virtually every case, there has been a substantial shift away from public transit as a means of reaching the CBD during the rush hours, even when the total volume of traffic into the CBD has increased or remained constant. The fact that the automobile accounts for much or most of any increase in the number entering during a peak hour also illustrates an important limitation on the preceding numbers; namely, that the number of people crossing a CBD cordon during the peak rush hour can increase even without a growth in downtown employment, simply because traffic in and out of CBD's may be better serviced than formerly, i.e., it takes less time to "clear" or "fill" the CBD because of improved transportation facilities. In general, because of increased transportation capacity, actual declines in the number crossing the CBD cordon at the evening peak often may reflect even greater proportional declines in actual CBD employment.

Changes in Central Office Locations

Both those who envisage an expanded and growing role for CBD's in U.S. metropolitan areas and those who envisage only decline agree that the magnitude of the CBD's role depends largely on its ability to maintain and expand its function as a control and central office center.[20] But the optimists and pessimists disagree over what the current trends are in CBD central office employment. The optimists often point to the recent boom

[20] The importance of office employment in determining the future of downtown areas is illustrated by a recent economic projection for Denver's CBD. (Real Estate Research Corporation, *Economic Survey and Market Analysis of Downtown Denver,* prepared for Downtown Denver Master Plan Committee, Denver, Colorado, September 1962). This study predicts that employment in Denver's CBD will increase during the 12-year period 1962–1974 by more than 26,000 persons, or 54 per cent, from 48,000 to 75,000. Of an estimated 1962–1974 increase of 26,271 in CBD employees, 24,521 (or 93 per cent of the increase) is represented by increased office employment. These increases in office employment were obtained from projections of SMSA office employment in 13 industry groups and were based on data from the 1950 and 1960 Censuses of Population. Estimates were then made of the portion of the increased SMSA office employment which would be located in downtown office space. The percentages of SMSA office employment that it is estimated will locate in the core area are of some interest in assessing these projections. During the period 1962–1968, 16.1 per cent of the SMSA increase in office employment is projected for the core; for the period 1968–1974, the share is 18.9 per cent; the percentage of total SMSA office employment in the core in 1962, however, is only 9.47. Thus the projected increase in office employment during the second period and, for that matter, all the projections of the report are predicated on a rate of accretion of new office employment of more than twice the average share in 1962, and on a first-period rate of accretion that is almost as large. If the percentage of the four county increases to go to the core was assumed to be the same as the average in 1962, the increase in office employment would be substantially smaller. The only support given in the report for using these very critical percentages in the projections is as follows: "Estimates were then made of the portion of the total four county increase in employment which would be located in downtown office space. In deriving these estimates, we were aided by the RERC downtown employee survey indicating the number in each category presently working in core areas. We then applied knowledge of trends to extrapolate the percentage of total county increase to allocate to downtown offices." (*Ibid.,* pp. 77, 83)

in office building construction. The less optimistic reply that much of the new construction is accounted for by the fact that space per office employee has risen rapidly in the postwar period.

There has been so little information on these points that one opinion has been as good as another. To shed some light on the question, RAND's Urban Transportation Group undertook a "directory study" of the locations of the central offices of large corporations in 1950 and 1960.[21] Listings of about 21,000 firms in the *1960 Dun and Bradstreet Million Dollar Directory* were matched with listings in the *1950 MacRae's Blue Book* and the *1950 Standard and Poor's Directory*. The match was not nearly as good as was hoped; only about 6000 of 21,000 Dun and Bradstreet listings were located for 1950. Of these, approximately 2000 had different street addresses in 1960 from those in 1950. The 2000 "movers" were coded by 1950 and 1960 locations. (Six locations were used: the CBD, the central city without the CBD, and the ring of SMSA's having more than a half-million population; the central city, and the ring of SMSA's having less than a half-million population; and the non-SMSA sites.) Table 8 gives the 1950 and 1960 numbers of central office movers located

TABLE 8

CENTRAL OFFICE "MOVER FIRMS" LOCATING IN NEW GEOGRAPHIC AREAS,[a] 1950–1960

Area	1950	1960	Difference	Percentage of change
All mover firms in sample (including New York)				
CBD (SMSA > ½ million)	876	727	−149	−17.0
CC (SMSA > ½ million)	447	418	−29	−6.5
Ring (SMSA > ½ million)	132	300	168	127.3
CC (SMSA < ½ million)	264	256	−8	−3.0
Ring (SMSA < ½ million)	43	70	27	62.8
Non-SMSA	142	133	−9	−6.3
39 large SMSA's (excluding New York)				
CBD	530	404	−126	−23.8
CC	394	392	−2	−0.5
Ring	102	235	133	130.4
New York SMSA				
CBD[b]	314	300	−14	−4.4
CC	31	12	−19	−61.3
Ring	20	45	25	125.0
SMSA	365	357	−8	−2.2

[21] Lawrence Schwartz, *An Econometric Study of the Relocation of the Central Office and Its Workers,* thesis submitted in partial fulfillment of the Ph.D. requirement, Department of Economics, Harvard University, 1963.

TABLE 8 (*continued*)

Area	1950	1960	Difference	Percentage of change
Chicago				
CBD	86	55	−31	−36.0
CC	98	76	−22	−22.4
Ring	15	66	51	340.0
SMSA	199	197	−2	−1.0
Philadelphia				
CBD	36	36	0	—
CC	44	22	−22	−50.0
Ring	4	28	24	500.0
SMSA	84	86	2	2.4
Boston				
CBD	55	32	−23	−51.1
CC	16	9	−7	−43.8
Ring	20	45	25	125.0
SMSA	84	75	−9	−10.7
Cleveland				
CBD	39	25	−14	−35.9
CC	25	34	9	36.0
Ring	1	4	3	300.0
SMSA	65	63	−2	−3.1
Los Angeles				
CBD	30	18	−12	−40.0
CC	26	33	7	26.9
Ring	8	24	16	200.0
SMSA	64	75	11	17.2
Detroit				
CBD	5	4	−1	−20.0
CC	41	28	−13	−31.7
Ring	5	14	9	180.0
SMSA	51	46	−5	−9.8
Dallas				
CBD	15	12	−3	−20.0
CC	4	10	6	150.0
Ring	1	0	−1	−100.0
SMSA	20	22	2	10.0

[a] CBD is central business district; CC is central city; and Ring is the metropolitan area less the central city.

[b] Manhattan Island south of Central Park.

in each geographic unit of the 40 largest SMSA's (the 39 previously analyzed in detail plus New York) and absolute and percentage changes between 1950 and 1960.

Analysis of the 2000 moving firms yielded some highly suggestive findings, but they must be carefully interpreted. Two-thirds of the 1960 Dun and Bradstreet firms are unaccounted for in 1950; the data include no information about the births and deaths of firms; and new firms may have much different locational propensities from those of survivor firms. For example, one hypothesis might be that new firms more often would be expected to locate in CBD's where a broader range of supporting services normally would be available.

Even with these reservations in mind, the findings in Table 8 are striking. In 1950, for example, 876 of the 2000 mover firms—just under 50 per cent—were located in the CBD's of SMSA's having more than a half-million population. In 1960, this number had declined to 727. At the same time the rings of these larger SMSA's increased their number of mover-firm central offices from 132 to 300.

CBD Retail Sales and Employment

Data are also available on postwar retail activity within CBD's. CBD retailing usually has been a major creator of urban transportation demands

TABLE 9

MEAN ANNUAL PERCENTAGE CHANGE IN RETAIL SALES (PRICE AND ANNEXATION CORRECTED) IN THE CBD, CENTRAL CITY, AND SMSA OF 39 LARGE SMSA'S, BY POPULATION GROWTH SUBGROUPS

(simple, unweighted averages of individual percentage changes)

Area	1954–1958	1948–1958
All		
CBD	−0.3	0.1
Central city	3.2	4.7
SMSA	5.2	6.7
CBD		
Highest	0.2	0.6
Medium	−0.8	−0.1
Lowest	−0.2	−0.1
Central City		
Highest	6.0	7.6
Medium	2.2	4.0
Lowest	1.3	2.4
SMSA		
Highest	7.6	9.8
Medium	4.2	5.5
Lowest	3.6	4.6

SOURCE: U.S. Department of Commerce, Bureau of the Census, *U.S. Census of Business: 1958*, vol. I, *Retail Trade-Summary Statistics*, U.S. Government Printing Office, Washington, D.C., 1961, Table 6-J, pp. 6–14, 6–15.

and an important source of off-peak transit revenues.[22] It is virtually certain that CBD retailing employment decreased in the postwar period, but it is hard to document the fact, since the 1958 Census of Retailing was the first to publish separate figures on CBD retailing employment. All three postwar Censuses of Retailing, however, list CBD retail sales and the number of establishments, from which data it is possible to infer something about the change in CBD retail employment.

Table 9 gives the mean annual percentage changes in retail sales in CBD's, central cities, and SMSA's for the 39 large SMSA's analyzed and for the three population growth subgroups. Retail sales for all 39 CBD's together increased 0.1 per cent a year from 1948–1958, an over-all rate of 1 per cent for the decade (although they declined 0.3 per cent a year from 1954–1958). During the same period, retail sales in the 39 central cities increased an average of almost 5 per cent a year and those of the SMSA's almost 7 per cent, so the ring increases must necessarily have been several times that large.

CBD retail sales by growth subgroups in Table 9 illustrate that only the 13 fastest-growing SMSA's enjoyed average increases in retail sales. The rest experienced declines.

During the postwar period large productivity increases in retailing were experienced. Thus, very small percentage changes in retail sales can be associated with substantial decreases in CBD retailing employment. In Chicago, for example, a 5 per cent decline in retail sales between 1948

TABLE 10

CBD SALES AS A PERCENTAGE OF SMSA SALES FOR CONVENIENCE GOODS STORES, SHOPPING GOODS STORES, AND ALL OTHER STORES, 1948, 1954, AND 1958

Type of store	1948	1954	1958
Convenience goods	11.9	7.3	5.9
Shopping	62.4	47.0	39.7
Other	19.0	11.0	9.5

SOURCE: U.S. Department of Commerce, Bureau of the Census, *U.S. Census of Business: 1958*, vol. I, *Retail Trade-Summary Statistics*, U.S. Government Printing Office, Washington, D.C., 1961, Table 6-J, pp. 6–14, 6–15.

[22] For example, even as late as 1962, approximately 7000 of Denver's 48,000 employees were engaged in retailing. Moreover, 48 per cent of the pedestrians interviewed in a pedestrian survey gave shopping as their main reason for being downtown. (Real Estate Research Corporation, *Economic Survey and Market Analysis of Downtown Denver,* prepared for Downtown Denver Master Plan Committee, Denver, Colorado, September 1962, pp. 44, 49, appendix)

and 1954 was associated with a 32 per cent decline in CBD employment.[23]

Table 10, which lists CBD sales as a percentage of SMSA sales for convenience goods stores, shopping goods stores, and all other stores for 1948, 1954, and 1958, provides some additional insights into these processes. Clearly, at least the relative importance of the CBD as a center of retailing has been declining steadily.

Transit Service and Central-City Growth

A major argument advanced for many postwar transit plans is that emphasis on highways and neglect of transit facilities have caused rapid decentralization of central-city population and employment. This movement, it is contended, is wasteful and inefficient and spawns unaesthetic and otherwise undesirable urban patterns. Adequate rapid transit, it is argued, would halt and reverse this trend. The implied hypothesis is that there should be some correlation between urban areas' levels of transit service and the rates at which they are decentralizing. That is, cities with little or no public transit should be decentralizing much faster than others.

To test this hypothesis, population and employment statistics for the 37 largest SMSA's other than New York, Newark, and Jersey City can be stratified into three groups, differing in transit usage: those with the highest, medium, and lowest percentages of central-city workers using public transit. As can be seen from Table 11, the central cities in the highest-usage group consistently exhibit the smallest percentage increases or the largest percentage declines in employment and population in *both* their central cities and rings. Their central-city retailing, for example, declined about 0.8 per cent a year over the entire decade, in contrast to only a 0.4 per cent a year decline for the intermediate group and a 0.2 per cent increase for the group whose workers use transit the least.

The population and employment growth rates of the metropolitan ring are also inversely related in most instances to the level of transit use in the central city. From this it seems apparent that neither central-city nor ring-growth rates are closely associated with public transit usage. Rather, the rates of central-city and ring growth seem to depend mainly on the over-all rates of SMSA growth. The inverse relationship observed between transit use and growth is probably attributable to the fact that central cities with well-developed public transit systems are usually older cities, which ordinarily are slower growing and have less vacant land. Still,

23 Employment data are available from a special census run for Chicago. See Evelyn M. Kitawaga and De Ver Sholes, *Chicago Lands Retail Market,* published by the Chicago Association of Commerce and Industry and Chicago Community Inventory of the University of Chicago, 1957.

TABLE 11

MEAN ANNUAL PERCENTAGE CHANGES IN EMPLOYMENT AND POPULATION (CORRECTED FOR ANNEXATIONS) IN CENTRAL CITY AND RINGS OF 37 LARGE SMSA'S,[a] BY TRANSIT USE SUBGROUPS[b]
(simple, unweighted averages of individual percentage changes)

Item	Central city			Metropolitan ring		
	1948–1954	1954–1958	1948–1958	1948–1954	1954–1958	1948–1958
Retailing						
Highest	−1.2	−0.2	−0.8	5.6	10.0	8.9
Medium	−0.4	−0.4	−0.4	10.4	15.2	15.8
Lowest	−0.1	0.9	0.2	20.8	17.9	26.3
Services						
Highest	1.0	4.2	2.4	12.3	10.2	15.0
Medium	1.7	3.7	2.8	17.9	19.8	24.9
Lowest	2.4	3.7	3.2	26.9	23.3	37.4
Manufacturing[c]						
Highest	−0.6	−2.8	−1.4	6.0	1.0	4.5
Medium	2.7	−1.6	1.2	10.6	7.7	13.4
Lowest	3.9	−0.1	2.5	25.7	14.1	30.5
Wholesaling						
Highest	0	−0.5	−0.2	23.5	13.8	28.6
Medium	1.3	0.3	0.9	21.1	16.4	21.1
Lowest	1.4	0.9	1.1	32.0	21.4	40.4
Population (legal boundaries)						
Highest	−0.1	0	0	5.8	4.2	5.9
Medium	0.6	0.7	0.6	8.1	5.3	8.1
Lowest	5.3	4.2	5.5	6.3	5.0	6.7
Population (1950 boundaries)						
Highest	−0.5	−0.4	−0.4	6.4	4.7	6.5
Medium	0	−0.2	0	9.3	6.9	10.1
Lowest	1.2	1.2	1.2	12.2	8.6	13.4

[a] Jersey City and Newark have been excluded from the previous group of 39 since their transit use pattern is so dependent on their close relationship to New York City. As before, New York itself has also been excluded, so these 37 SMSA's are the largest in the nation, with the exceptions in the greater New York–New Jersey area.

[b] The central cities with the highest percentage of transit use were Atlanta, Baltimore, Boston, Buffalo, Chicago, Cleveland, Milwaukee, New Orleans, Philadelphia, Pittsburgh, Rochester, St. Louis, San Francisco–Oakland.

The medium group encompassed Cincinnati, Columbus, Dayton, Detroit, Kansas City, Louisville, Memphis, Miami, Minneapolis–St. Paul, Portland, Seattle, Washington, D.C.

Those with the lowest percentage of transit use were Akron, Dallas, Denver, Fort Worth, Houston, Indianapolis, Los Angeles–Long Beach, Oklahoma City, Phoenix, San Antonio, San Diego, Tampa.

[c] Manufacturing data pertain to the years 1947–1954 and 1947–1958.

transit is obviously not a sufficient, or perhaps even a necessary, condition for central-city development.

Analysis of the absolute changes in central-city employment and population, as listed in Table 12, yields similar findings. Except for services, the largest absolute declines occurred in central cities experiencing highest transit use. During each year of the decade, these central cities lost an average of 739 retail employees, 2564 manufacturing employees, 82 wholesaling employees, 2000 in population within legal boundaries, and

TABLE 12

MEAN ANNUAL ABSOLUTE CHANGES IN EMPLOYMENT AND POPULATION (CORRECTED FOR ANNEXATIONS) IN CENTRAL CITY AND RINGS OF 37 LARGE SMSA'S,[a] BY TRANSIT USE SUBGROUPS[b]
(simple, unweighted averages of individual percentage changes)

	Central city			Metropolitan ring		
Item	1948–1954	1954–1958	1948–1958	1948–1954	1954–1958	1948–1958
Retailing						
Highest	−1,176	−83	−739	1,097	2,367	1,605
Medium	−346	−314	−333	893	1,612	1,181
Lowest	118	393	228	992	2,497	1,594
Services						
Highest	366	1,086	654	461	795	594
Medium	213	594	365	365	650	479
Lowest	586	727	643	573	1,167	810
Manufacturing[c]						
Highest	−1,514	−4,402	−2,564	2,392	850	1,832
Medium	58	−2,805	−983	1,619	13	1,035
Lowest	1,977	39	1,272	2,858	2,994	2,908
Wholesaling						
Highest	−130	−399	−82	541	902	690
Medium	159	252	−1	255	379	304
Lowest	266	510	68	367	908	583
Population (legal boundaries)						
Highest	−3,000	−2,000	−2,000	34,000	34,000	34,000
Medium	1,000	1,000	1,000	25,000	29,000	26,000
Lowest	17,000	20,000	18,000	20,000	26,000	22,000
Population (1950 boundaries)						
Highest	−5,000	−4,000	−4,000	36,000	36,000	36,000
Medium	−1,000	−3,000	−2,000	27,000	33,000	29,000
Lowest	8,000	8,000	8,000	30,000	38,000	33,000

[a] See note a, Table 11.
[b] See note b, Table 11.
[c] Manufacturing data pertain to the years 1947–1954 and 1947–1958.

4000 in population within 1950 boundaries. Offsetting these losses was a yearly increase of 654 in service employment. By contrast, the central cities whose workers relied on transit the least gained employment in every category: an average of 228 retailing employees, 643 service employees, 1272 manufacturing employees, and 68 wholesaling employees each year over the decade; population gains were 18,000 a year within legal boundaries and 8000 a year within 1950 boundaries.

On the other hand, the growth of ring population and employment was, on the average, as large or larger in absolute terms for the more transit-oriented cities than for the two groups of less transit-oriented areas.

In Table 13 data are shown for 1950 to 1960 on the absolute and percentage changes in the number of central office "movers" (as defined previously) for CBD's, central cities, and rings of each transit subgroup. Again, the conclusion seems to be that a high level of transit use by central-city workers is not a guarantee against the decline of central cities and CBD's; in particular, it is apparent that it is not a *sufficient* condition to keep central offices from moving to less central locations.

These statistics do not imply, of course, that the extent and type of available transit have no influence on land use; they only refute the more extreme claims made for transit as a device for reshaping and modifying urban locational choices. In short, these choices are a function of many influences: income levels, family characteristics, population age distribution, industrial technology, and so on, as well as transit availability.

TABLE 13

CENTRAL OFFICE MOVER FIRMS LOCATED IN THE CBD, CENTRAL CITY, AND RING, 1950 AND 1960: ABSOLUTE AND PERCENTAGE CHANGE, 1950–1960, BY TRANSIT USE SUBGROUPS[a]

Area	1950	1960	Absolute change	Percentage change
CBD				
Highest	356	277	−79	−22.2
Medium	78	57	−21	−26.9
Lowest	83	60	−23	−27.7
Central city				
Highest	251	222	−29	−11.6
Medium	84	85	1	1.2
Lowest	47	78	31	66.0
Ring				
Highest	57	156	99	173.7
Medium	12	22	10	83.3
Lowest	10	25	15	150.0

[a] See note b, Table 11.

Projections of Future Urban Growth

A common justification for new investments in urban transit is that urban population will grow so enormously over the next few decades that even if there is *relative* decentralization of urban activities there will still be *absolute* growth in central cities and in the number of people working in CBD's. In essence, proponents of this argument grant all that precedes about urban location trends, but argue that absolute declines in CBD's will be reversed in the future by simple population growth.

It is difficult to evaluate such a hypothesis, dealing as it does with the distant and uncertain future. In question are the locational choices and travel perferences of future generations of urban households and businesses, choices depending on a host of economic, social, and geographic considerations. Furthermore, data are not systematically collected on some of the more fundamental of these variables, such as real estate prices and the location of vacant land.[24]

Despite the hazards, an attempt to forecast future urban population and employment patterns was undertaken in the RAND Urban Transportation Study. The device employed was a model of an urban community based on land-use and transportation interrelationships within urban areas. The model's most important aspect is almost exclusive preoccupation with structural estimation and diagnosis as an objective. While the model can be used for broad forecasting purposes, it is not intended to foretell the values of specific variables at specific locations; that would require a fundamentally different design. In a pure forecasting model, for example, the strong autocorrelation probably present in many of the model's variables could and should be used as a simple means of improving forecast accuracy.[25]

Highly pertinent to the questions discussed in this chapter is one of the submodels, or components, of the over-all model, entitled "Workplace Location and Nonresidential Land Use." Two versions of this nonresidential land-use model have been completed.[26]

These models were used to make projections, for 1965 and 1975, of a metropolitan area with the average characteristics of the 39 areas ana-

[24] For an attempt to meet some of these data needs, see J. H. Niedercorn and E. F. R. Hearle, *Recent Land-Use Trends in Forty-eight Large American Cities,* The RAND Corporation, RM-3664-FF, June 1963.

[25] The model also is not designed to provide direct and quick solutions to specific policy or planning problems. Hopefully, it will provide some helpful insights into such problems, but the model is so geographically general or unspecific that its translations to the planning processes of a particular urban area may be difficult.

[26] A discussion of the first model may be found in J. H. Niedercorn and J. F. Kain, *Suburbanization of Employment and Population, 1948–1975,* The RAND Corporation, P-2641, January 1963. A discussion of the second and more complex model may be found in Niedercorn and Kain, *An Econometric Model of Metropolitan Development,* The RAND Corporation, P-2663, December 1962.

lyzed in earlier sections of this chapter. Various time-paths of the exogenous explanatory variables (that is, variables determined outside the model) were used or hypothesized in making these projections.[27] The procedure was carried out in two steps: first the exogenous variables were projected over time and then, by solving the model's equations with respect to time, changes were estimated for the dependent variables during the time periods 1954–1965 and 1954–1975.

Using the first version of the model, two sets of projections of the explanatory variables, a high and a low, were obtained. The low projections are based on an extrapolation of what actually happened, on the average, during the years 1954–1958. Since 1958 was a year of moderately severe recession, a second and higher set of projections incorporating more favorable developments in SMSA population and manufacturing employment were also used. Exogenous projections of vacant land, however, were the same for both sets. The high and low projections assumed for the exogenous or independent variables are listed in Table 14. Initially, vacant land was hypothesized to be 27 per cent of total

TABLE 14

PROJECTED ANNUAL CHANGES IN EMPLOYMENT, POPULATION, AND VACANT LAND FOR U.S. METROPOLITAN AREAS

Variable	Low projection (per cent)	High projection (per cent)
Manufacturing employment		
Growing areas	3.0	5.0
Declining areas	−1.1	−0.5
Population	2.6	3.5
Vacant land ratio	−5.9	−5.9

central-city land area in the manufacturing equation, and 22 per cent in the population equation.[28] Since a zero level of annexations was assumed in making the projections, all forecasts refer to constant 1954 areas.

The projections of cumulative absolute change over the periods 1954–1965 and 1954–1975 are presented in Table 15, along with actual 1954 average figures for the 39 SMSA's (to facilitate comparisons). The projected changes are, of course, consistent almost by construction with the simpler descriptive statistics presented earlier. Significant central-city declines of manufacturing employment are projected when either high or

[27] Niedercorn and Kain, *Suburbanization of Employment and Population, 1948–1975.*

[28] These figures were obtained from land-use data collected by Kain and Niedercorn from the 39 cities included in the study.

TABLE 15

PROJECTED MEAN ABSOLUTE CHANGES IN SELECTED EMPLOYMENTS AND POPULATION FOR 39 CENTRAL CITIES AND METROPOLITAN RINGS, 1954–1965 AND 1954–1975

Variable	Low projections 1954–1965	Low projections 1954–1975	High projections 1954–1965	High projections 1954–1975	1954 actual average totals for 39 large SMSA's
			Central city		
Manufacturing					
Total	−12,568	−25,084	−5,238	−10,429	98,718
Growing areas	5,052	5,333	7,734	13,519	59,373
Declining areas	−26,273	−48,742	−15,327	−29,056	132,442
Wholesaling	803	1,240	1,385	2,358	25,909
Retailing	2,638	4,328	4,037	7,019	48,753
Services	12,639	27,034	17,229	38,780	20,288
Total employment	3,512	7,518	17,413	37,728	193,668
Population	−6,174	−20,974	12,002	13,971	724,315
			Metropolitan ring		
Manufacturing					
Total	13,536	28,210	34,692	88,873	70,918
Growing areas	28,861	59,410	74,824	193,992	52,192
Declining areas	1,617	3,943	3,479	7,115	86,969
Wholesaling	7,508	16,691	10,484	24,572	5,148
Retailing	24,415	53,961	33,694	78,532	23,626
Services	9,199	21,306	13,926	33,824	6,726
Total employment	54,658	120,168	92,796	225,801	106,418
Population	461,706	1,020,117	636,770	1,483,727	656,052

low values of the exogenous variables are used. These are offset by employment increases in wholesaling, retailing, and, especially, services, so that when the high values of the exogenous variables are used, total central-city employment increases slightly. With a single exception (manufacturing employment in declining areas), growth of the metropolitan rings is rapid when either the high or low values of the exogenous variables are used.

Understanding of these projected changes in urban structure is further facilitated by Table 16, which expresses them in percentage terms and permits comparison of the percentage rate of change in central cities and rings from 1954 through 1965, and 1954 through 1975. When the most optimistic set of values of the exogenous variables is used, central-city employment increases 19.5 per cent for the employment categories included in the study (representing approximately 60 per cent of urban

TABLE 16

PROJECTED MEAN PERCENTAGE CHANGES IN EMPLOYMENT AND POPULATION FOR 39 CENTRAL CITIES AND METROPOLITAN RINGS, 1954–1965 AND 1954–1975

Variable	Low projections		High projections	
	1954–1965	1954–1975	1954–1965	1954–1975
		Central city		
Manufacturing				
Total	−12.7	−25.4	−5.3	−10.6
Growing areas	8.5	9.0	13.0	22.8
Declining areas	−19.8	−36.8	−11.6	−21.9
Wholesaling	3.1	4.8	5.3	9.1
Retailing	5.4	8.9	8.3	14.4
Services	62.3	133.2	84.9	191.1
Total employment	1.8	3.9	9.0	19.5
Population	−0.8	−2.9	1.7	1.9
		Metropolitan ring		
Manufacturing				
Total	19.1	39.8	48.9	125.3
Growing areas	55.3	113.8	143.3	371.7
Declining areas	1.8	4.5	4.0	8.2
Wholesaling	145.8	324.2	203.7	477.3
Retailing	103.3	228.4	142.6	332.4
Services	136.8	316.8	207.0	502.9
Total employment	51.4	112.9	87.2	212.2
Population	70.4	155.5	97.1	226.2

nonagricultural employment) in the twenty-one years from the end of 1954 through 1975. When a low set of values is used, total central-city employment increases only 3.9 per cent during the same period. The percentage increases in ring employment for 1954 through 1975, by contrast, are estimated at more than 112 per cent under the low or pessimistic conditions. Without the projected 133 and 191 per cent increases in selected service employments in central cities (which could well be incorrect), the contrasts between city and ring would be even more substantial.

In the second version of the model, the importance of the availability of suitable vacant land for urban development was tested more thoroughly.[29] On the basis of this version of the model, it would appear that as the quantity of vacant land in the central city decreases, less and less of the SMSA increment of manufacturing employment goes into the central city. For example, if 20 per cent of all of a central city's land is vacant, about 40 per cent of any increase in SMSA manufacturing will

[29] Niedercorn and Kain, *An Econometric Model of Metropolitan Development.*

go to the central city; if 10 per cent is vacant, only about 20 per cent of the increase will go to the central city. Furthermore, if SMSA manufacturing employment is declining, the central city suffers about 72 per cent of the loss, regardless of vacant land percentages. Similarly, with SMSA population increments, if 10 per cent of the central-city land zoned for residences is vacant, only 4 per cent of the newcomers find homes there.

Distributional characteristics must be taken into account if these average figures or projections are to be translated into transportation policy recommendations.[30] With the notable and important exceptions of Los Angeles, San Francisco, and Houston, the rapidly growing SMSA's among the 39 analyzed tend to be average or smaller than average in present population. This suggests that a "leveling process" is in motion which will promote a larger number of approximately equal-sized regional centers. Such a development seems compatible, of course, with the often-noted trend toward a more even geographic distribution of manufacturing employment.[31]

A final argument frequently offered against the hypothesis that densities in urban cores will tend to decline in the future is that recent historical tendencies toward decentralization will be reversed by urban renewal programs. That is, urban renewal programs now under way or even actually completed will reverse recent tendencies toward urban decentralization. However, using data from 297 urban renewal projects in an "advanced state of planning" in 102 U.S. cities, E. F. R. Hearle and J. H. Nieder-

[30] Simple trend extrapolations of population growth in central cities and rings for 12 Eastern Seaboard cities were made as part of a transportation demand study of the Eastern Seaboard corridor or "megalopolis" done of the U.S. Department of Commerce by the Systems Analysis and Research Corporation of Boston, Mass. These extrapolations, on the whole, were very pessimistic about central-city prospects. In the same vein, the New York Metropolitan Region Study Group projected a decline in Manhattan population from 1,650,000 in 1960 to 1,600,000 in 1985; for all of New York City they extrapolate a slight decline from 8,037,000 in 1960 to 7,810,000 in 1985. By contrast, they estimate that the inner ring of the New York region (Nassau, Essex, Westchester, Bergen, Union, Passaic, and Richmond) will increase its population from 4,919,000 in 1960 to 8,093,000 in 1985; the outer ring (Fairfield, Suffolk, Middlesex, Monmouth, Morris, Orange, Dutchess, Somerset, Rockland, Putnam) is expected to experience a phenomenal growth from 2,999,000 in 1960 to 7,809,000 in 1985. Total employment in New York City is expected to rise slowly from 3,899,900 in 1956 to 4,406,500 in 1985; inner-ring employment is extrapolated to increase from 1,453,600 in 1956 to 2,715,700 in 1985; finally, a rise in outer-ring employment from 775,000 in 1956 to 2,034,500 in 1985 is forecast. (Raymond Vernon, *Metropolis 1985* [Harvard University Press, Cambridge, Mass., 1960], pp. 234–239.)

[31] Victor R. Fuchs, "The Determinants of the Redistribution of the Manufacturing in the United States since 1929," *Review of Economics and Statistics,* 44:167–177 (May 1962); Richard A. Easterlin, *Population Redistribution and Economic Growth in the United States, 1870–1950,* vol. 2, *Analysis of Economic Change,* American Philosophical Society, 1960, pp. 108, 110; and Harvey S. Perloff *et al., Regions, Resources, and Economic Growth* (The Johns Hopkins Press, Baltimore, Md., 1960), p. 394.

corn in a research project[32] undertaken as part of the RAND Urban Transportation Study found a rather mixed pattern, namely:

> Within project areas, the major impact of renewal is to double the land area devoted to industrial uses and to triple the area used for public purposes. Residential area is sharply reduced, commercial area increased, and street area left about the same.
>
> Residential population densities . . . also . . . decline slightly—from 55.96 to 51.40 dwelling units per acre . . . Since residential *acreage* also is being reduced by urban renewal, the effect is reinforced—lower densities on fewer acres.
>
> It should be clear . . . that urban renewal projects, if current practice continues, are changing substantially the land-use character of the areas where they are located. Since such projects occur mainly in older sections, and such sections tend to be toward the centers of the cities, urban renewal appears to accelerate rather than retard the decentralization of residential population. Urban renewal areas are more and more becoming places to work rather than places to live. Indeed, urban renewal may well create expanded locational choices for industries finding central areas previously unattractive because of difficulties in acquiring multiple parcels in diverse ownership. However, it is not clear that increases of industrial acreage will bring about an increase in industrial employment because increases in land area per employee are possible.

Renewal thus works toward the creation of central areas that in some respects are more like their surroundings than was the case before renewal. In many ways, this is hardly surprising, and certainly not lamentable, since it suggests that the urban renewal programs may have facilitated adjustment of urban core areas to modern circumstances.

In sum, while it is clear that population and employment growth and urban renewal are powerful forces, it is not obvious that they will create insuperable transportation problems in the central parts of U.S. urban areas in the very near future. By any standards of comparison, the far more difficult urban transportation problems of the future seem likely to occur in the metropolitan rings, where prospective employment and population increases are likely to be so large as to border on the overwhelming.

Summary and Conclusions

This chapter has presented empirical information on changes in the location and distribution of employment and population within SMSA's. Most of this information, and certainly the most systematic, was for central cities and suburban rings only. Particular attention was focused on location trends within the 39 largest SMSA's, excluding New York. The

[32] E. F. R. Hearle and J. H. Niedercorn, *The Impact of Urban Renewal on Land Use,* The RAND Corporation, RM-4186-RC, June 1964.

data strongly verified the existence of the tendencies toward decentralization hypothesized in chapter 2. In recent years, most large central cities have been losing employment and population, both relatively and absolutely, particularly when "annexation effects" are eliminated. The most notable exceptions appeared to be the newer cities of the West and Southwest. On the other hand, service employment has been increasing in almost all central cities, reflecting the vastly increased importance of services in the American economy in general. However, this one major offset to declining employment in central cities seems, under the most favorable assumptions, barely sufficient to maintain present central-city employment and population levels in the future.

It is possible, of course, that these adverse general trends may mask quite different rates of change for specific parts of cities and, in particular, favorable growth rates for CBD's. While the statistical information available on CBD population and employment trends is admittedly unsystematic and fragmentary, it is sufficient to contradict the hypothesis that the figures on changes in central-city employment and population could mask large increases in core activity. In no instance is there any evidence of sharp increases in CBD employment. Similarly, there is every indication that the number of downtown shoppers has declined as well. Overall, the evidence points to frequent declines in CBD employment and other activity levels, frequent instances of stagnation, and only a few instances of moderate growth in central-city activity.

It is even doubtful that central office employment has been growing in CBD's—and nearly everyone interested in these problems agrees that the future of downtown areas heavily depends on central office employment. While no very reliable information is available on location trends in central office activities, the fragmentary information available indicates a moderate trend toward suburbanization. At a minimum, the CBD's relative advantage as a central office location apparently has not increased much in recent years. Of course, even with a net loss in the number of central offices, the level of CBD office employment could continue to increase if the number of workers per central office establishment increased. Still, the shift toward suburbanization makes caution advisable in postulating any large increases of this kind, and they must be offset against well-substantiated decreases in CBD wholesaling, manufacturing, and retailing employment.

Transit availability, moreover, does not seem to be a sufficient condition for creating density or downtown growth, nor does it seem to be a major deterrent to the development of new employment opportunities in the suburban ring. Other factors seem much more important. In short, the available data, however interpreted, strongly confirm the impression that employment opportunities in urban areas are becoming increasingly dispersed, both relatively and absolutely, in turn modifying the demand pattern for urban transportation.

Finally, it seems improbable that even with very large increases in urban population in the next few decades the absolute level of downtown employment and population will increase much, if at all. At a minimum, it seems undeniable that the great needs for new transport facilities will be much more in the very rapidly expanding metropolitan rings and suburbs than in and near CBD's.

Chapter 4 | Recent Trends in the Supply of Urban Transport and Highway Financing

An important fact about the supply of transport facilities is the time it takes to bring many components into being. It can take months or even years, for example, merely to acquire the land needed for rights-of-way, because of technical, legal, and political difficulties. The construction of rail and highway facilities also can be time-consuming, as witness the fifteen years or more needed to complete the interstate highway program, and the anticipated 10-year construction period for the San Francisco rail transit system. In general, various transport system components require varying amounts of time to construct and to meet deficiencies in supply. For example, it is relatively easy and requires little time to meet most equipment or rolling-stock needs, but it is considerably more difficult and time-consuming to eliminate an undersupply of rights-of-way and related roadbed or highway facilities.

In this chapter, some of the more pertinent aggregative figures on postwar rates of adjustments of urban transportation facilities in the United States are placed in historical perspective, along with some data on the supply of urban highways and recent developments within the urban public transit industry. Following this, an evaluation of highway financing is undertaken. Financial considerations help explain why urban highway facilities are currently supplied as they are and, more importantly from the standpoint of policy planning, shed light on the prospects for future urban highway development. Moreover, urban highway planning and financing almost invariably involve the difficult question of whether urban highway users are receiving subsidies from public funds. It is useful, at least, to try to define the extent of any "subsidy," not only of urban highway users in the large, but also of specific parts of the urban highway system and their use at particular hours of the day. Obviously, the prime importance attached to peak-hour utilization of centrally located urban expressways suggests that the subsidy status, or more precisely, the relationship between user charges and costs for these facilities, deserves special attention.

The ultimate test of any urban transportation system is, of course, its ability to perform the function for which it is designed or used. The public normally judges the success of financial, political, and other arrangements for providing urban transportation facilities by the degree to which the resultant systems and facilities meet the public's needs. A third section of this chapter entitled "Performance of Urban Highway Systems" is devoted to these issues.

Supply and Use of Urban Transportation Facilities

World War II almost completely halted the construction of urban transportation facilities, private vehicles, mass transit vehicles, and highways. Gasoline and tire rationing, coupled with booming employment, led to an all-time high in the use of public transit during the war years. As shown in Table 17, transit use has declined nearly 64 per cent since 1945. The

Table 17

Total Transit Passengers in the United States, by Types of Service: At 5-Year Intervals, 1935–1950, and Annually, 1950–1963 (millions)

	Railway					
Calendar year	Surface	Subway and elevated	Total	Trolley coach	Motor bus	Grand total
1935	7,276	2,236	9,512	96	2,618	12,226
1940	5,943	2,382	8,325	534	4,239	13,098
1945	9,426	2,698	12,124	1,244	9,886	23,254
1950	3,904	2,264	6,168	1,658	9,420	17,246
1951	3,101	2,189	5,290	1,633	9,202	16,125
1952	2,477	2,124	4,601	1,640	8,878	15,119
1953	2,036	2,040	4,076	1,566	8,260	13,902
1954	1,489	1,912	3,401	1,367	7,624	12,392
1955	1,207	1,870	3,077	1,202	7,250	11,529
1956	876	1,880	2,756	1,142	7,043	10,941
1957	679	1,843	2,522	993	6,874	10,389
1958	572	1,815	2,387	843	6,502	9,732
1959	521	1,828	2,349	749	6,459	9,557
1960	463	1,850	2,313	657	6,425	9,395
1961	434	1,855	2,289	601	5,993	8,883
1962	393	1,890	2,283	547	5,865	8,695
1963	329	1,836	2,165	413	5,822	8,400

SOURCE: American Transit Association, *Transit Fact Book*, 1964 edition.

extent of the decline, however, is almost surely magnified by the comparison with swollen wartime usage.

While the number of transit passengers declined in the postwar period, the route-miles of rapid or grade separated rail transit service have increased slightly since 1945—about 2 per cent. At the same time, bus round trip route-miles of service have increased about 30 per cent. On the other hand, surface rail and trolley coach service have both decreased substantially; even so, over-all route-miles of transit service have increased about 11 per cent since 1945.[1]

An alternative measure of over-all transit passenger service is the amount of revenue-vehicle or car mileage provided by transit operations. Here, there has been a substantial postwar decrease. Since 1950, over-all transit vehicle and car mileage has dropped more than 30 per cent (about 38 per cent since 1945); most of the drop, however, is a result of a sharp reduction in surface railway car mileage and trolley coach mileage. Rail rapid transit car mileage decreased slightly more than 12 per cent after 1950, while bus mileage fell just over 19 per cent. Obviously, since route mileage has increased and vehicle or car mileage has decreased, less frequent transit service is now offered, both by rail rapid transit and bus.[2]

While declining demand has been a major postwar difficulty of public transit, a problem with automobiles has been the rapidly increasing demand for limited highway facilities. Beginning in 1946, there were notable differences between the production rates of vehicles and highways. Although only 610 new private passenger vehicles were produced in 1944, over 2 million private automobiles were marketed in 1946 and over 6.75 million in 1950. From 1946 to 1950, inclusive, 21 million passenger cars were produced, exceeding by more than a million the total production from 1935 to 1946. With the end of wartime tire and gasoline rationing, the increase in miles of travel, particularly urban travel, was even more dramatic. From 1945 to 1950, travel in urban areas by passenger vehicles increased 73 billion vehicle-miles a year (from 111 to 184 billion). The increase over prewar levels was only slightly less impressive: the 184 billion figure for 1950 was 54 billion greater than the figure for 1940.[3] Nor was this increase geographically uniform. These aggregate figures understate the relative expansion in automobile ownership and travel in the largest and fastest-growing urban areas.

[1] American Transit Association, *Transit Fact Book,* 1964 edition, Table 19.

[2] Since more and more large buses have been bought in recent years, the total bus seating capacity and total bus seat miles may actually have increased, though probably not.

[3] U.S. Department of Commerce, Bureau of the Census, *Historical Statistics of the United States: Colonial Times to 1957,* U.S. Government Printing Office, Washington, D.C., 1958, pp. 462–463.

Highway capacity did not grow at the same pace. First of all, the war years saw a nearly absolute moratorium on the construction and even maintenance of highway facilities; the United States emerged from the war with about the same highway capacity it had at the beginning. Furthermore, annual postwar highway construction expenditures per vehicle were less than prewar, as can be seen in Table 18. In the 1920's the expenditure level was $85 a year per vehicle, rising to $101 by 1941. In the first postwar period, the figure was $48 per vehicle (in constant prices). In the later postwar period it rose to $65. Similarly, the Bureau of Public Roads estimates that by the end of 1948 the depreciated investment in

TABLE 18

HIGHWAY CONSTRUCTION EXPENDITURES AND INVESTMENT PER REGISTERED MOTOR VEHICLE FOR SELECTED PERIODS, 1921–1958, EXCLUDING TOLL FACILITIES

Item	1921–1927	1928–1934	1935–1941	1946–1952	1953–1958
Motor vehicle registration					
Annual average for period (million)	17.3	25.4	30.5	44.6	63.0
During last year of period (million)	23.3	25.3	34.9	53.3	68.3
Construction expenditures[a]					
Annual average for period ($ million)	1468	2521	3066	2120	4089
Annual average per registered motor vehicle during period ($)	85	99	101	48	65
Total remaining investment, undepreciated[b]					
At end of period ($ billion)	12.9	28.8	47.7	57.3	74.2
Amount per registered motor vehicle at end of period ($)	554	1138	1367	1075	1086
Total remaining investment, depreciated					
At end of period ($ billion)	10.2	21.9	34.0	34.8	47.1
Amount per registered motor vehicle at end of period ($)	438	866	974	653	690

[a] Adjusted to price level of last half of 1956.
[b] Accumulative construction expenditures less retirements.
SOURCE: E. H. Holmes, *Highway Transportation: U.S. Transportation, U.S. Transportation Resources, Performance and Problems*, National Academy of Sciences, National Research Council, Publication 841-S, Washington, D.C., p. 63, using data from unpublished estimates, Bureau of Public Roads.

highways was $690 per vehicle—about the level attained in 1931, and less than that in 1941.

To the extent that economies of scale and technological improvements are operative in the provision of highways, and that considerable excess capacity may have been previously in existence, these figures may not, of course be as unfavorable as they appear. In fact, some strong arguments can be made in favor of decreasing expenditures per registered motor vehicle over time. Given the fact that the great bulk of early highway expenditure was made on rural highways, one can argue that system or divisibility effects alone should result in decreased expenditures per vehicle.[4] Still, the actual decline in expenditures per vehicle probably exceeds a level that is attributable to scale economies or system effects alone.

Patterns in Highway Finance

Some presumption, in short, exists that the provision of highway services, located in the government sector and facing substantial design and planning problems, was less responsive to consumer demands than was the provision of passenger vehicles during the early postwar period. These imbalances may have been aggravated in urban areas, moreover, by certain practices used in financing highway construction and maintenance. There is evidence that the urban transportation problem, like many other urban problems, has been made more difficult by the urban-rural political imbalance in many state legislatures.

Three questions enter into discussions of highway financial practice as it relates to urban transportation: whether highway users as a class pay more or less than the costs of the facilities they use; whether *urban* highway users as a special class of automobile drivers pay more or less than

[4] Here of course we are referring to volume and capacity relationships. For example, virtually all rural highways have daily volumes below 10,000 vehicles a day. (See Theodore M. Matson *et al., Traffic Engineering* [McGraw-Hill, New York, 1945], Figs. 5–1 and 5–3.) The average daily vehicular volume on all main primary rural highways is around 1000 vehicles a day. Under these circumstances, it is evident that even a 2-lane highway, which can handle volumes of at least 1000 vehicles *per hour,* hardly needs to be expanded under most conditions. Interestingly enough, the average daily volumes on most urban highways are well below 10,000 vehicles a day, again indicating that the rate of growth of highways probably should be decreasing—because of divisibility. For example, a study of 44 urban areas in Los Angeles County found an average highway volume of only 7423 vehicles a day, even on those roads and streets whose volume carried at least 200 vehicles a day. In San Francisco, for daily volumes recorded at 1400 locations, the average was only 7214 vehicles a day, and less than 30 per cent of the locations had volumes over 10,000, and less than 10 per cent had volumes over 20,000. Under these conditions, it is evident that considerable excess capacity is available in most sections of our urban areas as well; of course, because of peaking, particular parts of urban systems can be considerably overworked for limited periods each day.

their costs; and whether urban highway users *during peak commuter periods* pay more or less than their costs.

The question of whether highway users are being subsidized involves the evaluation of a host of difficult and controversial issues, such as what accounting methods should be employed for government activities and what constitutes equitable distribution of certain policing and administrative charges normally incurred by state and local governments. For example, highway-oriented groups often contend that highway users are charged a disproportionate share of police costs in many states. Others contend that highway users do not pay their fair share of the general administrative and legislative costs of conducting government, particularly at the state level.

It is not the province of this study to assess these issues fully, but a brief commentary may be worth while. First of all, it appears that the so-called diversion of *state* highway taxes to other uses in recent years has amounted, on a simple average for all states, to approximately 8 per cent of total state highway user tax receipts, amounting to over $500 million per year. This average, however, comes from a highly skewed distribution; for a preponderance of states no diversion, or a less than 1 per cent diversion, occurs.[5] Only a few states have made substantial diversions of highway tax revenues into general governmental funds in recent years; specifically, about eight states usually divert from 12 to 59 per cent of their total highway-related tax receipts.[6]

To strike an over-all balance between highway user and state general funds, figures on highway tax diversion must be compared, of course, with their opposite, diversions of general funds into highway expenditures. At the state level these diversions have been negligible, usually averaging as low as 1 or 2 per cent for all states, and seldom exceeding 10 per cent for single states.[7] In rare instances, however, such as in recessions, general funds are sometimes used to speed up highway programs to offset unemployment. Similarly, municipalities have often borne highway expenses out of general funds. Thus, at the state and local level, it might be possible to assert that highway users as a class incur net costs 5 to 10 per cent more than they now pay in local taxes.

Any imbalance at the state and municipal level, however, is offset to some extent at the federal level. Expenditures from the Federal Highway Trust Fund in recent years have run $1 to $2 billion below *total* federal revenues from taxes on motor fuel, lubricating oil, vehicles, automotive

[5] Automobile Manufacturers Association, *Automobile Facts and Figures,* 1965 edition, p. 56.

[6] *Ibid.*

[7] These estimates are based on figures reported annually by the U.S. Department of Commerce, Bureau of Public Roads, in *Highway Statistics,* U.S. Government Printing Office, Washington, D.C.

products, and the like.[8] At the moment, almost the entire discrepancy is a result of excise taxes on automobiles which, as a matter of conscious policy, are assigned to the general fund rather than the highway trust fund. Furthermore, reported expenditures from the highway trust fund may not represent the full cost to the federal government of its highway program because of insufficient allowance for the general overhead of operating government. On balance, though, the safest and most reasonable conclusion for the nation as a whole would appear to be that highway users are neither overly pampered nor punished by the present level of highway user taxes.

This roughly equitable state of affairs, however, does not seem to apply to *urban* highway users as a specific class. There is considerable evidence that states (in using both federal and state funds) have devoted less than a fair share of automobile user tax revenues to urban areas, in view of the requirements and contributions of urban residents. It is almost irrefutable, in fact, that urban drivers as a whole have been paying more than the costs of the facilities they use, and certainly more, relatively, than do users of rural highways and roads.

Some favoring of rural roads probably is justified, however, on the basis that a highway system should provide access and connections among all important population centers and other points of interest within an area. In short, the rural roads may be of benefit to the urbanite even if he seldom uses them. Still, the relationship between user tax contributions and highway expenditures does provide at least some rough guidelines to the adequacy of expenditures made on different parts of a highway system. A highway system is a constantly evolving concept, not something planned, built, and left untouched for all time; relative use of facilities has always been a prime criterion used by highway engineers in evaluating alternative schemes for expanding a system. To put the argument in economists' terms, it usually would be considered good economic practice to expand the capacity of a service that yields revenues in excess of its costs, rather than to expand services that do not. At a minimum, the relationship between user tax contribtuions on a particular portion of a highway system and the costs of providing the system is at least

[8] It has been estimated that the federal government previously diverted almost 60 per cent of all federal highway income to other governmental purposes. See Philip H. Burch, Jr., *Highway Revenue and Expenditure Policy in the U.S.*, Rutgers University Press, New Brunswick, N. J., 1962. Use of gasoline taxes as a general revenue source rather than as a user charge to achieve efficient use of highway facilities is also a relatively regressive form of taxation. It has been estimated that while 26 per cent of general governmental revenues are contributed by those having family incomes of less than $5000 per year, this group pays 47 per cent of the gasoline taxes. The contribution to general revenues by households having family incomes of over $10,000 per year is estimated at 39 per cent, while they pay only an estimated 14 per cent of gasoline taxes. *Ibid.*, p. 43.

one relevant piece of data to be taken into account when planning highway facilities or, more accurately, considering the advisability of expanding certain portions of a highway system. The relationship between user tax contributions and highway costs in urban areas is further pertinent because it is one available measure for assessing the empirical validity of arguments that urban highway users are discriminated against or, contrarily, subsidized.

Examples of disproportionate sharing of highway revenues between urban and rural areas abound. For instance, Lyle Fitch of the Institute of Public Administration has summarized the situation as follows:

> Roadway-user taxes appear to balance roadway expenditures for the country as a whole, but the picture varies when we look at segments of the country. In urban areas generally, more revenues are generated by highways than are expended on roads within the areas. There are heavy transfers of highway-generated revenues from urban to rural states. For large central cities, however, it appears that highway-related expenditures within dense urban centers by all units of government often exceed highway-generated revenues.
>
> There is little question but that on net balance a considerable proportion of revenues generated by motor-vehicle use in urban areas is and historically has been diverted to rural areas (owing partly to the strength of rural interests in state legislatures). This has had two effects: (1) it has probably reduced the supply and quality of road space in urban areas over all, and (2) it has obliged municipalities to finance highway and street expenditures from nonhighway-related sources.[9]

Confirmation of Fitch's position is provided by figures compiled by G. P. St. Clair of the Bureau of Public Roads; St. Clair's figures pertain to the year 1960, and his user tax receipts and highway expenditures are for all levels of government. For forty-six large SMSA's in the United States St. Clair estimates total user taxes on highway use within the SMSA's to be at a level of $1.650 billion, while total expenditures on highways in these same SMSA's amounted to $1.491 billion in 1960. Furthermore, St. Clair's figures indicate that the excess of user taxes over total expenditures tends to rise with the size of the city, both in relative and absolute terms. Indeed, he reports a slight deficiency in user tax receipts as compared with highway expenditures for SMSA's under 250,000 in population.[10]

In discussing urban-rural shares of highway revenues, P. H. Burch concludes that "over the years, most metropolises have received short shrift in the allocation of state aid." He argues that by and large the apportionment of highway revenue should follow the distribution of the

[9] Lyle Fitch and associates, *Urban Transportation and Public Policy* (Chandler Publishing Co., San Francisco, 1964), pp. 32 and 129.

[10] G. P. St. Clair, "Congestion Tolls—An Engineer's Viewpoint," *Highway Research Record,* No. 47, 1964, pp. 93 and 95.

population, but that while 60 per cent of the American people dwell in urban centers (using 10,000 as the rural-urban division), and while 48 per cent of the total annual vehicle mileage is tallied in urban areas, less than 25 per cent of state aid allocations is earmarked for city streets and highways.[11] Using the data in Table 19 to illustrate his points, Burch argues that American cities should be entitled to a median level of about 47 or 48 per cent of all motor fuel and registration receipts.

Rather similar conclusions were reached by R. W. Harbeson in a study comparing allocations or expenditures with realization of fuel taxes by broad classifications of highways. While using data that admittedly embodied many difficulties and imperfections, he concluded:

For the United States as a whole in 1960 the allocation of state user charge revenue to state highways was only slightly in excess of the amount justified by traffic volume, as measured by fuel consumption; whereas, on the same basis,

TABLE 19

PROPORTION OF TOTAL STATE HIGHWAY DEPARTMENT FUNDS EXPENDED ON URBAN STATE HIGHWAYS, IN RELATION TO URBAN TRAFFIC AND URBAN POPULATION STANDARD

State	Percentage of total traffic in urban areas, 1956	Percentage urban population, 1960 (minus, as a rule, 20 per cent)[a]	Percentage urban of total state highway department expenditures (as of the first year or years for which reliable figures are available)	Percentage urban of total state highway department expenditures (1957–1959 average)
Maine	25.8	26.5	3.1 (1947)	12.1
New Hampshire	24.3	38.7	1.1 (1947)	5.8
Vermont	26.0	13.2	1.3 (1950)	1.4
Connecticut	56.5	58.6	5.2 (1945)	43.7
Delaware	19.4	45.2	2.1 (1951)	14.6
Maryland	31.2	53.1	11.1 (1950)	6.6
Massachusetts	51.0	63.7	4.0 (1946)	44.3
New Jersey	66.1	59.0	54.8 (1947–49)	45.0
Rhode Island	76.5	66.7	23.0 (1950)	69.8
Illinois	63.0	55.6	6.6 (1945)	41.3
Indiana	38.3	41.7	11.3 (1945)	7.3
Michigan	38.0	52.7	27.9 (1949)	29.3
New York	60.0	63.3	12.6 (1950)	43.6
Ohio	50.4	50.6	16.9 (1948)	32.7
Pennsylvania	38.3	45.6	12.5 (1945)	13.9
Wisconsin	40.8	41.7	3.8 (1945)	23.4

[11] Philip H. Burch, Jr., *Highway Revenue and Expenditure Policy in the U.S.* (Rutgers University Press, New Brunswick, N. J., 1962), p. 123.

TABLE 19 (*continued*)

State	Percentage of total traffic in urban areas, 1956	Percentage urban population, 1960 (minus, as a rule 20 per cent)[a]	Percentage urban of total state highway department expenditures (as of the first year or years for which reliable figures are available)	Percentage urban of total state highway department expenditures (1957–1959 average)
Alabama	48.3	34.8	4.6 (1948)	15.1
Arkansas	29.0	23.4	6.0 (1950)	17.4
Florida	49.6	48.7	9.8 (1952)	30.2
Georgia	46.9	35.4	9.2 (1949)	19.0
Kentucky	20.8	25.9	3.3 (1945)	14.8
Louisiana	37.8	42.1	8.7 (1951)	15.4
Mississippi	32.0	21.0	6.5 (1950)	4.9
North Carolina	31.6	24.4	5.2 (1945)	7.5
South Carolina	26.1	22.8	3.6 (1950)	9.6
Tennessee	31.8	34.7	21.2 (1947)	21.4
Virginia	33.8	40.0	3.1 (1945)	9.2
West Virginia	28.6	22.3	2.8 (1950)	13.2
Iowa	43.9	29.5	3.8 (1945)	18.8
Kansas	40.5	38.7	2.0 (1945)	9.9
Minnesota	45.8	39.1	20.8 (1945)	39.7
Missouri	47.6	42.5	6.1 (1948)	15.7
Nebraska	36.4	34.8	1.8 (1948)	3.4
North Dakota	30.4	17.0	1.1 (1945)	4.5
Oklahoma	24.8	39.4	4.5 (1949)	11.5
South Dakota	14.9	17.1	4.1 (1950)	8.0
Texas	47.2	50.8	4.7 (1947)	21.4

[a]The underestimate of 20 per cent is to compensate for purported extra travel by urbanites on rural roads, except in 10 western mountain states where 40 per cent has been deducted.

SOURCE: Philip H. Burch, Jr., *Highway Revenue and Expenditure Policy in the U.S.* (Rutgers University Press, New Brunswick, N.J., 1962), pp. 166, 170.

the amount allocated to county and local roads was approximately 50 per cent greater than was justified and the amount allocated to city streets less than half the amount that was justified. On the basis of relative traffic volume approximately $135.6 million less should have been spent on state highways in 1960, $331.4 million less on county and local roads, and $467 million more on city streets . . . A materially different picture emerges when fuel consumption is compared with the allocation of *total* highway revenue from all sources, including not only state user charges but also Federal aid and other sources of revenue. State primary rural roads show a substantial overallocation of revenue in relation to fuel consumption thereon, whereas state secondary rural roads and other state rural roads show a very large underallocation on this basis. County and township roads show a slight overallocation in relation to fuel consumption . . . The showing with respect to urban facilities is especially significant. Expenditures on municipal extensions of state highway systems conform closely to the amount indicated as desirable on the basis of fuel consumption, whereas other city streets show a particularly serious underallocation on this basis.[12]

Estimates by the Bureau of Public Roads also point up some interesting aspects of the costs of urban and rural highway facilities. Table 20 gives the Bureau of Public Roads estimates of annual highway ownership and operating costs (the fund flow needed to amortize the capital investment, meet interest costs, and cover maintenance and administration charges) per route-mile and per vehicle-mile for the rural and urban

TABLE 20

ANNUAL OWNERSHIP AND OPERATING COSTS (AT 5 PER CENT INTEREST), COSTS PER MILE, AND COSTS PER VEHICLE-MILE AS OF 1975 FOR ALL ROADS AND STREETS IN THE UNITED STATES[a]

Highway system	Annual costs ($ million)[b]	Miles in service in 1975[c]	Annual Cost per mile ($)	Estimated 1975 travel (million vehicle-miles)[d]	Annual Cost per vehicle-mile (mills)
Interstate					
Rural	1,503	34,037	44,158	169,174	8.8843
Urban	983	4,697	209,283	93,430	10.5212
Total	2,486	38,734	64,181	262,604	9.4667
Other Federal aid primary					
Rural	3,406	202,363	16,831	246,944	13.7926
Urban	1,147	17,412	65,874	112,591	10.1873
Total	4,553	219,775	20,717	359,535	12.6636
Federal aid secondary, state					
Rural	2,070	289,334[e]	7,154	101,371	20.4200
Urban	184	5,809	31,675	19,675	9.3520
Total	2,254	295,143	7,637	121,046	18.6210
Federal aid secondary, local					
Rural	1,189	327,830[f]	3,627	51,030	23.3000
Urban	112	7,076	15,828	13,470	8.3148
Total	1,301	334,906	3,885	64,500	20.1705

[12] Robert W. Harbeson, "Some Allocational Problems in Highway Finance," Paper presented before the Conference on Transportation Economics, April 26 and 27, 1963, sponsored by Universities-National Bureau Committee for Economic Research.

TABLE 20 (*continued*)

Highway system	Annual costs ($ million)[b]	Miles in service in 1975[c]	Annual Cost per mile ($)	Estimated 1975 travel (million vehicle-miles)[d]	Annual Cost per vehicle-mile (mills)
Other state highways					
Rural	697	75,271[g]	9,260	19,731	35.3251
Urban	179	5,614	31,885	17,057	10.4942
Total	876	80,885	10,830	36,788	23.8121
Other roads and streets					
Rural	3,755	1,757,231	2,137	95,862	39.1709
Urban	3,316	376,876	8,799	212,228	15.6247
Total	7,071	2,134,107[h]	3,313	308,090	22.9511
Summary					
All rural	12,620	2,686,066	4,698	684,112	18.4473
All urban	5,921	417,484	14,183	468,451	12.6395
Total	18,541	3,103,550	5,974	1,152,563	16.0868

[a]Excluding Hawaii and Alaska; including District of Columbia.

[b]Includes estimated average annual costs for capital outlay, maintenance, and administration. Includes average annual costs for the 2102-mile extension of the interstate system. Does not include costs for toll facilities. Costs adjusted to price level of last half of 1956 and at 5 per cent interest rate.

[c]Does not include toll-facility mileage.

[d]Does not include toll-facility travel.

[e]Excludes 1520 miles of unsurfaced road having an annual capital cost less than $50,000.

[f]Excludes 69 miles of unsurfaced road having an annual capital cost less than $50,000.

[g]Excludes 1411 miles of unsurfaced road having an annual capital cost less than $50,000.

[h]Excludes 529,850 miles of unsurfaced road having an annual capital cost of $18,600,000, applicable to only a small portion of the mileage.

SOURCE: Bureau of Public Roads.

portions of various highway systems as of 1975, when the interstate system will be completed, using a 5 per cent rate of interest. These Bureau of Public Roads estimates have some inadequacies. For example, they probably underestimate total capital costs because even a 5 per cent rate of interest is probably below the opportunity cost of the funds employed. On the whole, however, the figures are carefully constructed and are about as good as any available. From Table 20 it can be seen that although the urban portions of the highway system are many times as expensive per route-mile as the rural portions, their costs per vehicle-mile are, for all but the interstate system, far less than for the rural parts of the same systems. Even the very expensive urban interstate system has an estimated cost per vehicle-mile that is not out of line with those for other high-performance facilities.

These figures also suggest a much different pattern of cross-subsidization among different portions of the highway system from that often depicted in popular discussions. Since total taxes on motor vehicle operations from all sources average close to 1.2 cents per vehicle-mile at present for all private automobiles[13] (and usually are higher on urban than on rural highways), and since user tax revenues from trucks, buses, and other heavy vehicles generally are over three times higher, the over-all relationship between urban user taxes and highway costs is such that urban roads and highways are probably not subsidized. If urban users are subsidized, apparently it is on local streets and roads rather than on the high-performance (and high per-route-mile cost) interstate and other federally aided facilities, which are often singled out for special attack as uneconomic by many opponents of urban highway construction. It would be premature, moreover, to argue that urban autoists are subsidized even on local streets, since buses and trucks may be underpaying. Furthermore, a good argument might be made for the apparent policy of normally financing a high proportion of local street costs from property taxes.[14]

In this regard, local streets serve many uses: general welfare; local access to abutting properties for both public and private transport vehicles; and through traffic. Inasmuch as a basic roadway would always be needed to serve the abutting properties with local access for fire and police vehicles, and usually trash, garbage, and other service vehicles as well, it seems reasonable to consider the costs of the basic roadway simply as a welfare service and thus to recoup them through property taxes and general revenue funds, rather than from vehicle taxation. Additional costs for the provision of access to the abutting properties, either by public or private transport vehicles, would be marginal and could as well be considered recoverable from property taxes as from user charges. Note, moreover, that local access is just as important and necessary to a trunk-line rail or bus commuter transit system as it is to a trunk-line automobile system; thus, municipal subsidy (through property taxes, let us say) of this portion of the local street system seems equally justifiable in the case of a well-developed transit system as in the case of an extensive highway network for private automobile transport. However, further expenditures to permit the local streets to be used for through-trip purposes, either

[13] U.S. Department of Commerce, Bureau of Public Roads, *Highway Transportation*, U.S. Government Printing Office, Washington, D.C., August 1960, Table 33, p. 64.

[14] For an elaboration of this argument, see J. R. Meyer, M. J. Peck, J. Stenason, and C. J. Zwick, *The Economics of Competition in the Transportation Industry* (Harvard University Press, Cambridge, Mass., 1959), pp. 65–85.

by bus transit or automobile, are almost certainly equitably allocated directly to the vehicle users and in proportion to the extent of usage.

Again, though, it must be emphasized that the evidence suggests that urban vehicles as a group actually may pay more in user taxes than *all* urban highway costs, including those for local streets. Under these circumstances, the fact that some municipalities use general tax funds to pay for local streets is no indication that urban highway users are subsidized. Rather, it suggests the existence of problems in allocating funds collected by one governmental agency among other agencies. Further, by no stretch of the imagination can a use of general tax funds for local streets be regarded as a legitimate precedent for justifying use of general tax funds for subsidizing trunk-line facilities for through trips.

While, on balance, urban highway users as a class seemingly do not receive any public subsidy, it may be true that people who use the urban highway system during certain hours of the day are subsidized, i.e. pay less than their allocable costs. Indeed, an important issue in urban transportation planning is whether peak-hour users of urban freeway and arterial facilities pay their fair share of costs. Since the full capacity of many of these facilities is often required only for a few peak hours, users during these periods might well be assessed the full cost of at least that portion of the extra capacity that is strictly attributable to their needs or demands (especially if we ignore the service benefits that accrue to off-peak travelers). For example, many urban freeways are built with 6 lanes—3 lanes in each direction; analysis of hourly use patterns often reveals, however, that 4 lanes can usually meet all off-peak requirements. In such circumstances, peak-hour users seemingly should bear at least the cost of creating the extra 2 lanes and probably a share of the costs of the basic 4-lane facility as well.

A major difficulty in determining whether peak-hour use is subsidized is that of defining highway design capacity in some reasonably precise fashion. Two approaches to the problem seem superior to most alternatives. The first, and most conventional, is to match highway capacity to the peak volume that can be handled with some reasonable level of safety while maintaining speeds at or near the maximum specified. For example, under a 50- or 55-mph speed limit on urban expressways, it is not too difficult to achieve an *average* speed of 45 mph; at this speed each lane can accommodate about 1200 to 1700 vehicles an hour, depending on local conditions.

The second approach is to define capacity in terms of the maximum volume that can be moved over the expressway, regardless of speed; under such a concept, capacity is effectively defined in terms of the speed and volume just short of which the facility begins to face traffic jams and other "flow coagulations" that limit or decrease capacity. These maximum-use figures are usually achieved at an average speed somewhere between 30 and 40 mph. The volume that can be moved at that speed will partly depend on driving conditions in various cities and regions, on the particular mix of vehicles encountered, and on the design and geometric layout of the facility; but generally speaking, the maximum capacity for an urban expressway at these speeds will range between 1400 and 1900 vehicles an hour.

The major difference between these two capacity concepts, of course, is that the former takes account of service differentials. An objective choice between the two concepts would require some knowledge of how commuters and other drivers value time savings achieved by having a facility that permits a higher maximum and average speed. Unfortunately, such information is difficult to obtain.[15] Furthermore, it should be evident that off-peak users benefit from this extra peak-hour capacity by having more driving freedom, comfort and safety. These considerations will not be explored here, however.

As an illustrative exercise, figures on the hourly distribution of traffic on Detroit's Lodge-Ford Expressway can be analyzed to show how different capacity concepts influence the determination of the presence or lack of a match between user tax revenues and costs on an urban expressway at different times of the day. The Lodge-Ford Expressway is a pertinent example because performance data on it are readily available and have been previously used to discuss the peak-hour urban highway subsidy question.[16] Table 21 embodies estimates of average hourly volumes for this expressway based upon 120,000 vehicles per mile moving daily over the facility. Because the Lodge-Ford Expressway has a relatively even balance in its traffic flows, these volumes are favorable to establishing that peak-hour revenues are sufficient to cover additional peak-hour capacity costs. Specifically, many other urban expressways are not used so heavily during off-peak hours. By way of perspective, while the Lodge-Ford Expressway experiences 28 per cent of its daily use during the four peak hours, this figure is 44 per cent for Memorial Bridge in Washington, D.C., 29 per cent for Route 128 around Boston, and 29.5 per cent for the Congress Street Expressway in Chicago; the corresponding highest single peak-hour percentages are 7.2 (Lodge-Ford), 12.8 (Memorial Bridge), 9.1 (Route 128), and 8.0 (Congress Street). As will shortly be shown, even with these favorable peaking characteristics, those peak-hour

[15] For some interesting efforts to estimate such numbers and an excellent discussion of the problems involved, see Leon N. Moses and Harold F. Williamson, Jr., "Value of Time, Choice of Mode, and the Subsidy Issue in Urban Transportation," *Journal of Political Economy,* 71:247–264 (June 1963).

[16] John J. Cummings, "Is the Peak-Hour Urban Freeway User Being Subsidized?" Paper presented at the 49th Annual Conference of American Association of State Highway Officials, Portland, Oregon, October 24, 1963.

TABLE 21

AVERAGE HOURLY VOLUMES ON DETROIT'S LODGE-FORD EXPRESSWAY, BASED ON 120,000 VEHICLES DAILY PER MILE

	Inbound traffic		Outbound traffic	
Hour ending at	Number	Percentage	Number	Percentage
1:00 a.m.	780	1.3	1,500	2.5
2:00	420	0.7	840	1.4
3:00	420	0.7	660	1.1
4:00	240	0.4	360	0.6
5:00	420	0.7	360	0.6
6:00	1,200	2.0	660	1.1
7:00	3,120	5.2	1,800	3.0
8:00	4,680	7.8	2,760	4.6
9:00	4,740	7.9	2,760	4.6
10:00	4,020	6.7	2,220	3.7
11:00	3,480	5.8	2,460	4.1
12:00	3,300	5.5	2,700	4.5
1:00 p.m.	2,880	4.8	2,760	4.6
2:00	3,060	5.1	3,120	5.2
3:00	3,300	5.5	3,840	6.4
4:00	3,720	6.2	4,620	7.7
5:00	3,660	6.1	4,920	8.2
6:00	3,720	6.2	4,500	7.5
7:00	3,420	5.7	4,080	6.8
8:00	3,120	5.2	2,820	4.7
9:00	2,040	3.4	2,760	4.6
10:00	1,560	2.6	2,760	4.6
11:00	1,500	2.5	2,460	4.1
12:00	1,200	2.0	2,280	3.8
Total	60,000	100.0	60,000	100.0

SOURCE: John J. Cummings, "Is the Peak-Hour Urban Freeway User Being Subsidized?" Paper presented at the 49th Annual Conference of American Association of State Highway Officials, Portland, Ore., October 24, 1963. According to Cummings, "Percentage distribution of inbound and outbound expressway traffic by hours is based on 24-hour traffic counts by the Detroit Department of Streets and Traffic on November 7, 8, and 9, 1962; daily volume per mile was 102,000 vehicles. Percentages then were applied to estimated 1967-onward average daily expressway volume of 120,000 vehicles per mile."

users requiring the extra lanes on the Lodge-Ford Expressway apparently do *not* pay the full cost of the additional capacity they require.

One quick but only approximate way to evaluate the contribution of additional peak-hour users to the additional costs of the capacity that they alone require is to juxtapose the percentage increment in costs for the extra facilities against the percentage increment in use attributable to peak-hour use (as was done in the previously cited evaluation).[17] For the

[17] *Ibid.*

Lodge-Ford Expressway, the extra costs of creating a six-lane rather than a four-lane highway were estimated to be 16 per cent of the total construction cost. If it is argued, using the first or service oriented definition of capacity, that these extra lanes are required whenever hourly traffic volume exceeds 3000 vehicles in one direction (1500 vehicles per lane in the "basic" two-lane highway, one way), then an estimate of the total percentage of traffic served by the extra lane can be obtained by adding together all volumes beyond 3000 vehicles an hour. This percentage is then to be compared with the 16 per cent of costs needed for the extra lane to determine if a subsidy exists. (An implicit assumption in making such a direct comparison is that the peak-hour traffic mix does not significantly differ from that in off-peak hours and explicitly yields about the same total of user taxes per vehicle-mile of travel.) Proceeding in this fashion, it can be easily established from Table 21 that just under 13 per cent of the total daily volume is accounted for by hourly flows beyond the stated 3000-vehicle capacity. Even this 13 per cent figure, though, probably overstates the traffic actually served by the extra two lanes. Indeed, if one were to use the 1500-capacity figure consistently, it would have to be argued that hourly flows of more than 4500 vehicles—the capacity of three lanes in one direction—cannot be legitimately counted (since a fourth lane should be added at that point). An adjustment to eliminate all volumes over 4500 vehicles an hour in one direction would reduce the 13 per cent figure by approximately one percentage point, so that 16 per cent of costs would be incurred to serve approximately 12 per cent of the total traffic volume.

It becomes even more improbable that peak-hour users of the Lodge-Ford facility are paying their "proportionate share" of the costs of the extra capacity they use if one adopts the second suggested definition of highway capacity—that based upon maximum achievable volume regardless of speed. For example, under the assumption that the Lodge-Ford Expressway could accommodate a maximum of about 1800 vehicles hourly per lane, the percentage of total daily volume accounted for by overcapacity utilization of a four-lane facility (more than 3600 vehicles in one direction) would be only 6 per cent. Using a capacity figure of 1600 vehicles per lane-hour, a figure which corresponds to the maximum lane volume in Table 21, the percentage of volume accommodated by the extra lanes (that is, the volume over 3200 vehicles an hour in one direction) would be 10 per cent—a figure well below the additional costs of 16 per cent.

These relationships between percentage use and percentage of total costs are only part of the story, however. If total user tax revenues on the expressway greatly exceeded the total costs of the expressway, user tax revenues during the peak hours could equal or exceed the additional capacity costs even if the percentages of use and total cost are quite unequal. In short, additional peak-hour capacity costs could be absorbed by peak-hour users alone if large overpayments on the basic facility exist.

For the Lodge-Ford Expressway it can be estimated that the traffic-mix and speed characteristics are such that the user tax revenue per vehicle-mile is approximately 11 mills.[18] To obtain a comparable cost estimate per vehicle-mile would require computing the ownership, maintenance, and other costs associated with this facility. The ownership costs, since they involve amortization of the investment and interest charges, would depend crucially upon the life-span assumed for the facility and the interest rate used in making the computations. For the 23.3-mile Lodge-Ford Expressway, if a liberal 35-year life is estimated for the pavement, a 75-year life for the structures, and a 100-year life for all other items, and if a 6 per cent interest rate is assumed along with an annual figure of $500,000 for other maintenance and administration costs for the entire facility, the *total* annual cost per mile (for all six lanes) averages out to about $584,000.

The proportion of this $584,000 that should be attributed to peak-hour users again will depend crucially on the definition of capacity and on the allocation of the basic highway costs. Under almost any circumstance, however, 16 per cent of the ownership and operating costs—the portion attributable to the building of the two extra lanes—could be allocated to peak-hour use. It might also be argued that peak-hour users should bear their proportionate share of the costs of building the basic road, which in this case will be defined as the 4-lane facility. Using 1500 vehicles an hour per lane as the measure of capacity, or 3000 vehicles hourly in one direction, it is clear from Table 21 that this capacity is exceeded during 13 hours of use in the inbound lanes and 6 hours in the outbound on the Lodge-Ford facility. These 19 hours would thus account for 57,000 of the total 104,580 of daily vehicle utilization for the basic facility (excluding the 15,420 attributable to excess use during the peak hours). Accordingly, on these definitions peak-hour users should defray 55 per cent of the 84 per cent of the total cost attributable to the basic 4-lane road (or 46.2 per cent of the total roadway costs), in addition to the entire 16 per cent of costs attributable to the extra two lanes. On these definitions, approximately 62 per cent of the total costs per mile would be attributable to peak-hour users. In dollar terms this would mean the peak-hour users should pay approximately $362,000 of the total annual costs of $584,000 per mile. Since the peak-hour users account for 72,500 daily vehicle-miles of use or, at the most, 26,462,500 vehicle-miles annually per mile of the expressway, this would mean that the cost per vehicle-mile of peak-hour use would be $362,000 divided

[18] Based on U.S. Bureau of Public Roads estimates for this class of facility. *Ibid.*

by 26,462,500 or approximately 13.7 mills per vehicle-mile—as compared with the estimated revenue realization of 11 mills. It should be recognized, however, that this figure is arrived at by applying a favorable definition of capacity, and by using somewhat longer estimated lives for the facilities than are desirable. Under the other capacity definition based on maximum volumes, assumed for this expressway to be about 1800 vehicles an hour in one direction per lane, the costs per vehicle-mile attributable to peak-hour users would rise to 15.6 mills.

Again, it must be remembered that the Lodge-Ford Expressway has unusually balanced traffic flows at different times of day, particularly during peak hours. It is all the more significant, therefore, that even when one uses *conservative* costing assumptions for this expressway, the result is a peak-hour cost assignment per vehicle-mile that still exceeds revenues.

It seems likely, then, that peak-hour users of *very-high-cost urban expressways* do not pay their full costs. (The 23-mile Lodge-Ford Expressway had capital costs exceeding $9 million a mile, a cost figure exceeded by very few urban highways of such length.) On the other hand, it is quite clear that some of the recently talked about cost estimates of 20 cents, 30 cents, or even more per vehicle-mile of peak-hour use are hardly typical.

The typical urban work-trip, of course, is likely to use both underpriced and overpriced portions of the highway system. This is particularly true when it is remembered that most work-trips involve at least some travel over suburban arterial and expressway facilities, which, as can be seen in Table 20, have low costs on a vehicle-mile basis. Putting all these considerations together, it seems likely that most urban highway users, except those traveling at the very peak of the rush hours *and* using the most centrally located and highest-cost express facilities, will pay very nearly the full cost of what they use.

Performance of Urban Highway Systems

While urban highways seemingly have lagged behind travel demands since the war, and urban highway users perhaps have not enjoyed their "fair" share of highway expenditures, the prevalent belief that urban highway systems have been rapidly deteriorating is probably not justified. By many criteria, over-all performance has not steadily worsened and seems unlikely to worsen even if immediate corrective measures are not taken. This conclusion is admittedly based on fragmentary evidence —but fragmentary evidence is very nearly the only evidence available. Most of the better evidence pertains to only three cities—Boston, Chicago, and Los Angeles—but the three do constitute a sample that has wide geographic coverage and encompasses a wide diversity, perhaps even some polar extremes, of American urban development.

Any fair evaluation of urban transportation performance must take account of system effects. In particular, it can be highly misleading to judge a transportation facility's contribution strictly by the performance of the facility itself. It is often asserted, for example, that freeway construction can never catch up with urban growth and the expansion of automobile ownership, and that it is therefore an absolute necessity to construct rail transit facilities. Those who espouse this argument point to peak-hour congestion on urban expressways. Thus, Darrell Ward states:

> Los Angeles is a classic example to prove that freeways built to handle more and more automobile traffic cannot do the job of moving people efficiently into and out of a thriving metropolitan Central Business District . . . Los Angeles developments have proved that freeways into the CBD provide only temporary relief because once the freeway is open, it invites more traffic and results in the same pattern of congestion and delay on a larger scale.[19]

The observation is certainly correct that a freeway invites more traffic as soon as it opens. It is certainly incorrect, though, to conclude that it results in the same pattern of congestion and delay on a larger scale. Such a conclusion reflects a misunderstanding of the dynamics of system operation and failure to view the system's performance on a 24-hour basis. Paul T. McElhiney has evaluated the contribution and performance of the same Los Angeles freeways Ward describes as failures.[20] McElhiney shows that although freeways in Los Angeles become overloaded during a few peak hours almost upon opening, they have significantly reduced congestion and utilization of paralleling arterials and have thus significantly improved general traffic flow both during peak and off-peak hours. In 1955, for example, prior to the opening of the Harbor Freeway, he reports that South Figueroa Street was carrying 46,000 vehicles a day. In 1956, following the opening of the Harbor Freeway, this figure dropped to less than 16,000 vehicles, and in 1958 to under 14,000. The paralleling Harbor Freeway meanwhile carried 160,000 vehicles in 1958. Similarly, Sunset Boulevard carried 35,000 vehicles a day in 1950, before the nearby Hollywood Freeway opened. This figure dropped to 18,500 after the freeway opened in 1952, and rose only to 21,000 by 1958. Meanwhile, the Hollywood Freeway carried an average of 77,000 vehicles a day in 1953 and 144,000 in 1958, or more than 200,000 per-

[19] Darrell Ward, "Los Angeles a Classic Example," *Metropolitan Transportation,* January 1962, pp. 15, 17.

[20] Paul T. McElhiney, "Evaluating Freeway Performance in Los Angeles," *Traffic Quarterly,* July 1960, pp. 296–313.

sons a mile daily. Other freeway openings in Los Angeles have had a similar impact on parallel arterials.

Direct comparisons over time are also available on travel times in Los Angeles. Los Angeles, of course, has experienced the largest absolute growth of any U.S. metropolitan area during the wartime and immediate postwar periods, and among the highest percentage rates of growth. It is therefore rather unfair to use Los Angeles as a touchstone in judging the effectiveness of urban transportation systems, especially since the city faced a monumental task in simply providing basic urban services for its growing population. Los Angeles is also the largest U.S. city that does not have a high-capacity, grade-separated, rail transit system.

Despite these many handicaps, the information available warrants the guarded conclusion that urban automobile transportation has improved qualitatively in Los Angeles in recent years (see Table 22). Peak and

TABLE 22

TRAVEL TIME COMPARISONS, LOS ANGELES AREA, 1936, 1957, AND 1960 (minutes)

From Broadway and Seventh Street to	1936 Off-peak[a]	1957 Off-peak[a]	1957 Rush-hours	1960 Off-peak[a]
Pasadena	31	21[b]		18
South Pasadena	26	15[b]	21	14
San Marino	30	22[b]		22
Monterey Park	25	21[b]		18
Sierra Madre	40	34[b]		34
El Monte	31	26		24
Whittier	35		44	
Woodland Hills	57		64	
San Fernando	43		50	
Van Nuys	45	39		28
Universal City	32	20		16
Hollywood	23	17		16
Torrance	34		31	
Playa del Rey	37		37	
Venice	40		30	
San Pedro	48	42		35
Wilmington	39	36		29
Bell	25	22		20
Downey	33	25		24
Norwalk	37	27		26

[a]For this table, off-peak hours are from 9:30 a.m. to 3:30 p.m.

[b]Information provided by supplemental test run.

NOTE: Vehicle registration figures for Los Angeles County: 1936 = 967,981; 1956 = 2,741,422; 1960 = 3,360,000 (est.).

off-peak travel times from the Los Angeles CBD to outlying areas are available for 1957 and 1960, and off-peak times are available for 1936.[21] Off-peak comparisons for all three studies show that 1957 off-peak times were shorter in every case than they were in 1936, and that 1960 off-peak times in turn were shorter than in 1957 for twelve cases and remained the same in the other two. These improvements should be viewed against an almost threefold increase in automobile registrations from 1936 to 1956, the addition of over one-half million more automobiles during the period 1956–1960, and the construction of 47 more miles of freeway between 1957 and 1960 in Los Angeles.

Favorable system effects also were found in a careful study of the impact of Chicago's Congress Street Expressway on arterial and local streets.[22] The Chicago study was a "before and after" study (1959 and 1961) of the traffic within the 16-square-mile area around the expressway. Significant benefits accrued to the local and through circulation pattern within the 16-mile area, but some benefits probably were more widely diffused, since total miles traveled within the area increased by more than a normal amount relative to other areas in the Chicago vicinity. The 21 per cent increase in total vehicle-miles of travel within the study area over the 2-year period is three times the normal Chicago increase of 3.5 per cent a year or 7 per cent for the 2-year period, as determined from traffic volume counts made in 1953, 1956, and 1959. Although some of the 14 per cent difference between the actual and the normal increase in vehicle-miles is unquestionably "induced" travel (that is, travel that would not have occurred in the absence of the highway improvements) most of the difference is probably a result of traffic attracted from arterial and local streets outside the 16-square-mile study area.[23]

[21] Automobile Club of Southern California, Engineering Department, *Los Angeles Metropolitan Peak-Hour Driving Study,* June 1957; also *Los Angeles Metropolitan Peak-Hour Driving Study, 1960,* June 1960.

[22] Frederick F. Frye, *The Effect of an Expressway on the Distribution of Traffic and Accidents,* Chicago Area Transportation Study Publication 66,549 (mimeographed), presented at the 42nd Annual Meeting of the Highways Research Board, Washington, D.C., January 1963.

[23] Induced travel is one of the elements that makes urban transportation planning difficult. A paper by Alan M. Voorhees, Charles F. Barnes, Jr., and Francis E. Coleman, *Traffic Patterns and Land Use Alternatives,* presented at the 41st Annual Meeting of the Highway Research Board in Washington, D.C., January 1962 (mimeographed), points out (p. 1), "It has been brought out in the past, particularly by studies made in the Baltimore area that the average trip length increases as transportation service improves. For example, in 1926 the average work-trip length in the Baltimore area was 2.6 miles; in 1946 it has increased to about four miles; and today it is over five miles. This continued increase in trip length is attributable, in large degree, to the improved transportation service in the Baltimore area." If these estimates are correct, they indicate that improved urban transportation in the postwar period led to an increase in peak-hour capacity needs in the Baltimore area upward of 20 per cent.

In the Chicago study it was estimated that approximately 37,500 vehicle trips, totaling 150,000 vehicle-miles of travel, were diverted to the Congress Expressway.

Despite this large increase in travel within the study area, however, paralleling arterial streets benefited from the Congress Street Expressway much as did Los Angeles arterials paralleling newly opened freeways. Table 23 lists the peak-hour volumes on east-west arterials paralleling the Congress Street Expressway in 1959 and 1961, and the relationships of peak-hour volume to design capacity for each paralleling arterial. Unfortunately, the study does not include "before and after" driving-time estimates. These actual volume-to-design-capacity ratios, however, enable us to infer a great deal about the "before and after" speeds on these paralleling arterials, because a notable feature of the

TABLE 23

RELATIONSHIP OF PEAK-HOUR TRAFFIC VOLUME TO DESIGN CAPACITY ON EAST-WEST ARTERIALS AT AUSTIN BOULEVARD SCREENLINE: CHICAGO, 1959 AND 1961

Arterial	Peak-hour design capacity	Peak-hour volume (5:00 to 6:00 p.m.)		Relationship of peak-hour volume to design capacity	
		1959	1961	1959	1961
Cermak	1,990	2,070	2,020	1.04	1.02
16th	700	1,240	1,100	1.77	1.57
Roosevelt	1,660	2,180	1,210	1.31	0.73
Jackson	1,220	1,750	980	1.46	0.82
Madison	2,200	2,660	1,450	1.21	0.66
Washington	1,260	2,100	1,220	1.67	0.97
Lake	1,080	1,220	1,000	1.13	0.92
Chicago	1,080	1,400	1,020	1.30	0.94
Augusta	1,200	1,290	700	1.08	0.58
Division	1,330	1,440	710	1.08	0.53
North	2,070	2,510	2,970	1.21	1.43
Total	15,770	19,870	14,380	1.26	0.91

SOURCE: Chicago Area Transportation Study paper prepared for presentation at the 42d Annual Meeting of the Highway Research Board, Washington, D.C., January 1963.

relationship between speed and the volume-to-design-capacity ratio is the extent to which travel times and speeds deteriorate at ratios of 1 or above. (Design capacity generally is defined as that capacity which will provide for travel "without undue delay or congestion" at the particular level of projected volume.) As shown in Table 23, in 1959 all eleven east-west arterials in the Chicago study area had peak-hour volume-to-design-capacity ratios exceeding 1; in 1961 only three had ratios larger than 1; and only one arterial had a ratio greater in 1961 than in 1959, despite a normal increase of 7 per cent and an actual increase of 21 per cent in total traffic in the area. As might be expected, the greatest benefits accrued to those arterials most closely paralleling the new expressway.

The study also pointed out that sizable benefits accrued to local streets as a result of the Congress Street Expressway opening. Specifically, traffic volume on local streets decreased 7 per cent. (Use of local streets by through traffic can offer a serious problem, sometimes increasing accident rates and lowering the desirability of abutting residential properties.)

New expressways, however, can cause secondary increases as well as declines on nearby arterials. The opening of the Congress Street Expressway, for example, led to significant volume increases on intersecting north-south arterials. From Table 24 it can be seen that volumes in-

TABLE 24

RELATIONSHIP OF PEAK-HOUR TRAFFIC VOLUME TO DESIGN CAPACITY ON NORTH-SOUTH ARTERIALS AT CONGRESS STREET SCREENLINE: CHICAGO, 1959 AND 1961

Arterial	Peak-hour design capacity	Peak-hour volume (5:00 to 6:00 p.m.)		Relationship of peak-hour volume to design capacity	
		1959	1961	1959	1961
Cicero	2,130	1,730	2,290	0.81	1.08
Laramie	1,640	1,790	1,540	1.09	0.94
Central	1,640	900	1,260	0.55	0.77
Austin	1,400	1,100	1,650	0.78	1.18
Ridgeland	1,550	1,200	1,200	0.77	0.77
Oak Park	1,110	1,080	930	0.97	0.84
Harlem	1,550	1,500	1,930	0.97	1.24
Des Plaines	1,000	800	900	0.80	0.90
Total	12,020	10,100	11,700	0.84	0.97

SOURCE: Chicago Area Transportation Study paper prepared for presentation at the 42d Annual Meeting of the Highway Research Board, Washington, D.C., January 1963.

creased on five of the eight intersecting arterials. Before the expressway opened, only one of the eight had a peak-hour volume-to-design-capacity ratio above 1, implying that the rest still had some excess peak-hour capacity. After the expressway opened, the ratio for three of the eight exceeded 1. The increased volumes undoubtedly led to some deterioration of service and speed on these arterials.

Evaluation of system effects was also a major concern in a Boston Travel Time Study, mainly directed to an evaluation of the Boston Central Artery built in the 1950's. The authors report that "differences in travel rates and average vehicle speeds between 1951 and 1960 for [parallel] routes seem to be dependent upon proximity . . . to the Central Artery, with largest benefits being achieved on the route parallel and adjacent to the Central Artery."[24]

Even more interesting were the system effects implied by the direct time-comparisons reported in the Boston Study. The opening of the Boston Central Artery had a broadly beneficial effect, reducing most average travel times by 25 per cent or more. A particularly interesting improvement was that during the morning peak a closer balance was achieved in 1960 than in 1951 in travel times and speed in the heavy and light volume directions. Average morning speeds in the heavy volume direction in 1951 were only about 60 per cent of speeds in the light volume direction; in 1961, this figure rose to over 90 per cent. Improvements in the afternoon peak, by contrast, were much smaller in the heavy volume direction.

Not all the reported changes between 1951 and 1960 in Boston were obviously for the better, however. A finding of the Boston Study particularly relevant to the problem of evaluating freeway performance is that a trip from Leverett Circle to South Station (a distance of about 1.4 miles) in the heavy-volume direction during the afternoon peak hour took nearly a minute longer in 1960 than it did by city street in 1951. It is just this kind of observation that leads some people to conclude that expressways are a failure; but the one-minute excess is partly because the expressway trip is slightly longer in miles; average vehicle speed on the expressway in 1961 was 7.8 mph as opposed to 6.7 mph by local streets in 1951. Even more important, however, are the system improvements resulting from the expressway; although the point-to-point trip was almost a minute longer by expressway in 1961, it was nearly five minutes shorter by city street. The decrease in city-street volumes caused by the expressway substantially reduced congestion and saved travel time on city streets, even though heavy peak-hour volumes on the expressway during the afternoon peak hour caused breakdowns and low expressway performance.

As noted, the data available for making direct comparisons in urban transportation performances between cities and modes are notoriously fragmentary. A primary problem is that the usually available data are limited to the CBD trip and to facilities radiating from the downtown.

[24] Alexander J. Bone and Frederick W. Memmott, *Travel Time Studies in Boston, 1960,* Joint Highway Research Project, MIT and Massachusetts Department of Public Works (Cambridge, Mass., January 1961).

Of somewhat more general relevance, however, are the results of a series of nationwide driving experiments conducted during the peak of the evening rush hour in the 25 largest U.S. cities in the mid-1950's.[25]

The results of these studies show that outbound auto traffic averaged about 20 mph in most of the cities. Only in three—Boston, St. Louis, and New Orleans—was the average speed as low as 16 mph for a 30-minute trip. The average by transit, using the busiest transit routes in the same cities, was about 13 mph; the slowest transit speed, 8 mph, was recorded in Pittsburgh and San Antonio. These slow transit speeds, of course, largely reflect the difficult conditions under which surface transit usually operates in the United States; but perhaps it is significant that Detroit and San Francisco, with exclusively highway-oriented transit systems, recorded transit speeds as high as those for private automobiles, while Boston, Chicago, and Cleveland, with substantial rail transit systems, all had transit speed performances below those for automobiles. While some reservations are in order about these data, Francis Bello, the author of the report, draws the conclusion that the automobile still moves with remarkable speed at rush hours in most American cities.

Bello is not sanguine, however, about the continuation of this favorable state of affairs for automobile commutation. He notes that motor vehicle registrations more than doubled between 1945 and 1958, and that by 1975 the United States should have over 100 million vehicles for a population of 220 million. He therefore worries that the ballooning number of vehicles demanding space on the streets during rush hours will necessitate an extremely large allocation of space to new freeway and other highway construction. He does note, however, that there are other ways to ease these problems, such as restricting on-street parking, using better signalization, and offsetting highway centerlines to increase the effectiveness of available highway capacity.[26]

Summary

It can hardly be overemphasized that the recent past is not a promising period in which to look for a high performance level in urban transportation. The early postwar years were marked by the struggle to

[25] Francis Bello, "The City and the Car," in The Editors of *Fortune, The Exploding Metropolis* (Doubleday, Garden City, N. Y., 1958), p. 58.

[26] Along these same lines, the authors of a study on urban transportation prepared for the Department of Commerce and the Housing and Home Finance Agency report that, by utilizing advanced traffic techniques and controls, Baltimore achieved during an eight-year period a threefold increase in traffic volume on some streets and savings of travel time up to 33 per cent. (Institute of Public Administration, *The Transportation Picture in Selected Urban Areas: A Supplement to Urban Transportation and Public Policy,* prepared for the U.S. Department of Commerce and the Housing and Home Finance Agency, 1961, p. 9.)

eliminate the abnormalities inherited from a war economy and rapid urbanization. The postwar responses in supplying various facilities were also widely disparate, with the production of vehicles and supplies for operating vehicles quickly outstripping new road construction. Bottlenecks were inevitable in urban highway systems; some are being eliminated only now.

Elimination of these bottlenecks has been further impeded by the relatively low share of highway funds allocated to urban areas. In fact, on the definition that a subsidy does not exist if the costs incurred by *all* levels of government are less than the payments made by users to *all* levels of government, the typical user of urban highway facilities seems to be overpaying and therefore is not subsidized. However, while a distinct over balance may exist *en toto* between payments by urban users of highways and the costs of these highways, some *particular* users of urban facilities apparently do not pay the costs of the highways they use. Most importantly, those using centrally located limited-access expressways during the peak commuter hours are probably underpaying.

Finally, not all recent trends in urban transportation have been unfavorable. For example, the route mileage of public transit systems has increased during the postwar period even though the vehicle miles of service have decreased. In particular there seems to be little immediate justification for the view that the present supply of urban transportation, taking all modes into consideration, is grossly inadequate. Performance data on urban highways suggest that some people's despair stems more from unfulfilled hopes than from any real deterioration of performance. The public, having found it convenient and useful to cross an urban area at speeds upward of 40 mph on new expressways during off-peak hours, understandably would like to repeat the experience during rush hours. With increasing affluence they might even be willing to pay the costs of achieving such service. If they so insist, and if automobile ownership continues to rise rapidly, a need would appear to exist for many new expressways in urban areas. The only alternative would be a diversion of urban traffic back to public transit. The feasibility of any such "transit solution" obviously depends to a large extent on the demand characteristics for urban transportation, the subject of the next chapter.

Chapter 5 | Trip Patterns and Demand

Ideally, it would be desirable to have accurate and detailed estimates of urban transportation demand functions, including all the relevant price and income elasticities and cross-elasticities for the various urban transportation modes and for closely complementary or competitive goods in urban consumer budgets, such as land and housing outlays. Unfortunately, scantiness of data and other limitations have severely hampered most direct attempts to obtain the needed empirical parameters, although a few highly ingenious studies have recently produced results that will be suggestive and useful until better estimates become available.[1]

A more limited and indirect approach has been adopted in this study. To begin, the aggregate levels of urban transportation demands and capacities in different American cities were examined. A specification of these aggregate demand levels is useful if for no other reason than that the relative efficiencies of transportation modes vary widely according to the volumes they must handle.

It is also crucial to understand the composition of urban transport demand, with emphasis on variations that might occur at different hours of the day and among urban trips with different purposes (for example, work-trips and social or recreational trips). Knowledge of the geographic dispersion of trips is useful as well. Finally, it is important to know which transportation modes will normally be chosen for different trip purposes and at what times of the day. These modal choice patterns permit at least some preliminary inferences to be made about the relative elasticities and cross-elasticities of demand.

[1] Walter Y. Oi and Paul W. Shuldiner, *An Analysis of Urban Travel Demands* (Northwestern University Press, Evanston, Ill., 1962); Stanley Leon Warner, *Stochastic Choice of Mode in Urban Travel: A Study in Binary Choice* (Northwestern University Press, Evanston, Ill., 1962); and Leon N. Moses and Harold F. Williamson, Jr., "Value of Time, Choice of Mode, and the Subsidy Issue in Urban Transportation," *Journal of Political Economy,* 71:247–264 (June 1963).

Aggregate Demand and Capacity Requirements

To begin, it must be recognized that it is not particularly meaningful to use maximum daily capacity as a measure of capacity or daily utilization as a measure of demand. According to these measures, urban transportation problems do not exist—every U. S. area has many, many times the capacity it needs. But fallacious or not, many discussions of the urban transportation problem are based exclusively on total daily trip generation and capacity requirements, which are misleading simply because urban travel is distributed very unequally in time and space. A single peak hour may account for more than 10 per cent of total daily travel while almost no trips are made during some other hours, especially between midnight and dawn.

To take an illustrative example, transportation capacity is often defined as the number of persons or vehicles that can be transported between two or more points per unit of time.[2] Thus a 4-lane limited-access highway that can carry 1500 automobiles an hour per lane, has a 24-hour capacity of 72,000 vehicles in each direction, and—with an average of 5 passengers per car—*can* supply 360,000 passenger-miles a day per mile. By comparison, the Chicago Area Transportation Study reported, on the basis of an interview study conducted in 1956, that Chicago residents traveled just over 49 million miles (airline distance) on an average 24-hour weekday.[3] If we divide this total by the 360,000 passenger miles of capacity for a mile of 4-lane highway as just calculated, it would appear that Chicago needs only 103.5 miles of such highway, and that an "extravagant" 517.5 miles would allow every traveler to drive his own automobile. Actually, Chicago in 1956 had about 10,000 miles of streets and highways and 1914 route-miles of transit facilities[4] so that available capacity thus measured obviously is well in excess of actual needs.

Numbers of trips may vary tremendously among locations as well as over time. For example, in Chicago in recent years as many as 3545 daily person-trips are made to each acre of manufacturing land in the Loop. By contrast, an average of only 1.5 person-trips per acre are made to public open space, parks, and the like when these are located an average of 24 miles from the Loop; over all, locations at that distance

[2] While the character of the service associated with the movement and capacity is also relevant, it will not be included at this point in the discussion.

[3] *Chicago Area Transportation Study, Final Report,* vol. 1, *Survey Findings,* December 1959, p. 47. By comparison, typical weekday travel in 1958 in Pittsburgh is estimated at about 8.9 million passenger-miles. See *Pittsburgh Area Transportation Study, Final Report,* vol. 1, *Findings,* Pittsburgh, Pa., November 1961, p. 19.

[4] *Chicago Area Transportation Study,* 1:76.

average only slightly more than 21 person-trips per acre.[5] For Detroit, an average of 1522 internal trips per acre are made to the core of the CBD; for developed land more than 12 miles from the core, the figure is 15. Similar quantities for Pittsburgh are 1315 trips per acre for the CBD and 3 trips per acre of land over 12 miles from the CBD.[6]

For determining capacity requirements and to account for the wide geographic and time-of-day variations, a more useful number is the single hour of maximum demand on the system, particularly for those facilities centering on the CBD. One optimistic note is that, for reasons explained in previous chapters, today's maximum employment and residential concentrations at central downtown locations may well be high-water marks for many U.S. cities. Accordingly, today's figures on CBD and other central cordon crossings[7] could well be reasonably good bases for long-term urban transportation planning.

A systematic analysis of the available data reveals that the maximum hourly CBD cordon crossings are surprisingly low for most major U.S. cities, though obviously they outstrip the demands at less centrally located cordons quite substantially. Table 25 gives the approximate number of persons leaving the CBD's of major U.S. cities during the evening peak hour. (The evening peak is used because in most CBD's it exceeds the morning peak, the evening commuters being joined by housewives returning home from various trips, students going home from school, etc.)

Not only are the maximum CBD cordon crossings surprisingly low outside of New York,[8] but highway and traffic engineers have been insisting for years that a large proportion of the vehicles and people entering CBD's are only passing through, even during peak hours. Accordingly, they have argued that adequate bypass or inner belt highways could eliminate a sizable portion of the downtown concentration. If so, the figures presented in Table 25 seriously overstate the actual number of potentially available passengers for high-capacity, CBD-oriented transportation systems.

[5] *Ibid.*, pp. 60, 64.

[6] Detroit Metropolitan Area Traffic Study, *Report on the Detroit Area Traffic Study,* part 1, *Data Summary and Interpretation,* Lansing, Michigan, July 1955, p. 41; *Pittsburgh Area Transportation Study,* vol. 1, pp. 55–56.

[7] CBD cordon counts are obtained by drawing a line around the CBD and counting the number of vehicles and persons entering and leaving by various modes.

[8] It is especially worth emphasizing the degree to which New York City's evening peak, with hourly volumes exceeding 800,000, far outstrips its nearest rival. In fact, the entire range from 250,000 to 800,000 peak-hour person-trips is an empty box, and the ranges from 150,000 to 200,000 and from 200,000 to 250,000 together have only four entries. In short, only five CBD's have peak-hour volumes over 150,000 persons; and New York's experience is so extraordinary that it is difficult to use in drawing inferences for other cities.

Table 25
Evening Peak-Hour Volumes Leaving CBD's of Major U.S. Cities

Number of persons	CBD		CBD area[a] (sq. mi.)	Approximate No. of Persons Leaving CBD per Peak Hr. in an Ave. Corridor
More than 800,000	New York		9.1	above 60,000
250,000 to 800,000	None			40,000 to 60,000
200,000 to 250,000	Chicago		1.0	30,000 to 40,000
150,000 to 200,000	Philadelphia		2.2	20,000 to 30,000
	Boston		1.4	
	Washington, D.C.		6.1	
100,000 to 150,000	Los Angeles		1.6	13,000 to 20,000
	San Francisco		1.3[b]	
75,000 to 100,000	Cleveland		2.0	9,000 to 13,000
	Detroit		1.1	
	Atlanta[c]		1.7	
	Pittsburgh[c]		0.7	
	New Orleans[c]		0.4[b]	
	St. Louis[c]		1.2	
	Baltimore[c]		0.8	
50,000 to 75,000	Dallas		0.6	6,000 to 9,000
	St. Paul		0.3[b]	
	Minneapolis		0.4[b]	
	Providence[c]		0.3	
	Fort Worth		0.3[b]	
	Milwaukee		1.2	
Less than 50,000	Miami	(17,000)	0.9	below 6,000
	Cincinnati		0.5[b]	
	Rochester	(34,000)	0.3[b]	
	Seattle		0.7	
	Kansas City	(12,000)	0.9	
	Denver		0.4[b]	

[a]Definitions vary widely. Sources used were American Municipal Association, *Collapse of Commuter Service;* H. S. Levinson and F. H. Wynn, "Some Aspects of Future Transportation in Urban Areas," *Highway Research Board Bulletin, no. 326*, 1962, p. 18; *Chicago Area Transportation Study*, vol. 1; and D. A. Gorman and S. T. Hitchcock, "Characteristics of Traffic Entering and Leaving the Central Business District," *Public Roads*, vol. 30, no. 9, 1959.

[b]Estimated by assuming 0.47 sq mi per million SMSA population(1960).

[c]These peak-hour volumes were estimated from 12- or 24-hour volumes. A maximum estimate was used in all instances. Some of these probably would fall in a lower volume group if more accurate data were available.

Some information on the number who might be bypassed is available from special CBD traffic studies and cordon counts, as in the following summary:[9]

(1) The Buffalo Board of Safety estimates that between 60 and 70 per cent of all vehicles passing through the downtown area have neither origins nor destinations there.

(2) In the downtown Milwaukee plan, the authors state: "Finally, the whole traffic problem in the central business district is aggravated by a serious conflict between local and through traffic. It is estimated that around 70 per cent of the vehicles entering the CBD have destinations there and the remaining 30 per cent are merely passing through."

(3) In New Orleans it was determined that "the 71,891 vehicles passing through the central business district without parking comprise 78 per cent of the inbound traffic between 10:00 a.m. and 6:00 p.m. on an average 1960 weekday."

(4) In Atlanta the daily numbers of persons passing through as against those destined for the CBD were found to be roughly equal in cordon counts performed in 1941, 1945, and 1948; furthermore, a count in 1953 revealed that the number just passing through had risen to 57 per cent of the total.

(5) In Detroit 25 per cent of the evening peak of about 73,000 person-trips consists of through trips; of the 18,200 through trips, 6800 are through transit trips.

By any standards, these data strongly corroborate the highway engineers' view that bypasses would alleviate downtown traffic and transport problems. They also indicate that the maximum capacity requirements for transit services into CBD areas are considerably below the maximum cordon crossing counts, which themselves are remarkably low.

Furthermore, few American cities would suffer absolute shortages in transport capacity if, during rush hours, they used highways entering their CBD's with anything approaching maximum efficiency. As will be shown later, even ten or eleven lanes of grade separated streets or highways in each direction and provided with proper terminal facilities set aside for buses could accommodate 250,000 people an hour; six or seven lanes could accommodate 150,000. Without grade separation, these lane requirements would be quadrupled or quintupled (assuming no standees in either case). Most cities of over one million population have more than 20 streets and highways entering their CBD's. Under the conservative estimate of only two lanes in each direction for such thoroughfares,

[9] See Buffalo City Planning Commission, *1958 Greater Buffalo Downtown Business Core,* 1959; *City of Milwaukee, Downtown Milwaukee, 1975,* May 1, 1957, p. 27; Wilbur Smith and Associates, *Parking Study, Central Business District, New Orleans, La.,* vol. 1, *Parking Demands and Need,* 1960, p. 15; City of Atlanta, City Planning Commission, *Why People Come Downtown.*

around 40 lanes are thus available.[10] United States urban areas therefore possess substantial reserves of highway capacity when measured on this basis.

Spatial, Time, and Trip Purpose Profiles in Urban Transportation

In view of the foregoing, the aggregate level of demand for transportation into CBD's should be easily manageable, even in the largest cities (where considerable rapid transit capacity is also usually already in existence). But the aggregate is only part of the story; the demand for urban transportation services is composed of complex and interdependent parts, some of the more important being the spatial, time, and service dimensions.

The choice among travel modes seems to depend as much on the quality of service as on simple price or cost comparisons. At least four considerations (aside from price) might be hypothesized to be especially important to urban travelers: over-all trip speed; convenience, particularly walking distance and frequency of service and thus the amount of waiting time necessary; privacy; and comfort. The relative importance of these qualities depends heavily on trip purpose, notably: commuting from home to work or school; shopping; business; and recreation.

It can be hypothesized or even postulated that the private automobile will usually dominate noncommuter travel to the CBD's of all but the very largest cities. Commuting, on the other hand, is likely to be a much more complex matter. Where the costs of private automobile operation are not too high, either in money or in traffic congestion, commuters too may prefer the automobile; elsewhere, they will probably find public transportation more attractive. Also, rising incomes presumably will work to the advantage of auto commuting.

The following discussion is an attempt to see how far these expectations can be empirically verified. Attention will be devoted to defining the choices among transportation modes for different trip purposes, the patterns these choices and relationships take over time and space, and the degree to which they are consistent with the hypotheses just advanced.

Time and trip purpose profiles are best discussed simultaneously.

[10] Of course, these streets and highways vary considerably in quality and in the amount of traffic they carry. In San Diego, for example, six of twenty-one streets crossing the CBD cordon carried 78 per cent of the total traffic in 1953. These six are very highly developed state highways with several lanes and flow control devices. See State of California, Department of Public Works, Division of Highways, *San Diego Traffic Survey, 1952–53,* compiled as a Highway Planning Survey project conducted by the U.S. Bureau of Public Roads and the Division of Highways, 1954, p. 49.

Table 26 is a breakdown by trip purpose of transit usage in twelve urban areas. It is apparent that transit is used most often for work-trips and least often for social-recreational trips, though here it must be noted that these are data for all urban area trips, rather than simply CBD-oriented trips.

A percentage distribution of trips in Detroit by trip purpose at the destination end of the trip further illustrates this principle, as shown in Table 27. In 1953 only 4.3 per cent of Detroit's transit trips were social-recreational trips, and 5.3 per cent were shopping trips. For auto drivers, the corresponding figures were 9.3 and 10 per cent, and for auto passengers 25.8 and 8.8.

TABLE 26

PERCENTAGE OF TRIPS USING TRANSIT IN SELECTED CITIES, BY PURPOSE

City	Year	Work	Business and shopping	Social and recreational
Chicago	1956	32.6	18.5	13.5
Detroit	1953	21.2	11.3	6.6
Washington	1955	30.3	17.1	11.7
Pittsburgh	1958	23.2	11.0	7.0
St. Louis	1957	20.1	10.5	7.4
Houston	1953	17.5	6.8	4.4
Kansas City	1957	7.4	5.4	3.2
Phoenix	1957	3.8	2.0	1.0
Nashville	1959	10.5	4.0	2.7
Ft. Lauderdale	1959	3.5	.7	1.0
Charlotte	1958	10.5	4.2	2.5
Reno	1955	2.7	1.6	1.3
Unweighted average		15.2	7.8	5.3

SOURCE: Wilbur Smith and Associates, *Future Highways and Urban Growth*, New Haven, Conn., 1961, Tables A-18 to A-20, pp. 348–350.

This specialization is even more clearly seen in Table 28 showing, for Detroit, breakdowns of the total trips of each kind according to transportation mode used. Perhaps the most striking figures are those for social-recreational trips: 54 per cent were made by auto passengers, and only 6 per cent by bus passengers.

Even at that, the data in Tables 27 and 28 probably understate how specialized in purpose transit travel has become. Since 1953 the percentage of transit trips has been declining most rapidly in off-peak trips, such as shopping and social-recreational trips. A recent Detroit study, conducted in connection with an experiment with more frequent transit

TABLE 27

PERCENTAGE OF TRIPS BY TRIP PURPOSE BY TRAVEL MODE: DETROIT, 1953

		Percentage		
Trip purpose	All modes	Automobile drivers	Automobile passengers	Transit
Home	42.4	41.5	41.6	46.3
Work	25.2	30.0	13.0	30.0
Personal business	5.5	6.3	4.6	4.0
Social-recreation	13.0	9.3	25.8	4.3
Eat meal	1.9	2.3	2.0	0.3
Shopping	8.8	10.0	8.8	5.3
School	3.2	.6	4.3	10.0
Total	100.0[a]	100.0	100.0	100.0

[a] Columns may not total to 100 because of rounding.

SOURCE: D. Gulyos, Sue Smock, and P. Pekpala, "Mass Transit Study, Interim Report I: Reliability of the Sample," Detroit Area Traffic Study, Wayne State University, Detroit, Mich., 1959 (mimeographed), appendix A, Table II.

TABLE 28

PERCENTAGE OF TRIPS USING EACH MODE: DETROIT, 1953, BY PURPOSE

	Travel mode				
Trip purpose	All modes	Automobile drivers	Automobile passengers	Transit passengers	Others
Home	100.0	53.2	26.9	16.3	3.6
Work	100.0	64.7	14.1	20.8	0.4
Personal business	100.0	58.9	21.4	12.0	7.4
Social-recreation	100.0	38.9	54.5	5.9	0.7
Eat meal	100.0	67.0	29.3	3.0	0.7
Shopping	100.0	61.8	27.3	10.5	0.4
School	100.0	8.9	36.3	54.8	0.0
All purposes	100.0	56.8	25.9	16.7	0.6

SOURCE: D. Gulyos, Sue Smock, and P. Pekpala, "Mass Transit Study, Interim Report I: Reliability of the Sample," Detroit Area Traffic Study, Wayne State University, Detroit, Mich., 1959 (mimeographed), appendix B, Table IV.

schedules sponsored by the Housing and Home Finance Agency, included new interviews with many people who also had been interviewed in 1953 for the Detroit origin-and-destination study, and thus furnished valuable comparative data on changes in travel habits by urban households.[11] The study determined that while work-trips as a whole declined

[11] Albert J. Mayer and Sue M. Smock, "Public Response to Increased Bus Service," paper presented at the 1963 annual meetings of the Highway Research Board.

6 per cent, bus trips to work declined 32 per cent and shopping trips by bus declined 64 per cent.

Similarly, although social-recreational trips rose 1 per cent, the number made by transit declined 62 per cent. Total school trips made by vehicle increased 111 per cent, automobile-driver school trips 336 per cent, and chauffeured school trips 147 per cent, while bus trips to school declined 35 per cent.

Trip purpose specialization for certain kinds of transit is extremely pronounced. For example, the Penn-Jersey Transportation Study conducted a postcard survey of inbound passengers at fourteen outlying suburban elevated stations and of outbound passengers at seven in-city railroad stations, yielding the results shown in Table 29.[12] (Here, of course, most of the trips have downtown origins or destinations.) Of the inbound trips made from the outlying elevated stations, 74 per cent were work-trips. Even more rail trips, 81 per cent, were work-trips; and when long-haul trips are omitted from the railroad summary, this figure rises to 84.1 per cent for all trips, and to 85.4 per cent for trips made from home.[13] Similarly, in the Chicago Metropolitan Area in 1956, 70 per

TABLE 29

PERCENTAGE OF PHILADELPHIA SUBWAY-ELEVATED AND RAILROAD PASSENGERS TRAVELING EACH WEEKDAY BY PURPOSE

	Fourteen subway-elevated stations (inbound)		Seven railroad stations (outbound)	
Trip purpose	Total trips	Trips from home	Total trips	Trips to home
Work	73.7	78.1	81.4	84.3
Shopping	3.0	3.2	2.5	2.8
School	11.4	8.3	5.6	5.9
Social-recreation	4.0	3.7	3.4	1.7
Personal business	7.1	6.0	6.4	4.8
Other	0.8	0.7	0.7	0.5
Total (per cent)	100.0	100.0	100.0	100.0
Number	149,111	108,886	58,973	47,583

SOURCE: Russell G. Berryman, *Mass Transportation Post Card Survey*, Penn-Jersey Transportation Study, Paper No. 16, May 7, 1962 (mimeographed).

[12] Russell G. Berryman, *Mass Transportation Post Card Survey*, Penn-Jersey Transportation Study, Paper No. 16, May 7, 1962 (mimeographed).

[13] The railroad survey does not include local riding between way stations, since it reflects only traffic passing through the seven principal stations. However, it does cover 90 per cent of all railroad passenger traffic within the study area to distant destinations. The subway-elevated check, covering only the outlying stations, encompasses about 69 per cent of the passengers using this mode of travel.

cent of the trips made by subway or elevated were work-trips, and 80 per cent of these work-trips were made to and from the central area.[14]

In short, a large and rising percentage of transit trips is made up of work-trips, particularly to the CBD, and only a small percentage is composed of social-recreational, personal business, and shopping trips.

This specialization in work-trips, together with the steady outward trend in urban employment locations, is the basis of much of today's financial problems of public transit. Work-trips usually strain the capacity of the transportation system during peak hours; most other trips are made during off-peak hours when there is an excess of capacity. The pronounced peaking of transit trips, in both absolute terms and relative to automobile trips, is illustrated by Figures 1 to 5. Figures 1 and 2 show,

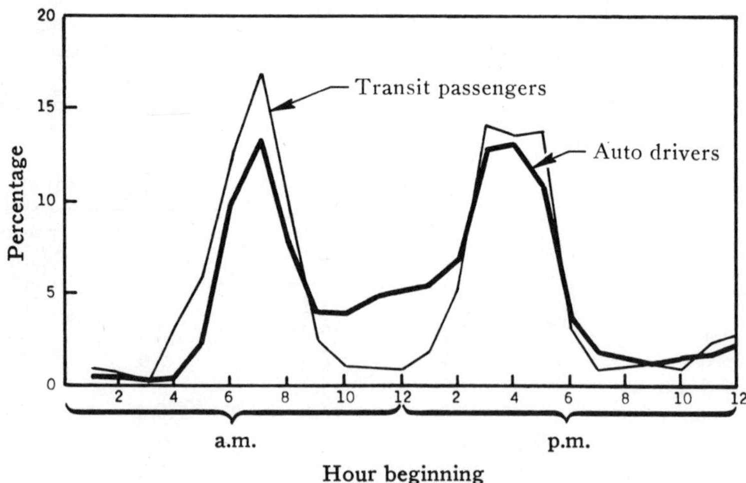

Figure 1. Detroit: percentage distribution of trips to and from work, by mode of travel and hour of trip origin. SOURCE: Detroit Metropolitan Area Traffic Study, *Report on the Detroit Area Traffic Study,* part 1, *Data Summary and Interpretation,* Lansing, Michigan, July 1955, Table 38, p. 124.

respectively, the percentage of trips to and from work, and the percentage of all trips by mode and hour of origin in Detroit. Figures 3, 4, and 5 present similar data for Pittsburgh, Washington, D.C., and Chicago. The Chicago Metropolitan Area data are particularly revealing of transit peaking, since Chicago is the only one of the four cities that possesses rail rapid transit service (as distinct from rail commuter operations). A substantial rapid transit system and high urban density, probably

[14] The central area includes the Loop and the immediate surrounding area. (*Chicago Area Transportation Study,* vol. 1, p. 72.)

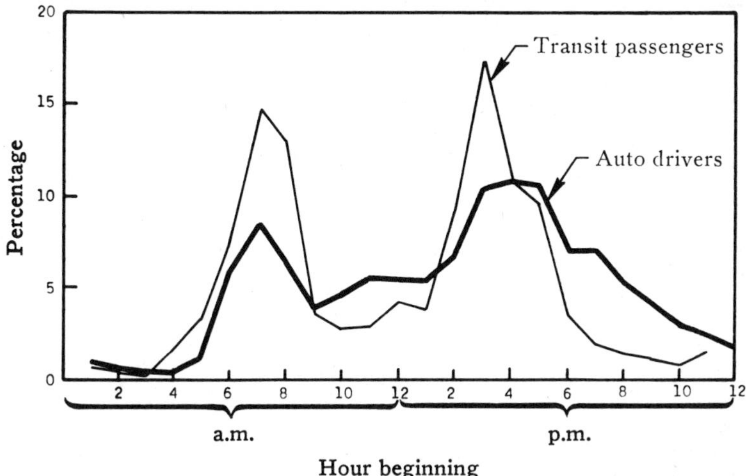

Figure 2. Detroit: percentage distribution of all trips, by mode of travel and hour of trip origin. SOURCE: Detroit Metropolitan Area Traffic Study, *Report on the Detroit Area Traffic Study,* part 1, *Data Summary and Interpretation,* Lansing, Michigan, July 1955, Table 38, p. 124.

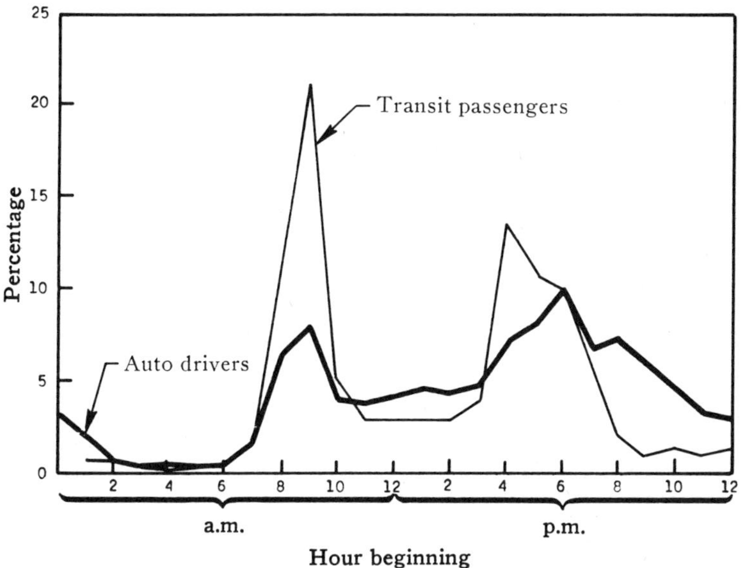

Figure 3. Pittsburgh: percentage of trips by hour and mode of travel. SOURCE: *Pittsburgh Area Transportation Study, Final Report,* vol. 1, *Study Findings,* Pittsburgh, Pennsylvania, November 1961, p. 23.

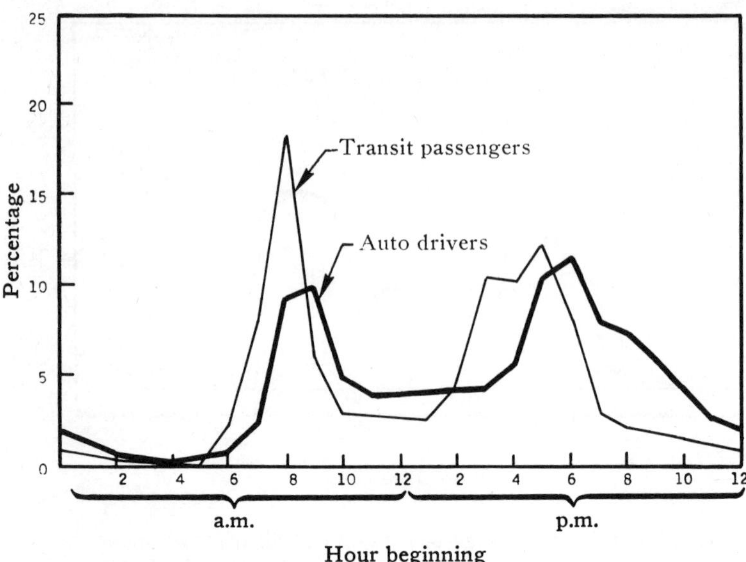

Figure 4. National Capital Region: hourly distribution of transit and automobile driver trips. SOURCE: *Mass Transportation Survey, Civil Engineering Report,* Washington, D.C., 1959, p. 28.

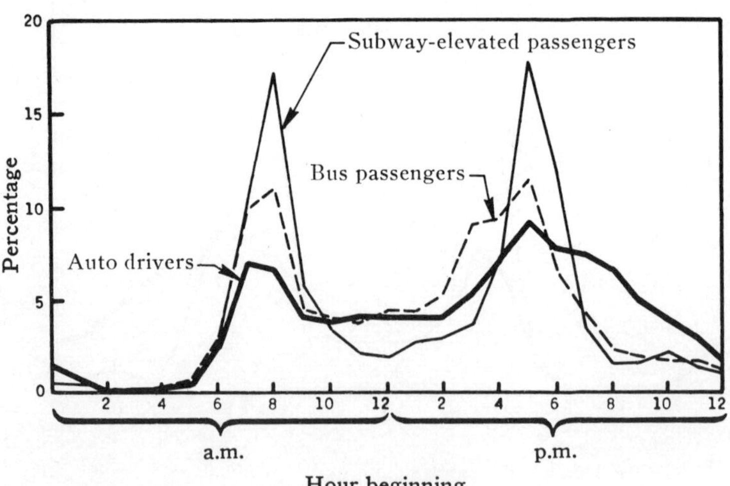

Figure 5. Chicago, 1956: hourly distribution of trips by mode. SOURCE: *Chicago Area Transportation Study, Final Report,* vol. 1, *Survey Findings,* Chicago, Illinois, December 1959, Figure 24.

coupled with high downtown parking costs and congestion, apparently creates a relatively low peaking for automobile travel in Chicago. The peak-hours for automobile *passengers* actually occur in Chicago between 7 p.m. and 9 p.m., reflecting the heavy use of automobiles for evening shopping and social-recreational trips.

TABLE 30

APPROXIMATE PERCENTAGE OF TRANSIT PASSENGERS OR VEHICULAR VOLUME TRAVELING DURING PEAK HOURS IN SELECTED CITIES

System and city[a]	Percentage of daily volume	
	During four peak hours	During maximum peak hour
Bus transit systems		
Chicago	40	—
Washington, D.C. (3 major lines)	53	16
Rail rapid transit systems		
Boston	44	—
New York City	49	14
Chicago	58	16
Toronto	51	18
Cleveland	58	19
Philadelphia	58	17
Railroad commuter systems		
Chicago	72	25
Washington, D.C. (Pennsylvania RR)	68	23
Philadelphia (Pennsylvania RR)	68	25
Highway systems		
Chicago	32	9
Detroit (Lodge-Ford Expressway)	28	7
Chicago (Congress Street Expressway)	30	8
Washington, D.C. (Memorial Bridge)	44	13
Boston (Route 128)	29	9

[a]Based on available data for 1959–1962 period.

Additional perspective on the relative peaking of different modes can be obtained from Table 30. It is apparent that rail transit and railroad commuter facilities experience relatively the highest peak-hour and the lowest off-peak demands. By contrast, private automobile travel has the highest percentage of its use during off-peak periods, as would be expected since this mode offers particular service advantages for non-commuter trips. Note also that the bus systems fare better off-peak than rail transit but not as well as automobile travel.

Passenger ridership and highway usage, moreover, are not equally distributed throughout the four rush hours. The maximum peak hour

TABLE 31

ANNUAL REVENUE-PASSENGER TRENDS ON RAPID TRANSIT AND BUS TRANSIT SYSTEMS
(Index: 1956 = 100.0)

	Rapid transit system ridership						Bus and surface transit system ridership	
Year	Cleveland	Toronto	New York	Chicago	Philadelphia	Boston[a]	Washington, D.C., bus transit	Chicago surface transit
1946			151.8	136.8	177.8	185.1	—	—
1950			121.9	95.2	137.3	140.2	202.2	—
1951			117.5	97.1	126.3	132.3	191.0	—
1952			114.1	97.0[b]	123.0	127.0	184.0	—
1953			114.0	96.1	114.8	122.8	141.9	—
1954			103.9	95.8	109.2	112.1	122.8	—
1955		97.0[c]	101.0	97.2	102.8	103.6	95.4	101.0
1956	100.0[c]	100.0	100.0	100.0	100.0[d]	100.0	100.0	100.0
1957	107.0	101.0	99.5[e]	97.2	95.6	96.6	100.2	92.8
1958	105.7	99.1	96.7	92.8	92.0	94.1	100.1	84.2
1959	121.0[f]	99.1	97.2	98.1[g]	89.5	92.4	100.5	85.5
1960	124.7	95.7	98.7	97.6	90.1	91.2[h]	99.9	83.4
1961	120.9	91.0	100.0	95.2[i]	92.9	88.5	98.9	78.0
1962	117.5	91.0[j]	100.5	98.9	89.4	(81.6)[k]	99.0	77.3
1963	115.1	100.8[m]	100.0	96.1	NA	(79.1)		75.4
1964	113.8	105.1	100.3	96.2	81.7	(80.5		75.0
1965	113.1	109.8	98.6	99.1	80.3	(78.8)		76.7

[a]Two extensions of existing lines have been made since 1947. [b]Milwaukee Avenue and Dearborn Line opened in 1951. [c]First full year of operation.
[d]Woodland Avenue extension opened in 1955. [e]Rockaway Line opened during 1956. [f]CTS Westside extension opened during 1958.
[g]Congress Street Line opened during 1958. [h]Highland Branch Line extension opened during 1959. [i]Congress Street Line extension opened during 1960.
[j]Estimate by Toronto Transit Commission, based on 11 months actual data (letter to authors).
[k]Parentheses indicate that indexes were computed on the basis of "revenue fares collected." (Fares are collected more than once from some passengers.)
[m]Original system extended 2 miles (or about 50 percent) within downtown Toronto during 1963.
[NA]Data not available.

largely controls capacity and equipment requirements. Data on this movement are also shown in Table 30. These percentages make it evident that the maximum-hour peaking of transit is very pronounced. Railroad commuter trains usually must carry almost 25 per cent of their total daily load during only one of the 24 hours, rail transit from 14 to 20 per cent, and bus only slightly less. By contrast, highways experience only about 10 to 15 per cent of their total usage during the maximum hour.

The over-all ridership trends on six major rapid transit systems and on two bus transit systems are shown in Table 31. In general, bus transit has suffered considerably larger ridership declines than rail transit over the past 15 years, but has not been beset by as heavy peaking characteristics. Buses also have usually enjoyed shorter trip lengths and higher revenue per passenger-mile.

To the deleterious effects of dwindling off-peak use of transit must be added an even more pronounced shift in weekend travel. (However, this latter shift does permit more nearly proportional cost reductions.) In Chicago, for example, while weekday riding on Chicago Transit Authority vehicles declined 16.8 per cent between 1956 and 1961, Saturday riding declined by 19.5 per cent and Sunday riding by 26.8.[15]

TABLE 32

PERCENTAGE OF TOTAL REVENUE-PASSENGER VOLUME CARRIED ON WEEKENDS: SELECTED RAPID TRANSIT SYSTEMS, 1947 THROUGH 1962

Year	Boston	Chicago	New York	Toronto	Philadelphia	Cleveland
1947	22.9	21.2	—	—	—	—
1948	22.3	20.1	—	—	—	—
1949	—	18.6	—	—	—	—
1950	20.4	17.7	—	—	—	—
1951	20.2	17.4	—	—	—	—
1952	19.4	16.8	—	—	—	—
1953	19.0	15.9	16.3	—	—	—
1954	18.4	15.8	15.6	—	—	—
1955	18.2	16.4	14.7	—	—	—
1956	17.9	16.4	15.2	15.7	—	—
1957	17.3	15.7	15.4	15.6	—	—
1958	16.6	14.9	14.3	14.9	—	—
1959	16.6	14.4	14.8	14.5	13.5	—
1960	17.4	14.5	14.5	14.4	—	13.7
1961	—	14.2	14.8	14.4	11.5	13.1
1962	—	—	14.9	14.3	—	12.2

[15] George Haikalis, "Non-Weekday Transit Riding," *CATS Research News,* vol. 4, no. 5, June 8, 1962.

TABLE 33

PERCENTAGE OF TOTAL 2-WAY HOURLY FLOW PROCEEDING IN MINOR DIRECTION DURING MAXIMUM RUSH HOUR, AT MAXIMUM LOAD POINT

System and city	Percentage of flow in minor direction
Rail transit	
Toronto, p.m., 1962	19.5
New York, p.m., 1961	13.5
Cleveland, p.m., 1961	16.0
Philadelphia, p.m., 1961	23.0
Chicago, p.m., 1960	19.5
Bus transit	
Washington, D.C. (3 lines), p.m., 1959	21.0
Railroad commuter	
Philadelphia (Pennsylvania RR), p.m., 1958	15.1
Highway systems	
Detroit (Lodge-Ford Expressway)	42.6
Chicago (Congress Street Expressway)	37.4
Washington, D.C. (Memorial Bridge)	36.3

The Executive Vice-President of the American Transit Association recently commented on this weekend decline as follows:

At one time, weekend and holiday transit riding was often almost as good as on weekdays. However, the prevalence of the 5-day week, combined with the automobile and other factors, has caused Saturday riding to drop to 61.2 per cent of the average weekday level in 1959. Sunday and holiday riding last year [1960] dropped to 30.2 and 33.8 per cent, respectively, of the weekday average for all cities.[16]

He added that in cities of less than 50,000 population, losses in Saturday riding had been relatively less than in larger cities. This difference, perhaps, is attributable to smaller cities adjusting earlier than large cities to high levels of automobile ownership and weekend automobile use.[17] This steady though small decline in weekend ridership on major rapid transit systems is illustrated further by the data in Table 32.[18]

16 George W. Anderson, "The Transit Industry—Its Resources, Capabilities and Problem Areas," in National Academy of Sciences, National Research Council, *U.S. Transportation, Resources, Performances and Problems,* Pub. 841-S, Washington, D.C., 1961, p. 172.

17 *Ibid.*

18 An Institute of Public Administration report, *The Transportation Picture in Selected Urban Areas, A Supplement to Urban Transportation and Public Policy,* December 1961 (prepared for the U.S. Department of Commerce and the Housing and Home Finance Agency), suggests that off-peak patronage is often sensitive to unexpected and special influences. Thus for Birmingham, Alabama, they report that

Another aspect of the peaking problem is the imbalance in the directional flow of many transit and highway operations. Extreme peaking and flow imbalance are particularly characteristic of rail commuter and transit systems, although certainly not unimportant for bus transit or private automobile travel. Table 33 summarizes data on the directional imbalance for various systems and modes, and clearly points out the relatively greater imbalance of transit compared to automobile experience. Generally, highways currently record about twice as much relative usage in the minor flow direction as do transit facilities.

Transit Improvement and Public Attitudes Toward Modal Choice

An often-suggested method to improve transit patronage and reverse the unfavorable trends just cited is to build new and more modern rail transit systems, the logic being that a "better" product will attract more customers, including significant numbers of automobile commuters. Two new rail rapid transit lines that came into use in the 1950's were the Yonge Street Subway in Toronto and the Congress Street Rapid Transit Line in Chicago. In commenting on the Yonge Street Subway, Francis Bello notes that although the subway was a replacement for the city's busiest streetcar route (which carried up to 12,000 riders an hour while the new facility is carrying 42,000) there appears to have been "no significant increase in the total number of morning and evening riders; it is just that they have discovered that more of them can now ride at one time."[19] If we accept Bello's assessment, it appears that the primary contribution of the Yonge Street Subway has been to shorten the duration of the peak. Table 34 lists the former modes of travel of 1960 riders on the Yonge Street Subway and the Congress Street Rapid Transit Line. In both cases, over 85 per cent of the new subway patronage came from previously existing transit.

Another commonly suggested method to increase transit patronage is to reduce the price of transit services by government subsidy. In any consideration of this method, attention should be given to what has actually happened when such practices have been instituted. First, almost all commuter railroads long have been forced to subsidize their passenger

---

while transit route-miles increased from 8 million in 1958 to 8.20 million for the 12 months ending June 30, 1961, revenue passengers fell from 24.6 million in 1958 to 23 million for the 12 months ending June 30, 1961. The authors point out that "peak-hour passenger traffic has increased during the past several years; but shopping passengers have decreased, in part because of the desegregation since many white shoppers refuse to ride desegregated buses."

[19] Francis Bello, "The City and the Car," in The Editors of *Fortune, The Exploding Metropolis* (Doubleday, Garden City, N. Y., 1958), p. 69.

TABLE 34

PREVIOUS MODES OF TRANSPORTATION USED BY 1960 RIDERS ON THE YONGE STREET SUBWAY, TORONTO, AND THE CONGRESS STREET RAPID TRANSIT, CHICAGO
(per cent)

Previous mode	Congress Street	Yonge Street
Surface transit	85.4	86.2
Automobile	12.5	12.9
Other	2.1	0.9

SOURCE: Philip H. Burch, Jr., *Highway Revenue and Expenditure Policy in the U.S.* (Rutgers University Press, New Brunswick, N.J., 1962), p. 286.

and commuter business at the expense of freight business and general profits; and while it is difficult to generalize on the extent of subsidy, it is perhaps instructive to note that the New Haven Railroad incurred an estimated annual deficit of $4 million for handling 15,000 daily commuters into Boston in 1959.[20] Similarly, in 1961 the Chicago and North Western Railway Company lost about $1.9 million on the 60,000 daily commuters using its suburban operations.[21] Despite subsidies of this nature, and a relative increase in automobile commuting costs, railroad commuting has decreased some 20 per cent since 1947 and at best has only remained stable in recent years.

A similar predicament besets rail transit operations. For example, large subsidies (whether explicit or implicit) are afforded to commuters on the Toronto, New York, Boston, Philadelphia, and Chicago rail rapid and bus transit systems. New York City "currently pumps over $120 million a year into its transit system for capital improvements, police protection, and other incidental costs."[22] The Boston Metropolitan Transit Authority incurred an operating deficit in 1963 of about $12 million, to be added to almost $7 million in fixed charges, producing a total annual deficit of slightly over $19 million which was paid by the 14 cities and towns served. In Chicago, the extent of subsidy to transit system passengers is

[20] Boston College, College of Business Administration, Seminar Research Bureau, *Problems of the Railroads*, Studies of Urban Transportation, Boston 1959, p. 8.

[21] *Northwest Chicago Corridor Transportation Study,* Engineering Report, prepared for C&NW and Chicago Transit Authority by Parsons, Brinckerhoff, Quade & Douglas, September 1962. According to more recent reports, though, this loss situation may have improved.

[22] Institute of Public Administration, *The Transportation Picture in Selected Urban Areas, A Supplement to Urban Transportation and Public Policy,* prepared for the U.S. Department of Commerce and the Housing and Home Finance Agency, December 1961.

not directly known; however, it is probably substantial since the Authority pays rental to the city only for trackage and subway equipment costs but not for interest and principal for subway and other fixed rail transit construction.

The Toronto transit system, and more particularly its rail rapid transit portion, is generally held to be self-supporting. This is not entirely correct. The first 4.6 miles of the system seem to be on a pay-as-you-go basis provided only that its costs accounting does not include any allocation of some $24 million expended on subway construction out of a reserve fund. As for recent extensions of this 4.6-mile section and for others now under way, only 45 per cent of the capital costs will be borne directly by transit users; the remainder will be borne by Metropolitan Toronto.

In Philadelphia, some of the capital costs for rail transit facilities are and have been borne by the private Philadelphia Transportation Company (PTC), while others are borne by the city. In fact, most of the subway and rapid transit facilities operated by the PTC are owned by the City of Philadelphia or the Delaware River Port Authority, and then leased to the PTC at less than full ownership costs. The extent of subsidy is not clear, however.

Cleveland is a notable exception in that its municipally owned transit system (CTS), including an eight-year-old (limited) rapid transit network, has to date been maintained on a pay-as-you-go basis, including debt service on the capital.

Over the last few years more explicit fare and service subsidy programs have been debated and considered, and a few have been placed into practice. For example, Philadelphia has had a large-scale effort under way for some time to draw commuters from automobile to rail by such means. So far, the $1.5-million annual investment in the Philadelphia projects, Operations Northeast and Northwest, has diverted 1500 car owners to transit on downtown trips.[23] Similar experiments in Boston have yielded much the same results. The demonstration projects on the Boston and Maine railroad, for example, financed by $2.2 million in annual government subsidies, appear to have diverted about 1500 peak-hour riders to the commuter railroad from other modes (70 per cent from automobiles) as a result of doubling scheduled service and slashing fares (generally in the region of 20 per cent).[24] The extent of the total subsidy involved is unknown in view of the substantial freight-to-passenger cross-subsidy already in existence. Even under the most modest of assumptions the sub-

[23] Philip H. Burch, Jr., *Highway Revenue and Expenditure Policy in the U.S.* (Rutgers University Press, New Brunswick, N.J., 1962), p. 276.

[24] Commonwealth of Massachusetts, Mass Transportation Commission, *Demonstration Project Progress Reports 3 and 4,* 1963.

sidy appears to be at least $200 a passenger per year or about 80 cents per round trip. Similarly, in a recent HHFA subsidized experiment, Detroit succeeded in increasing bus patronage somewhat by more frequent scheduling and the institution of more express services, but at a cost of about $2.50 per additional bus ride taken—a figure comparable to taxi fares.

The results of these experiments should of course be regarded as only preliminary. For one thing, the experiments may have been hampered bcause the public knew they were only temporary, or because the service improvements were not large enough. It would be premature to use these results as the basis for any final conclusions about the sensitivity of urban transportation demands to price and service offerings; but so far, at any rate, they offer little support to the argument that subsidies to or improvements in rail commuting or other transit operations will attract many automobile commuters to public transit.

Evidence broadly confirming these findings (notably, little price or schedule frequency elasticity for transit travel, but considerable income elasticity for automobile travel) has also been provided by a few exploratory econometric studies of urban transportation demand. For example, insensitivity of transit ridership to increases in service frequency is noted in a study by J. F. Kain.[25] Similarly, evidence of a very low price elasticity of demand for urban transportation was reported by L. N. Moses and H. F. Williamson.[26] Moses and Williamson's findings suggest that the cross-elasticity of demand between private automobile and public transportation might be so low that actual cash payments would have to be made to automobile riders to induce any considerable number to shift from automobile to transit. Also, Oi and Shuldiner report a very high income elasticity of demand for urban automobile transportation services, but a low one for transit services.[27]

Additional information on the attitudes of urban commuters toward service considerations was obtained in a *Fortune* survey of automobile commuters in Los Angeles, San Francisco, and Washington, D.C., all described by the editors of *Fortune* as cities "where the automobile is king." An interesting aspect of the results (summarized in Table 35) is the importance commuters attach to transit time (as envisioned by the

[25] J. F. Kain, "A Contribution to the Urban Tranportation Debate: An Econometric Model of Urban Residential and Travel Behavior," *The Review of Economics and Statistics,* 46:55–64 (February 1964).

[26] Leon N. Moses and Harold F. Williamson, Jr., "Value of Time, Choice of Mode, and the Subsidy Issue in Urban Transportation," *Journal of Political Economy,* 71:247–264 (June 1963).

[27] Walter Y. Oi and Paul W. Shuldiner, *An Analysis of Urban Travel Demands* (Northwestern University Press, Evanston, Ill., 1962), chap. 6.

TABLE 35

RESULTS OF *Fortune* MAGAZINE SURVEYS OF AUTOMOBILE COMMUTERS IN LOS ANGELES, SAN FRANCISCO, AND WASHINGTON, D.C.
(in per cent)

	Los Angeles	San Francisco	Washington
How they feel about their work-trip:			
Do not enjoy driving in today's traffic; would almost certainly switch to public transportation if it came reasonably close to competing with automobile trip in time, cost and convenience	34	39	32
Driving to work convenient, but would seriously consider switching to a first class transit system	32	39	37
Enjoy driving; can't imagine switching to public transit	34	22	31
Could now use public transportation to commute to work, but do not	42	90	85
Believe transportation and traffic problem in their area best solved by:			
New public rapid transit system	66	78	47
New highways and expressways	34	22	53
Type of transit system preferred:			
Bus system	35	21	41
Rail system	65	79	59
Would use transit system of choice:			
If round trip travel time matched present driving time	64	68	60
Only if it offered a substantial round trip time saving (ranging from 10 to 60 minutes)	19	18	22
Doubt would use under any circumstances	17	14	18
Facts about present automobile trip:			
Belong to car pool (per cent)	12	46	54
Average 1-way distance (miles)	11.4	14.1	9.1
Average travel time home-to-work (minutes)	27	29.5	28.5
Average travel time work-to-home (minutes)	32.5	33.5	33.5
Average speed for homebound trip in mph (from above figures)	21	25	16

SOURCE: The Editors of *Fortune*, *The Exploding Metropolis*, Doubleday & Company, Inc., Garden City, N.Y., 1958, pp. 79–80. The surveys included 840 automobile commuters in Los Angeles, 370 in San Francisco, and 1395 in Washington, D.C.

individual traveler, of course). This emphasis shows up in several ways. First, there is the apparently strong preference for rail over bus transit, probably to be explained by the fact that present-day bus systems almost always operate more slowly than rail systems. Even more striking is the high percentage of automobile drivers—60 per cent or more for all three cities—who claim they would use transit if their round-trip travel times matched their present driving times; and almost 20 per cent more say they would use transit if it substantially shortened their travel times. In general, the results of the *Fortune* survey suggest a substantial diversion to transit from autos *if* a transit system can be designed that will offer automobile commuters over-all home-to-office travel times that are the same as or shorter than they now enjoy.

Such a transit system does not seem to be a likely possibility, however. As can be seen from Table 35, the trip home for automobile commuters in these three cities (the slower of the two trips between home and work) takes a little over 30 minutes at an average speed of 16 to 25 mph, over a distance of about 9 to 14 miles. For transit to equal this record, its performance would have to be considerably superior on the line-haul portions of the trip—that is, between downtown and the suburban transfer point—to make up for time the transit traveler probably would lose in transfers, waiting time, walking, and in suburban feeder bus or park-and-ride operations. For example, it might be hypothesized that an average transit trip will involve at least one transfer, taking about 2 minutes; a commuter will have to walk for 2 or 3 minutes between the feeder stop and his home (if only a block and a half or less apart); he will have to wait 2 or 3 minutes to catch a feeder bus (assuming a 10-minute and well-defined schedule frequency); and the feeder bus, making stops in the suburbs to pick up and drop off passengers, will consume 3 to 7 minutes more than a private automobile between the line-haul stop (or suburban transfer point) and the commuter's local bus stop. Under these assumptions, the transit system suffers at least a 10-minute initial handicap compared with the automobile.

Of course, if the transit system could drop the commuter off downtown at a point closer to his work than his parking lot, it could offset some of this time disadvantage.[28] However, if the trend toward wide dispersal of workplaces continues, automobiles may almost always get people closer to their workplaces and sooner than transit. If workplaces became widely enough dispersed, in fact, feeder buses would be required at the work-

[28] Such a circumstance seems very unlikely in view of the large number of parking lots and their dispersal. Few blocks, for example, would not have at least one parking lot or garage (other than in New York City), but it is seldom that even local buses stop at every block.

place as well as the residential end of the trip. On balance it seems a conservative conclusion that existing types of transit will neither greatly improve nor deteriorate time performance at the work place end of the typical commutation trip, as compared with automobile travel.

Thus, if we assume 10 miles of line-haul for the typical work-trip[29]—the only remaining segment in which the transit system has a chance to outcompete the automobile—transit must gain 1 minute per mile over the auto to counterbalance a 10-minute disadvantage, as described above. Thus if the automobile's line-haul average is 20 mph, the transit facility must achieve 30; if the automobile's average is 24 mph, transit must achieve 40; and so on.

For reasons documented in chapters 8 and 9 and in the appendixes, average over-all speeds of 35 to 40 mph are about the maximum achievable by a well-designed rapid transit system with 1-mile station spacing. The main obstacle to improvement is the simple fact that the train, and to a lesser extent the bus, must make passenger stops every mile or so and incur time losses for braking, acceleration, loading, and unloading. Therefore, barring some dramatic breakthrough in transit technology or operational changes of the character outlined in chapter 12, the automobile will probably maintain its time-in-transit supremacy.

The public's implicit recognition of this likelihood is suggested by a recent poll of Los Angeles residents, in this case not restricted to automobile commuters.[30] This questionnaire, as contrasted with the *Fortune* survey, said nothing about levels of transit service; instead, 709 families representing a "scientific sample" of the *Los Angeles Times* Reader Panel were merely asked, "If by some miracle, a rapid transit system were in effect tomorrow morning, would you ride to work on it?" In response, 50 per cent said they "wouldn't, definitely, flatly." Another 10.8 per cent said they probably would not, while only 4.7 per cent said they definitely would, and another 2.6 per cent said they probably would. On the other hand, an overwhelming number—86.8 per cent—said they believed Los Angeles needed a new rapid transit system! In short, the respondents did not want a new system for themselves, but apparently thought it was a good idea for everybody else or for occasional usage.

The strong contrast in the responses given in the two different surveys might be attributable to the fact that the second questionnaire postulated no specific hope or guarantee that transit would considerably improve the

[29] This assumed length is well above the 6-mile average for the United States as a whole. Shortening the assumed length works still further to the time disadvantage of transit, which then has even less distance in which to compensate for the time loss described.

[30] Richard Bergholz, "Public Wants Rapid Transit—But No Taxes," *Los Angeles Times,* June 12, 1963, sec. II, p. 4.

quality of the commutation trip.[31] In this connection, comments in the report are perhaps especially suggestive:

> The public would have to see enough advantages cost-wise and time-wise and then be re-educated in the use of this type of transportation. Angelenos have too long found that private cars are faster and more comfortable than outdated public vehicles now in use and it will take a long time to prove otherwise.

The moral seems to be that a promotional effort would be necessary to win the Los Angeles public over to a transit system, which would also have to prove its superiority over automobile travel on the freeway.

Summary

Since supply and demand characteristics lie at the heart of urban transportation problems, it would be ideal to have a complete set of empirical estimates of all the relevant income, service, and price elasticities and cross-elasticities that determine consumer choices. The available data fall far short of that ideal, however. Accordingly, an alternative two-stage strategy was employed here. First, the aggregate level of demand for urban transportation was investigated, particularly peak-period demands in the central parts of the city. These demands crucially affect the maximum capacity requirements for urban transportation facilities in most cities. The second stage consisted of erecting hypotheses about urban transportation choices and testing the forecasts they yielded against available data on the types of transportation used for making various types of trips. In essence, the procedure was to hypothesize the modal choices urban travelers would make if they behaved in accordance with certain fundamental economic axioms.

On the whole, the hypothesized and the empirical data closely agreed. As expected, for example, it was found that the automobile will predominate more for shopping, social-recreational, and personal business trips, for which its service advantages are greatest and its cost disadvantages least or nonexistent. Two effects of these developments are a greatly increased specialization of public transit in commuter trips, and a serious over-all decline in transit use. These two facts undoubtedly go a long way toward explaining the present financial difficulties of much of the urban transit industry.

The evidence with respect to price elasticities of demand, while not clear-cut, is indicative. The automobile dominates when automobile costs

[31] Other possible explanations are the fact that the Los Angeles freeways improved in the period between the surveys, and the fact that the questionnaire was not restricted to commuters (although this should have been largely offset by the inclusion of people who were already commuting by transit).

are about the same as or below those of public transit, as they seem to be for many family shopping excursions and social-recreational trips. For the work-trip made to high-density workplaces, however, in which the cost advantage still seems to lie with public transit (ignoring service differentials), the evidence is less clear; what evidence there is strongly suggests that the choice of mode for the work-trip is very insensitive to price changes. Final judgment on this issue must await more complete information.

In short, to use the jargon of the economist, the demand functions for urban transportation seem to be such that income elasticities are substantially positive for private automobile transportation and inconsequential or possibly even negative for public transit; certainly there has been a long-term negative trend in public transit. Also, the price elasticities and cross-elasticities are relativcly less important, at least within the recent range of historical experience.[32]

[32] Of course, the recent range of historical experience may not have been entirely relevant if the argument is accepted that the urban highway commuters have been heavily subsidized while public transit riders have not. There seem to be no overriding reasons for accepting the argument, however. The public transit industry has not been very profitable in recent years, and has often been subsidized by government, by stockholders, or by funds earned by private companies from other activities. Furthermore, as chapter 4 demonstrated, urban highway users do not seem to be subsidized, possibly excepting those using the most central facilities during peak hours. On the whole, then, it seems relevant and reasonable to make price comparisons between private and public transportation. The only major exception would arise if there were pronounced external economies or diseconomies associated with one form of transportation as opposed to another. A discussion of such factors is to be found in subsequent chapters.

Chapter 6 | The Interrelationship of Housing and Urban Transportation

In analyzing the interrelationships between urban residents' expenditures for transportation and for housing, an obvious initial hypothesis is that urban households choose their housing locations and urban transportation modes so as to maximize their total real incomes, though probably in an imperfect way. In particular, households can make substitutions between outlays for transportation and housing and among alternative transportation media. Many urban households, for example, find it possible to get the housing and yard space they want cheaper, if they are willing to spend more money on transportation and travel farther. Longer commuter trips also may enable consumers to obtain certain other services, particularly of a public character, cheaper or at least seemingly cheaper.

Given that workers employed at central urban locations can usually save money on housing by making longer work-trips, the amounts they save will depend on the kinds of housing they buy; the larger savings normally will accrue to workers who want to consume lower-density housing services (more residential space). Work-trips thus should vary in length, at least broadly, according to the various quantities and types of housing that workers consume, and where in the city their workplaces are. It also seems probable (although no direct evidence is presented here) that the cost of other residential attributes, such as the quality of the structure and perhaps the level of community services, may vary significantly from one part of an urban area to another and these will condition trip choices.

Substitutions also may be made between travel time and travel costs. These substitution possibilities are interdependent, moreover, with workers' choices of housing and workplace location. For example, a worker can save money by using a transportation medium that may be slower but is cheaper. The dollars he can save in this way will depend partly on the kind of transit service available, and this, in turn, depends on where he works and the housing and yard space he consumes. In brief, a worker's use of public transportation, or the probability of it, largely depends on certain data about himself, on his housing location and consumption, and the employment density of his workplace.

While the hypotheses of this chapter apply to both whites and nonwhites, the empirical evidence presented is mainly applicable to white workers. However, evidence on nonwhite workers (for these data, they represent 10 per cent of the total) is considered separately in the next chapter, since segregation in the housing market can be expected to cause differences in white and nonwhite travel and residential behavior. (Chapter 7 also considers the effects of segregation upon the travel and residential behavior of white workers.)[1] Much, though not all, of the empirical evidence in this chapter and in chapter 7 pertains to Chicago and Detroit, consisting as it does of an analysis of data gathered by origin and destination surveys conducted there; but an attempt has been made to formulate hypotheses and to analyze the empirical information in such a way as to render the findings applicable to other cities.[2] The analysis proceeds in three stages: first, a general analysis of recent housing market development; second, evaluation of the relationships between housing and work-trip choices; and third, study of the way in which choice of urban transport mode is conditioned by workplace and household locations.

The Urban Housing Market: Recent Trends and a General Appraisal

One of the many charges leveled against private automobile transportation is that it has created a great wasteland or ugly "urban sprawl" around our cities. There is abundant evidence, however, that the automobile is not the sole cause of low residential densities, although it undoubtedly aided and abetted the course of low-density urban residential

[1] The terms "nonwhite" and "negro" are used interchangeably in this book, since the overwhelming majority of nonwhites residing in U.S. cities in recent years have been negroes.

[2] Much of the analysis presented in this and the next chapter is based on approximately 60,000 home interviews obtained in 1956 by the Chicago Area Transportation Study and approximately 40,000 home interviews obtained in 1953 as part of the Detroit Area Traffic Study. For the Chicago analysis approximately 57,000 linked first work-trip cards, 53,000 household cards, 23,000 block land-use cards, 5000 summary land-use cards, and a number of smaller card decks were obtained and analyzed. The Detroit analysis is based on approximately 50,000 first work-trip cards and 40,000 household cards, as well as summary information on land use and characteristics of the Detroit area transit system. Use of magnetic tape permitted combining the household and work-trip information and cross classification of household and trip characteristics in a way previously not possible with information for the Chicago or Detroit studies. The trip information presented here refers only to "internal work-trips." Internal trips are defined as trips having both their origin and destination within the study area.

development. Other important factors contributing to suburbanization are cheap and easily available home financing, higher income levels, and dispersed employment locations. In the postwar period, what appeared to be a preference among large numbers of Americans for home ownership and low-density arrangements also became a matter of Federal Government policy. In short, the FHA loan insurance and the VA guaranty programs combined with rising incomes, increasing automobile ownership, and decentralized employment to extend home ownership and occupancy of single-family and other low-density living arrangements.

TABLE 36

PERCENTAGE OF U.S. POPULATION OWNING AND RENTING, BY DECADES

Year	Percentage owning	Percentage renting
1890	36.9	63.1
1900	34.6	65.4
1910	37.1	62.9
1920	40.0	60.0
1930	45.3	54.7
1940	41.1	58.9
1950	53.4	46.6
1957	60.0	40.0

SOURCE: U.S. Savings and Loan League, *Savings and Loan Fact Book, 1958*, Chicago, 1959, Table 4, p. 14.

In large measure, moreover, these postwar developments only reemphasized long-standing trends in American living patterns. Table 36 shows the rising proportion owning rather than renting at each decile census from 1900 to 1957. These figures suggest a sharp rise in single-family dwelling since the economics of rental operation are such as to make the maintenance and operation of single-family rental units expensive. (Only in the past five years have cooperative apartments and other ownership arrangements for units in multifamily structures begun to make headway in this country.) More direct confirmation of this point is obtained from Table 37 which lists the number and percentage of single- and multiple-family nonfarm housing construction starts by five-year intervals from 1900 to 1959. For the five-year periods from 1935 to 1959, single-family starts exceeded 80 per cent of total new private housing starts.

The postwar rise in family income was certainly very important in expanding home ownership and the number of single-family dwellings. Also, home ownership in higher-income groups has become more pro-

TABLE 37

PRIVATELY OWNED PERMANENT NONFARM HOUSING STARTS, 1900–1959

Period	Dwelling units (thousands)			Percentage of total		Type of financing[a] (percentage of total starts)	
	Single-family	Multifamily	Total	Single-family	Multifamily	Government	Conventional
1900–1904	852	419	1272	67	33	—	100
1905–1909	1557	778	2334	67	33	—	100
1910–1914	1285	767	2052	63	37	—	100
1915–1919	1025	519	1543	66	34	—	100
1920–1924	2002	1174	3176	63	37	—	100
1925–1929	2269	1589[b]	3858	59	41[b]	—	100
1930–1934	717	220	937	77	23	—	100
1935–1939	1376	334	1709	81	19	23	77
1940–1944	1434	288	1772	84	16	45[b]	55
1945–1949	3070	547	3617	85	15	39	61
1950–1954	4992	719	5711	87[b]	13	44	56
1955–1959	5022	859	5682	85	15	39	61

[a]The FHA made its first inspections in 1935, the VA in 1945. All data given here are worked from the rounded number of starts.

[b]All-time high.

NOTE: Because of rounding, the numbers of sales and rental units may not add precisely to the totals shown.

SOURCE: U.S. Housing and Home Finance Agency, *Housing Statistics*, *Annual Data*, *March 1960*, U.S. Government Printing Office, Washington, D.C., 1960.

TABLE 38

HOUSING STATUS OF NONFARM FAMILIES, 1949 AND 1957
(Percentage distribution by income)

Family income before taxes	Own home		Rent home		Other[a]	
	1949	1957	1949	1957	1949	1957
Under $1000	39	42	30	30	31	28
$1000 to 1999	31	40	41	41	28	19
$2000 to 2999	33	39	38	35	29	26
$3000 to 3999	43	40	44	42	13	18
$4000 to 4999	51	50	39	40	10	10
$5000 to 7499	55	64	37	31	8	5
$7500 to 9999	64	76	30	23	6	1
$10,000 and over	75	83	20	17	5	—
All nonfarm families	44	54	38	33	18	13

[a]Families living with relatives, receiving housing as part of compensation, etc.
SOURCE: U.S. Savings and Loan League, *Savings and Loan Fact Book*, *1958*, Chicago, 1959, Table 5, p. 15.

nounced recently than in the past. Table 38 gives the housing status of nonfarm families in 1949 and 1957 by income classes, from which it can be seen that during the period the percentage of homeowners increased in all but two income classes: $3000 to $3999 and $4000 to $4999. The same period also had a general rise in family income, so that more families entered the higher-income classes for which home-ownership is more common.

In recent years, however, some reversal of the tendency toward single-family dwelling may have occurred. As indicated by Figure 6, multiple-dwelling-unit construction in metropolitan areas has increased relatively as well as absolutely, from a low of 8.5 per cent of all housing starts in 1955 to a high of 31.0 per cent in 1962. These figures reveal a steady expansion of multifamily construction from 1945 to 1949, and a steady decline from 1949 to 1956, followed once more by a rapid expansion. In interpreting Figure 6 it should be remembered that during the late 1950's and early 1960's the relatively few "depression babies" were new entrants to the 25- to 45-year age group (the backbone of the market for single-family homes), while the large numbers of World War II babies were entering the 18- to 25-year age group (an important segment of the market for multifamily units). Also, the sharp increase in the absolute and relative number of multifamily starts in 1949 was a result almost entirely of liberal financing under FHA Section 608 loans, which made it possible for entrepreneurs to construct multiple units with little or no equity. Because of high foreclosure rates resulting from excesses in the

608 program, it was discontinued in 1954. In retrospect, it appears that the program's incentives were too attractive—so much so that some contractors failed to use good judgment in selecting and planning projects.[3] This experience strongly suggests the importance of the mortgage credit structure in determining the character of postwar urban housing.

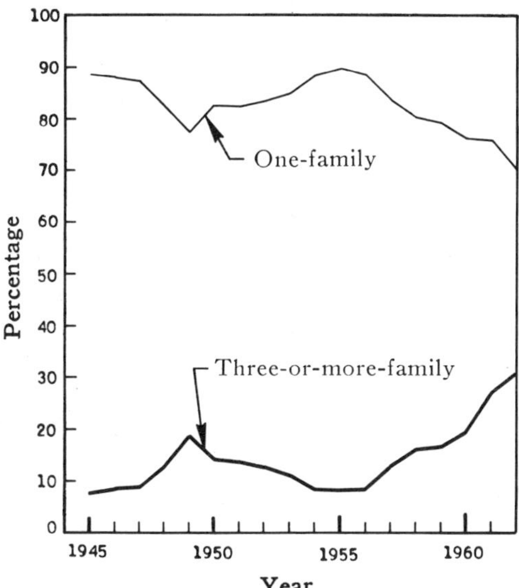

Figure 6. Percentage of nonfarm housing units started, by structure type and year. SOURCE: U.S. Housing and Home Finance Agency, *Housing Statistics, Annual Data, May 1963,* U.S. Government Printing Office, Washington, D.C., 1963, Table A–3, p. 2.

It appears, however, too early to determine what has caused the most recent upsurge in construction of multifamily and rental dwellings. It may be merely a cyclical movement or a temporary response to special tax incentives, family formation, or other matters. It could also be a fundamental shift in underlying consumer preference patterns or a response to increasing land values in many rapidly growing cities. Some of the problems involved in making these assessments are well documented by Louis Winnick in his book, *Rental Housing: Opportunities for Private Investment.* Winnick in 1958 predicted a fairly high level of rental construction by the 1970's but was pessimistic about the level of multifamily

[3] For an interesting discussion of the foibles of this program and of its successes, see Miles L. Colean, "Realities of Today's Real Estate Investment," *Architectural Forum,* 102:110–112 (June 1955).

starts in the late 1950's or early 1960's. "It is conceivable that by the 1970's the share of rental construction may increase from its 1956 level of 9 or 10 per cent to a sustained average of 20 per cent or even more of a larger aggregate of dwelling unit starts." [4]

Commenting on the then barely visible 1957 upturn in multiunit starts, he added, "It is highly improbable that, despite the 1957 upturn, the immediate future will see a vastly greater volume of private rental construction. Rapid population growth in the large cities, which, among other factors, fed the rental boom of the pre-1920 era, appears to be a thing of the past." [5] If we assume multifamily housing starts to be equivalent to rental housing starts (see Figure 6), rental housing starts during the period 1957–1962 have exceeded Winnick's 20 per cent projection for the 1970's in every year since 1958, and have averaged 26.5 per cent of nonfarm housing starts since 1957.

Winnick's optimism about a high level of rental and thus multifamily starts during the 1970's is based largely on an analysis of demographic trends. He argues that future populations will include increased numbers and proportions of young married couples as the World War II babies mature, increased numbers and proportions of people who live alone (mostly widows and widowers), increased numbers and proportions of older people, and the like, all of whom represent markets for rental housing.[6] Also favorable to rental housing, he argues, are changes in labor force composition—such as increases in the proportion of professional, managerial, and white-collar workers and in the number and proportion of working wives, as well as rising suburban land costs and a more cheerful view of rental housing on the part of investors as the depression experience recedes further into the past. Although admitting that it would be a mistake to consider the popularity of suburban living as a mere fad, he also insists that "the suburban way of life is losing some of its admirers," and that it is "hard to deny entirely the impression that there is growing dissatisfaction with the suburbs, and that there exists a possibility of a return movement to the cities."[7]

In fact, the very recent revival of multifamily construction has been seized upon by numerous observers of the urban scene as evidence of a recentralization trend and as justification for rail rapid transit solutions to the urban transportation problem. Obviously, though, the exact urban location of new multifamily construction is important in evaluating these arguments. It is particularly pertinent whether the construction is located in the central city near the core, as in the past, or in the suburbs. Table

[4] Louis Winnick, *Rental Housing: Opportunities for Private Investment* (McGraw-Hill, New York, 1958), pp. 212–213.

[5] *Ibid.*, p. 212.

[6] *Ibid.*, pp. 213–218.

[7] *Ibid.*, pp. 225–226.

39 presents information on the proportions of single-family, 2- to 4-family, and 5- or more-family dwelling units constructed in the central cities and suburban rings of U.S. metropolitan areas in 1956, 1957, and 1958. It is apparent from these data that the suburbs are getting a large and increasing proportion of new multiunit construction. More than half of 2- to 4-family starts were made in the suburbs in both 1957 and 1958, and the percentage of suburban starts on 5- or more-family units increased from 31 per cent in 1956 to 39 per cent in 1958.

TABLE 39

PERCENTAGE OF NEW HOUSING UNIT STARTS IN SUBURBS AND CENTRAL CITY, BY STRUCTURE TYPE[a]

	Suburbs			Central city		
Structure type	1956	1957	1958	1956	1957	1958
1-family	74.0	72.0	71.2	26.0	27.6	28.8
2 to 4-family	—	51.7	52.6	—	48.3	47.4
5- or more-family	30.6	34.5	38.8	69.4	65.3	61.2
All structures	68.5	64.8	63.2	31.5	35.2	36.8

[a] Central City and Suburb percentages may not add to 100 because of rounding.
SOURCE: Mary F. Carney, "Suburban and Central City Building in Metropolitan Areas, 1957," *Construction Review*, vol. 4, no. 5, May 1958, pp. 13–16; and *Construction Review*, vol. 5, no. 7, July 1959.

A somewhat similar finding is suggested by Table 40, which presents housing data for 39 large metropolitan areas (as listed in chapter 3). The unweighted percentage of SMSA multiunit family starts taking place in the central cities analyzed is 60 per cent, as opposed to 28 per cent of single-family and 41 per cent of all starts. The central city's predominance in multifamily construction is hardly astonishing, but the extent of multifamily construction in the suburbs—40 per cent—may come as a surprise. The variation from city to city is also dramatic. In Tampa and Washington, D.C., 88 and 84 per cent of multifamily starts were in the suburbs; in Baltimore and Houston the figure was only 4 per cent. And, again, it appears from the data in Table 39 that the suburban proportion of multifamily units is increasing.

Table 40 also includes averages for the SMSA population growth and transit use subgroups analyzed in chapter 3. From 30 to 50 per cent of multiunit starts (defined as 3- or more-family units) of all population growth and transit use subgroups were in the suburbs. It would appear from Table 40, though, that cities enjoying the greatest transit use do have a higher average proportion of multiunit to all starts—46 per cent, as compared to 28 and 26 per cent for cities with medium and low transit use. (The higher density and therefore higher land cost of the cities with higher transit usage would seem to explain this in part.) On the other hand, SMSA's with the lowest transit use (the latter heavily weighted by the Los Angeles–Long Beach metropolitan area) have a higher average number of 1961 multiunit starts and have a higher percentage of multiunits in the central city than do the SMSA's with the greatest transit use.

TABLE 40

NUMBER AND PERCENTAGE OF SINGLE-FAMILY AND MULTIFAMILY HOUSING STARTS IN 39 SMSA'S AND CENTRAL CITIES, 1961

	Starts, SMSA		Percentages in central city		
SMSA	All structures	Percentage 3-or-more-family	All structures	Single-family	3-or-more-family
Akron	3,258	16.5	39.9	34.2	49.4
Atlanta	12,689	29.2	35.1	20.1	71.5
Baltimore	10,614	40.4	44.2	8.5	96.1
Boston	9,754	53.3	17.8	7.9	25.6
Buffalo	2,846	82.6	10.3	5.5	55.5
Chicago	39,372	51.6	39.0	19.4	56.2
Cincinnati	6,250	45.4	42.8	15.1	75.3
Cleveland	9,503	52.0	24.6	15.9	35.1
Columbus	6,719	20.8	64.6	57.9	93.9
Dallas	16,605	29.8	81.9	44.9	86.7
Dayton	3,593	14.3	12.4	6.7	46.7
Denver	19,373	45.2	46.1	7.6	39.9
Detroit	4,525	33.4	33.7	26.4	45.5
Fort Worth	2,672	18.4	68.7	69.4	66.3
Houston	10,855	40.6	92.5	90.0	95.8
Indianapolis	5,957	12.8	43.1	42.5	47.2
Jersey City	1,875	60.9	56.4	44.2	60.4
Kansas City	7,288	19.7	39.6	33.8	82.2
Los Angeles–Long Beach	92,564	51.3	28.8	2.0	36.2
Louisville	3,929	21.0	42.8	29.8	91.2
Memphis	5,059	25.7	53.5	36.9	95.2
Miami	10,181	36.4	17.8	3.6	38.4
Milwaukee	5,529	53.3	61.5	37.4	76.7
Minneapolis–St. Paul	11,264	51.4	36.8	9.8	59.9
New Orleans	6,274	33.8	47.1	24.7	82.7
Newark	9,834	72.4	26.9	2.2	35.9
Oklahoma City	4,418	13.6	77.5	75.6	93.0
Philadelphia	17,543	51.8	67.5	58.3	71.8
Phoenix	15,024	19.9	36.5	28.5	61.2
Pittsburgh	3,628	26.0	27.8	14.9	65.0
Portland	6,111	16.9	17.2	12.2	33.6
Rochester	2,901	28.6	14.5	3.4	40.4

TABLE 40 (*continued*)

SMSA	Starts, SMSA: All structures	Starts, SMSA: Percentage 3-or-more-family	Percentages in central city: All structures	Percentages in central city: Single-family	Percentages in central city: 3-or-more-family
St. Louis	7,342	39.0	20.2	4.9	44.3
San Antonio	3,356	18.4	97.7	99.1	91.0
San Diego	10,975	26.4	59.9	55.7	71.5
San Francisco–Oakland	32,256	55.3	20.4	7.7	30.0
Seattle	8,379	1.9	25.4	13.9	68.8
Tampa	11,750	15.4	13.5	13.8	11.7
Washington, D.C.	26,039	51.5	9.5	2.5	16.0
Total quantity	468,104				
Mean percentage		35.2[a]	40.9[a]	27.9[a]	60.1[a]
Means[a] for population growth subgroups[b]					
High	18,369	31.0	50.2		60.0
Medium	8,391	29.0	41.4		70.4
Low	9,247	45.9	31.1		49.9
Means[a] for transit use subgroups[b]					
High	12,327	45.9	33.1		57.8
Medium	8,278	28.2	33.0		62.2
Low	16,400	25.7	57.2		62.5

[a]Unweighted.

[b]See chap. 3 for definitions of the groups.

SOURCE: U.S. Department of Commerce, Bureau of the Census, *Construction Reports, Building Permits, New Housing Units Authorized by Local Building Permits, Annual Summary 1960–61*, Pub. C-40-38, U.S. Government Printing Office, Washington, D.C., 1962, pp. 73–110.

Also indicative of the tendency for much new multifamily dwelling construction to be in the suburbs is the spatial distribution of multifamily starts within the Los Angeles–Orange County Metropolitan Area in 1960–1961, as shown in Figure 7. By way of perspective, the Los Angeles area had more multifamily starts in 1960–1962 than any of the other 38 SMSA's analyzed, that is more than in any SMSA other than New York.[8] Another index of the relative importance of the Los Angeles area is the fact that multiunit starts there accounted for 25 per cent of all multiunit starts for the 39 metropolitan areas listed in Table 40. The striking feature of Figure 7 is the uniformity with which multifamily starts were dis-

[8] As might be expected, the New York area has the largest number of new 3-or-more-family starts (approximately 65,000 in 1961 as compared to the approximately 47,000 starts in the Los Angeles–Long Beach Metropolitan area).

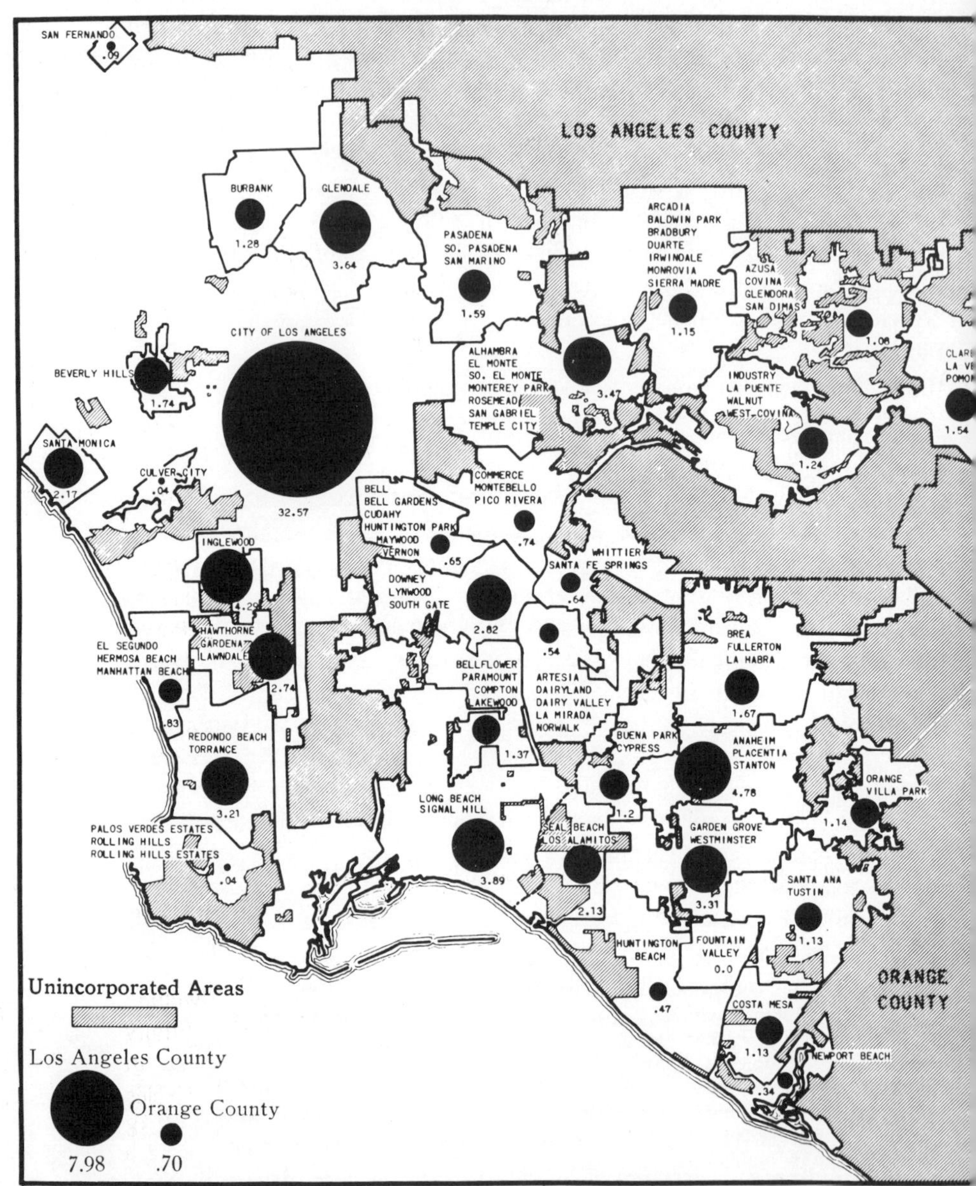

Figure 7. Percentage of multiunit (3-or-more-family) housing starts, by political subdivision, Los Angeles urban area, 1960–1961. SOURCE: U.S. Dept. of Commerce, Bureau of the Census, *Construction Reports, Building Permits, New Housing Units Authorized by Local Building Permits,* C–40–38, Government Printing Office, Washington, D.C., 1962, pp. 73–74.

tributed over the area. The only political subdivisions to obtain more than 5 per cent of the total were the City of Los Angeles (32.57 per cent) and the unincorporated part of Los Angeles County (7.98 per cent). Both are geographically very large (the City of Los Angeles includes some 450 square miles of land area, for example), and it seems quite likely that their multifamily starts were fairly widely dispersed within their extensive boundaries. In short, it would be somewhat premature to forecast that the recent rise in the relative number of multiple-family dwelling units portends any fundamental change in American consumption patterns, and it would be almost certainly fallacious to use these data to prove that a "recentralization" of urban populations is now occurring.

Work-Trip and Residential Choice Relationships

In urban areas, transportation expenditures and housing costs are substitutable in varying degrees. As noted, workers employed at high-density workplaces have an option between higher transportation expenditures and higher housing costs and many choose to make longer and costlier work-trips from the suburbs in order to obtain more cheaply the housing and yard space they want. It is therefore irrelevant to point, as some do, to figures like those in Table 41 showing a rise in the proportion of the total household budget spent on transportation, as evidence of the waste inherent in a system of private transportation and, by implication, its distortion of consumer values. Overlooked are many considerations, such as increases in the quality of transportation service which have accompanied these cost increases. Also, such simple comparisons ignore some important questions about consumer choice and interdependencies of consumer budgets and expenditures. To no small extent, consumers' willingness to spend more money on transportation may be simply traceable to the lowered costs of complementary goods, such as housing, that can thereby be achieved.[9]

[9] The complementarity between transportation and housing costs is often overlooked even by housing market analysts. Louis Winnick, for example, in *American Housing and Its Use: The Demand for Shelter Space* (John Wiley & Sons, New York, 1957), completely ignores the interdependence of housing and transportation costs. He notes that the $600 annual cost of automobile ownership (capital and operating) estimated by the Bureau of Labor Statistics in 1950 is actually higher than average contract rent for that year. From this fact he concludes (p. 72): "If the average home owner (to whom such a choice would be unthinkable) were to substitute more and better housing for his car, such a sum could have financed a house nearly twice as expensve as the one he is currently occupying." In this comparison Winnick fails even to allow any expenditure for access by an alternative mode, such as public transit, let alone consider the possibility that transportation expenditures and use of private automobiles may affect the price of various kinds of housing services. In addition, his statement implicitly assumes that the marginal cost of new housing will be the same as the average historical cost of housing, a seemingly dubious proposition in a period of sharp price inflation.

TABLE 41

PERCENTAGE DISTRIBUTION OF PERSONAL CONSUMPTION EXPENDITURES, 1930–1959

Period	Total expenditure	Housing and household operation			Clothing and shoes	Food and alcoholic beverages	Transportation and travel[b]	Other goods and services
		Total	Housing	Housing operation[a]				
1930–1934	100.0	30.8	16.4	14.4	10.8	24.9	8.5	24.9
1935–1939	100.0	27.7	13.1	14.6	10.5	29.0	9.4	23.4
1940–1944	100.0	26.0	11.7	14.3	12.2	31.7	7.1	23.0
1945–1949	100.0	24.7	9.9	14.8	11.7	32.2	9.2	22.2
1950–1954	100.0	26.9	11.5	15.4	9.7	28.5	12.2	22.7
1955–1959	100.0	27.7	12.5	15.2	9.0	26.0	12.6	24.7

[a]Includes furniture and household equipment, semidurable furnishings and other nondurable goods, and services.

[b]Includes automobiles and parts, gasoline and oil, and transportation.

SOURCE: U.S. Housing and Home Finance Agency, *Housing Statistics, Annual Data, March 1960*, U.S. Government Printing Office, Washington, D.C., 1960, Table A-35, p. 38.

Some general perspectives on housing choices and work-trip patterns can be obtained by looking at work-trip data gathered as part of the Chicago and Detroit origin and destination surveys.[10] These two cities differ in a number of important ways in their urban transportation characteristics. In Detroit the only public transportation is bus service; Chicago has a complex mix of public transportation services including buses, grade separated rail transit, and railroad commuter facilities. Detroit is a relatively young city. Most of its growth has occurred in the automobile era and has been largely a result of the automobile industry. Chicago is much older, with much of its growth taking place in the preautomobile era. There is also an important disparity in the number of people employed in the respective CBD's: only a little over 100,000 for Detroit compared with 250,000 for Chicago.

Nonetheless, the work-trip patterns are remarkably alike in the two cities in most important aspects, and it appears that they are conditioned by similar forces; also, these patterns seemingly resemble those found in other cities for which reasonably good travel data are available.[11] Among the more important constants, in spite of the frequent references to and actual relative increase in reverse commuting and cross-hauling, is the continued importance of work-trips made between central workplaces and less-central or peripheral residential areas.[12]

The number of workers employed and residing in each of several concentric workplace rings in Chicago and Detroit are shown in Figures 8 and 9. Workplace and residence locations are divided among six concentric distance rings in Detroit and eight in Chicago (see Figures 10 and 11). The divisions indicated by lighter lines and running across the ring divisions designate sectors. (For Chicago, Sector 0 also equals Ring

[10] For a more complete and comprehensive analysis of household travel and residential behavior based on these surveys, see J. F. Kain, *The Journey-to-Work as a Determinant of Residential Location Behavior,* The RAND Corporation, P-2489, December 1961 (also published in the *1962 Proceedings of the Regional Science Association*); *idem, Commuting and Residential Decisions of Chicago and Detroit Central Business District Workers,* The RAND Corporation, P-2735, April 1963 (presented at the Conference on Transportation Economics sponsored by the National Bureau of Economic Research in Evanston, Illinois, April 26–27, 1963).

[11] For example, Raymond Vernon, in "The Economics and Finance of the Large Metropolis" (*Daedalus,* Winter 1961, pp. 31048), points out the existence of similar patterns in New York; see also Joseph M. C. Leiper, "Suburban Rail Transit in the New York Metropolitan Region," excerpts from a report to the Regional Plan Association, January 23, 1961, p. 1; and Louis K. Loewenstein, "Commuting and the Costs of Housing in Philadelphia," *Traffic Quarterly,* 17:302–319, (April 1963).

[12] "Reverse commuting" applies to workers who commute to outlying workplaces in low-density areas from centrally located high-cost and high-density residence areas. "Cross-hauling" refers to work-trips made across the area rather than along a line radial from the central business district, which historically has been and still is the main transportation axis in most urban areas.

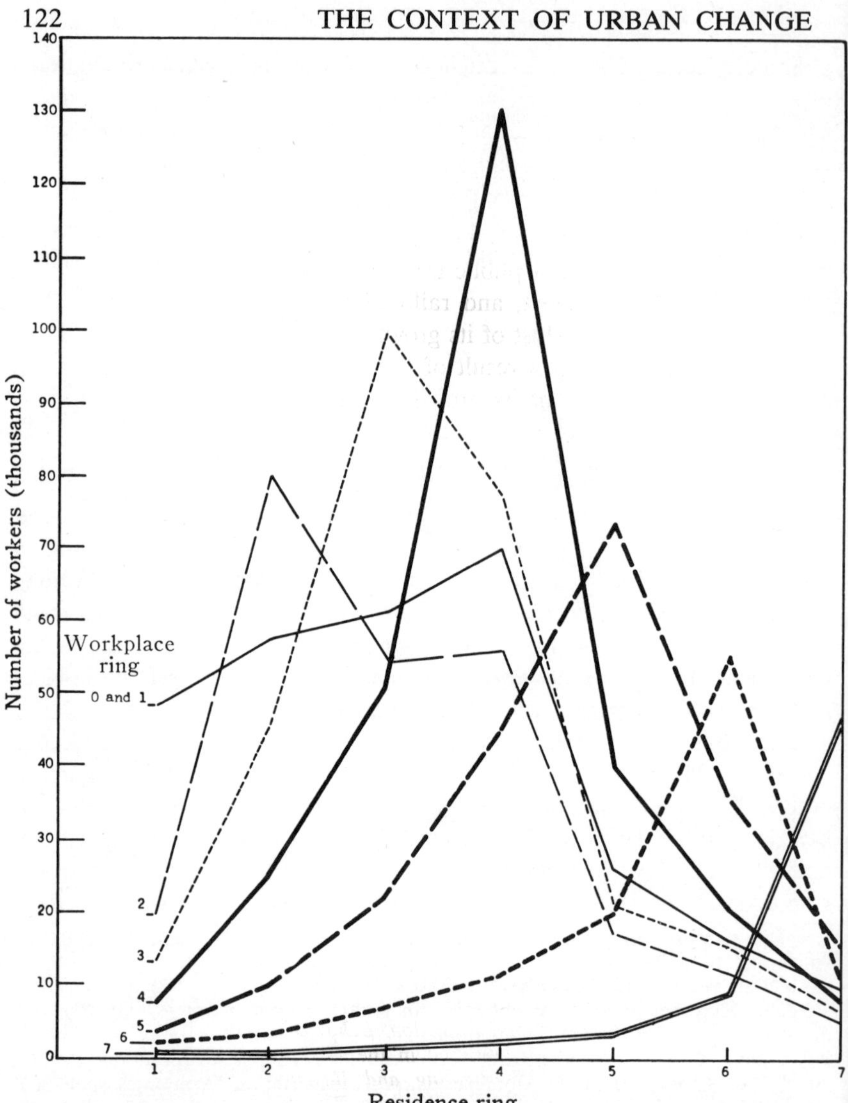

Figure 8. Number of Chicago white workers residing in each ring, by workplace ring. SOURCE: Tabulated from Chicago "first work-trip" file.

1 and Ring 0 equals the CBD.) With a few exceptions for the innermost rings, the residence ring housing the largest proportion of each workplace ring's workers is also the same ring in which they are employed. In short, workers tend to live in their workplace rings; furthermore, this tendency is greater for outer than inner workplace rings. This suggests that a tendency exists to try to economize on transportation outlays for work-trips

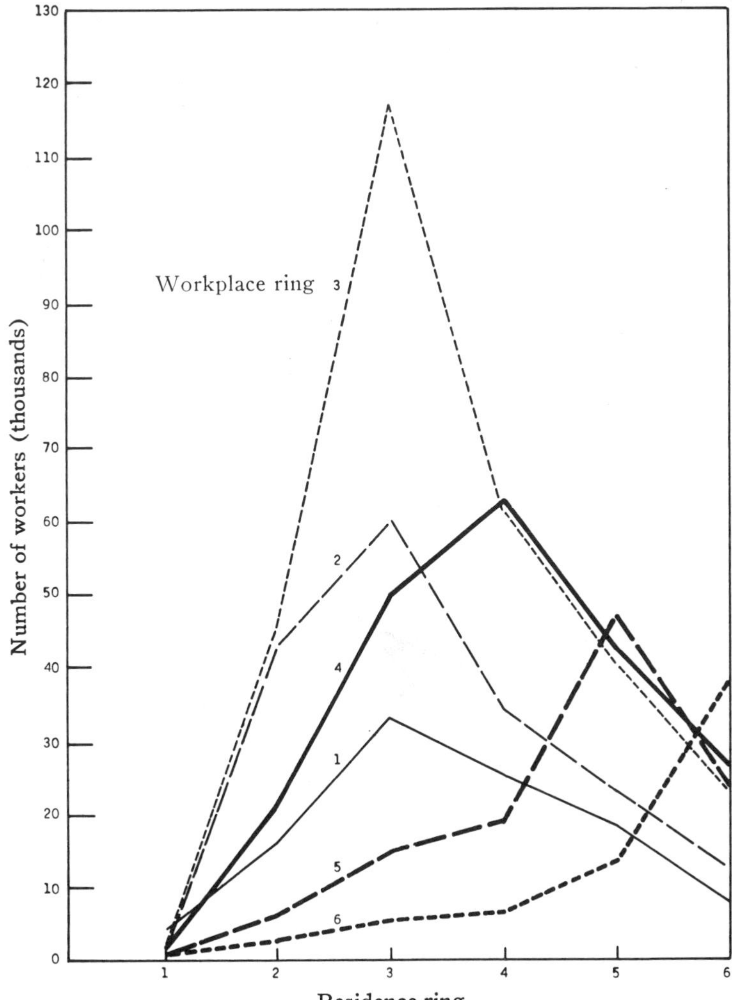

Figure 9. Number of Detroit white workers residing in each ring, by workplace ring. SOURCE: Tabulated from Detroit "first work-trip" file.

and that this may be somewhat easier to achieve if one's workplace is at a distance from the CBD.

The interrelationships between outlays for transportation and housing may be observed from other evidence as well. Specifically, if the same kind of housing costs less with distance from the city center, there should be resultant differences, by ring, in the proportions of workers choosing to live in the various types of housing. Tables 42 and 43, in support of this supposition, list the percentage of Chicago and Detroit workers employed

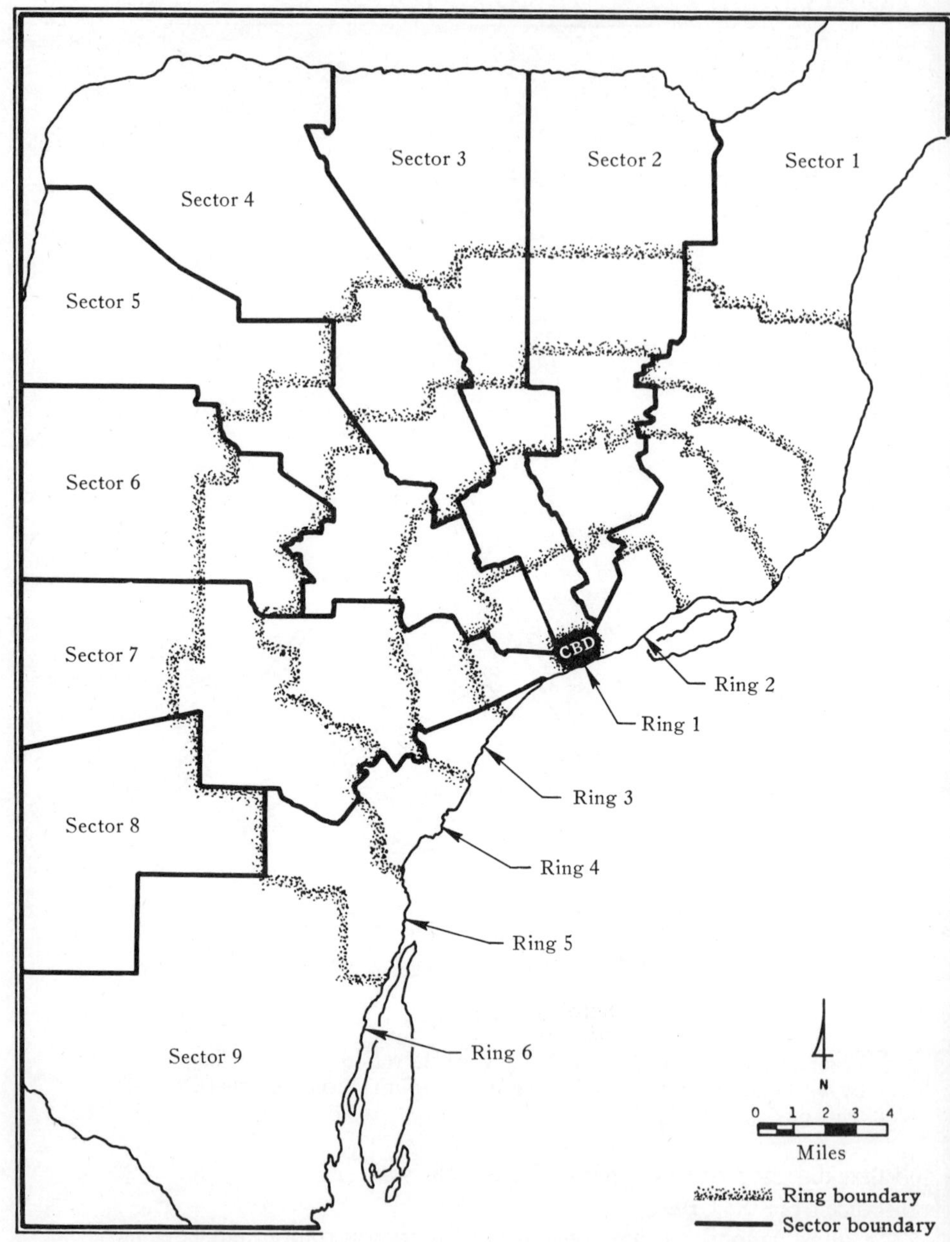

Figure 10. Detroit: analysis rings and sectors.

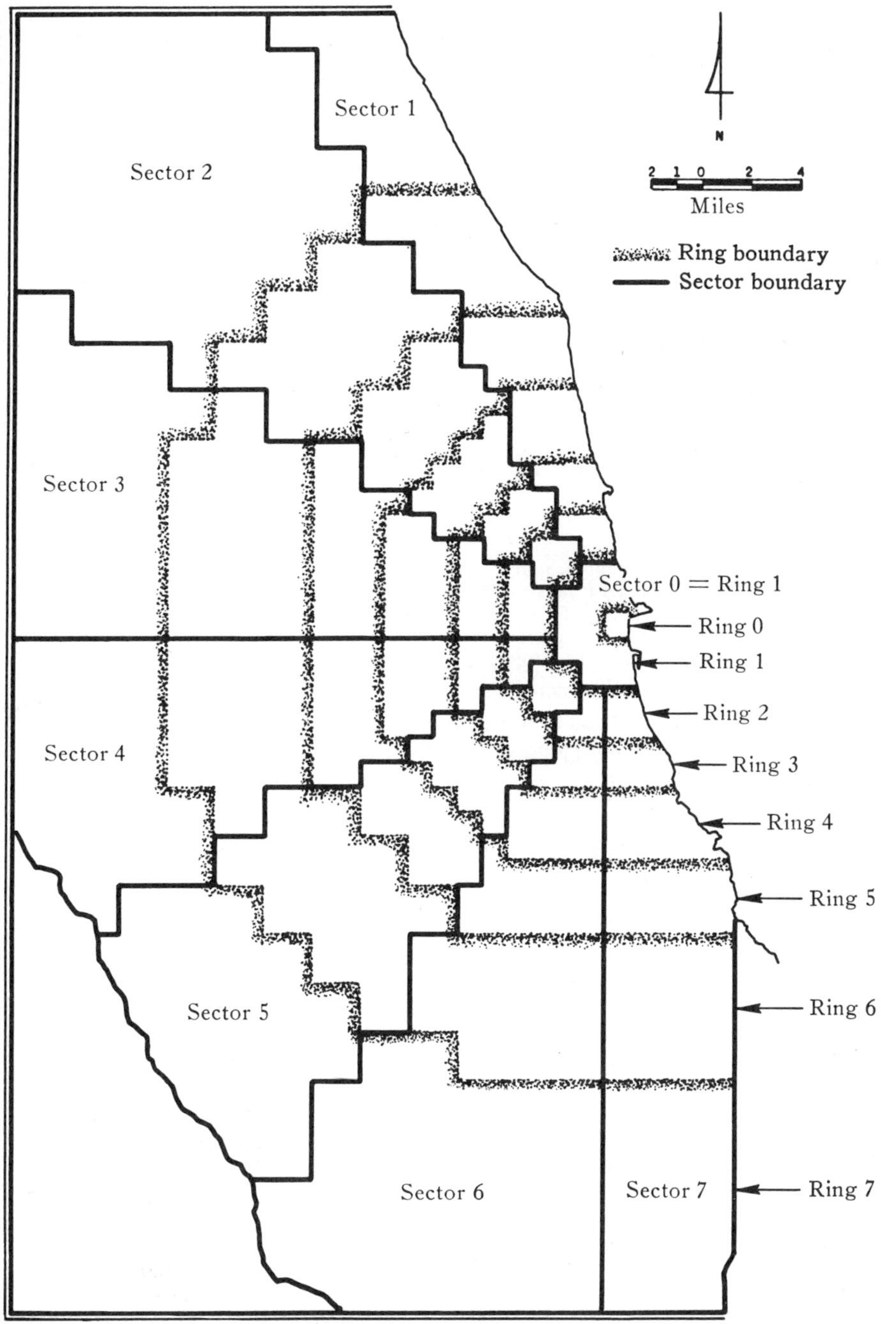

Figure 11. Chicago: analysis rings and sectors.

TABLE 42

PERCENTAGE OF CHICAGO WHITE WORKERS RESIDING IN EACH STRUCTURE TYPE, BY EMPLOYMENT RING

	Employment ring							
Structure type	0	1	2	3	4	5	6	7
1-family	36.5	29.8	28.2	34.0	41.6	54.9	63.9	69.4
2-family	15.0	18.4	21.8	23.2	19.9	17.1	14.3	15.6
Multiunit	41.4	43.3	44.3	37.6	34.7	24.9	17.4	12.5
Hotel	5.1	4.8	2.4	2.6	1.4	0.9	0.6	0.8
Motel	—	—	—	0.1	—	—	0.1	0.1
Rooming house	1.3	2.4	2.2	1.7	1.2	0.9	0.5	0.4
Institution	0.1	0.4	0.5	0.1	0.3	0.2	0.5	0.2
Trailer	0.1	0.1	—	0.1	0.3	0.5	1.0	0.4
Other	0.5	0.7	0.8	0.6	0.6	0.6	1.5	0.8
Total	100.0	100.0	100.0	100.0	100.0	100.0	100.0	100.0

NOTE: Columns may not total to 100 because of rounding.
SOURCE: Tabulated from the Chicago "first work-trip" file.

at various distances (by ring) from the city center, who reside in 1-family, 2-family, multiple, and other structures. In both cities, residence in lower-density structures tends to increase with distance from the CBD.

Similarly, Figures 12 and 13 illustrate the differences in residential location patterns of Chicago whites employed in Rings 1, 3, and 6 and of Detroit whites employed in Rings 1 through 6, according to type of residence—single-family, 2-family, or multiple-unit. It can be seen from these figures that, by and large, centrally employed workers (that is, those with workplace Ring 1 or 2 in Detroit, or Ring 1 in Chicago) who con-

TABLE 43

PERCENTAGE OF DETROIT WHITE WORKERS RESIDING IN EACH STRUCTURE TYPE, BY EMPLOYMENT RING

	Employment ring					
Structure type	1	2	3	4	5	6
1-family	57.7	57.0	60.2	68.6	78.6	77.0
2-family	18.6	21.8	21.0	18.4	12.1	10.9
Multiunit	17.7	17.1	15.7	10.5	7.1	8.0
Other	6.0	4.1	3.1	2.4	2.3	4.2
Total	100.0	100.0	100.0	100.0	100.0	100.0

NOTE: Columns may not total to 100 because of rounding.
SOURCE: Tabulated from the Detroit "first work-trip" file.

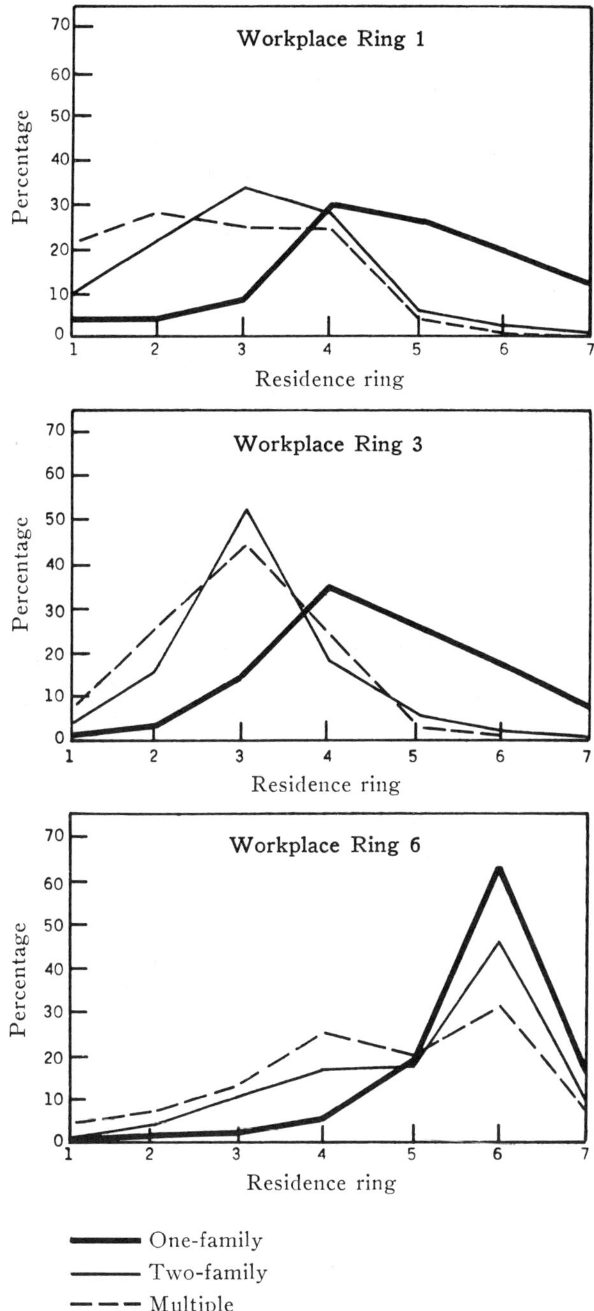

Figure 12. Percentage of Chicago white workers residing in each ring, by workplace ring and structure type. SOURCE: Tabulated from Chicago "first work-trip" file.

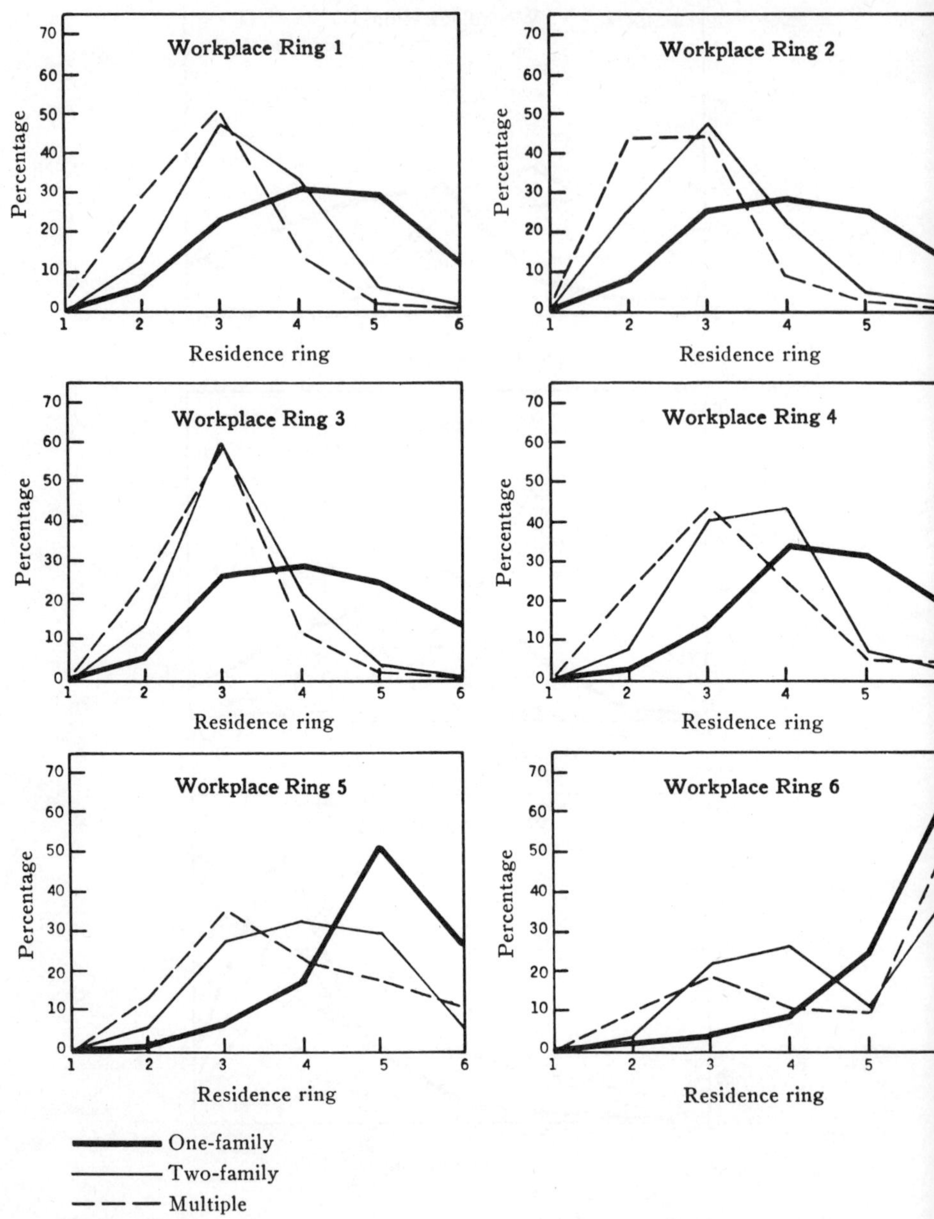

Figure 13. Percentage of Detroit white workers residing in each ring, by workplace rings and structure type. SOURCE: Tabulated from Detroit "first work-trip" file.

sume the most residential space also commute the farthest. From these residence profiles it can also be seen that, of workers employed in outlying workplaces, those residing in multiple-dwelling units, and slightly less often those residing in two-family units, are often reverse commuters; that is, they commute from central residences to outlying workplaces. These workers in many cases belong to childless households, and a disproportionate number belong to households with two or more wage-earners.[13] Both groups could have significant cost incentives for living in central areas, even though housing costs are likely to be higher there (on a unit-space basis). For example, the first group—single people and childless married couples—may have more time for the cultural and recreational activities found in more central areas. For the second group, the attempt of two or more wage-earners to minimize their joint transportation and housing costs may dictate their locating near the workplace of one wage earner and in an area with good public transportation service. Moreover, the cost disincentives for both groups may be less because of smaller residential space needs; the increase in housing costs of a central location is, of course, less for those preferring higher-density residences than for those preferring lower densities. In fact, in those cases where small apartments are suitable, housing costs may be cheaper at a central location if small apartments in outlying areas are less available.

TABLE 44

PERCENTAGE OF CBD WORKERS (WHITE AND NONWHITE) RESIDING WITHIN CERTAIN DISTANCES FROM THE CBD CENTER

Distance from CBD (miles)	Percentage of CBD workers residing less than distance shown from CBD	
	Chicago	Detroit
2	5.8	11.5
4	15.9	27.3
6	23.0	49.8
8	58.8	70.5
10	74.0	83.9
12	82.3	93.2
14	88.3	97.6
16	91.4	99.5
18	94.1	100.0
20	95.9	100.0
22	100.0	100.0

[13] A more complete discussion of this matter will be found in an unpublished study by John F. Kain on commuting and housing choices.

Another aspect of extreme importance concerns the residence patterns of downtown CBD workers, particularly since they contribute so importantly to the rush-hour patronage of present-day and most proposed rail transit systems. These downtown workers, not too surprisingly, tend to live much closer to the CBD than do noncentral workers and, in fact, live within closer proximity than one might expect. Table 44 summarizes on a cumulative percentage basis the residential location pattern for downtown CBD workers in Chicago and Detroit. Importantly, about 74 per cent of the Chicago CBD workers and 84 per cent of the Detroit CBD workers live less than 10 miles from the downtown; only 12 per cent of the Chicago group and less than 3 per cent of the Detroit group live at distances of 14 miles or more from downtown. It should be apparent, then, that in the face of this pattern the potential market for downtown-oriented transit systems would not be seriously enhanced by extending routes much beyond a distance of 10 miles from the city center.

Modal Choices in Relation to Residential and Workplace Locations

Substitutions are possible among transportation modes with various average speeds, costs, degrees of comfort, and the like. The cost of the worker's final choice of mode in time, comfort, convenience, and money will depend to a considerable degree (though indirectly) on how much residential space he consumes and what levels and types of transit services are available at home and work. (Chapter 10 discusses how residential density affects the costs of residential collection and distribution by various transportation modes.) Rapid transit services may be excellent for workers in high-density workplaces, offering such savings in time and money that workers are very likely to use them eagerly (especially if their employers do not provide parking lots). At low-density workplaces poorly serviced by public transportation, and where parking is inexpensive, the probability is very high that workers will be attracted to the private automobile. In broad outline, this is confirmed by the modal split of trips made by workers employed in various parts of the Chicago and Detroit urban areas as shown in Tables 45 and 46. In these two metropolitan areas the proportion of public transit trips declines sharply with the workplace ring's distance from the center of the city. For example, approximately 17 per cent of work-trips from Chicago's Loop or CBD, Ring O, are by automobile; 25 per cent by bus; 34 per cent by grade separated rail transit; and 22 per cent by commuter rail. By contrast, of work-trips from Ring 7, the outermost ring, 80 per cent are by automo-

TABLE 45

PERCENTAGE OF WORK-TRIPS MADE FROM EACH WORKPLACE RING, BY TRAVEL MODE USED AT WORKPLACE: CHICAGO

	Workplace ring							
Workplace mode	0	1	2	3	4	5	6	7
Automobile driver	12.5	34.1	42.8	45.3	52.0	60.3	63.7	61.8
Automobile rider	4.4	8.5	10.9	11.5	11.8	16.1	16.3	18.6
Rail	22.4	6.3	0.8	0.8	0.7	0.6	1.5	1.9
Elevated or subway	33.8	9.4	2.1	2.5	2.0	0.8	0.2	[a]
Bus	25.4	34.0	31.4	28.6	22.4	14.7	7.6	3.1
Walked to work	1.4	6.7	10.9	10.3	9.6	6.4	9.0	12.8
Worked at home	0.1	1.0	1.0	1.2	1.5	1.0	1.7	1.8
Total	100.0	100.0	100.0	100.0	100.0	100.0	100.0	100.0

[a]Less than 0.1 per cent.
NOTE: Columns may not total exactly because of rounding.
SOURCE: Tabulated from the Chicago "first work-trip" file.

bile; 3 per cent by bus; less than 0.1 per cent by rapid transit; and 2 per cent by commuter rail. These differences reflect the lower employment densities in outer rings and differences in parking costs and travel conditions between central and outlying locations; however, they are also caused by differences in patterns of housing consumption by workers employed in the various distance rings.

The percentage of Detroit white workers employed in each ring, by structure type, who use public transit is shown in Table 47. Two types of

TABLE 46

PERCENTAGE OF WORK-TRIPS MADE FROM EACH WORKPLACE RING, BY TRAVEL MODE USED AT WORKPLACE: DETROIT

	Workplace ring					
Workplace mode	1	2	3	4	5	6
Automobile driver	31.2	50.9	48.6	57.7	64.7	69.5
Automobile passenger	10.0	13.3	16.3	16.2	17.8	19.2
Bus passenger	52.7	26.6	26.8	21.9	12.0	4.8
Walked to work	5.2	8.0	8.0	4.0	5.0	5.7
Other	0.9	1.2	0.3	0.2	0.5	0.8
Total	100.0	100.0	100.0	100.0	100.0	100.0

SOURCE: Tabulated from the Detroit "first work-trip" file.

TABLE 47

PERCENTAGE OF DETROIT WHITE WORKERS USING TRANSIT, BY WORKPLACE RING AND STRUCTURE TYPE

	Structure type		
Workplace ring	Multiple	2-family	1-family
1	60.7	58.7	50.6
2	28.5	28.6	19.5
3	29.4	26.8	18.9
4	27.3	23.1	14.4
5	17.8	11.1	8.4
6	5.8	4.1	3.5

SOURCE: Tabulated from the Detroit "first work-trip" file.

relationships are evident from the table. Transit use declines both with the workplace distance from the CBD and the amount of residential space consumed. The latter is probably in part an indirect expression of economic level and ability to afford private transportation, and is related to quality and cost of public transit. In addition, the comparative costs of transit and automobile shift in favor of the automobile as employment density, residential density, and channel volumes decrease. As shown in chapters 8 through 11, a necessary condition for low-cost transit operations with at least some reasonable schedule frequency is a relatively high volume between a given pair of origins and destinations.

This same relationship between housing density and modal use is illustrated in a slightly different form in Figure 14. Plotted for 100 Chicago residential areas is the relationship between the use of the automobile as a residential collector and three measures of residential density: percentages of workers residing in single-family units, percentages residing in multiple units, and the average quantity of residential space consumed as measured in square feet of land per dwelling unit.[14] Again, it is quite obvious that auto use rises as residential density falls.

Further insight into the tradeoffs possible between residential and transit modal choice is provided by the data in Table 48 on average residential space consumption (square feet of land per dwelling unit), family income, family size, elapsed time spent traveling, airline distance between home and work, and speed in miles per hour (over the airline distance) for all Chicago workers using a transit mode for one or more

[14] This measure is computed by assigning to each worker an average space consumption per dwelling unit, obtained by dividing the number of acres in 500 geographic analysis areas by the estimated number of dwelling units in the area.

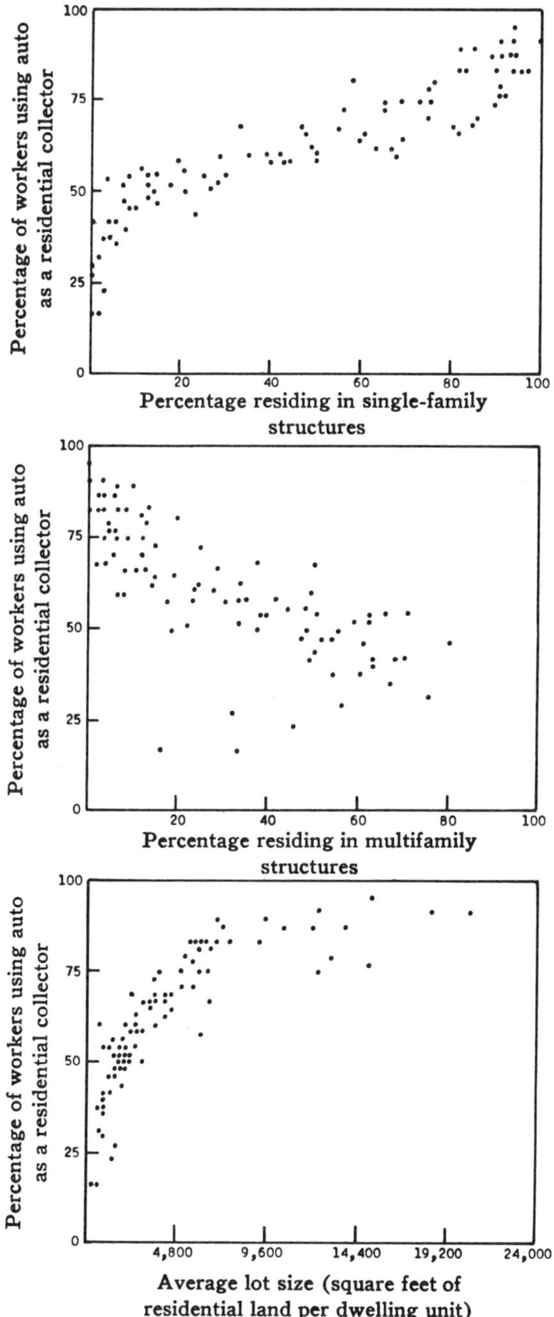

Figure 14. Percentage of Chicago white workers using automobile as a residential collector, by density characteristics of residential area.

TABLE 48

MEAN NUMBER OF SQUARE FEET PER DWELLING UNIT, FAMILY INCOME, FAMILY SIZE, ELAPSED TIME, DISTANCE TRAVELED, AND SPEED, BY LINE-HAUL AND RESIDENTIAL COLLECTION MODES

Residential collection mode	Line-haul mode	Residential land per dwelling unit (sq ft)	Family income ($)	Family size	Elapsed time (hr)	Average distance (mi)	Average speed (mph)
Automobile		3830	7696	3.6	0.85	9.2	10.8
Rail		—	—	—	—	—	—
Rapid	Rapid	1126	6456	3.0	0.67	6.6	9.8
Bus		1800	7003	3.4	0.89	7.4	8.3
All		1676	6850	3.2	0.79	7.2	9.1
Automobile		7542	7325	3.7	0.87	13.5	16.5
Rail	Rail	4434	7453	3.3	0.76	11.1	14.6
Bus		3879	7066	3.5	1.10	13.8	12.5
All		5903	7425	3.5	0.87	13.5	15.5
Automobile		3763	6405	2.7	0.89	9.3	10.4
Rail	City bus	—	—	—	—	—	—
Bus		1425	6766	3.3	0.62	3.9	6.3
All		1466	6789	3.3	0.62	4.0	6.4
Automobile		1456	5956	4.0	0.50	5.2	10.4
Rail	Suburban bus	—	—	—	—	—	—
Bus		3427	6904	3.5	0.60	4.6	7.7
All		3108	6683	3.5	0.59	4.6	7.8

SOURCE: Tabulated from the Chicago "first work-trip" file.

segments of their work-trips.[15] Commuter rail is the fastest of these modes, with an average airline distance speed of 15.5 miles per hour, followed by rapid transit averaging 9.1 mph, the suburban bus averaging 7.8 mph, and the city bus averaging 6.4 mph. (These speeds are somewhat greater than actual speeds, since over-the-road distance is invariably greater than airline distance, particularly for the bus modes.) When the line-haul modes are disaggregated by residential collection modes, the fastest combined residential collection line-haul mode is the automobile and commuter-rail combination (16.5 mph), and the slowest is the suburban-bus city-bus combination (6.3 mph).

Comparisons of the average square feet of land per dwelling unit of travelers using different line-haul modes are also as might be expected: city bus, 1466 sq ft; rapid transit, 1676 sq ft; suburban bus, 3108 sq ft; and commuter rail, 5903 sq ft. Family incomes vary little among line-haul bus and rapid transit travelers, but are almost 10 per cent higher for railroad commuters. Disaggregating by residential collector mode within line-haul mode sharpens these relationships considerably. Of travelers on the combination modes carrying significant proportions of work-trips (greater than 0.1 per cent of total Chicago work-trips), users of the rapid-rapid combination of residential collector and line-haul facilities reside at the highest average density, and have the second lowest mean incomes and the smallest mean family size. Countrariwise, those combining automobile and rail reside at the lowest average density (have the largest average lot size), and possess the second highest average income and the highest average family size.

The relationship between use of residential collector modes and residential space consumption is further illustrated by Table 49, in which the percentages of Chicago workers residing in single-family, two-family, multiple, and other dwelling units for each residential collection and line-haul combination are given. The automobile-commuter-rail combination has by far the most users residing in single-family units (86 per cent). Except for the combination of rapid and rail, which carries only an

[15] Family income was not obtained in the Chicago home interview study. For this research a family income variable was defined and coded to each worker. Family income was defined as the sum of the mean occupational earnings of those employed in the worker's family:

$$O_{1kj} + O_{2kj} + \ldots + O_{nkj},$$

where O_{kj} is the estimated mean earnings of Chicago workers employed in the kth occupation by race j, and where 1, 2, . . . , n refers to the workers in the family. It is apparent that this is an extremely crude income measure. In spite of its shortcomings, however, it is probably better than no result at all; and it appears to provide reasonably consistent results in this study and elsewhere when it is employed. Moreover, comparisons of the income distributions obtained in this way with comparable ones obtained from the 1960 census of population yield reasonably consistent results.

TABLE 49

PERCENTAGE OF CHICAGO WORKERS RESIDING IN EACH STRUCTURE TYPE, BY COMBINED LINE-HAUL AND RESIDENTIAL COLLECTION MODES

Residential collection mode	Line-haul mode	1-family	2-family	Multiple	Other	All	Estimated number
Automobile		53.4	18.3	27.1	1.2	100.0	13,179
Bus	Rapid	26.2	21.9	48.1	3.8	100.0	76,504
Rapid		9.3	12.4	68.3	10.0	100.0	69,703
Automobile		85.7	6.7	7.3	0.3	100.0	39,477
Bus	Rail	48.3	17.2	30.9	3.6	100.0	6,406
Rail		49.7	11.1	35.2	4.0	100.0	50,322
Rapid		9.1	9.1	63.7	18.1	100.0	342
Automobile	City bus	55.2	14.6	28.2	2.0	100.0	6,001
Bus		17.5	20.3	53.5	8.7	100.0	30,164
Automobile	Suburban bus	24.6	11.1	56.1	8.2	100.0	2,905
Bus		48.5	11.7	34.5	5.3	100.0	20,580
Automobile	Auto	44.2	16.5	32.4	6.8	100.0	619,990
All	All	35.5	17.1	40.6	6.8	100.0	1,252,592

SOURCE: Tabulated from the Chicago "first work-trip" file.

estimated 300 or so workers (probably mostly domestics traveling in the direction of reverse flow), the combination of rapid-rapid has the fewest riders residing in single-family units (9.3 per cent) and the most residing in multiple and other dwelling units (68.3 and 10.0 per cent). By contrast, for those using automobiles for the entire trip, the percentages residing in each structure type are: single-family, 44.2; two-family, 16.5; multiple, 32.4; and other, 6.8.

To illustrate these same points further, some results of a study of Detroit travel behavior are summarized in Table 50.[16] The elasticities shown in the table indicate the changes in the percentages of automo-

TABLE 50

ELASTICITIES AT THE SAMPLE MEANS FOR THE PERCENTAGES OF DETROIT WORKERS WHO ARE AUTOMOBILE DRIVERS AND TRANSIT RIDERS

Item	Automobile drivers (61.4 per cent)	Transit riders (17.5 per cent)	Sample mean
Percentage belonging to families with more than two members	0.20	−0.53	(70.2%)
Percentage male	0.32	−0.99	(71.4%)
Percentage belong to families with a single wage earner	0.23	−0.88	(48.2%)
Mean family income ($ hundred)	0.21	−0.76	(50.4)
A proxy variable for the price of residential space[a]	−0.04	0.11	(4.34)
Level of transit service at the workplace[b]	−0.06	0.31	(1.37)

[a]11.5 minus the workplace distance from the CBD, with a minimum value of 0.5.
[b]Coach-miles of bus service in each workplace zone during a 24-hour day, divided by number of acres in the workplace zone.
SOURCE: John F. Kain, "A Contribution to the Urban Transportation Debate: An Econometric Model of Urban Residential and Travel Behavior," *The Review of Economics and Statistics*, 46: 55–64 (Feb. 1964).

bile drivers or of transit users that result from a 1 per cent change in certain explanatory variables tested. These elasticities were obtained from the reduced forms of a multiple-equation econometric model estimated from the Detroit data. The dependent and independent variables measure attributes of white workers employed at 254 workplace zones, or attributes of the workplace zones themselves. According to Table 50, for

[16] John F. Kain, "A Contribution to the Urban Transportation Debate: An Econometric Model of Urban Residential and Travel Behavior," *The Review of Economics and Statistics,* 46:55–65 (February 1964).

example, a 1 per cent increase in the mean family income of workers in a given work-place zone would lead to a 0.21 per cent increase in the percentage of automobile drivers and 0.76 per cent decline in the percentage riding transit. (The effects of housing structure variables were incorporated indirectly in these estimates through the structural equations from which the elasticities were obtained.) In general, the results reported in Table 50 agree with the hypotheses outlined earlier. Not only do higher incomes seem conducive to more automobile commuting, but, also, males who are the only wage earners in their families and who have larger families seem to prefer automobile commuting.

Functional Specialization of Modes

The relationships just outlined between modal and residential choices imply that a considerable degree of specialization should exist in the use of urban transport technologies. The rationale behind these specializations derives from both demand and cost considerations. The relevant demand characteristics have been discussed previously; the cost aspects will be developed in chapters 8 through 11.

That there is a considerable functional specialization among transit modes, at least in Chicago, can be seen from the cumulative percentage-distance profiles by transit mode shown in Figure 15.[17] The profiles differ markedly and appear closely related to the mode's speed and coverage characteristics. For example, the commuter railroad has a cumulative distance profile which exhibits marked tendencies toward long trips: 50 per cent of rail commuter trips exceed 11.5 miles, while less than 4 per cent are shorter than 4 miles and about 40 per cent are between 7 and 12 miles.

The distributions of trips by bus and rapid transit display a similar though different specialization. Bus riders typically make considerably shorter trips, as measured by distance, than do rapid transit riders. Of city bus riders, 50 per cent make trips less than 2.4 miles long, while 50 per cent of suburban bus riders make trips of less than 2.2 miles. The median rapid transit trip, by contrast, is 6.7 miles long. The elapsed time, cumulative percentage profiles for the four line-haul transit modes (see Figure 16), although they have the same order, differ from the distance profiles in that they are closer together.

[17] The terms "residential collector," "line-haul," and "destination mode" are used in the following discussion to relate more closely to the cost analyses presented in part II. The residential collection mode is the mode by which the worker originates his work-trip at his residence; the line haul mode is the one he uses for the major through portion of the trip; and the destination mode is the one by which he reaches his workplace from the line haul facility. Actually, a single mode is used for most trips, but a sizable proportion require two or three modes.

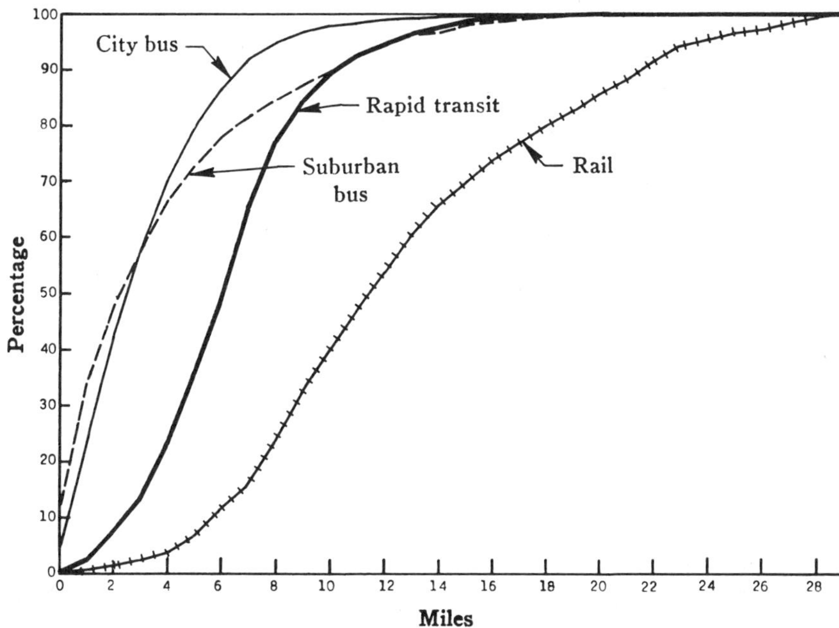

Figure 15. Cumulative percentage of Chicago white workers making work-trips less than given distances, by line-haul travel media. SOURCE: Tabulated from Chicago "first work-trip" file.

These principles are illustrated in a slightly different way in Table 51, which gives the characteristics of Chicago's CBD commuters according to their travel media. The first two rows, which give mean elapsed distances and times, illustrate the differences in the time and distance characteristics of the five transportation modes serving these commuters. While the differences in mean travel time by the five modes are small, the differences in mean distance traveled are large. In particular, if commuters use rail or automobile, they may travel nearly twice as far in only slightly more time than they would require by the other modes.

From the statistics in Table 51, residents of single-family structures more often appear to use the longer distance and faster modes. Automobile riders make the longest trips (12.4 miles) and reside in the highest proportions in single-family residences (63.3 per cent); automobile drivers average 12.0-mile trips and also display a strong tendency to reside in single-family residences (53.1 per cent). Of the three long-distance forms of commuter transportation, rail (with 11.7-mile trips) has the smallest proportion of users residing in single-family units (48.6 per cent). Of all forms, rapid transit has by a substantial margin the smallest proportion of users residing in single-family units (11.5 per cent) and the largest proportion residing in multiple units. Buses also draw large

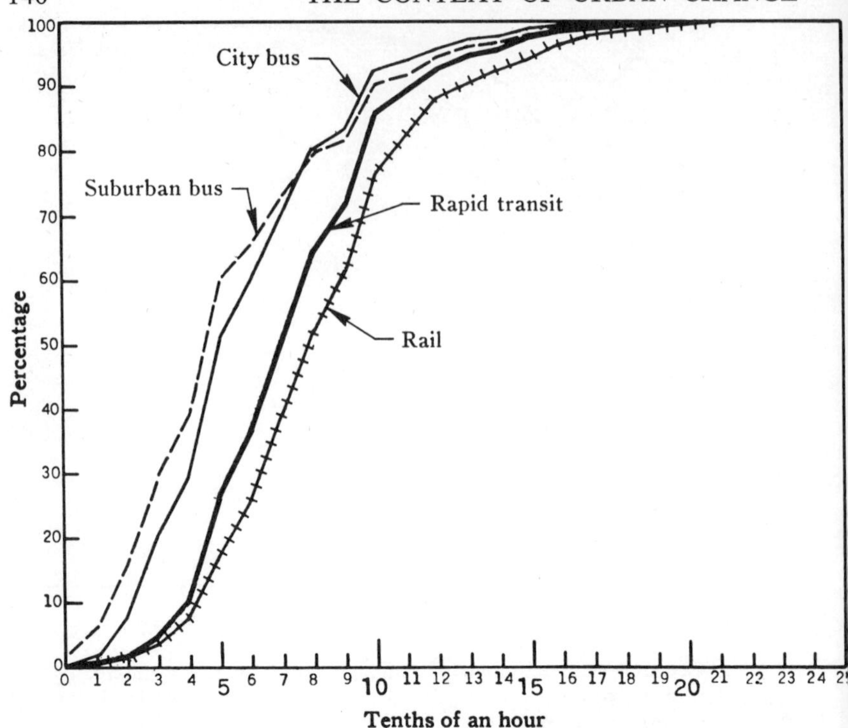

Figure 16. Cumulative percentage of Chicago white workers making work-trips of less than various elapsed time, by haul-line mode. SOURCE: Tabulated from Chicago "first work-trip" file.

percentages from multiple-unit and two-family structures. They also serve significantly more single-family dwellers than rapid transit does. If the percentages residing in multiple units are compared, only 8 per cent more bus users than rail commuters reside in multiple units. These figures undoubtedly reflect the fact that buses here include both local and suburban buses.

The statistics on occupational groups indicate that higher-income workers lean toward the faster and more expensive forms of transportation while lower-income workers more often use buses and rapid transit. As pointed out previously, there are two reasons for this phenomenon: higher-income workers consume more residential space in outlying suburbs, and they probably value their time and convenience more. (Of course, a relatively high proportion of salesmen and certain craftsmen drive automobiles because their work requires it.)

The interrelationship between automobile use and automobile ownership is also shown in Table 51: 45 per cent of bus riders and 42 per cent of rapid transit riders belong to households that do not own automobiles, while, as might be expected, less than 1 per cent of automobile drivers

TABLE 51

CHARACTERISTICS OF CHICAGO CBD COMMUTERS, BY TRAVEL MODE AT RESIDENCE

Item	Automobile driver	Automobile passenger	Rail commuter	Rapid transit	Bus
Work-trip length					
Mean distance (mi)	12.0	12.4	11.7	6.6	6.4
Mean elapsed time (hr)	0.8	0.8	0.8	0.6	0.7
Structure type (per cent)[a]					
Single-family	53.1	63.3	48.6	11.5	25.0
2-family	13.2	10.3	9.2	13.7	20.4
Multiple unit	30.3	23.9	37.6	67.8	45.7
Other	3.4	2.5	4.6	7.0	8.9
Occupation (per cent)					
Professional, technical	22.3	21.5	20.5	14.8	11.6
Managers, officials	24.3	17.1	14.0	9.9	7.3
Clerical	15.7	42.1	46.4	46.3	48.8
Operatives	2.4	2.4	1.3	4.4	5.0
Service	3.9	3.3	3.2	7.3	11.4
Sales	20.0	9.2	9.2	11.5	8.6
Craftsmen, foremen	10.5	3.6	5.2	5.2	6.4
Laborers	0.9	0.7	0.2	0.6	1.0
Automobile ownership					
Mean number of passenger cars	1.3	1.2	0.9	0.6	0.6
Percentage of families *not* owning passenger cars	0.6	8.0	28.6	41.8	44.8
Mean family size	3.4	3.5	3.3	2.8	3.0

[a] Percentages may not total 100 due to rounding.
SOURCE: Tabulated from the Chicago "first work-trip" file.

and only 8 per cent of automobile riders belong to families without automobiles. Nearly 30 per cent of rail commuters have no family car. The data on the family size of Chicago CBD workers in Table 51, as well as those previously presented for Chicago transit users generally in Table 48, again illustrate the economizing procedure used by households in making housing choices: those using the more expensive transport modes (automobile and rail) have the largest families and travel farthest, apparently to secure economical housing of their choice.

Another factor influencing modal choice and specialization is the distance people will walk to various residential collection facilities. As will be shown in chapter 10, the distance walked greatly affects the residential collection costs incurred at various residential densities or for given trip origination rates. Chicago commuters' walking distances are

TABLE 52

CUMULATIVE PERCENTAGE OF CHICAGO WORKERS WALKING GIVEN DISTANCES FROM THEIR RESIDENCES, BY RESIDENTIAL COLLECTION AND LINE-HAUL MODES

Residential collection mode	Line-haul mode	Blocks walked from residence			
		Less than 1	Less than 2	Less than 3	Less than 4
Rail	Rail	7.7	23.8	46.1	65.5
Bus	Rail	33.6	73.1	90.3	95.2
Rapid	Rapid	11.2	35.7	90.3	95.2
Bus	Rapid	33.3	65.3	89.3	95.8
Bus	City bus	35.6	69.2	90.2	96.2
Bus	Suburban bus	33.7	62.2	83.7	92.7

SOURCE: Tabulated from the Chicago "first work-trip" file.

shown in Table 52. The figures for bus users are perhaps the most interesting. Of those using city buses for their entire work-trips, 90 per cent have to walk less than three blocks between their homes and their bus stops. While it is true that the bus has a lower line-haul speed, the average city bus trip is short (4.0 airline miles against 13.5 for commuter rail facilities). Also, while a disproportionate amount of bus travel time is spent in picking up and dropping off passengers, Chicago buses may more than compensate by greater coverage with a concomitant reduction in walking distances and times. Seen in this way, the overall speed performance of city and suburban buses can be considerably better than one would surmise from comparative line-haul speeds alone.

SUMMARY

The empirical interrelationships observable between housing and urban transportation choices seem to fit a pattern that is explainable through reasonably conventional economic hypotheses. American urban households apparently have a choice between spending more for transportation and less for housing (quality held constant), or the reverse. The typical urban commuter can also choose among the different travel modes with their various costs and quality. Large housing cost savings per mile traveled for those residing at the lowest densities encourage long-distance travel. As the distance traveled increases, commuters are encouraged to spend more money on transportation in order to garner the time savings obtainable from using faster modal combinations. In addition, as residential density decreases, the travel time, cost, inconvenience, and sheer technological incapabilities of the various public residential collectors increase rapidly (particularly for rail rapid transit and to a lesser extent buses for reasons outlined in chapters 8 through 11). For people who choose to reside at high density, potential housing cost savings from commuting longer distances are diminished and they have little incentive to spend much time or money on transportation. Since terminal time (waiting, walking, transferring, parking, and so forth) makes up a large proportion of total time spent on short trips by all modes, the travel time savings obtainable from the faster and costlier travel combinations are often too small to justify larger expenditures by those residing close in at high densities. Moreover, many consumers with small space needs employed in central business districts served by rapid transit can use the relatively high-speed rapid transit mode for the entire trip and walk to residences located near the rapid transit line.

Given these basic cost characteristics and tradeoffs, a rational consumption pattern for urban housing and transportation services can be outlined. First, workers with higher incomes and larger families normally will desire a considerable amount of housing and yard space, which costs less with distance from the city center. If they work in central areas they will be willing to make long commuter trips in order to purchase such housing at reasonable prices. If their incomes are high enough, they can afford the faster and more comfortable transportation modes for making this journey, for example, the automobile and commuter rail. Lower-income people working in downtown areas will accept either higher residential densities closer in, or very long trips (in time or distance) to obtain the housing services they desire. They are also more likely to use slower but cheaper transportation.

Extensive empirical agreement with this pattern was found for workers residing in Chicago and Detroit. Appropriate tests were possible for these two cities because very detailed origin and destination surveys have been made. There is no obvious reason for believing Chicago and Detroit to be untypical of large American cities. In fact, the only major deviation from these rational economic patterns in housing and transportation consumption would appear, superficially, to be among nonwhite urban workers. However, as chapter 7 will explain, even nonwhites conform to a rational pattern in these matters once the special circumstances created by racial segregation in housing are taken into account. In short, the empirical evidence presented in this chapter strongly supports the view that urban workers, at least in Chicago and Detroit, consume housing and transportation in a pattern that would be predicted on the basis of a simple economic model in which income and price are the important economic variables and in which crucial sociological factors of family status are taken into account.

Chapter 7 | Race and the Urban Transportation Problem

A number of works on racial segregation and discrimination in urban areas have appeared in recent years, notably the series of books and monographs produced under the sponsorship of the Committee on Race and Housing and the direction of Davis McEntire.[1] Most were authored by urban sociologists; notable exceptions particularly pertinent to the present study are Laurenti's investigation of race and property values,[2] the Rapkin and Grigsby analysis of housing market experience in racially changing areas of Philadelphia,[3] and several important studies of relevance to these problems completed in recent years at the University of Chicago.[4]

[1] Davis McEntire, *Residence and Race, Final and Comprehensive Report to the Commission on Race and Housing* (University of California Press, Berkeley and Los Angeles, 1960); Eunice Grier and George Grier, *Privately Developed Interracial Housing: An Analysis of Experience* (University of Cailfornia Press, Berkeley and Los Angeles, 1960); Nathan Grazer and Davis McEntire, *Studies in Housing and Minority Groups, Special Report to the Commission on Race and Housing* (University of California Press, Berkeley and Los Angeles, 1960).

[2] Luigi Laurenti, *Property Values and Race: Studies in Seven Cities, Special Research Report to the Commission on Race and Housing* (University of California Press, Berkeley and Los Angeles, 1960).

[3] Chester Rapkin and William G. Grigsby, *The Demand for Housing in Racially Mixed Areas: A Study of the Nature of Neighborhood Change, Special Report to the Commission on Race and Housing, and the Philadelphia Redevelopment Authority,* prepared in the Institute for Urban Studies, University of Pennsylvania (University of California Press, Berkeley and Los Angeles, 1960).

[4] Gary Becker, *The Economics of Discrimination* (University of Chicago Press, Chicago, Ill., 1957); Beverly Duncan and Philip M. Hauser, *Housing a Metropolis: Chicago* (Free Press, Glencoe, Ill., 1961); Beverly Duncan, *Population Growth in the Chicago Metropolitan Area: 1950–57* (Department of City Planning, City of Chicago); Beverly Duncan, *Demographic and Socio-Economic Characteristics of the Population of the City of Chicago and of the Suburbs and Urban Fringe: 1950* (Chicago Community Inventory, University of Chicago, Chicago, Ill., 1954); Otis Dudley Duncan and Beverly Duncan, *The Negro Population of Chicago* (University of Chicago Press, Chicago, Ill., 1957).

Few authors of studies of racial problems, however, have considered the fact that housing market segregation may affect both the nature of the urban transportation problem and the appropriateness of various public transportation policies. The thesis of this chapter is that it can do so. Specifically, it will be hypothesized that if housing available to nonwhite workers is centrally located, as it usually tends to be in most U.S. cities, the nonwhite population with centrally located jobs will commute less far on the average than if housing were not segregated. That is, because of housing segregation, centrally placed nonwhite workers will not commute as far as they otherwise would in search of housing that fits their needs and incomes. These centrally employed nonwhites will not effect as much of a substitution of travel for housing costs as would be the case in the absence of segregation; they thus incur somewhat higher housing costs and lower transport costs than if housing choices were not racially constrained. On the other hand, noncentrally employed nonwhites will find that housing segregation leads them on the average to commute farther and spend more on transport, and possibly to pay higher housing costs. Since central employment is still much more common than noncentral employment for most urban nonwhites, the net transport effect is probably to reduce over-all urban transport requirements of nonwhites. Of course, if employment opportunities continue to decentralize, this balance could shift in the future.

For whites employed at central locations, the hypothesis would be just reversed: in their case, housing segregation, by tending to preempt or reduce housing opportunities for whites near the core, increases transport costs. The centrally employed white thus spends more on transport and perhaps less on housing than he would if the housing market were racially unconstrained. The noncentrally employed white, on the other hand, is little affected in his housing and transport choices by housing segregation.

In essence, these hypotheses imply that whites pay a price for housing segregation mainly in the form of higher transport costs, but only if they are centrally employed. Nonwhites, on the other hand, probably spend less on urban transport than they would freely choose to do if their housing choices were not constrained. (The social costs of serving urban transport needs of nonwhites probably are further reduced by the fact that housing segregation tends to create considerable reverse commuting by nonwhites—out in the morning and in in the afternoon—that uses capacity that would otherwise be unused.) It is to the testing of these hypotheses, in an admittedly imperfect way because of lack of data and inability to control all the relevant influences, that the rest of this chapter is devoted. Again, the Detroit and Chicago origination and destination studies are relied upon as the best sources of available data.

Journeys to Work by Whites and Nonwhites

The distance profiles of residences and workplaces of Detroit's and Chicago's white and nonwhite workers are shown in Figure 17. In both Detroit and Chicago it is apparent that as a group nonwhite workers live closer to the CBD than do whites, and that nonwhite employment is likewise closer to the CBD than it is for whites; and, except for the residence and workplace pattern of nonwhites in Detroit, workplaces tend to be somewhat closer to the CBD than do residences for all groups.[5] An extremely important aspect of these distributions is that the radial or ring separation between residences and workplaces is considerably smaller for nonwhites than for whites. As a consequence, for work-trips where radial movement is involved (that is, movement from one ring to another within one sector) it seems that on the average negroes travel less distance and incur less expense than do whites.

Figures 18 and 19 show residential locations by workplace ring and thus permit a more intensive analysis of the above conclusion. For example, in both Detroit and Chicago about 30 per cent of nonwhites and whites work in the two innermost rings, or in central locations. In these cases, because nonwhite housing is more centrally located, it is clear that nonwhites travel less distance to work than do whites—and particularly so if account is taken of the fact that the innermost rings are closer together than the outer ones. Also, for those workers making strictly radial trips to workplaces in the first three rings in Detroit and in the first four rings in Chicago, nonwhites would experience less travel distance than whites; however, the reverse holds for the remainder of the rings in the two cities with regard to radial type trip-making (that is, travel between homes and workplaces in the same sector). More importantly, those three rings in Detroit and four in Chicago which show the radial or ring separation between homes and workplaces to be less for the nonwhite than for the white include 67 per cent of the nonwhite employment and 59 per cent of the white employment in Detroit; and 72 per cent of nonwhite employment and 61 per cent of white employment in Chicago. Thus, for a considerable proportion of the work-trips, negroes seem to incur shorter work-trip journeys than whites. Also, it is evident that larger percentages of negroes than whites reverse-com-

[5] Extreme care must be taken, incidentally, in comparing or drawing inferences from these profiles: eight rings are used for Chicago and only six for Detroit, and the Chicago study area is much larger. The greater peaking exhibited by the Detroit profiles is therefore partly because of differences in definitional units and in metropolitan size. For Chicago's workers to live within a given distance of the CBD in the same percentages as Detroit's workers, Chicago's residential densities would have to be several times as great, because of differences in the size of the study area. This tendency is further reinforced by the greater amount of nonresidential land use around Chicago's CBD than around Detroit's. Nonetheless, useful comparisons can be made. It is legitimate to point out, for example, that the racial profiles are similar for the two cities.

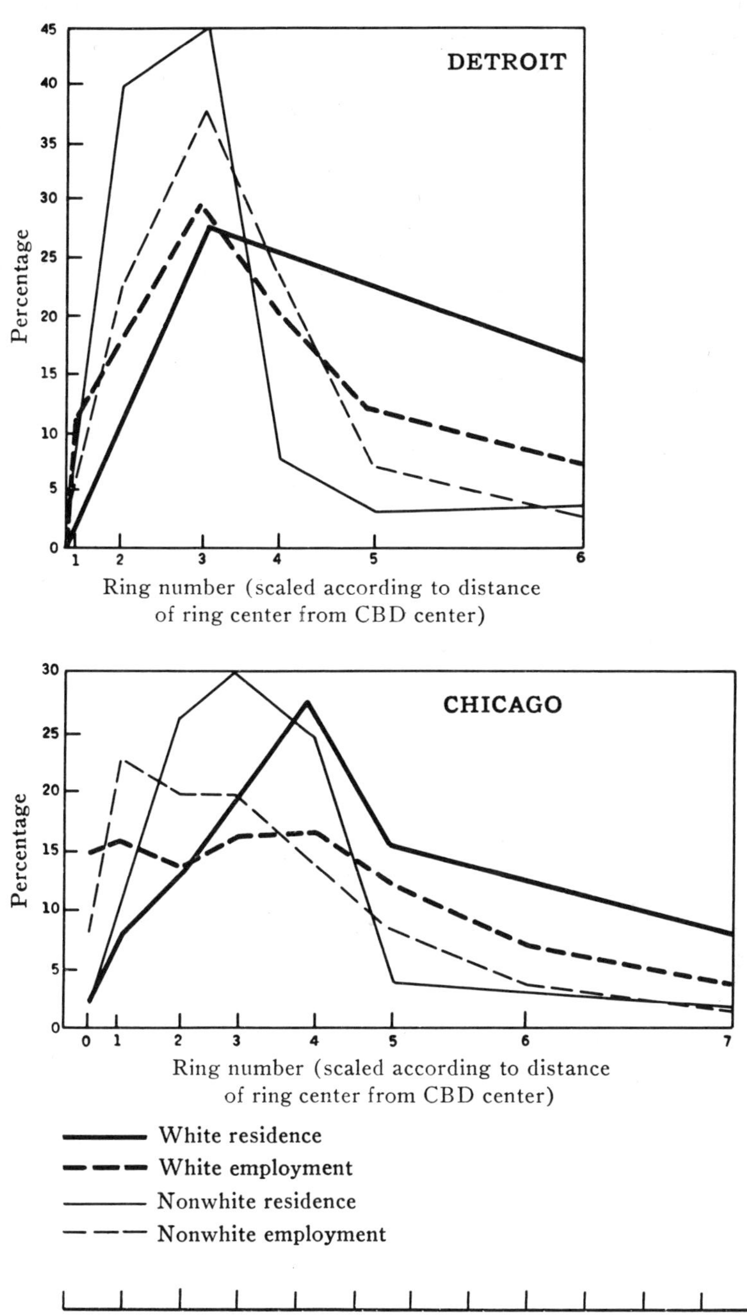

Figure 17. Percentage of Detroit and Chicago workers residing and employed in each distance ring, by race.

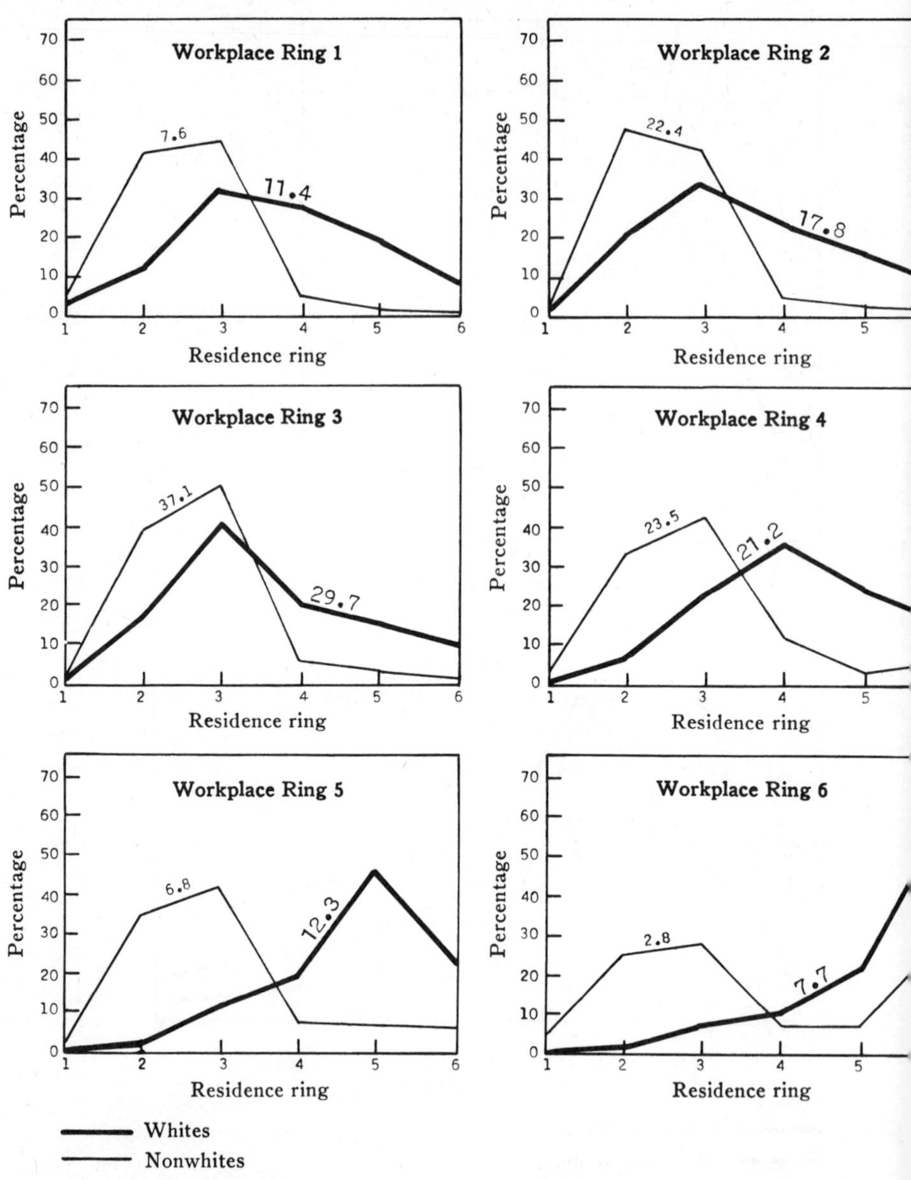

Figure 18. Percentage of Detroit white and nonwhite workers residing in each ring, by workplace ring. Percentages of total employed whites and nonwhites working in the ring are shown on the curves.

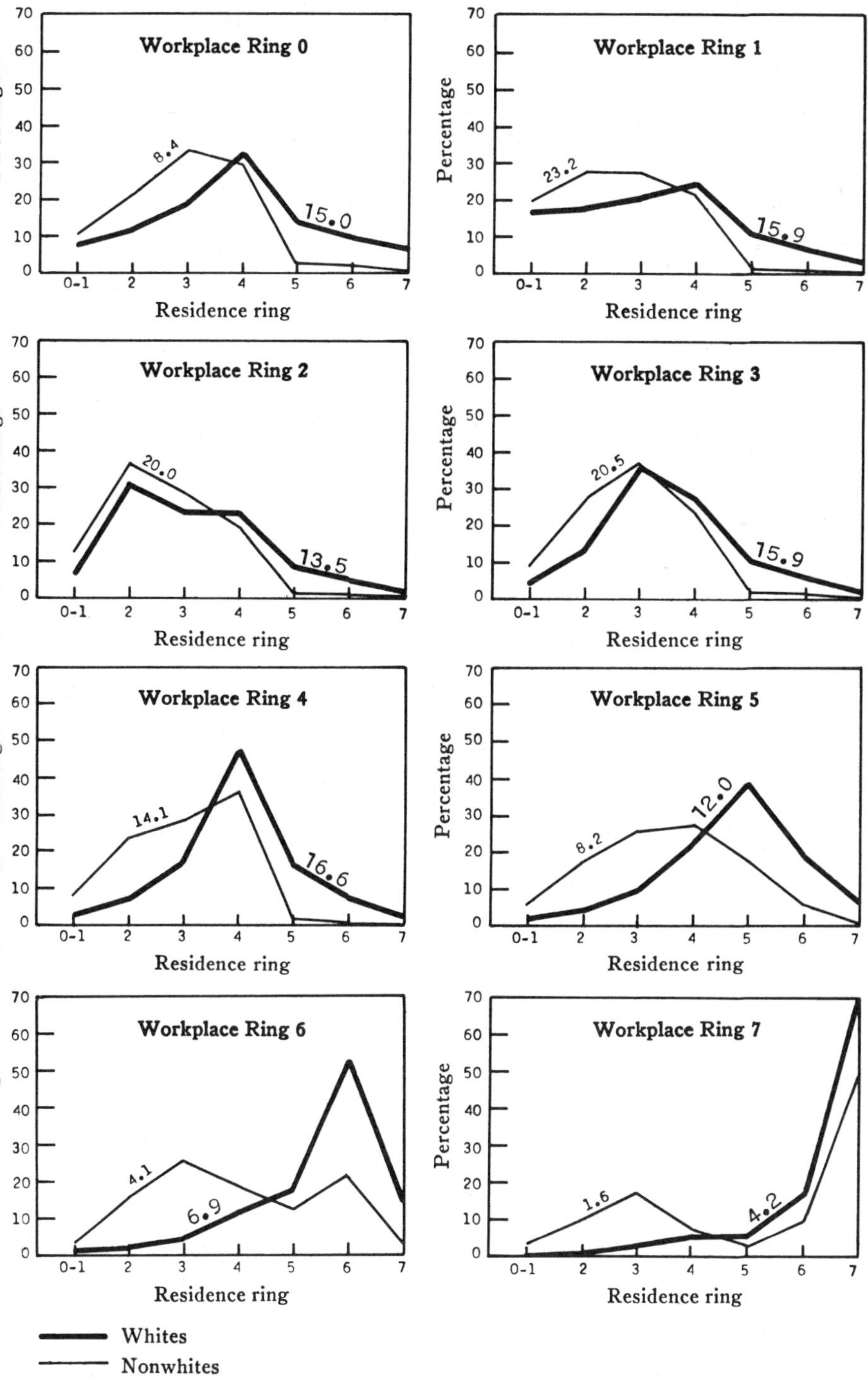

Figure 19. Percentage of Chicago white and nonwhite workers residing in each ring, by workplace ring. Percentages of total employed whites and nonwhites are shown on the curves.

mute. For example, about 80 per cent of nonwhites, but only 30 per cent of the whites employed in Detroit's Ring 4 (about 7 1/2 miles from the CBD) reside in rings closer to the CBD. The situation is similar in Chicago: 80 per cent of the nonwhites employed in Ring 5 (about 12 miles from the CBD) reside in rings closer to the CBD; the figure for whites is 40 per cent.

Differences in housing and work-trip patterns may be ascribed to several factors, of course, including income levels, preference patterns, and segregation. That racial segregation in housing does exist (regardless of the underlying factors) in Chicago and Detroit is evident from data shown in Figures 20 and 21. Chicago's pattern of segregation is largely sectoral; the negro housing market mostly consists of Chicago's South Side. The secondary portions are near the CBD, with the second largest just north and west of the Loop, and within Sector 0; only 20 per cent of Chicago's nonwhite workers live elsewhere. By contrast, Detroit's nonwhite areas are more concentric, with heavy concentrations in Rings 2 and 3, but with considerable sectoral development northeast along Woodward Avenue.

The way in which these segregated housing patterns and differences in housing and employment affect travel distances and costs cannot be determined, however, without examining both the ring *and* sectoral distributions. For example, whereas negroes employed in central locations or those engaging entirely in radial movement evidently travel less distance than whites, the cross-hauling that results from intersectoral movement must be examined for the two classes of commuters and balanced out. For these questions, the data on Chicago in Tables 53, 54, and 55 are helpful.

If the hypotheses in chapter 6 about the determinants of journey-to-work patterns are correct (for example, that some workers accept longer journeys to work to economize on housing expenditures), homeward-bound work-trips would be expected to be primarily unidirectional—away from the CBD. Also, because of the usual location of transport facilities, there should be a tendency for these journeys to be made along a line drawn through the CBD and the employee's workplace, so that this radial type of movement usually might be expected to remain within a single sector between home and workplace. Furthermore, the percentage of workers residing in the sectors in which they work should increase in the outer rings because of larger sector width. According to the data in Table 53, Chicago white workers clearly observe these suggested patterns, especially in the outer rings (reaching a high of 79 per cent for Ring 7, Sector 6). For nonwhites, the patterns are irregular; generally, though, for other than Sector 7 a much smaller percentage of nonwhite than of white workers live and work in the same sector. Also,

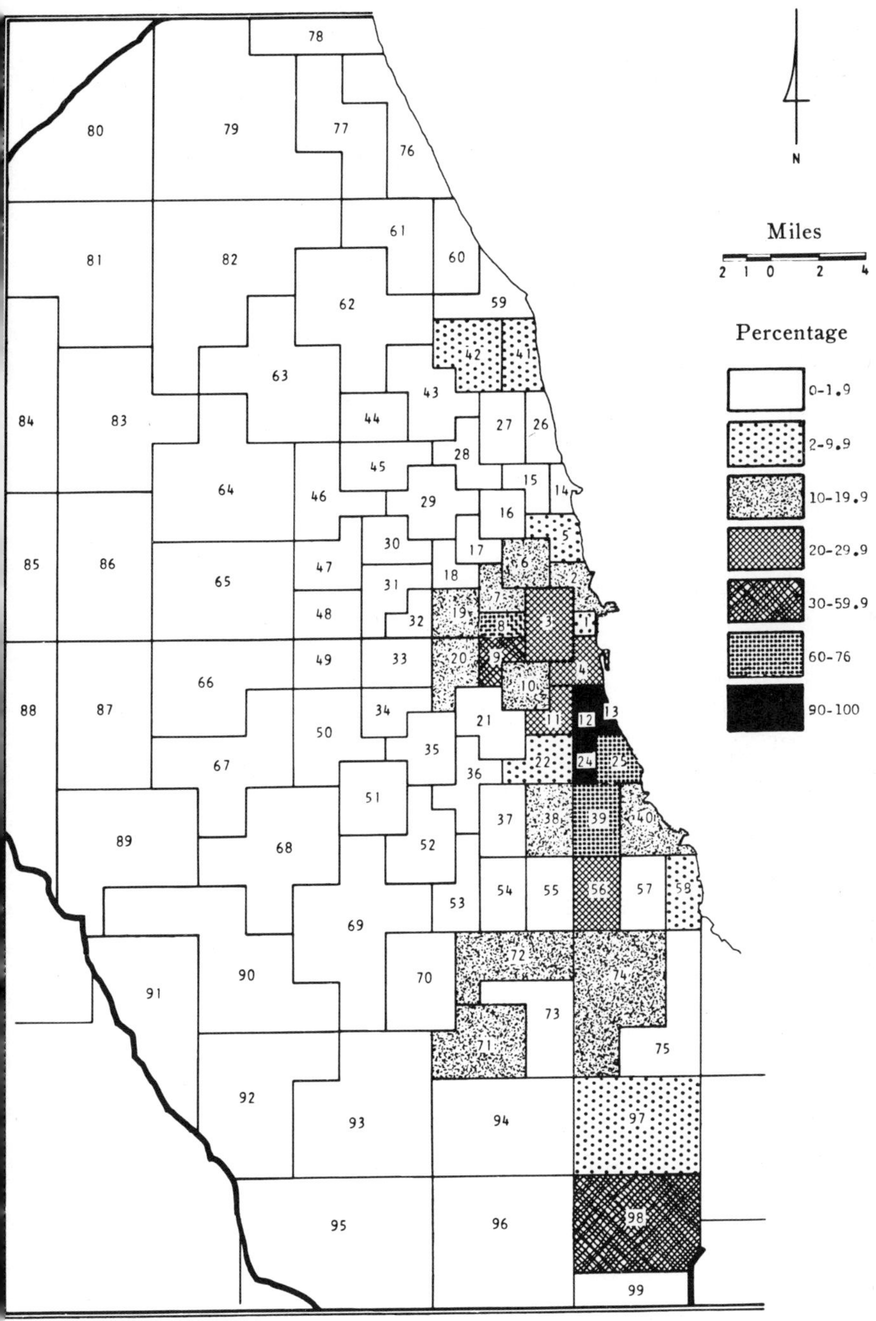

Figure 20. Nonwhite workers residing in each Chicago analysis area, as a percentage of all workers residing in the analysis area, 1956.

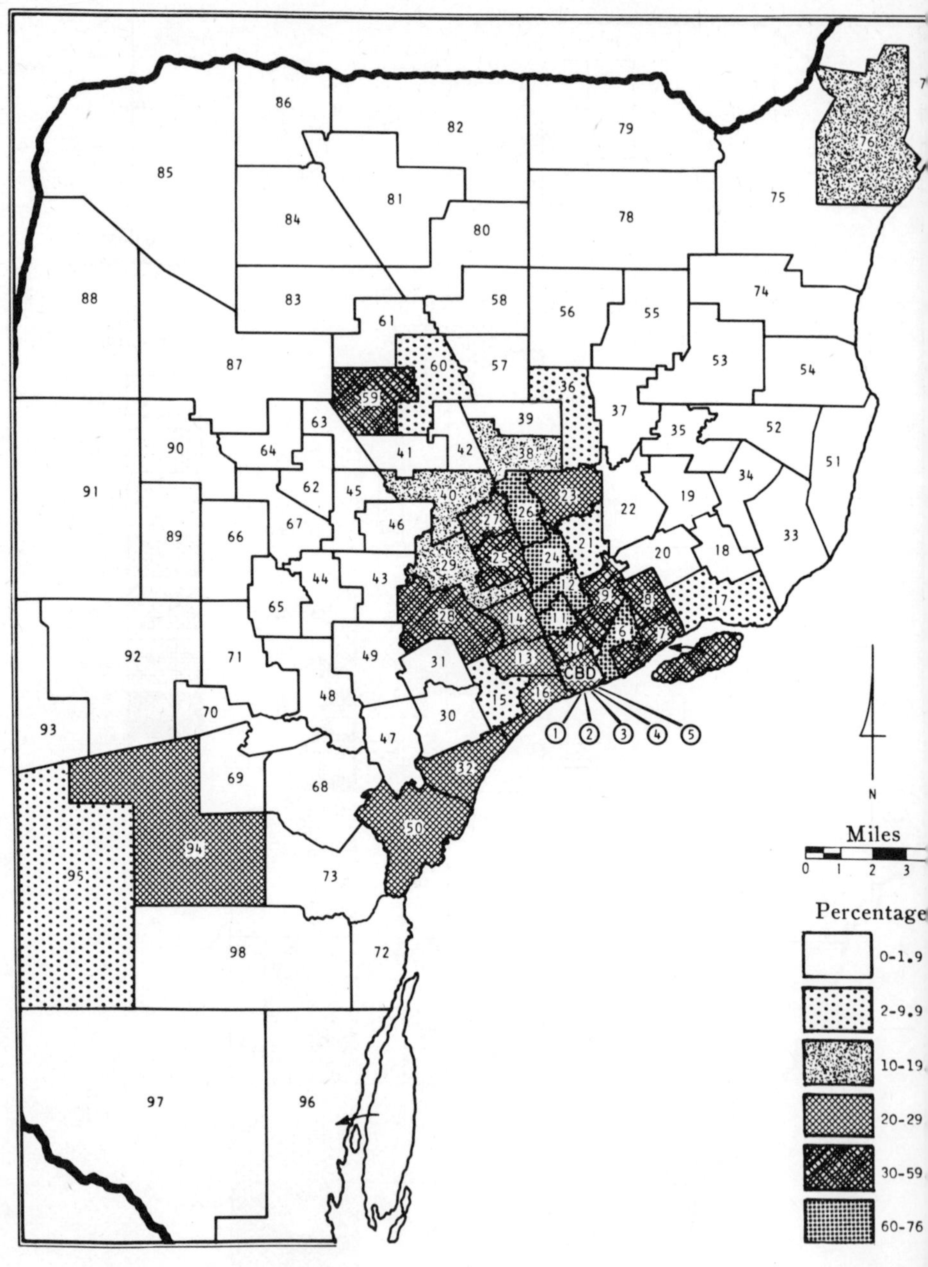

Figure 21. Nonwhite workers residing in each Detroit analysis area, as a percentage of all workers residing in the analysis area, 1953.

TABLE 53

PERCENTAGE OF CHICAGO WHITES AND NONWHITES EMPLOYED IN SPECIFIED RING AND SECTOR WHO RESIDE IN SAME SECTOR AS EMPLOYED

Workplace ring	Race	Workplace sector						
		1	2	3	4	5	6	7
2	White	59.2	46.0	42.6	22.3	29.6	47.1	29.3
	Nonwhite	20.5	2.4	34.5	46.4	0.9	5.9	86.2
3	White	67.0	46.6	47.7	42.3	34.5	57.3	55.5
	Nonwhite	20.0	1.0	19.9	29.7	0.5	8.6	90.1
4	White	65.6	55.4	57.0	54.5	37.8	62.1	57.0
	Nonwhite	15.5	—	34.8	28.2	2.2	17.8	87.6
5	White	68.6	55.0	64.6	55.8	43.2	62.7	73.2
	Nonwhite	43.1	—	49.4	22.5	6.5	32.7	81.7
6	White	74.3	70.4	68.4	65.6	39.7	71.7	72.3
	Nonwhite	50.4	—	27.2	50.6	—	46.7	81.8
7	White	78.3	77.2	76.1	67.9	50.4	78.8	46.4
	Nonwhite	18.6	—	—	—	—	18.1	79.3

this differential between Chicago whites and nonwhites increases in the outer rings. In Sector 7, though, from 80 to 90 per cent of the nonwhite workers also reside in that sector. Thus, one can conclude that work-trips by whites tend to be more radial in character than do work-trips by nonwhites, and that nonwhites experience more intersector travel than do whites in Chicago. In a somewhat more limited fashion, the data in Tables 54 and 55 also aid in identifying these intersectoral relationships. For example, a difference between the percentage of nonwhites working in a given sector and the percentage residing in that same sector obviously means that intersectoral travel results. Thus if absolute percentage points of difference for a sector between workplaces and residences for each race are accumulated, a rough measure of cross-hauling in Chicago will be provided (though the absolute extent of cross-hauling will remain indeterminate). Excluding the CBD and Sector 0, both of which are central zones, the cumulative percentage points of difference are about 27 per cent for Chicago whites and 63 per cent for nonwhites. (These numbers represent the absolute differences of the percentages reported in the last two rows of Tables 54 and 55 cumulated over the seven sector columns.) These figures are somewhat misleading, however, because few workers reside in the CBD and Sector 0 where substantial percentages are employed; specifically, 30.9 per cent of the whites are employed in these two areas, which is not too dissimilar to the 27 per cent of cumulative excess of residences over em-

TABLE 54

PERCENTAGE OF CHICAGO WHITES AND NONWHITES RESIDING IN EACH RESIDENTIAL SECTOR, BY WORKPLACE RING

Work-place ring	Race	Residence sector 0	1	2	3	4	5	6	7	Total[a]
0	White	7.4	27.0	14.9	14.7	7.1	4.2	13.0	11.7	100
	Nonwhite	10.2	3.9	—	5.3	6.6	0.1	5.7	68.2	100
1	White	16.1	20.9	16.5	15.5	7.1	6.0	10.0	7.9	100
	Nonwhite	19.8	1.6	0.5	6.9	12.8	0.2	4.1	54.0	100
2	White	6.6	18.3	20.4	17.8	8.4	10.7	13.2	4.7	100
	Nonwhite	12.5	0.9	0.3	9.9	14.2	0.4	3.9	57.9	100
3	White	4.0	14.4	18.8	20.1	13.0	10.8	12.7	5.9	100
	Nonwhite	9.2	1.2	0.2	7.4	12.0	0.2	4.6	65.3	100
4	White	2.2	14.3	16.6	17.5	12.1	8.6	17.8	10.9	100
	Nonwhite	7.8	1.2	0.2	6.9	8.8	0.2	7.2	67.9	100
5	White	1.4	14.9	15.2	18.4	9.9	9.7	14.6	15.8	100
	Nonwhite	5.9	5.6	0.2	7.2	9.0	2.9	9.9	59.4	100
6	White	0.9	9.7	14.9	16.1	9.9	4.7	23.0	20.8	100
	Nonwhite	3.4	5.9	0.3	6.7	10.5	0.6	17.4	55.2	100
7	White	0.4	12.3	13.8	13.3	10.3	3.7	33.9	12.2	100
	Nonwhite	3.6	2.8	—	2.1	7.0	0.7	14.5	69.2	100
All	White[b]	7.1	17.5	16.8	17.0	9.7	7.8	15.1	10.6	100
	Nonwhite[b]	11.6	2.5	0.3	7.4	11.4	0.5	5.9	61.1	100

[a] Rounded.
[b] All workplace rings.

ployment in Sectors 1 through 7. On the other hand, the total nonwhite employment of 31.4 per cent in these two central areas is substantially below the 63 per cent of the cumulative nonwhite discrepancies between residences and employment in Sectors 1 through 7. This cumulative percentage point figure also would not differentiate between intersectoral travel involving trips through the downtown sector (such as between Sectors 1 and 7, which are very similar to radial-type trips) and those between two outlying districts in different sectors not directly served by connecting radial facilities.

As a consequence, the data in Table 53, involving only outlying Rings 2 through 7, were weighted according to the percentage of *total* Chicago employment (by race) employed in the specified rings and sectors to obtain weighted average percentages of those people residing in the same sector in which they work. These showed that of all Chicago nonwhite workers, some 28.5 per cent work in Rings 2 through 7 and reside in

TABLE 55

PERCENTAGE OF CHICAGO WHITES AND NONWHITES EMPLOYED IN EACH EMPLOYMENT SECTOR

	Employment sector									
Race	CBD	0	1	2	3	4	5	6	7	Total[a]
White	15.0	15.9	9.5	11.5	12.6	9.4	8.3	9.4	8.2	100
Nonwhite	8.3	23.1	6.2	4.6	8.0	7.1	8.3	10.6	23.9	100

[a] Percentages may not total 100 because of rounding.

the same sector in which they work; of all Chicago white workers, 37.5 per cent work in Rings 2 through 7 and reside in the same sector in which they work. Viewing just those persons who work in Rings 2 through 7, about 54 per cent of the whites live in the same sector where they are employed; the comparable figure for nonwhites is only 42 per cent. Summing, it is clear that Chicago negroes do more cross-hauling or intersectoral travel than do whites.

It is difficult to estimate whether this cross-haulage more than offsets the shorter travel distances of the negro workers who are employed in the central zones. From Figures 17 and 19 the weighted average distance between residence and workplace can be computed for those Chicagoans who work either in Ring 0 (CBD), or in Ring 1 (Sector 0). For whites, the weighted distance is approximately 8.3 miles (and includes about 31 per cent of the white work force), and for nonwhites the distance is about 5.4 miles (and includes about 32 per cent of the nonwhite work force). Since the remaining nonwhite workplaces (in Rings 2 through 7) relative to those for whites are much closer to the CBD, the average intersectoral trip by nonwhites might be shorter than the average intersectoral trip by whites because outlying sectors are considerably wider than inner ones. On the other hand, more intersectoral trips by whites may terminate in adjacent sectors than do trips by nonwhites. Still, to expect the net over-all work-trip to be longer for the Chicago negro than for the white would at best be doubtful given the substantially greater average commuting distance of centrally employed whites than nonwhites.

THE NEGRO'S DECISION-MAKING CALCULUS

It seems reasonably clear from the evidence presented that whites and nonwhites having the same or similar workplace locations make different residential choices and undertake different types of commuter trips. Clearly, these differences are functions of many considerations besides housing segregation. For the most part, however, these other explanations of racial differences in residential choice patterns can be attributed, with at least reasonable validity, to differences in the opportunities available to the different races as the ultimate causal factors; for example, much of the difference observed in average incomes between races can be fairly ascribed to racial differences in educational and employment opportunities. The possibility still exists, though (at least on a strictly conceptual level), that even if all income, educational, and housing barriers were eliminated, housing choices of negroes would be different from those of whites because the negroes would have a fundamentally different set of values or utility calculus applicable in such matters. For example, negroes might prefer spending more on housing and less on transportation than whites.

Figures 22 and 23 aid in the examination of these possibilities. First, it is evident that nonwhite residential location distributions by structure type and employment location are not overwhelmingly different from those for whites. However, centrally employed nonwhites living in single-family residences live closer to the downtown area than whites and almost as close as nonwhites living in multiple-family homes. By contrast, centrally employed whites living in single-family homes as a group reside almost twice as far from their work as those living in multiple-family structures. Also, for each structure type, centrally employed nonwhite workers live closer to the CBD than white workers. Centrally employed nonwhites thus either exhibit different housing-transportation behavioral choices than whites, preferring to spend less on transportation expenses but more (on a unit and adjusted quality space basis) for housing, or the nonwhite worker, by virtue of housing segregation, is placed in the situation of paying more for housing (and saving on transportation).

In differentiating between these two possibilities it is significant that for workers employed in outlying rings, a quite different pattern seems to exist. In the outer employment rings the nonwhite residences are located closer to the CBD (where location rents are usually higher) than those for white workers. It would appear, therefore, that nonwhites working in outlying rings incur *both* higher housing costs (again, on a unit space and quality basis) and transportation expenses. For these outlying nonwhite workers, conserving on transport outlays would dictate a residence away from the city center. Since it seems difficult to imagine that fundamental changes in consumer preferences are created by changes in workplace, this shift in nonwhite residential and travel choices between central and outlying employment locations suggests that housing segregation is more important than racial differences in preference patterns in explaining racial differences in housing.

Of course, nonwhites might simply prefer to live at central locations, regardless of cost, but this is difficult to reconcile with the commonly

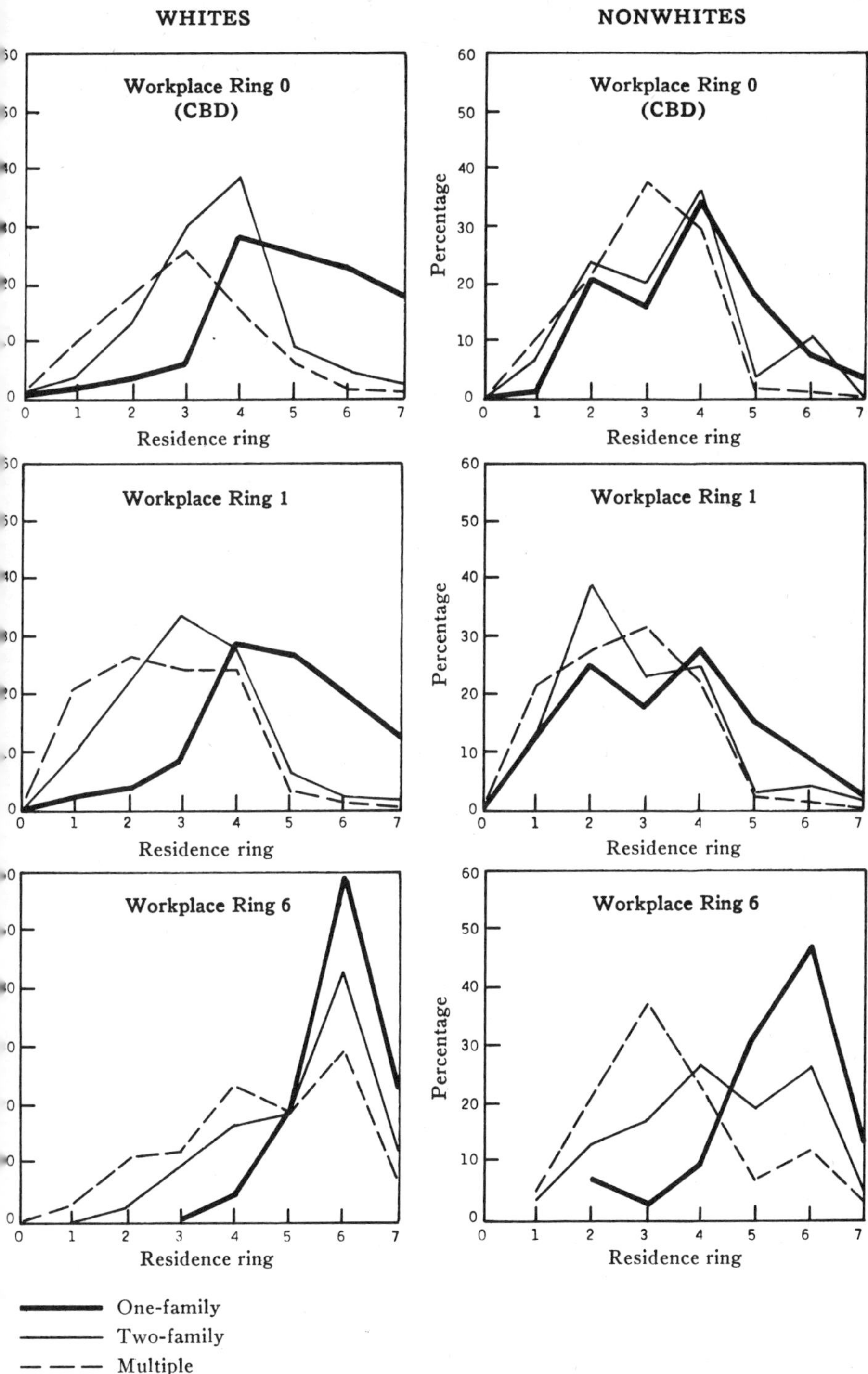

Figure 22. Percentage of Chicago white and nonwhite workers residing in each ring, by structure type and workplace ring.

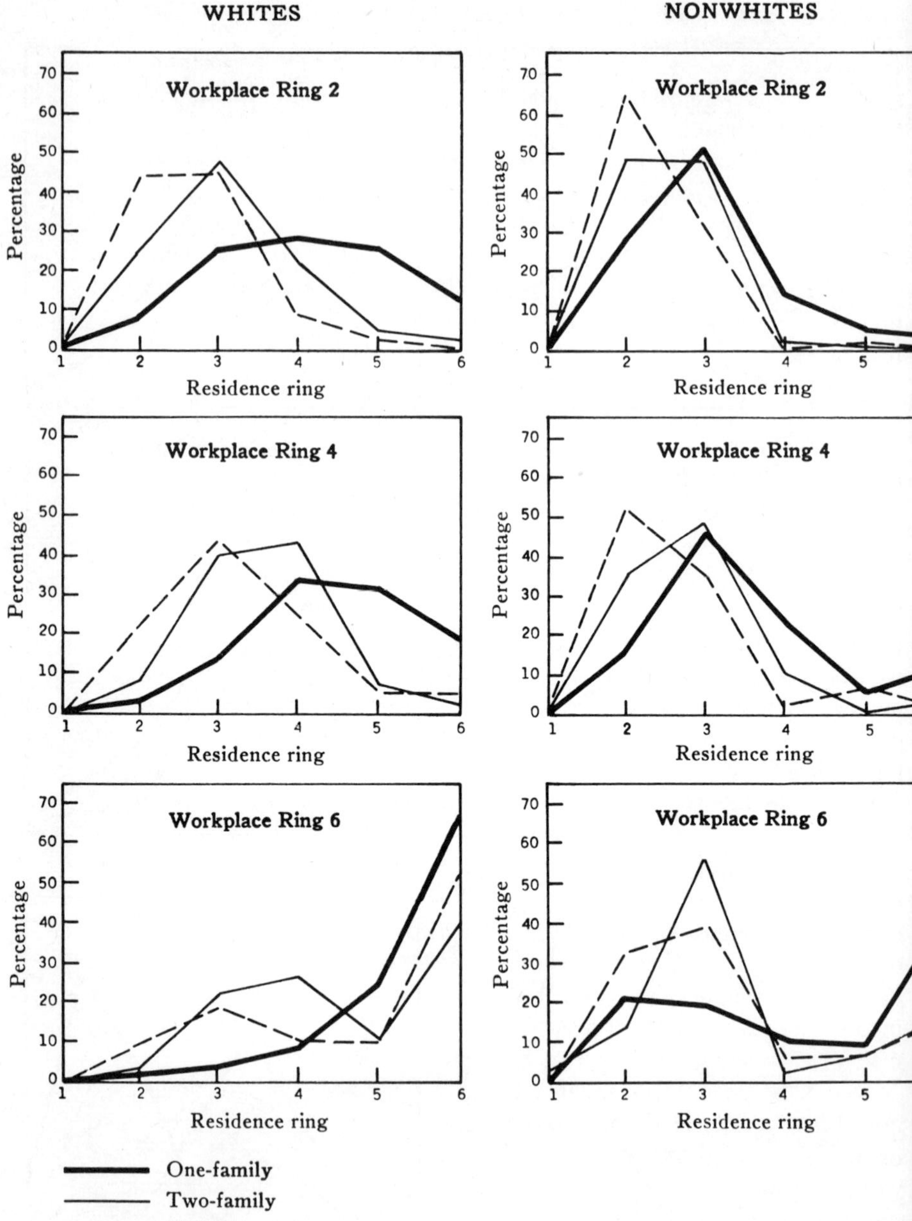

Figure 23. Percentage of Detroit white and nonwhite workers residing in each ring, by structure type and workplace ring.

expressed desires by negro groups for more housing opportunities in suburbs. It is also somewhat inconsistent with observed differences in the housing choices of nonwhites by income groups, which suggest that decentralized housing is considered a superior good by many wealthy negroes just as much as it is by many whites. Much the same arguments can be made against the proposition that negroes segregate themselves (that is, that they "want to live among their own kind"). At any rate, this is an argument for their living in one group; it provides no explanation of why they should choose to live in relatively high-cost central residential locations and to spend less on transportation.

Another remotely plausible explanation might be that the average size of outlying residences is so large that the total housing costs in outlying areas are above what negro incomes can tolerate (that is, whereas in-town housing cost per unit of space is higher than that for the suburbs, the availability of smaller-sized apartments and homes in the city results in lower total housing costs). Such an argument, however, subsumes considerable inflexibility in housing markets, and runs counter to common observation of housing market trends. Furthermore, it is an argument for finding relatively fewer nonwhites in the suburbs but not well-defined or demarcated all-negro districts; even though median and average incomes of nonwhites are markedly lower than those of whites, considerable overlap still exists in the income distributions for the different races.

These income effects are illustrated by the data in Figures 24 and 25 which show the residence locations of workers employed in various rings by race and occupational groups corresponding roughly to high-, medium-, and low-income groups (used in lieu of mean or median family or worker income levels that were not available). Since the income levels of nonwhites for all three groups are lower than those for whites, the data are incomparable to a certain extent. (For example, the median income for "low-income" whites is about 23 per cent higher than the median income for all nonwhite workers.)

It can be seen from Figure 24 that, for both Chicago whites and nonwhites, residence in the suburbs is associated with higher occupation or income levels. Approximately 30 per cent of Ring 1's nonwhite workers who belong to the high-income occupational group reside in the four most suburban rings, as compared to about 25 per cent of those in the middle-income occupational group, and 15 per cent of those in the lowest group. According to Figure 25, which provides the same information for workers in Detroit's Ring 2, somewhat the same relationships hold for Detroit. Similarly, as shown in Table 56, nonwhites employed in the suburbs of both Chicago and Detroit consume more residential space—that is, live in lower-density structures—than do non-

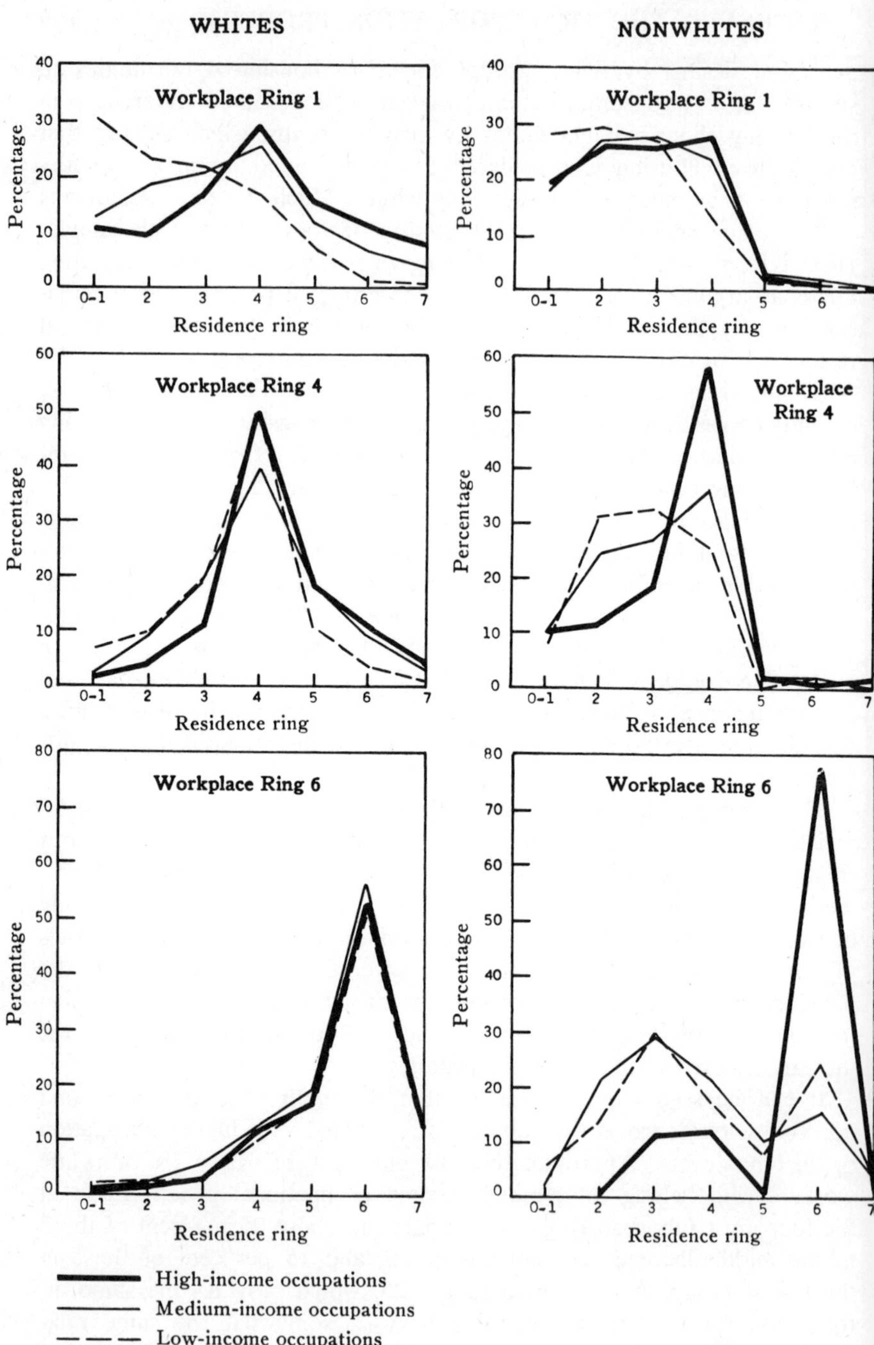

Figure 24. Residence profiles of Chicago white and nonwhite male workers, by income occupation group and workplace ring. (In each occupation group, the incomes for nonwhites are much lower than those for whites.)

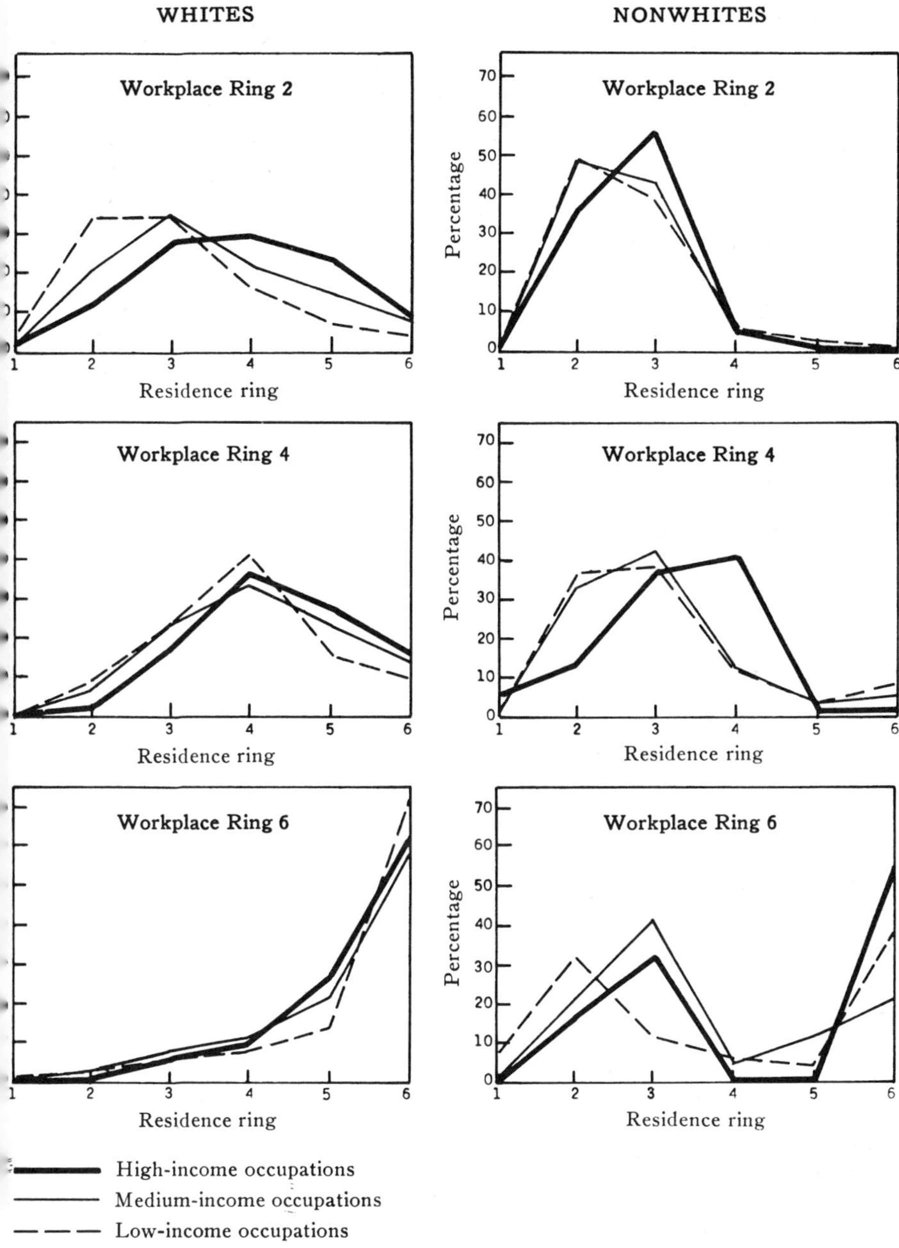

Figure 25. Residence profiles of Detroit white and nonwhite male workers, by income occupational group and workplace ring. (In each occupation group, the incomes for nonwhites are much lower than those for whites.)

TABLE 56

PERCENTAGE OF DETROIT AND CHICAGO WHITE AND NONWHITE WORKERS RESIDING IN EACH STRUCTURE TYPE, BY WORKPLACE RING[a]

Workplace ring	Race	Structure type: 1-family	2-family	Multiple	Other
		Detroit			
1	Nonwhite	30.2	30.0	28.7	11.1
	White	57.7	18.6	17.7	6.0
2	Nonwhite	31.2	36.8	27.0	5.0
	White	57.0	21.8	17.1	4.1
3	Nonwhite	32.2	36.4	27.5	3.9
	White	60.2	21.0	15.7	3.1
4	Nonwhite	35.9	34.5	23.6	6.0
	White	68.6	18.4	10.5	2.4
5	Nonwhite	40.5	30.1	23.4	6.0
	White	78.6	12.1	7.1	2.3
6	Nonwhite	56.0	21.8	11.1	11.1
	White	77.0	10.9	8.0	4.2
		Chicago			
0	Nonwhite	8.9	9.4	73.3	8.4
	White	36.5	15.0	41.4	7.1
1	Nonwhite	7.6	12.6	72.5	7.3
	White	29.8	18.4	43.3	8.5
2	Nonwhite	6.4	12.5	72.2	8.9
	White	28.2	21.8	44.3	5.7
3	Nonwhite	8.2	11.5	73.0	7.3
	White	34.0	23.2	37.6	5.2
4	Nonwhite	7.0	12.3	71.9	8.8
	White	41.6	19.9	34.7	3.8
5	Nonwhite	13.2	17.5	62.4	6.9
	White	54.9	17.1	24.9	3.1
6	Nonwhite	21.2	15.2	58.6	5.0
	White	63.9	14.3	17.4	4.4
7	Nonwhite	23.5	30.2	44.0	2.3
	White	69.4	15.6	12.5	2.5

[a] Percentages may not total 100 because of rounding.

whites employed at more central locations. Again, all these choice patterns are quite consistent with and similar to those for whites.

In sum, the evidence suggests that, within income and housing constraints, negroes display about the same housing and transportation choices as whites. It also indicates that the simple transportation and housing cost trade-off model, if properly modified to include constraints caused by housing segregation, provides useful insights into both negro and white behavior. Furthermore, the income and housing-type classifications further buttress the conclusion that for central employees, nonwhites live closer to the place of employment than whites. Conversely, for noncentral employees, nonwhites live closer to the central area (relative to the ring of employment) than whites.

Some Hypothetical Residential Distributions of Nonwhites

A further check on the effects of race on urban housing and travel patterns can be obtained by considering what housing patterns of nonwhites might be if there were no housing discrimination and if nonwhite workers, on the average, achieved incomes at least equal to those of whites in lower-income occupations. The lumping of these income and discrimination effects for analytical purposes is at least somewhat justified by the circumstance of their interdependence.

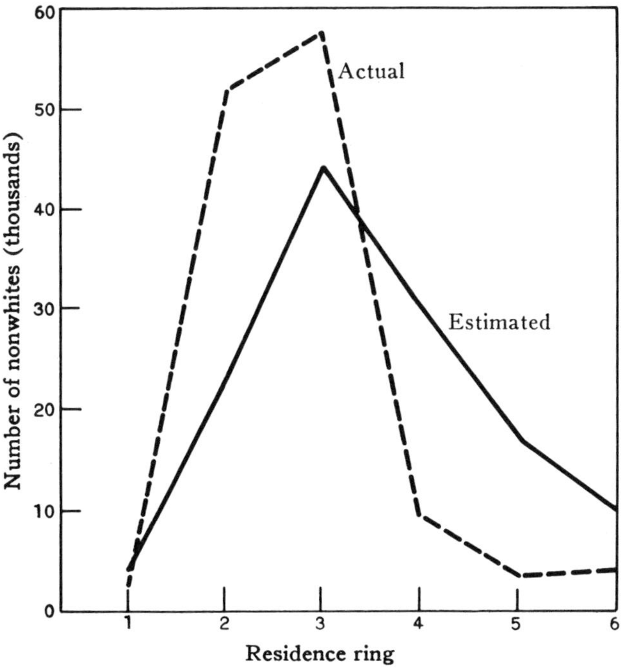

Figure 26. Detroit nonwhites actually residing in each ring and the estimated distribution in the absence of racial income differences and housing discrimination. (The estimated distribution assumes that nonwhites have income levels and housing preferences similar to those of low-income whites and thus similar residential patterns.)

Figure 26 portrays the actual distribution of nonwhite residences in Detroit and what the distribution would be if nonwhites resided in each ring in the same proportions as do lower-income whites employed in the same workplace rings.[6] The hypothetical numbers for nonwhites were obtained by multiplying the proportion of a workplace ring's lower-income whites residing in each residential ring by the number of nonwhites employed in the same workplace ring, and summing those distributions over the six workplace rings. The results imply that as many as 40,000 nonwhites might move out of Detroit's inner three rings if racial and economic differences did not exist, and if preference patterns of low-income whites and negroes were similar.

Figure 27 presents the results of a slightly more complex analysis of actual and estimated residential patterns of Chicago nonwhites. Because of the overwhelming importance of the sectoral pattern of segregation in Chicago, actual and estimated distributions by distance ring are given for all sectors, the heavily nonwhite Sector 7 (the South Side), and all sectors excluding Sector 7. The estimated values for Sector 7 were calculated by assuming that nonwhites would reside there in the same proportion as do all workers, and that the distance they reside from the CBD would correspond to the residence location relationships for low-income

[6] The estimated values in Figs. 26 and 27 were calculated from the following equations, where

$i =$ residence ring,
$j =$ workplace ring,
$W =$ number of white workers,
$N =$ number of nonwhite workers,
$T =$ total number of workers (whites and nonwhites),
$P =$ estimated values,
$7 =$ residence Sector 7,
$0\text{–}6 =$ residence Sectors 0 through 6,
$k =$ low-income whites,
$\alpha, \beta =$ arbitrary parameters as defined below.

(1) $$\beta_{ij}^{k} = \frac{W_{ij}^{k}}{W_{i}^{k}}.$$

(2) $$N_{ij}^{P} = \beta_{ij}^{k} N_{j}.$$

(3) $$N_{i}^{P} = \sum_{j=0}^{7} N_{ij}^{P}.$$

(4) $$\alpha_{ij7} = \frac{T_{ij7}}{T_{j}}.$$

(5) $$N_{ij7}^{P} = \alpha_{ij7} N_{j}.$$

(6) $$N_{i7}^{P} = \sum_{j=0}^{7} N_{ij7}^{P}.$$

(7) $$N_{i0-6}^{P} = N_{i}^{P} - N_{i7}^{P}.$$

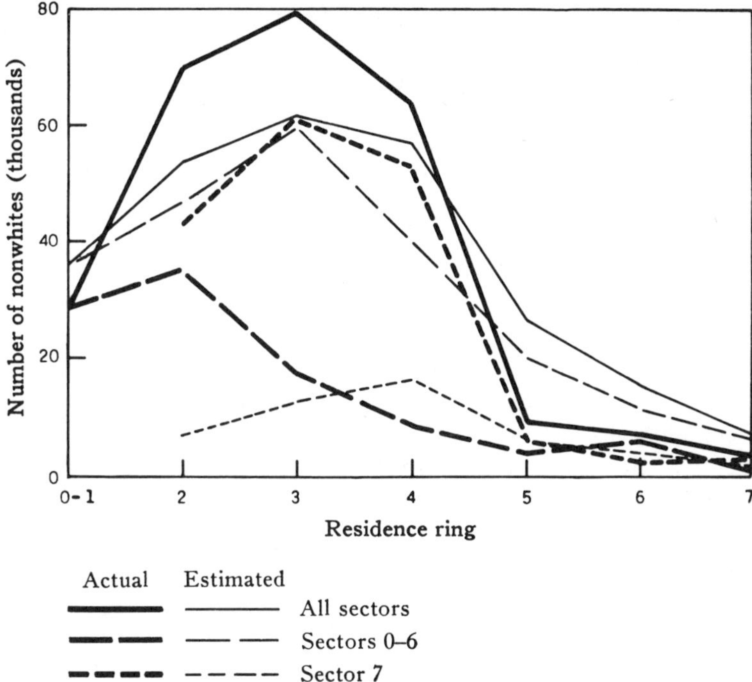

Figure 27. Chicago nonwhites actually residing in each ring and the estimated distribution in the absence of racial income differences and housing discrimination. (The estimated distribution assumes that nonwhites have income levels and patterns similar to those of low-income whites and thus similar residential patterns and sectoral employment locations.)

workers used in calculating the estimated values for all sectors in both Figures 26 and 27. The hypothetical distributions for all Chicago sectors shown in Figure 27 resemble those for Detroit nonwhites shown in Figure 26. For example, Chicago Rings 2, 3, and 4 now house approximately 36,000 more nonwhites, and Rings 5, 6, and 7 approximately 29,000 fewer than would be expected if nonwhites resided there in the same proportions as do low-income whites employed in the same workplace rings. According to the actual and estimated residential distributions, 112,000 nonwhites would move away from Sector 7, Chicago's South Side, if employment and economic conditions for low-income whites and nonwhites were similar, if there were no discrimination, and if preference patterns were the same for both groups. While nonwhites are underrepresented in every ring in Sectors 0 to 6, the extent of underrepresentation increases with distance from the center (with the exception of Ring 6). The percentages of actual-to-estimated residence levels are: Ring 2, 75 per cent; Ring 3, 32 per cent; Ring 4, 22 per cent; Ring 5, 19 per cent; Ring 6, 45 per cent; and Ring 7, 9 per cent.

If these hypothetical redistributions should be approximated over time by a reduction of present inequalities in economic opportunities for negroes and elimination of housing segregation, the effects on urban form and transport needs could be quite profound. Above all else, a considerable dispersion of residences for negroes could occur. Unless offset by an influx of whites to central locations, the result would be a further decline in central-city residential densities and probably some increase in urban transport requirements. The latter, in fact, would almost surely occur unless the elimination of racial differences were accompanied by a considerable dispersion of job opportunities. Actually, some offsetting influx of whites and decentralization of employment would seem reasonably certain, but it seems doubtful that these would be sufficient to neutralize fully the effects on transportation requirements of a reduction in housing segregation.

Summary

In several ways housing market segregation affects the travel behavior of urban residents and the magnitude and character of the urban transportation problem. In general, the hypotheses advanced at the beginning of this chapter seem sustained by the empirical evidence. Centrally employed nonwhites make short work-trips and probably shorter than they would freely choose if the housing market were not segregated. Centrally employed whites seem to do just the opposite. Noncentrally employed nonwhites, on the other hand, seem to travel relatively long distances to work while noncentrally employed whites usually manage to live reasonably close to their work. In general, the evidence is that discrimination forces minority groups into a disproportionate amount of cross-hauling and reverse commuting. Ghettos and their counterparts are usually near CBD's; accordingly, since more and more workplaces are located at the fringes of cities, more and more negroes will be traveling to and from work in directions opposite to the main commuter streams unless housing discrimination is lessened.

While income differences between the races partially explain some of the differences in residential patterns of whites and nonwhites, there is little to sustain the contention that they are attributable to basic racial differences in preference patterns. Nonwhites living in the suburbs are, like whites, usually those who have higher incomes and want more residential space. The residents of central nonwhite areas, regardless of where they are employed, are typically those who have lower incomes and who could be expected to have lower space preferences. The determinants of nonwhite travel and residential behavior do not appear essentially different from those of whites, except for the apparent constraints imposed by housing segregation.

This chapter has also attempted to enumerate and evaluate some of the obvious and less probable costs of racial segregation. The higher transportation cost imposed on nonwhites employed at outlying locations is one of the more obvious costs. The pattern of housing discrimination and the artificially maintained nonwhite demand for central locations also seem to force centrally employed whites to make longer average journeys to work than they would if the market were unsegregated. These same factors may make nonwhites purchase or rent more centrally located housing than they really desire and perhaps also pay more per unit of housing consumed. In general, the evidence suggests that housing segregation imposes extra transport costs on whites and additional housing costs on nonwhites. An obvious corollary is that public policies to alleviate urban housing problems (for example, by increasing its supply) are likely to have a different benefit incidence from those aimed at amelioration of transport difficulties. In particular, the housing and workplace location of nonwhites is such that suburban extensions of rail transit systems or continuance of railroad commuter services hardly will befit the needs either of many nonwhites or, for that matter, of most low-income groups.

PART II | COMPARATIVE COSTS

Chapter 8 | Costing Procedures and Assumptions

Perhaps no aspect of urban transportation planning has been talked about so often but examined so poorly as the cost of providing comparable urban transport services by different kinds of technologies. In this chapter a framework for conducting more rational urban transport cost analyses is outlined.

The central (but not exclusive) focus of these cost analyses is the provision of services to commuters traveling between home and downtown workplaces during rush hours. The systems analyzed thus incorporate high-performance, high-volume capabilities seldom encountered or needed on other than urban radial, CBD-oriented transportation facilities.

The total CBD commuter trip pattern (between home and downtown) can be separated into three functional components for analysis: residential collection; line-haul service; and downtown distribution. The first pertains to the collection and distribution of travelers at the residential end of the trip. It can require an entirely separate feeder service (and a passenger transfer), as in most rail and some express bus systems. Other technologies, though, can provide continuous movement, with no transfer at the intermediate point between residential collection and the line-haul.

The line-haul component connects the residential and downtown services. For the present analyses, the line-haul function is considered to be performed on a grade separated, high-speed transportation facility, usually with private right-of-way and with access limited to stations or ramps 1 mile apart.

Downtown distribution is the movement of passengers between the points where they get off the line-haul system and their final destinations. They may walk, or use private automobiles, taxis, transit service, or other means. Automobiles, taxis, and transit may use either city streets or grade separated facilities. A downtown distribution system may be connected directly with a line-haul system and thus provide "no transfer" service, or may be completely separate.

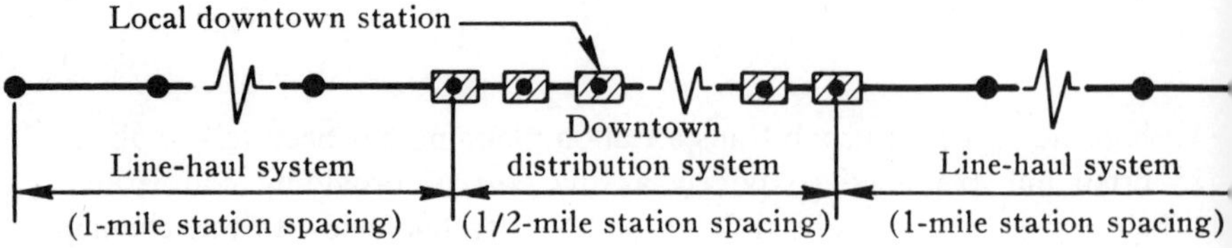

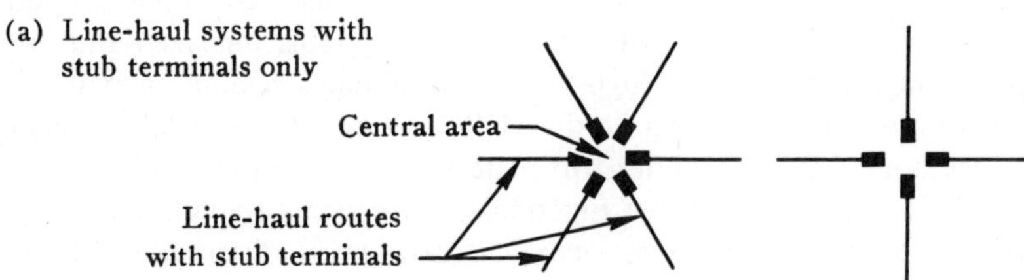

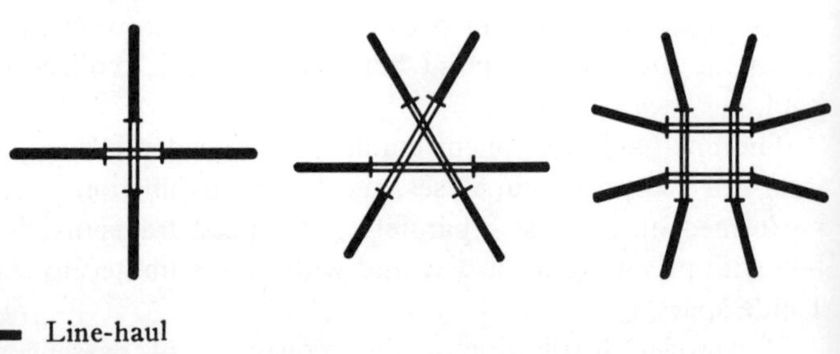

Figure 28. Some general layouts of urban transportation systems.

Figure 28 illustrates some general schematic layouts of line-haul and downtown distribution systems. Part (3) of the figure suggests several general configurations for integrating line-haul routes, or combining line-haul and downtown distribution routes, into larger-scale and perhaps regional rapid transit systems.

Basic Cost Model

The cost of performing a particular urban transportation function tends to vary with the number of vehicular units it requires, the miles these units have to travel, and the costs of providing needed structures. Also, it is often useful to express some administrative and operating costs, particularly for maintenance, as a function of track-miles or lane-miles of roadbed or roadway needed. These functional cost relationships can be expressed notationally as follows:

(1) $$TC = \alpha n U + \beta M + \gamma L + S,$$

where TC = total cost for some specified time period (usually, for convenience, taken to be one year);

U = number of basic vehicle groups needed;

M = miles of vehicle travel during the period;

L = lane-miles or track-miles of roadway or roadbed needed;

S = structure and related costs (for example, highways, roadbed, right-of-way);

n = the number of vehicular units operating as a coordinated group or train (that is, n usually equals 1 for bus and auto operations today and is usually greater than 1 for rail);

α = costs per period per vehicular unit employed;

β = direct costs assignable on the basis of miles of travel performed;

γ = costs assignable on the basis of miles of roadway or roadbed required.

By far the easiest of these quantities to estimate is M, total miles of vehicular travel. It is almost invariably necessary for other purposes to estimate the average distance traveled on each round trip by each vehicle employed in a particular transportation service, and the number of round trips each vehicle can make during a peak hour. Thus, since there are normally 255 workdays in a year and four peak hours in a workday, the total *peak-hour* mileage per year, M, can be expressed as:

(2) $$M = 1020\, drnU,$$

where d = average distance of a round trip (in the service analyzed);

r = average number of round trips each vehicle performs in one peak hour (four peak hours are usually assumed here—two in the morning and two in the afternoon);

1020 = peak hours in a year (255 workdays times four peak hours).

The average distance traveled on each round trip also can be estimated, as a rule, by fairly straightforward methods. For example, when rail line-haul services are being analyzed, this distance can be approximated by twice the total length of the route served; the only exceptions will occur when volumes are high enough to make it worth while to run some trains only part of the total route length, providing crossovers for them to switch back at intermediate points along the route. Similarly, the average distance of a round trip on an express bus line-haul service can usually be approximated by the total line-haul route length plus 1 mile. In this case, the service would be differentiated so that one bus run would serve the line-haul station located 1 mile from the CBD, the second bus run would serve the line haul located 2 miles from the CBD, and so forth. Only residential feeder services offer moderately complex distance estimation problems; in such services the average distance of a round trip will depend on the volume of traffic served, the distance people will walk, and the density of trip originations in the area served. (The complexities of residential cost and trip length analyses are explained in chapter 10.)

An essential part of any urban transportation cost analysis is determining U, the number of vehicular groups needed or scheduled during the peak hours. (Obviously the total fleet requirement will be larger because of allowances for maintenance time.) A basic function to such analyses is

$$R = \frac{V}{nc}, \tag{3}$$

where R = total number of transit round trips or automobile one-way trips required every peak hour;

V = major direction peak-hour passenger volume served;

c = capacity as measured by number of passengers each vehicular unit actually carries in the major direction.

In the cost analyses of this study, uniform population or traffic origination densities are usually assumed so that it is often easier to formulate Eq. (3) in terms of volumes at one particular point in the system, for example, a line-haul station or stop at some neighborhood curbside. In such a case, V would pertain to a specified proportion of the total volume, and the total number of round trips and vehicles required would simply be some multiple of the number found in the specific analysis. An immediate advantage of expressing Eq. (3) in terms of volumes originating at a particular point or at a group of stations (served by one train or bus run) is that it provides a check on one of the most crucial service considerations in urban transportation analyses: scheduled frequency or headways. Specifically, it is often deemed desirable that a specific condition of the following type be met:

$$R_i = \frac{V_i}{nc_i} \geq h, \tag{4}$$

where V_i = some specified portion of V;

R_i = the number of transit round trips serving the same specified portion of V_i;

c_i = the capacity of units available and serving point i (or a run ending at the ith station);

h = the minimum rush-hour service frequency specified as "tolerable."

If the condition of Eq. (4) is not met, then c_i, the capacity of the units available for serving the location in question, usually is modified downward until the condition is satisfied. In most cases this modification will simply take the form of a reduction in average load factor.

Once R, the number of one-way or round trips required every peak hour is known, the total number of vehicular units needed, U, can be quickly obtained if r, the number of round trips each vehicle can perform per hour, is also known. That is, the following relationship must hold:

$$U = \frac{R}{r}, \quad \text{or} \quad U_i = \frac{R_i}{r_i}. \tag{5}$$

To determine r or r_i for transit systems the only information needed is how long it takes to complete a round trip in the service under analysis. The basic function for making such a determination is as follows:

$$t = t_1 + t_2 + t_3 + t_4, \tag{6}$$

where t = total time (in seconds) per round trip;

t_1 = running time at top operating speed (basically a function of the distance traveled, d, and the operating speed of the vehicle);

t_2 = time for acceleration, deceleration, and opening and closing doors (all functions of the number of stops made on each round trip, the first two also being a function of operating speed);

t_3 = loading and unloading time (essentially a function of the amount of door space in each vehicle and the number of passengers carried);

t_4 = turnaround time.

As is obvious from the above description, t_1, t_2, and t_3 are all functions of other basic characteristics of the system. On the other hand, t_4 is usually best treated as a constant. Accurate estimation of the constitutent items in this basic time equation is often difficult, and it can involve very different considerations in different circumstances, though the analytical essentials tend to be similar in all cases.

Total time spent on each round trip, t, will also largely determine the average time that individual travelers must spend on each trip while en-route. Like scheduled frequency, this average time per trip will be an important determinant of the value of the service rendered by a transportation system. Accordingly, it is often desirable to subject t to a boundary constraint, that is, of being equal to or less than some specified level. The actual form of this constraint can be expressed in different ways, the simplest of which is to assert that t must be equal to or less than some arbitrarily specified value. Alternatively, the constraint can be expressed as a function of the distance traveled, d; for example, it might be asserted that the over-all travel time for the entire trip should not be at an over-all speed (including stopping time) less than so many miles per hour.

To estimate the number of round trips each transit vehicle can perform in one rush hour once t is known, it is necessary only to divide the total number of seconds in an hour, 3600, by t. Thus, $r = 3600/t$, and by substitution Eq. (5) can be expressed as

$$U = \frac{Rt}{3600}. \tag{7}$$

Determining L, the number of single track-miles or lane-miles required, is essentially a matter of comparing track-mile or lane-mile capacity with requirements for every mile in the system, and then summing to obtain an estimate of total needs.

The structural costs, S, invariably include two essential components: right-of-way and the costs of constructing a roadway or roadbed on it. Both costs will be functions of width and length and of the intensity of urban development. In the present analyses, attention is confined almost exclusively to systems that extend radially from the CBD so that the distance from the CBD and the length of the system are interchangeable quantities. This technique makes for simplicity, since right-of-way real estate costs tend to vary inversely with distance from the urban center. Similarly, the closer a roadbed or roadway is to the CBD, the more likely it is that expensive elevated or tunneled structures will be used; in general, construction costs are likely to rise with population and employment densities and therefore with proximity to urban centers. Right-of-way and construction costs are also likely to vary widely among cities with different geographical and population characteristics. In the analyses that follow, population density is used as a simple, though admittedly imperfect, proxy for expressing all the effects on cost attributable to greater urban development.

The structural cost analyses could be formulated with reasonable accuracy in several different ways. For present purposes the approach will be to develop a basic unit cost of acquiring right-of-way or constructing roadbed or highway for a basic eight-lane highway or two-track facility at a specified population density, and to express the costs of smaller or larger facilities or of facilities located at other population densities as multiples of this base figure. Essentially, the procedure is to develop an index relationship between the basic units and all other units included in the system.

Since structure costs (and equipment expenditures, too) usually involve capital investments of some longevity, these costs must be placed on a per-period basis. Placing all costs on the same time basis is indispensable in performing cost analyses and comparisons. In this study annual cost equivalents were computed by using capital recovery factors conventional to engineering economy analyses. These are convenient and seem at least as sensible as any obvious simple alternative. Capital recovery factors for a yearly time period are defined by

$$\text{(8)} \qquad \text{CRF} = \frac{i(1+i)^n}{(1+i)^n - 1} = \frac{i}{(1+i)^n - 1} + i,$$

where n = life in years, and i = the rate of interest.

Wherever reference is made in succeeding pages to annual capital costs, these have been obtained by multiplying total capital cost by the appropriate capital recovery factor (CRF). The rate of interest is assumed to be 6 per cent for all systems analyzed, probably a very reasonable estimate of the alternative opportunity value of investment funds. It should be noted, morever, that opportunity rather than borrowing costs are considered relevant, particularly since the latter are often implicitly or explicitly subsidized to municipal transit systems. The assumed lives and capital recovery factors used for computing the annual capital costs are summarized in Table 57 for all modes.

Many aspects of these annual capital cost calculations are controversial or at least questionable. There is, for example, the already mentioned problem of properly defining the interest rate to be used. Similarly, the service life estimates are rough approximations at best, though every effort has been made to render them as realistic as possible and, more importantly, to preclude their unduly biasing the results in favor of one

TABLE 57

CAPITAL RECOVERY FACTORS AND ASSUMED SERVICE LIVES FOR URBAN TRANSPORTATION INVESTMENTS

Capital item	Service life (yr)	CRF at 6 per cent interest
Rail		
Rolling equipment	30[a]	0.07265
Yards and shops	50	0.06344
Line-haul stations and downtown terminal	50	0.06344
Line-haul construction		
Track structure, etc.	50	0.06344
Right-of-way (land acquisition)	infinite	0.06000
Bus		
Right-of-way (land acquisition)	infinite	0.06000
Line-haul roadway construction[b]	35	0.06897
Yards and shops	40	0.06646
Stations, terminals, and subways	50	0.06344
Rolling equipment[c]	12	0.11928
Automobile		
Right-of-way (for roadway and parking)	infinite	0.06000
Roadway construction[b]	35	0.06897
Parking garage construction	40	0.06646
Parking lot construction	15	0.10296

[a] Stretching this service life to 40 years would reduce the annual service charges on the rolling-stock debt by only 8½ per cent, and the total annual system costs by less than 2 per cent.

[b] About 80 per cent of these costs are for capital items (structures, grading, drainage) with lives of approximately 40 to 50 years, whereas the base and surface need replacement considerably sooner, at about 20 years. Thus a reasonable composite is 35 years.

[c] According to A. Mongini, these buses "will reportedly go 300,000 to 400,000 miles in 6 to 8 years and retain a market value of 50 per cent of original price." ("The Physical and Economic Characteristics of Express Bus Urban Transit Systems," S.B. thesis, MIT, Cambridge, Mass., June 1961.) His source was a letter from F. L. Bates of the G.M.C. Truck and Coach Division. At 6 per cent interest, this implies an economic life of 12 years. On the other hand, data from the Cleveland Transit System (as of March 1962) show an average bus age (as contrasted with life) of about 9 years for a fleet of almost 900 buses; this suggests that our 12-year life is overly conservative. Increasing the life to 16 years would reduce annual service charges on the rolling-stock debt by 17 per cent, and total annual costs by less than 2 per cent.

mode or another. On the whole, the estimated *economic* lives are probably somewhat favorable to rail transit and slightly unfavorable to bus transit.

The use of capital recovery factors as a procedure might also be challenged. For example, it is almost certainly incorrect to make the implicit assumption that all capital assets follow a one-horse-shay pattern of service. Normally, most facilities in their first years offer better service, lower maintenance, and even lower operating costs, than they do later on. This implies that the returns yielded by the investment decline over time and that the use of capital recovery factors exaggerates annual capital costs. Similarly, it often takes a long time to construct transit and highway facilities and put them into use, especially the forms that require elaborate structures or tunneling. Taking these gestation periods into account would tend to increase annual capital costs, since total costs of the investment would be increased by the interest charges placed against these investments for the period before they became productive. These two biases in the use of capital recovery factors obviously tend to offset one another, but the extent to which they are offsetting will vary in different situations. Indeed, there are so many imperfections in the construction of the annual capital cost estimates, not the least of which is obtaining a reasonably accurate estimate of the actual cost of specific investments, that it seemed unnecessary to use more sophisticated capital cost calculations.

The basic structural cost equations can generally be expressed as follows:

$$S_{\text{row}_i} = W_{\text{row}_i} f(X_i), \tag{9}$$

and

$$S_{c_i} = W_{c_i} g(X_i), \tag{10}$$

where S_{row_i} = the costs per period of acquiring right-of-way (ROW) needed for the *i*th mile of a particular system;

S_{c_i} = the costs per period of constructing needed highway or roadbed facilities for the *i*th mile of a system;

$f(X_i)$ = a function expressing the relationship between basic ROW costs per period and population density over the *i*th mile;

$g(X_i)$ = a function expressing the relationship between basic construction costs per period and population density over the *i*th mile;

W_{row_i} = an index expressing the multiple of basic ROW costs that the *i*th mile costs will be because of width;

W_{c_i} = an index expressing the multiple of basic construction costs that *i*th mile costs will be because of width.

Total system cost estimates can be obtained by summing these costs for every route-mile in the system.

It should be obvious that these formulations cannot be a substitute for careful or detailed analysis of right-of-way and construction characteristics needed to estimate costs accurately in real situations. Specifically, these functional relationships constitute a fairly simple and consistent basis for making rough cost comparisons among different modes. Again, it should be stressed that structure costs will vary widely under different geographic and urban circumstances and that the figures presented in subsequent analyses are representative of the range of possible costs rather than any "fundamental truths" applicable to specific situations.

Another important category of costs, that associated with the provision of station or terminal facilities, is also usually grouped conveniently with structural costs. Terminal costs largely depend on the number of passengers or vehicles arriving at each line haul or CBD station during a rush hour or some other specific time period. Thus, terminal costs can usually and very conveniently be expressed as functions of R or R_i, the number of round trips required per peak hour to serve the system or a particular stop on a system, since the number of round trips implies the number of vehicle arrivals that can be expected at a terminal facility. As the number of *vehicle* or car (as distinguished from *train*) arrivals goes up in the case of rail transit, the increase normally should be handled by lengthening platforms to accommodate the longer trains that result from such an increase. For bus transit, by contrast, the accommodation normally will be made by widening the terminal facilities to provide more platforms of a fixed length. To determine terminal costs in the case of rail transit it is therefore necessary to know exactly how the vehicles are grouped together into trains, and to have the train length expressed as a function of the number of cars in the longest train, as well as the number of train arrivals. The relationship of terminal costs to the number of train or bus arrivals tends, moreover, to be basically a step function since discrete increments usually must be added to terminal facilities as arrivals per period exceed some specified design level. With bus transit, for example, a single bus terminal platform or slot might be able to accommodate 70 buses an hour (assuming centralized fare collection, triple-door buses, and a terminal design somewhat as shown in Figure 61 in appendix B); a second slot would be required for anything over that number, and a third slot if the number rose above 140. Thus bus terminal requirements, like lane- or track-mile requirements, are determined by comparing total needs with the capacity of each unit. Because of these many complexities, the cost relationship for terminal costs will be expressed here only in a general functional notation:

$$S_T = f(nR \quad \text{or} \quad nR_i), \tag{11}$$

where S_T is the cost per period of providing needed terminal facilities.

At this point it should be obvious that the complete expression for structural costs will normally be of the following type:

$$S = S_{\text{row}} + S_c + S_T. \tag{12}$$

Actually, specific treatment of structural costs will be omitted for all residential transit systems wherein the highway facilities are shared by transit and private vehicles. The usual practice is to recoup the costs of the shared highway and related right-of-way by charging a gasoline tax or similar user tax; such a procedure essentially converts the structural costs into a variable charge assessed on a per-mile basis, so that such charges are readily incorporated into the β coefficient of the fundamental cost equation, Eq. (1). In such circumstances it is also not unusual for a bus system to use the curb of a public street or highway as its terminal facility so that terminal costs become negligible, or at least unassignable except on a per-mile basis; however, there can be exceptions to this rule, so terminal costs may sometimes be treated specifically even when right-of-way and highway costs are recouped by mileage charges.

It is also useful to note that the total costs, TC, for some specified time period can be converted into other measures of unit cost, such as cost per mile of revenue service rendered, cost per mile of total operation, or cost per trip. Costs per passenger-trip, and in the particular case of this study, costs per peak-hour passenger-trip, are often a particularly relevant measure for evaluating the performance of an urban transportation system. If TC has been computed on an annual basis, such a cost estimate would be obtained in the present case simply by dividing TC by $1020V$. Similarly, TC/M would yield the costs incurred per mile of total annual vehicle travel. These different unit costs measure, of course, very different aspects of system performance. Unit costs, moreover, often can be obtained very simply by reducing the total cost formula to a per-mile basis expressed in general terms, for example as a function of distance and time required for each trip.

Specification of System Service and Design Variables

Each community has its own set of travel conditions, land-use pattern, and economic level, and thus its own unique transport requirements; and travelers in one community may be unable or unwilling to afford the same level or quality of transportation service as another. Thus there can be no single "optimum" system or mode, or even level of system investment, for all communities. Even so, it is reasonable—and in fact necessary—to specify the broad limits and conditions under which certain system designs and technologies generally are most economic; such specifications aid in the selection of the more promising system alternatives (in terms of layout, mode, and service) for deeper and more intensive investigation by individual communities, and decrease the chances of failing to consider certain systems of high potential.

In specifying the particular systems to be costed for this study, many design and operating variables were considered and many performance or service capabilities specifically were taken into account. Also, a critical need was felt to exist to include evaluations of systems different from the norm and systems of varying operational or service capability. Too often, in fact, planners have arbitrarily concluded that certain kinds or amounts of transport service must be provided, without measurement and evaluation of the consequences of not providing a service. Consider, for example, such often-heard statements as "We must eliminate urban traffic congestion," or "We must eliminate highway accidents and fatalities," or "We cannot afford to abandon commuter railroads," or "We must improve our urban transit systems." Similarly, it is often said that urban transit systems "must provide service for those travelers who cannot afford private automobiles," or "must provide service for school children," or "must provide 'along-the-line' service, outbound service," and so forth. It should be clear that one relevant issue is the expense of satisfying any one of these conditions. Inspection may reveal that the expense is so high that the resulting economic, social, and political "benefits" do not seem worth the cost to the community.

In the present cost analyses, therefore, the emphasis is on evaluating different technological systems for carrying specific passenger volumes under approximately the same conditions of service. The cost data may be considered precise only for the assumed conditions of service, volume, and design. Change the input variables—volume levels, route lengths, design speed, schedule frequency, and the like—and the costs almost invariably change too.

Further, only those systems that seem realistic in terms of consumer preference patterns of today or tomorrow were evaluated. The following are examples of major input variables that were considered relevant: transport type, hourly volume level (and its origin-and-destination pattern and distribution), route length, station (or ramp) spacing, over-all trip speed or travel time, schedule frequency, seating space (or comfort level), and walking distance to stations.

The choice of transport types was restricted to those in current use: automobile, bus, and rail transit. In each case attention was concentrated on that representative of each type which seemed best suited for the peak-hour commuter function. For cases in which this choice was at all ambiguous, either the alternatives were explicitly costed or an indication was given of what the cost effects would be (if any) of using a particular transport type with somewhat different technological characteristics. Usually, however, substitution among these representatives within the same group makes little impact on the reported cost comparisons.

The choice of specific volume levels, while arbitrary, was directly related to available peak-hour cordon count data for most urban downtown or core areas throughout the nation. As reported in Table 25, only the

New York CBD among 26 of the largest metropolitan areas encounters peak-hour passenger volumes of over 250,000, and only four other cities have volumes of over 150,000. When these data for our largest cities are placed on an approximate sector or radial corridor basis, existing peak-hour corridor volumes (excluding New York City) range from 3000 or 4000 up to 40,000. Apart from the four or five largest cities (in terms of peak-hour downtown passenger volumes), only a few approach corridor volumes of 30,000 passengers an hour and most cities report corridor counts mostly below 20,000. The corridor volume limits used in the reported cost analyses—5000 to 50,000 an hour—therefore cover most American cities, plus an allowance for extremely high peaking or potential growth. Another assumption was that these volumes are distributed uniformly over geographic areas and rush-hour periods. Specifically, once an hourly volume was stated, it was hypothesized that the flow implied by this volume appeared at terminals at a uniform rate over the hour. Similarly, hypothesized trip origination densities at the residential end of commuter trips were assumed to be the same at all points within the area analyzed. (However, residential densities of properties abutting line-haul facilities were varied according to distance from the CBD.) These assumptions, while unrealistic to some extent, greatly simplify the computations and probably do not alter the basic results significantly; however, they are obviously inappropriate for specific applications and may limit the generality of the reported findings.

As a point of departure to illustrate service effects on costs, the following special volume characteristics were assumed in the initial analyses (but were always relaxed later): (1) hourly passenger capacity is required and provided only in the major flow direction; for example, in the morning peak hours no outbound capacity is provided; (2) for express bus line-haul operations *only,* hourly passenger volumes entering (or leaving) the line-haul stations are destined for (or originate at) the downtown area; for example, no morning peak-hour passengers get off the line-haul system before reaching the downtown area; (3) maximum passenger capacity is provided for a two-hour period in the morning and a two-hour period in the afternoon; and (4) no capacity is provided during other hours.

Many will voice an alarmed concern about using these initial assumptions, asserting that no such method of operation is or ever would be used. Unfortunately, this assertion may well be correct—unfortunately, because of the underlying resistance it reveals to change and to analysis of alternatives, however urgently needed. Many seem to insist that certain transport services must continue to be provided merely because they have been in the past. Even worse, it is rarely recognized that providing a service to one customer may impose a disservice on many others. While there may be strong political or even economic justification for perpetuating present practices, the conscientious transport analyst should at least open them to question.

Even these initial assumptions are not as restrictive, moreover, as might be suspected. Regarding passenger service in the minor flow direction during peak hours, conditions vary from city to city and line to line. In Pittsburgh, for example, at the maximum load point for the system as a whole, the minor direction volume (as a percentage of the total two-way peak-hour volume) is about 15 per cent for transit and about 25 per cent for private automobile; and at the most central area, the minor direction volume is only 10 per cent of the total two-way flow.[1] At the maximum load point for three major lines of the Washington, D.C. bus transit system, the outbound volume during the morning peak hour is about 16.5 per cent of the total two-way volume. Data for some other lines, all rail transit, are as shown in Table 58. The importance of these data is simply that the outbound volumes usually are not significantly high relative to the inbound flows during morning peak hours. Thus, unless the incremental costs of providing the additional service are correspondingly low, as they often are, justification must often derive from other than economic grounds. In a later chapter, the costs of providing this minor direction service are computed to permit a more exact assessment of the economics of such services.

As for the provision of along-the-line service, the data in Table 58 indicate that there is little present demand for it on some rail transit systems. In this respect, Toronto's Yonge Street Line must be considered a special case because of its shortness (about 4.5 miles) and particular locational characteristics; in a very real sense, it operates as a downtown-distribution subway for much of its length rather than as a line-haul facility.

However, bus line-haul systems have been designed and evaluated in this study both with and without along-the-line service, the object being to determine the extra costs of providing such service. The nature of rail transit operations is such that along-the-line service in the direction of major volume flow is almost automatically provided at little extra cost and is identical with the through (or downtown-oriented) service in terms of both speed and schedule frequency; therefore rail transit without such service has not been separately analyzed.

The third assumption about volume characteristics pertains to the provision of passenger capacity only during the morning and afternoon rush-hour periods, each two hours long. This assumption is actually one of the least critical in the study from the standpoint of determining the

[1] *Pittsburgh Area Transportation Study, Final Report,* vol. 1, Study Findings, Pittsburgh, November 1961, Fig. 55.

TABLE 58

PERCENTAGE OF MORNING PEAK-HOUR RAIL TRANSIT PASSENGERS BOUND FOR AREAS OTHER THAN DOWNTOWN

Rail system and line	Outbound passengers as a percentage of total 2-way flow[a]	Percentage of inbound passengers dismounting before reaching downtown[b]
New York City		
Manhattan–Brooklyn	8	—
Bronx–Manhattan	11	—
Queens–Manhattan	7	—
East–Westside at 60th Street	12	—
Chicago		
Congress–Douglas Park–Milwaukee	21	13[b]
North leg of North–South line	40	—
South leg of North–South line	13	—
Cleveland		
Westside	—	4
Eastside	—	9
Both lines	14	6
Toronto		
Yonge Street	10	30
Philadelphia		
Entire system	23	—

[a]Data from transit authorities (letters to authors).
[b]Walter S. Rainville, Jr., *et al.*, "Preliminary Progress Report of Transit Subcommittee, Committee on Highway Capacity," *Highway Research Board Proceedings*, 40: 532–533 (1961).

relative costs of providing transport by one mode of travel or another, particularly for transit modes.

The relative costs of alternative systems can be computed and meaningfully compared on any time basis desired, whether it be four or twenty-four hours or a year, so long as all the volume and service characteristics for all systems are kept equal during the period of comparison. If volume and service conditions are controlled, relative costs will be little altered by the use of a twenty-four hour period for costing rather than only the four rush hours.

It is interesting to speculate, nonetheless, how the relative and absolute costs for each of the rush-hour, downtown-oriented travel systems analyzed would change if off-peak volumes and service characteristics were incorporated into the cost calculations. The answers involve evaluation of both supply and demand characteristics. During off-peak hours the *relative* demand pattern for downtown-oriented travel by different modes might be hypothesized to remain the same as that during the peak hours, providing that equivalent service and relative cost structures were retained for basic systems.[2] For reasons explained and documented in previous chapters, however, it is clear that the off-peak utilization of different modes is not equivalent, in large part because origination-destination and trip purpose patterns are different during off-peak hours and because the avoidance of discomfort, inconvenience, and other travel conditions seem to be more important to off-peak than peak travelers. (See Figures 1 through 5 and Table 30.) Off-peak travel is relatively less by transit modes than by private automobile. The specific rank ordering seems to be that long-distance rail commuting is most highly concentrated during the rush hours, rail rapid transit is second, and bus transit third, while automobile travel is the least rush-hour-oriented of all the major modes. Therefore, the net result of placing the cost analyses on a twenty-four-hour rather than a four-hour basis would certainly be to reduce the costs of automobile travel most and rail modes least.

Equally important in determining the relevant time period for a cost analysis is the matter of for whom are the system costs incurred, and therefore to whom should they be charged. If the basis of design and justification of downtown-oriented systems is the rush-hour flow, as it usually seems to be, then it can be argued that the full costs of providing the capacity needed for that service should be charged to rush-hour travelers. In particular, if the rush-hour downtown movement were not of high volume and highly peaked, it is doubtful whether the construction of expensive, high-capacity, and inflexible (in the sense of not serving all types of regional trips) rail or other specialized transit systems ever would be considered. Consequently, the costs of constructing facilities to meet highly peaked, downtown movements probably should be charged largely to rush-hour passengers. (This point is more fully elaborated in chapter 13.) Under these circumstances, the result is that little net effect will be made on rush-hour costs,[3] relative or absolute, by the inclusion of off-peak travel.

Different route lengths were specified for costing in order to provide data for different sizes of communities (in terms of geographical distribution and density) and to categorize in quantitative form any changes in the relative positions of alternative technological systems which might

[2] This is a very tricky assumption, of course, and one hard to validate without actually examining detailed cost structures. The additional transit expenditures—both capital and operating—should be small compared to the peak-hour costs, and the same would hold true for automobile travel. For automobiles, additional parking, ownership, and accident costs would be small because of joint use and cost sharing (that is, high turnover in parking garages, use of automobiles for vacation trips, and so forth); further economies would result because of higher car occupancy during off-peak hours.

[3] In this connection, it is vital to distinguish between cost and price.

TABLE 59

LINE-HAUL FACILITY ROUTE LENGTHS

Type of facility and location	Approximate route length (mi)
Rail transit lines	
Chicago, Congress St.	10.0
Chicago, Congress St.–Milwaukee	15.5
Cleveland, Westside	7.1
Cleveland, Eastside	7.8
Boston, Highland Branch	12.0
Philadelphia, Market–Frankford	13.0
South Jersey (proposed)	14.5
Washington, D.C. (proposed in 1962)	
N.W. Bethesda	9.2
Petworth–Columbia	3.6
Silver Spring–Rockville	19.8
Queens Chapel–Route 95	13.8
Anacostia–Henson Creek	11.0
Alexandria–Springfield	13.0
Rosslyn–Route 66	17.2
Express bus lines on mixed traffic expressways	
Washington, D.C. (proposed in 1962)	
GWMP (Maryland)	10.3
Route 95	6.0
Suitland Parkway	7.4
Henson Creek	2.3
Bolling	3.9
Shirley Highway	5.5
Dulles Airport	16.9
Highway routes (average distance to outer belt)	
Washington, D.C.	10.0
Baltimore	5.0+
Boston	10.0
St. Louis	15.0
Philadelphia	10.0

occur because different route lengths were required. Some data on route lengths for highway and transit line-haul facilities are shown in Table 59. Figures 29, 30, and 31 provide information on trip length useful in evaluating route lengths needed for urban transportation facilities. On the basis of these present-day data, it appears that the three route lengths employed in the present cost-analyses—6, 10, and 15 miles—include most relevant cases,[4] both present and future.

[4] It should be noted that attention generally was restricted to urban rapid transit technologies and does not include consideration of longer-length commuter railroad operations.

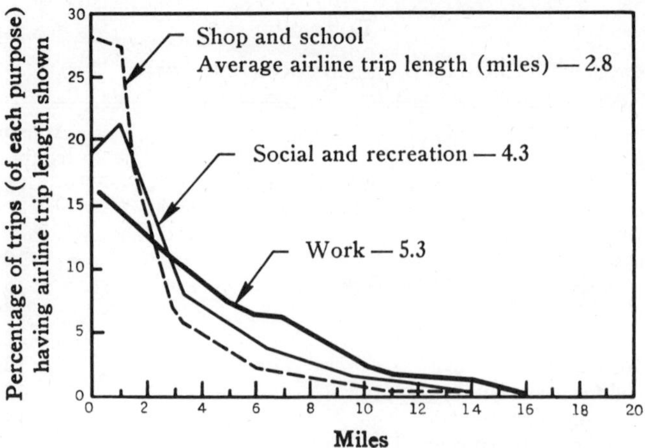

Figure 29. Trip length by purpose in Chicago, 1956. SOURCE: *Chicago Area Transportation Study, Final Report,* vol. 1, *Survey Findings,* Chicago, Illinois, December 1959, p. 38.

For the cost analyses, 1-mile station spacing (or ramp entrances and exits) was assumed for each of the route lengths. The older rapid transit systems in this country generally average about 1/2-mile station spacing, while most of the newer ones have considerably increased the spacing to permit travel speed increases. The new Congress Street rail transit line in Chicago, for example, has spacing of about 0.7 mile, the Cleveland rail transit system about 1.2 miles, and the proposed (in 1962) Washington, D.C., rail transit about 1.2 miles.

No very definite conclusions can be reached about "optimal" systems without varying this spacing and testing its impact on costs and market demands. The assumed 1-mile spacing is something of an arbitrary compromise among considerations of over-all travel speed, flexibility, and convenience.

Longer spacing offers higher over-all travel speeds, but reduces convenience by lengthening the average trip between home and line-haul station; shorter station spacing does the opposite. It is difficult to say precisely how different spacings would affect the market, and it is not at all clear that higher line-haul speeds do offer the great advantage (relative to the loss of convenience) so often assumed in specific transit plans.

Spacing of stops for residential feeder services is, of course, the same type of problem as station spacing. To be done intelligently, it must be decided how far people can be expected to walk. Data collected as part of the Chicago Area Transportation Study and other surveys in recent years strongly suggest that people actually using transit vehicles for work-trips are willing to walk an average of two or three blocks but not very much

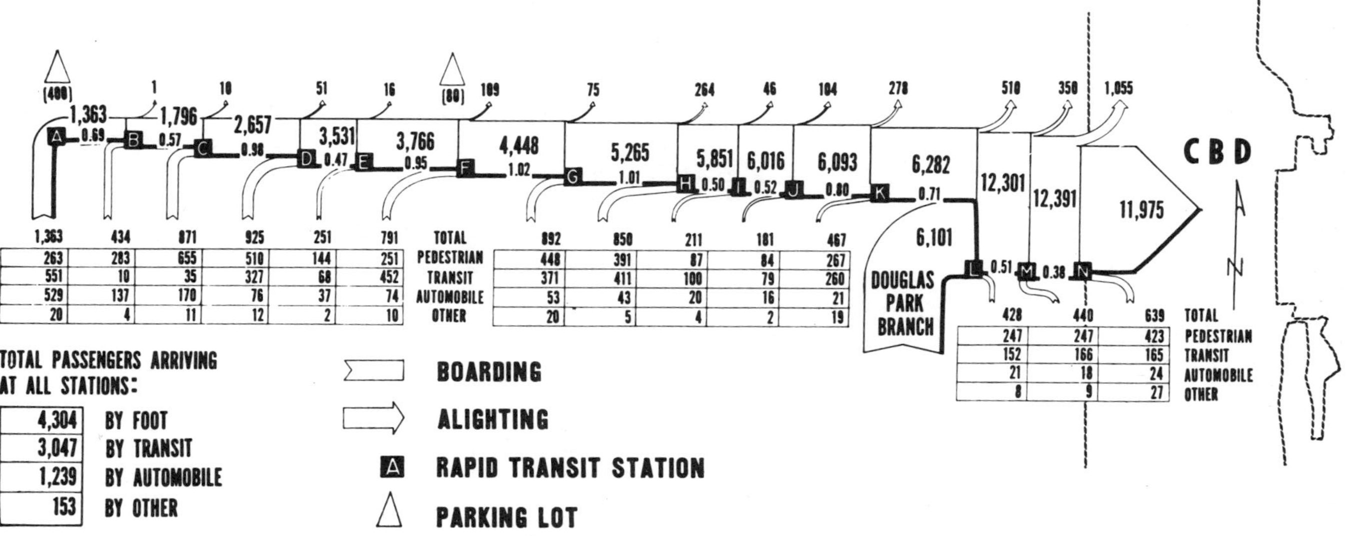

Figure 30. Inbound peak-hour passenger flow on Congress Street rail rapid transit line, Chicago; typical weekday (May 1959). SOURCE: W. S. Rainville, Jr., *et al.*, "Preliminary Progress Report of Transit Subcommittee, Comittee on Highway Capacity," *Highway Research Board Proceedings,* vol. 40, 1961, **p. 532.**

more.[5] Since the purpose of this study is to analyze the costs of different urban transportation modes under approximately equal service conditions, a two- or three-block maximum walking distance will be specified for the public transit vehicles in most of the subsequent cost analyses; the only important exceptions will be cases in which trip origination densities are so low that adherence to the two- or three-block radius would result in both exorbitant costs and an obvious deterioration of service as measured by travel times. (Deterioration can occur, for example, when there is a drop in the number of people who can be expected to board a bus at any one stop; normally, the result is an increase in the number of stops necessary to fill a bus for economical operations, and therefore also in the bus round trip travel time.)

The number of blocks that will be served by one specific transit stop can be expressed as

$$b = 2w^2, \tag{13}$$

where b is the number of blocks served by one stop and w is the maximum number of blocks people will walk. Strictly speaking, such a formulation will hold only for uniform densities (as already assumed) and a gridiron layout of residential streets (also assumed throughout subsequent analyses). Also, a uniform block spacing of 12 blocks to the (lineal) mile always will be assumed. From Eq. (13) it is apparent that if people have to walk no more than two blocks to reach a transit stop, one transit stop will serve the equivalent of eight full blocks. Under these assumptions it also follows that transit stops themselves must be spaced $2w$ apart in order to cover the area served.

As noted previously, travel time constraints can be expressed either directly as specific maximum times or as average travel speeds. Both constraints are combined in most of the analyses to follow. For example, in the line-haul analyses, the approximate objective will be that total travel times per vehicular round trip, t, be either less than ten minutes or at a level which does not permit the average speed for the entire distance traveled (over the line-haul facility) to fall below 35 mph, whichever is the greater. Thus, if an average speed of 35 mph indicates a total line-haul round trip travel time of less than ten minutes, the ten-minute constraint is used; if more than ten minutes, the 35-mph constraint is honored. The ten-minute constraint is generally binding on route lengths of 2 miles or less and the 35-mph constraint on all others. It should be noted that t pertains to the total time for a round trip for the transit modes; thus the total travel time incurred by individual transit travelers

[5] These averages were computed as part of the RAND study from data tapes supplied by these transportation studies. These same calculations indicated that people will walk farther to reach high-speed transit facilities.

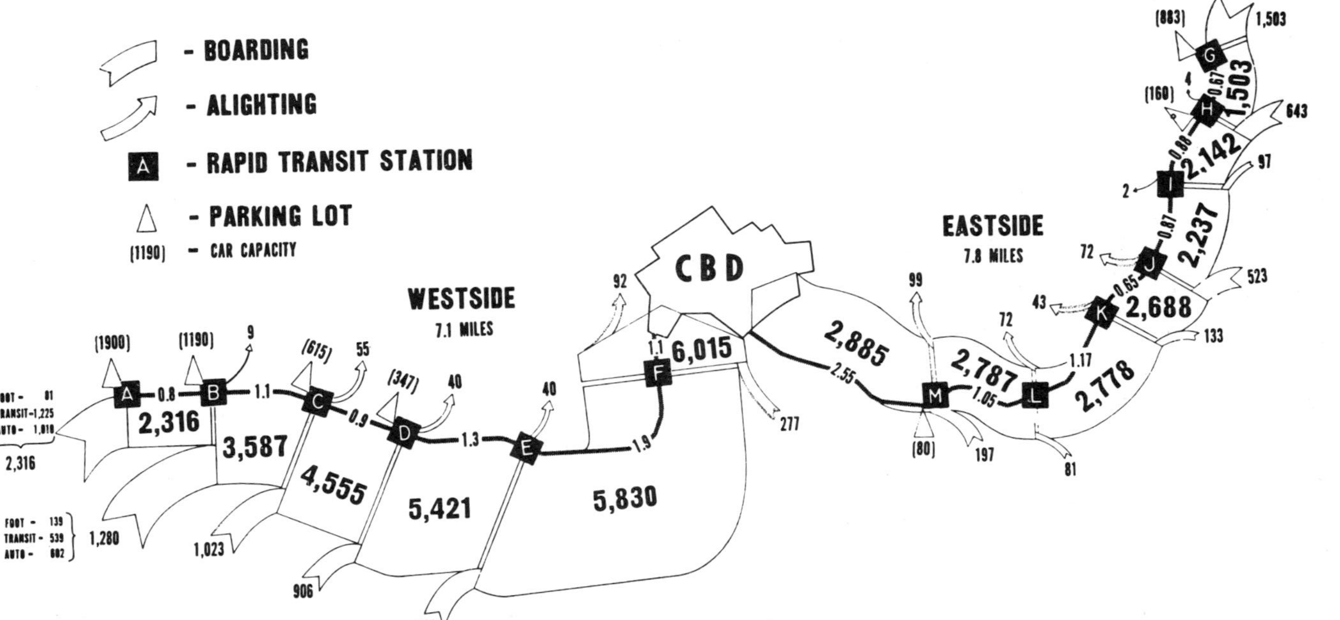

Figure 31. Inbound peak-hour passenger flow on Cleveland rail transit lines, typical weekday (January 1960). SOURCE: W. S. Rainville, Jr., *et al.*, "Preliminary Progress Report of Transit Subcommittee, Committee on Highway Capacity," *Highway Research Board Proceedings*, vol. 40, 1961, p. 533.

under a ten-minute constraint should rarely exceed five minutes. The resulting average travel time for all travelers will vary for the different route lengths, ranging from about seven minutes for 6-mile routes to about fourteen minutes for 15-mile routes.

A 35-mph over-all speed performance represents a considerable improvement over the usual transit speeds, even on high-performance rail line-haul systems or by private modes. (See Tables 35, 48, and 60.) At the same time, there is considerable evidence that urban travelers are willing to pay for better service (lower travel time) than they are now offered (see chapters 4 and 5). The choice of 35 mph, then, is an implicit reflection of the supposed market structure of the present and near future.

Selection of a particular travel time or speed constraint (together with the related station spacing) can be extremely critical in determining the relative economy of travel modes. For example, as required over-all speeds increase—particularly above 35 mph—private automobile travel enjoys a marginal cost advantage over transit; a reduced requirement would reverse these relative cost positions, primarily to the relative disadvantage of automobile travel, and secondarily to that of bus transit travel. In any realistic situation, of course, several speed levels should be chosen for design and costed in detail for determination of the most nearly "optimal."

The last two service variables considered in the system cost analyses —schedule frequency and seating space (or vehicle seating capacity)— are also important in determining the relative economy of the different

TABLE 60

AVERAGE SPEEDS ON EXISTING AND PROPOSED RAIL RAPID TRANSIT SYSTEMS

System and city	Approximate average over-all speed (mph)
Existing systems[a]	
Toronto	16.0
New York City	18.0
Philadelphia	21.0
Chicago	22.0
Cleveland	28.9
Proposed systems	
Washington, D.C.	36.0

[a]A. S. Lang and R. M. Soberman, *Urban Rail Transit*, MIT Press, Cambridge, Massachusetts, 1964, Table 6.2.

modes. Of the two, schedule frequency is probably the most difficult to specify with any degree of reliability. The basic problem is to set a minimum frequency of service for all the modes costed; that is, each mode must provide service at each line-haul station (or feeder bus stop) at certain specified intervals so as to retain service comparability between modes. If one mode offered service every five minutes and another every thirty minutes, with all other service variables for the two modes held constant, it is clear that the two systems would not be comparable and no direct conclusions could be reached regarding relative costs, unless travelers were assumed to place no value on additional service frequency.

Obviously, the automobile offers the utmost in schedule frequency and flexibility, particularly when there is no car-pooling. The minimum schedule frequencies for the transit modes were chosen so that the differential between automobile and transit service did not appear so large as seriously to affect modal choice. No reliable information is available that can be used for establishing this frequency criterion; thus it was necessary to rely largely and rather arbitrarily on judgment. In the costing, two types of schedule frequency standards normally were used: a maximum vehicle or train interval (headway) of two minutes at each line-haul station; and a maximum vehicle interval of ten minutes at each feeder bus stop (for the residential collection system service). Since it is difficult to justify these choices other than in a general and intuitive fashion, the next three chapters incorporate sensitivity analyses of the effects of changing schedule frequency.

Setting controls on seating space and "comfort" requirements for the various travel modes is difficult but not impossible. At present, rail transit operators allocate less vehicle floor space to seated passengers than do bus operators. Of course, differentials for present-day operations are partly a result of the two modes providing different types of service and having different trip length, loading factor, and speed characteristics. If the rail and bus transit modes were to perform identical functions and handle the same volumes at equivalent levels of service, there would be no obvious justification for permitting a higher percentage of standees on one mode than another. In short, both modes should furnish the same amount of floor space per passenger in a comparison of their performances in a specified service. In the present analyses, the more generous bus seating standards were used in computing rail transit car seating capacities.

In recognition of what consumer preference patterns apparently are today and what they even more likely will be over the life of any new transportation investments, system capacities were designed at levels that would provide a seat for every passenger. Many will argue that "no one operates a transit system this way." This argument is generally correct, except for suburban rail commuter lines, but it is regrettable that such an alternative is entirely excluded from analysis, since the public at least conceivably might be willing to pay for better service, particularly in view of rising real incomes.[6]

An interesting paradox has developed regarding the design standards transit operators ordinarily use in setting the percentage of standees in bus and rail transit operations. Transit experts often assert that passenger accommodation at peak hours and maximum load points should be based on 200 per cent of seating capacity for rail vehicles and 150 per cent for buses. However, the limited data available on trip length characteristics reveal that rail transit travelers apparently make considerably longer trips than do bus transit riders; thus, not only do more rail transit riders have to stand, but they have to stand for greater distances as well. Of course, they often travel at higher speeds than bus riders, so a correction should be made by comparing the mean time in transit for the two modes. Generally, though, both mean trip length and transit time are shorter by bus than by rail transit. It therefore might seem reasonable to reverse the usual loading standards for bus and rail. In any case, there is no reason to believe that rail and bus transit systems being proposed and designed for the next twenty years or more cannot or should not be designed on a no-standee basis, merely because no system is now operated in that fashion and because travelers today will tolerate standing during peak hours.

It is no mean task, of course, to try to place the seating space and "comfort" requirements of automobile and transit modes on an equivalent or comparable basis, since the two have rather inherent differences in comfort, convenience, and privacy. Automobile drivers have more comfortable seats, can smoke and listen to the radio, and can choose to ride alone or with others. On the other hand, transit travelers (and automobile riders as distinguished from drivers) are free of the driving task and can read. Given this wide set of variables to balance, the problem again was resolved somewhat arbitrarily by using a passenger car "seating capacity" or occupancy of 1.6 passengers per vehicle for automobile systems, and 1.1 per automobile for park-and-ride residential analyses.[7]

Another difficult factor that had to be considered in specifying car occupancy was the inconvenience and time delay involved in picking up riders, probably not at all negligible to either driver or rider. For exam-

[6] Apropos to these possibilities, in the recently proposed Washington, D.C. rail transit system design the requirements were based on the assumption that approximately 50 per cent of the peak-hour travelers would be willing to stand during the design year, 1980.

[7] Caution must be exercised when comparing these figures with recorded data in the literature. Virtually all car occupancy data are recorded by purpose of trip rather than by period of travel. Since these analyses are concerned with rush-hour travel over a two-hour period, it would be incorrect to compare with car occupancy for work-trips alone.

ple, if there was a delay of five minutes in picking up each rider, the average automobile driver would be delayed three minutes with a car occupancy of 1.6 (driver plus an average of 0.6 riders), and both driver and rider would be inconvenienced by adjusting to each other's schedules. On a pure time scale, this pick-up delay would equal the average delay in waiting for feeder buses with a headway of six minutes. From the standpoint of comfort, however, the automobile delay may well be considered superior by car-pool riders since they are protected in most cases from the weather while they wait.

Concluding Remarks

Many will characterize the systems that have been designed, the service conditions imposed, and the volume characteristics assumed for analytical purposes in this study as unrealistic, particularly when compared to rapid transit and passenger automobile systems as they are *presently* designed, built, and operated. It will be argued that "no one operates a system that way," or that we must provide this or that service that is not included. It must be granted that there is some truth in such arguments; however, to argue that certain kinds or levels of transport service must be provided, or to argue that we cannot operate a system in one fashion or another without also considering and evaluating alternatives, with different costs and market structures, is to wish away the problem of rationalizing urban transportation. For too long it has been arbitrarily concluded that certain urban transportation services must be provided or not provided.

The essential problem is one of determining when, if ever, it is profitable—in economic, social, or political terms—to provide certain urban transportation services or to improve upon them and to pay the associated costs. An obvious first step in meeting this problem is to determine the costs of providing various services at different volume levels, for different route lengths, and under specified conditions of speed, frequency, convenience, and comfort. At least the initial phase in this decision process is dealt with in the cost analyses presented in the next few chapters.

Chapter 9 | Line-Haul Systems

A central feature of all urban transportation systems must, of course, be some means of transporting people along the "line haul" from residential areas to workplaces, particularly in the CBD. Important as it is, however, this feature often can command undue attention in popular discussions and professional analyses as well, with the line-haul operation depicted as virtually the entirety of the urban transportation problem. As the following chapters will show, this is an oversimplification and overlooks the cost and service aspects of both residential collection and downtown distribution. These other functions may be just as important as, if not more important than, the line-haul component in determining traveler choices and the relative efficiency of different transport modes.

While such other components as feeder buses and automobiles must usually be combined with a transit line-haul system in order to provide a complete urban transportation service and cost evaluation, it is meaningful to examine line-haul operations separately. For the present, it is specifically assumed that regardless of the mode of the line-haul system it is served in the residential and downtown areas by common collection and distribution systems whose costs do not affect the cost of the basic line-haul systems.

This chapter presents cost analyses for three current line-haul modes: private automobile, bus transit, and rail transit. The route lengths analyzed are 6, 10, and 15 miles, with hourly passenger volumes at the maximum load point varying between 5000 and 50,000. High and medium population densities along the route length have also been considered because facility construction and right-of-way costs vary with such densities. The chosen ranges of route length, volume, and population density encompass most circumstances relevant to American cities.

Basic System Characteristics

The specific service, volume, and operating characteristics hypothesized for these cost analyses are: (1) Passenger volumes are distributed uniformly along route lengths; doing so simplifies the cost analyses and does little harm to the generality of the findings and analytic techniques employed. (2) Cost comparisons are made both with and without along-the-line and reverse or minor direction service being incorporated into the systems. This permits a determination of the costs of providing such services and sheds light on how the provision of these services can modify the quality of the service as measured in other dimensions; for example, the provision of along-the-line service almost invariably reduces the quality of the service rendered to through travelers moving from a line-haul station directly to the CBD. (3) At all line-haul stations, at least one bus or train must run every two minutes. (4) Equal seating space standards are used for rail and bus transit and a seat is provided for every passenger carried, using bus standards of spacing. An automobile always is assumed to have an average capacity or use of 1.6 passengers. (5) Line-haul stations are located at 1-mile intervals, with the first station 1 mile from the downtown stub terminal.

In addition, each mode has its own important characteristics. In the rail transit design, for example, additional trackage is sometimes provided in the direction of maximum passenger flow, but only as much as is necessary because of large volumes or as can be justified because of the operating economies thereby effectuated. Only a single track is used in the direction of light volume flows—outbound from the CBD in the morning and inbound in the afternoon—even when two tracks are required for major direction flows. When trains are empty or nearly empty, either they may be coupled into longer trains than would be permissible when every coach must be occupied, or every station stop must be made; or headways can be reduced safely if station-stop delays are eliminated or trains are "traveling light." In short, the rail transit operation has been closely tailored to provide only the track capacity that efficiency demands.

The line-haul bus systems evaluated are operated either over grade separated highways reserved exclusively for buses, or over mixed-traffic expressways with input control devices to prevent congestion, so that maximum speeds and efficiency can be attained. The closest actual bus operation of this type would be so-called freeway fliers, express buses operating on freeways or other high-performance facilities; ordinarily, however, buses using such facilities are hampered by congestion and other obstacles since the lack of input control permits backward-bending capacity and delay situations. The idealized congestion-free conditions were assumed attainable (with the use of input control devices) in an effort to place rail and bus transit systems on roughly equivalent grounds; if, in practice, flow were not controlled, it is likely that congestion would result and would negate the cost analysis and comparability of this freeway flier design with rail transit.

The assumed 2-minute schedule frequency restriction does not materially affect rail transit operations and costs, but it strongly affects bus operations and costs at low-volume levels, specifically at levels of 5000 and 10,000 passengers an hour at the maximum load point. Extra buses must be operated at such volume levels merely to meet the 2-minute headway restriction. Accordingly, alternative operating schemes are considered for the bus in which transfers and multiple stops are permitted, thereby affording significant economies in certain low volume cases (though, at the sacrifice of service to through travelers).

An underground downtown stub terminal is also included for the bus systems analyzed. This has been designed to provide sufficient capacity to dissipate and minimize both deceleration and acceleration requirements and loading and unloading delays that are common around large bus terminals. To this end, roadways are widened in the CBD terminals in much the same way as toll roadways are widened at toll booth plazas. A more complete description of this terminal design is included in appendix B and is illustrated in Figure 61.

Two other features of some importance related to bus terminal design and operation are employed: fares are collected (whenever it is more economical) in the terminal mezzanine much as they now are on rail transit systems, and a third door is added to each bus and double-side loading and unloading is permitted. These changes greatly reduce loading and unloading times, reduce the terminal area lengths required, increase utilization rates for bus equipment and labor, and thereby reduce both capital and labor costs. These changes, it should again be noted, amount to adapting some principles of rail transit and high-capacity toll facility operations to buses; when coupled with the improvements permitted by operation over grade separated and exclusive use highways, it should be evident that the passenger can be offered high-speed and high-quality bus transit service many times superior to the poor, local street bus service so common today.

No real innovations are assumed for the automobile system analyzed, but the car occupancy and parking requirements assumed are powerful determinants of final system costs. The occupancy rate is particularly important because of its service implications and the effect on system costs. Virtually proportional reductions in automobile travel costs could be achieved by increasing the occupancy rate.

Parking charges or costs are the single most important cost item entering into the automobile cost estimates; in fact, they can occasionally account for some 40 per cent or more of total passenger car system costs. Actually, it is in a sense unfair to include parking charges in line-haul cost comparisons between automobile and transit systems. In most cases, parking charges incorporate some of the costs that would be associated with downtown collection and distribution operations, and such costs have not been included in the public transit system line-haul analyses. On the other hand, it would be misleading to ignore automobile parking charges completely since downtown storage of the automobile during the workday is obviously an integral part of using it for the line haul. (In this connection, it should be noted that partially offsetting charges for underground stub terminals and for storage yards and shops are included in the transit cost estimates.)

An important set of cost estimates for the line-haul analyses is that associated with acquiring rights-of-way and constructing highways and railways. These costs are basic to the cost estimates for all three modes and in many specific essentials are very similar, particularly the important relationship between the level of these costs and urban density. The next section, therefore, makes a rather detailed presentation of the sources and means by which these construction and right-of-way estimates were developed. Following that, operating and other cost characteristics of the three different modes are reported. A separate treatment is then presented, for each mode, of the underlying functional characteristics that define each system. Finally, in a concluding section, the cost estimates for the different modes are compared and evaluated.

It should be noted that the presentation of equations in this chapter departs somewhat from that employed in other chapters. The equations have been numbered and lettered as if they belonged to three separate systems, one pertaining to rail, one to bus, and one to auto. (The only exceptions are a few equations applicable to all systems, which have been numbered sequentially in the usual fashion.) Each equation is designated by an alphabetic characterization of the mode: A for automobile, B for bus, and R for rail transit. Furthermore, a C is inserted in the alphabetic-numeric designators of cost functions or equations in order to differentiate between cost functions and those pertaining to definitions of operating characteristics; for example, the first rail cost equation has been designated (RC-1), and the first functional equation for rail is (R-1). The set of equations for each mode is numbered sequentially in the complete summaries of rail and bus transit systems presented in appendixes A and B, and the equation-numbering scheme used there has also been employed in this chapter to facilitate cross-referencing. There is no separate appendix for the automobile system as its basic characteristics are so simple that a separate appendix did not seem necessary.

COST PARAMETERS: ROADWAY, RIGHT-OF-WAY, AND TERMINALS

Estimation of roadway and structures costs for the line-haul cost models is a most uncertain exercise. These costs hinge largely on traits peculiar to each area—on topography, for example, and, more importantly, on the kind and intensity of urban development. Despite the importance and variability of these capital costs, little systematic analysis of their characteristics has been conducted. For urban rail systems, there is little cost experience in recent years on which to base cost estimates—and even less systematic analysis of how these costs might vary under different circumstances. The only recourse is to rely on engineering estimates of unknown quality and on the few instances of actual postwar construction. In the cost analyses that follow, therefore, the emphasis is on synthesizing the available information on right-of-way and construction costs, so as to indicate the approximate range of costs in various urban situations and to specify where further analysis and data are most needed. The estimates for the alternative systems also have been constructed as far as possible as indexes of one another so that errors in estimating the level of costs will penalize or benefit competing systems more or less equally.

Roadway Construction

Highway construction costs appear to be a nonlinear function of the number of lanes constructed, with the costs of additional lanes increasing less than proportionally with the addition of lanes. These costs normally also have an important relationship to the intensity of urban development, rising as intensity increases because of demands for more frequent and more elaborate bridges, underpasses, overpasses, utility relocations, and the like. For line-haul bus analyses, however, urban density should not be as influential because of the simplicity of line-haul stations, relative to the more elaborate interchanges for general traffic access.

The estimates of highway construction and of both highway and rail right-of-way costs used in this study are based primarily on a predictive formula obtained for the Chicago area by Hyman Joseph. Joseph fitted least squares regressions to data on construction costs of the Congress Street, Edens, and Calumet-Kingery Expressways as a function of net residential density (NRD), defined in thousands of persons per square mile of residential land,[1] the latter being accepted as a fairly good proxy for the over-all intensity of urban development. Joseph obtained the following regression:

(1) $$Y = \$999{,}000 + \$70{,}800X,$$

[1] Hyman Joseph, "Construction Costs of Urban Expressways," *CATS Research News,* vol. 4, no. 1, December 19, 1960. See also P. W. Aitkin, "Cost of Constructing Transportation Facilities in the Chicago Standard Metropolitan Area," *CATS Research News,* 1:8–12 (August 2, 1957) The NRD figures for Chicago were computed on the basis of the "districts" within which the facility was located. The Chicago study area consists of 44 districts covering 1237 square miles of land area. The average district had 28 square miles of land and about 4 square miles of residential land.

where Y is the construction cost per mile for a standardized eight-lane facility in dollars, and X is the net residential density in thousands of persons per square mile. In adjusting the costs of facilities of other than the standardized eight lanes, Joseph assumed that bridge costs were the same regardless of the number of lanes and that other construction costs are proportional to the number of lanes. Because Joseph's data mainly pertained to 4- and 6-lane facilities, finer adjustment for these effects probably would increase costs estimated for 8-lane highways.

More importantly, the Joseph model fails to take into account differences in ramp and interchange spacing at different distances from the CBD; large cost increases normally result from closer spacing. Furthermore, since both the interchange design and spacing stem directly from residential density, use of the model in this form implies a reduction in ramp spacing with an increase in residential density; obviously this is undesirable for present purposes since the ramp spacing was set at 1 mile for all cases. The result should be some tendency to overestimate construction costs for bus systems and to underestimate these costs for automobile systems.

It would be preferable to have an estimating function based on a wider range of experience and encompassing a larger number of urban situations than that of Chicago alone. More particularly, it would be desirable to have a function that better accounted for the independent effects of the intensity of urban development, the ramp and interchange spacing, block length, and the number of lanes. The Joseph function tends to intermix all these effects, with the final results being cost estimates that are probably reasonably, *though somewhat fortuitously,* accurate.

Certain construction costs would be expected to be invariant to width, some variable with width, and some directly variable with the number of lanes. Figure 32 and Table 61 illustrate the general relationship between the right-of-way width for *depressed* highway and rail facilities and the number of lanes or tracks that were used in the present analysis. The crucial fact illustrated by Figure 32 and Table 61 is that the width of both *depressed* rail and highway facilities is clearly not proportional to the number of lanes or tracks. A somewhat similar relationship would prevail between facility width and number of lanes for earth-fill or embankment structures, though for viaduct structures the relationship would be much more directly proportional.

Construction costs for facilities with various numbers of lanes can be estimated by assuming that all but base and paving costs are proportional to width, and that base and paving costs are proportional to the number of lanes. The costs of constructing expressways with varying numbers of lanes thus can be derived from Eq. (1) by substracting the costs of providing base and paving for eight lanes at $86,000 per lane-mile and

Bus transit or auto

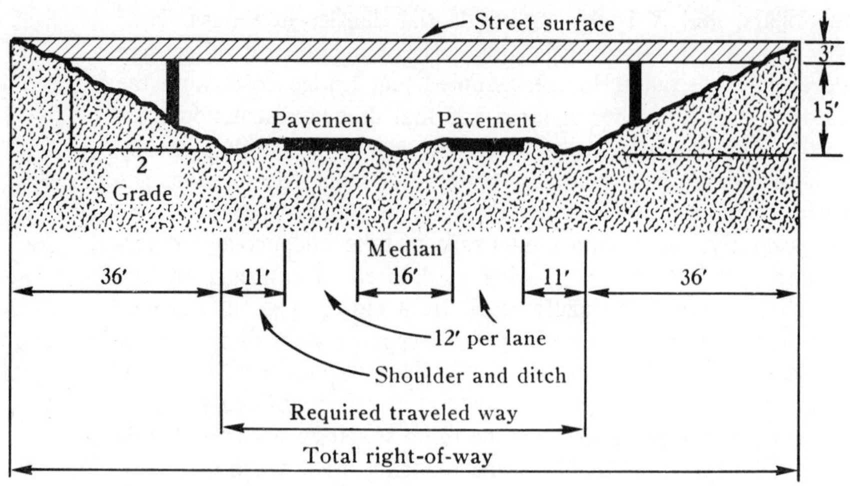

Rail transit (2-track)

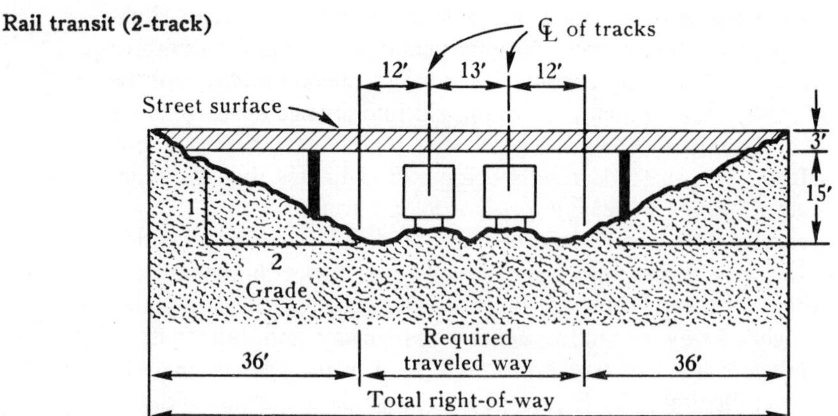

NOTE: Not to scale.

Figure 32. Widths of depressed rail and highway facilities.

TABLE 61

RIGHT-OF-WAY REQUIREMENTS FOR DIFFERENT URBAN TRANSPORTATION FACILITIES

Facility	Between stations or ramps			Extra ROW required for stations or ramps[a] (ft)	Average total ROW required	
	Width of traveled way required (ft)	Total ROW between stations				
		Width (ft)	W_c		Width (ft)	W_{row}
2-track rail transit	37	109		7	116	0.386
3-track rail transit	50	122		9	131	0.436
2-lane highway	62	134	0.65	126	260	0.860
4-lane highway	86	158	0.77	122	280	0.933
6-lane highway	110	182	0.88	108	290	0.966
8-lane highway	134	206	1.00	94	300	1.000

[a]The additional ROW required for stations or ramps (and yards and shops) has been distributed along the entire distance between stations or ramps for the purpose of computing ROW costs; it was further assumed, for simplicity, that all rail transit stations are 500 feet long.

making these costs dependent on the number of lanes.[2] Construction costs of a mixed-traffic expressway facility (that is, one for joint use by cars, buses, and trucks) are thereby:

$$(2) \qquad Y_k = W_c(\$311{,}000 + \$70{,}800X) + \$86{,}000k,$$

where Y_k is the construction cost in dollars per mile for k lanes, X is net residential density (NRD) in thousands of persons per square mile, and W_c is as given in Table 61 and is an index of the width of different facilities as a ratio of the width of an 8-lane facility. (It should be noted that the NRD should be computed for land areas of somewhat similar size to those used for developing Eq. (1) as noted in footnote 1.)

Equation (2), converted to a yearly cost basis with a 6 per cent interest rate and a composite life of 35 years, becomes

$$(3) \qquad y_k = W_c(\$21{,}451 + \$4883X) + \$5931k,$$

where y denotes annual costs per mile for construction.

Several independent checks were made of the consistency of the highway construction cost model in Eq. (2). One of these is reported in Table 62 which presents construction costs per mile and the net residential density implied by Eq. (2) for a sample of roadway segments assembled by the Bureau of Public Roads and pertaining to over 340 miles of urban interstate highway in several large cities. Although this is obviously not an exact test, the implied residential densities appear reasonable in a comparison of facilities of various widths and of urban areas of various sizes. (See Figure 33 for some relevant actual densities for Chicago, Detroit, and Pittsburgh.) In general, the imputed data support the functional relationship between the number of lanes and net residential density. Also, it would appear that when residential densities are controlled, less than proportional increases in construction cost can be anticipated with increases in the number of lanes. However, it may be that the cost estimates provided by the model are somewhat low; any realistic upward revision of these figures, however, would have very little effect on the relative cost relationships reported subsequently.

Highway cost allocation studies provide a basis for estimating the costs of constructing facilities for various weight classes of traffic.[3] These

[2] The base and paving costs of \$86,000 per lane-mile is an average cost for 6-lane suburban and urban limited-access highways developed by the Penn-Jersey Transportation Study. See James E. Watt, Jr., and Marshall F. Reed, Jr., *Preliminary Cost Estimate of Construction and Right of Way for Rail and Highway Facilities in Alternative Regional Transportation Plans,* Penn-Jersey Transportation Study Paper no. 19 (mimeographed).

[3] The increments of total mixed-traffic highway construction cost occasioned by vehicle type as a percentage of total highway construction cost items for 6- or 8-lane highways are estimated to be: grading for bus, 100 per cent, and for passenger car, 96.6 per cent; bases and surface for bus, 97.8 per cent, and for

Table 62

Construction Costs for 4-, 6-, and 8-Lane Highways, and Implied Residential Density, for Selected Segments of the Interstate System Within Urban Areas

Highway width and city	(1) Cost per mile ($ million) Average	High	Low	(2) Implied net residential density[a] (thousand/sq mi) Average	High	Low	Miles of facility
4-lane							
Philadelphia	3.4	8.3	1.8	52.0	142.6	22.5	9.5
Youngstown	2.4	—	—	33.6	—	—	9.2
Norfolk	2.4	—	—	33.6	—	—	4.4
Louisville	1.7	2.3	1.5	20.6	31.7	17.0	9.4
Savannah	1.7	—	—	20.6	—	—	5.1
Montgomery	1.5	—	—	17.0	—	—	8.2
Tucson	1.1	1.4	0.8	10.0	15.1	4.0	12.8
Pueblo	1.0	—	—	7.7	—	—	5.8
Butte	0.9	—	—	6.0	—	—	5.3
Winston–Salem	0.8	—	—	4.0	—	—	6.1
6-lane							
Louisville	9.4	10.5	8.3	138.2	155.8	120.5	4.9
Philadelphia	5.6	15.9	1.8	77.2	242.5	16.2	17.3
Milwaukee	4.9	7.1	0.7	66.0	101.3	—	12.2
Cleveland	4.2	8.5	3.0	54.7	123.8	35.5	22.0
Mobile	3.7	—	—	46.7	—	—	7.0
Minneapolis–St. Paul	3.2	9.0	2.3	38.7	131.8	24.2	4.0
Richmond	3.0	—	—	35.5	—	—	2.9
Tulsa	3.0	—	—	35.5	—	—	11.0
Norfolk	2.7	2.7	2.6	30.6	30.6	29.0	8.4
Memphis	2.4	—	—	25.8	—	—	9.6
San Diego	2.3	2.7	1.9	24.2	30.6	17.8	12.1
Albuquerque	2.3	3.4	1.3	24.2	41.9	—	7.9
St. Louis	2.0	—	—	33.5	—	—	10.5
Salt Lake City	1.8	2.0	1.6	16.2	33.5	13.0	12.0
8-lane							
Baltimore	11.7	14.0	9.1	151.0	183.6	114.4	16.4
Philadelphia	9.1	11.9	7.6	114.4	154.0	93.2	15.1
Cleveland	5.8	8.9	3.0	67.8	111.6	28.2	15.8
Cambridge–Boston	5.7	12.4	2.4	66.4	161.0	19.8	33.6
Seattle	5.2	7.4	3.2	59.3	90.4	31.1	7.4
San Diego	4.1	4.7	1.3	43.8	52.2	4.2	9.1
St. Louis	3.3	4.7	2.4	46.6	52.2	19.8	14.9
Houston	3.1	3.8	2.8	29.7	39.5	25.4	14.0

[a]Computed using Eq. (2) and data from column (1).

studies suggest that the construction costs related to number of lanes, or base and pavement costs, for a 6- or 8-lane, all-passenger-car highway are only about 61.5 per cent of those for a mixed-traffic highway. The equivalent figure for an all-bus highway is about 97.8 per cent. The remaining costs (for grading and structure), assumed here to be related to width, are approximately 80.9 per cent of the mixed-traffic highway grading and structure costs for auto, and 92.6 per cent for bus. Application of these percentages to Eq. (3) yields the following estimates of the yearly costs of constructing *exclusive* automobile and bus highways (per mile) as a function of net residential density and number of lanes:

$$\text{(AC–1)} \qquad SA_{c_i} = W_{c_i}(\$17{,}354 + \$3950X_i) + \$3648k_i;$$

$$\text{(BC–6)} \qquad SB_{c_i} = W_{c_i}(\$19{,}864 + \$4522X_i) + \$5800k_i,$$

where SA_{c_i} is the yearly construction cost of the ith mile of an exclusive automobile highway and SB_{c_i} of the ith mile of an exclusive all-bus highway; in both cases the formulas apply at net residential density X_i (in thousands) and with k_i lanes. Another highway system of interest is one on which express buses use a controlled limited-access freeway facility serving mixed traffic. The yearly cost for construction of a bus on a mixed-traffic expressway system (using an 8-lane facility) with a full capacity usage assumed to be 480 buses per lane[4] or 1675 passenger cars

---

passenger car, 61.5 per cent; and structures for bus, 89.5 per cent, and for automobile, 74.4 per cent. These construction cost items are assumed to constitute the following percentages of total construction cost of a 6- or 8-lane facility: grading, 23.7 per cent; bases, 20.9 per cent; structures 55.4 per cent. Deduced from: U.S. Department of Commerce, Bureau of Public Roads, *Highway Cost Allocation Study, Supplement to Part IV-B: A Preliminary Allocation of Cost Responsibility by the Incremental Method,* U.S. Government Printing Office, Washington, D.C., March 1961, and U.S. Department of Commerce, Bureau of Public Roads, *Highway Statistics—1960,* U.S. Government Printing Office, Washington, D.C., 1962.

[4] The lane capacity of a highway reserved exclusively for buses is not well established. Research by the Port of New York Authority indicates that a through or non stop express bus lane could handle up to 720 buses an hour (per lane) at running speeds of 40 to 60 mph. (See Nathan Cherniack, "Transportation—A New Dimension of Traffic Engineering," *1963 Proceedings,* Institute of Traffic Engineers, Washington, D.C., p. 44). This figure is substantiated by data recorded in New York City by the Port of New York Authority. "For example, in the Port Authority Bus Terminal in Manhattan, more than 450 buses arrive regularly on weekdays between 8 and 9 a.m. and bring into the terminal, at an average of about 45 passengers per bus, about 20,000 to 25,000 bus passengers in that rush hour. *The 450 buses or so utilize only a portion of a lane in the Lincoln Tunnel* [emphasis added] with which the Bus Terminal is connected by ramps. More buses could without difficulty be accommodated in one lane, if it were allocated exclusively (or even preferentially) for buses in any one rush hour." (See Nathan Cherniak, "Passenger Data for Urban Transportation Planning," *Journal of the Highway Division,* American Society of Civil Engineers,

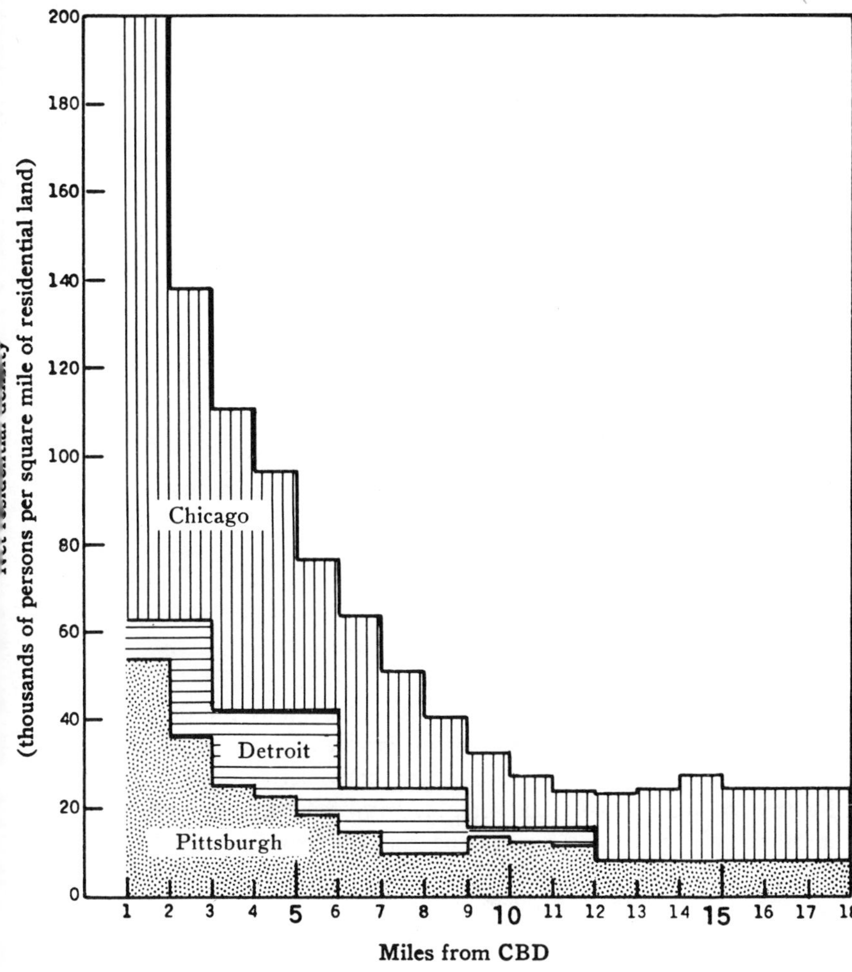

Figure 33. Net residential density, by distance from the CBD. SOURCE: Chicago—*Chicago Area Transportation Study, Final Report,* vol. 2, *Data Projections,* July 1960, Table 29, p. 112; Detroit—computed from Detroit Metropolitan Area Traffic Study, *Report on the Detroit Area Traffic Study,* part 1, *Data Summary and Interpretation,* Lansing, Michigan, Table 8, p. 30, and Table 36, p. 123; Pittsburgh—*Pittsburgh Area Transportation Study, Final Report,* vol. 2, *Forecasts and Plans,* Pittsburgh, February 1963.

per lane, or a combination thereof, can be approximated by:

$$\text{(BC–10)} \qquad SBE_{c_i} = \$35.90\left(R + R_i - \sum_{x=1}^{i} R_x\right) + \$2.54X_i\left(R + R_i - \sum_{x=1}^{i} R_x\right).$$

SBE_{c_i} again is the yearly construction cost for the *i*th mile of limited-access highway, R_i or R_x is the hourly number of bus round trips entering (or departing) at the *i*th or *x*th line-haul station, and X_i is the corresponding net residential density in thousands of persons per square mile. It should be noted that this equation implies full use of the highway for the four peak hours. Since these costs are on a per-highway-mile basis, they must, of course, be aggregated over an entire system to obtain total cost estimates.

In this chapter, line-haul systems are costed for two sets of urban densities, one high and one medium. Figure 33 illustrates the net residential densities in thousands of persons per square mile of net residential land in Chicago, Detroit, and Pittsburgh by distance from the CBD. The Chicago gradient was used in the cost calculations for the high-density system, and Pittsburgh's gradient for the medium-density system.

Like the estimates for urban highway construction costs, cost estimates for the construction of grade separated rail facilities are somewhat crude approximations. In addition to the roadbed construction and structure costs similar to those for highways, rail rapid transit systems require capital expenditures for electrification, amounting to \$250,000 to \$350,000 per single track-mile in existing plans, and for signals and train control facilities ranging from as low as \$50,000 per single track-mile for con-

---

December 1959, page 50). More recent studies of the capacity of an exclusive bus lane reported by Bureau of Public Roads and General Motors researchers emphasize how conservative a bus lane capacity of 480 would be; the BPR study indicated (possible) bus lane capacity to be 1300 to 1450 buses per hour at speeds ranging between 25 and 35 mph, not unlike the General Motors research. In fact, Rothery and others report, "The results of these [Detroit] measurements demonstrated that flow levels comparable to those obtained on the [GM Proving Grounds] test track can be realized on an expressway. For example, on I-96, a four-lane divided highway, a flow level of 1400 buses/hour at a speed of 45 miles/hour was measured. Even at the relatively high bus speed of 55 miles/hour, flow rates of 1100 buses/hour were realized." (See R. Rothery, *et al.*, "Analysis of Experiments on Single-Lane Bus Flow," *Operations Research*, Nov.–Dec. 1964, page 932; also, see E. Hodgkins, "Effect of Buses on Freeway Capacity," *Highway Research Record* No. 59, Washington, D.C., pp. 66ff.) Finally, it is important to note that the *actual* hourly bus volumes per lane for this costing analysis seldom approach our assumed design capacity figure of 480, thus rendering the costing results even more conservative.

ventional signals to $175,000 or more for automatic train operation.[5] In addition, per-mile trackage costs must be taken into account. One approach to obtaining comparative costs would be to use the highway construction cost model with a narrower right-of-way, with an incremental cost for electrification and train control, and with corrections for the difference between roadbed trackage and roadway pavement costs. Instead, however, the present analyses use estimates of average rail transit construction costs for open cut (or fill), elevated, or subway construction, as given in Table 63; for the line-haul analyses, it is assumed that elevated construction would be necessary at net residential densities above 40,000 persons per square mile, and that open cut (or fill) construction would be suitable at lower densities. With a 6 per cent interest rate and a 50-year life (rather than the 35-year life used for highway construction), a yearly capital cost for construction of $251,000 a mile is obtained for 2-track rail systems at densities of over 40,000 per square mile and $209,000 at lower densities. The annual capital costs for 3-track systems were taken to be $380,000 per mile (50 per cent more than the high-density 2-track system, plus an allowance for extra switches, crossovers, and signaling).

TABLE 63

RAIL CONSTRUCTION COSTS PER MILE

Type of construction	(1) Without right-of-way and without allowances for engineering and contingencies[a]		(2) Without right-of-way but with allowances for engineering and contingencies[b]	
	Double track	Single track	Double track	Single track
Tunnel	$15,300,000		$19,125,000	
Cut and cover	14,000,000		17,500,000	
Elevated	3,168,000	$1,584,000	3,960,000	$1,980,000
Open cut (or fill)	2,640,000	1,320,000	3,300,000	1,650,000

[a]These unit costs are based primarily on data from *Mass Transportation Survey, Civil Engineering Report*, Washington, D.C., 1959, Tables B-1 through B-6, pp. 82–83. (The unit costs vary little from those included in Praeger-Cutting-DeLeuw, *Cleveland Subway-Operating and Engineering Feasibility*, Board of County Commissioners, Cuyahoga County, Ohio, December 1955, or A. S. Lang and R. M. Soberman, *Urban Rail Transit*, MIT Press, Cambridge, Mass., 1964.)

[b]Engineering and contingency fees as a percentage of the basic construction cost normally run from 20 to 40 per cent; here we have assumed them to be 25 per cent, and have increased the basic cost in column (1) by this amount.

[5] See, for example, James E. Watt, Jr., and Marshall F. Reed, Jr., *Preliminary Cost Estimate of Construction and Right of Way for Rail and Highway Facilities in Alternative Regional Transportation Plans,* Penn-Jersey Transportation Study Paper no. 19 (mimeographed), Table 3; and George A. Hoffman, *Urban Underground Highways and Parking Facilities,* The RAND Corporation, RM-3680-RC, August 1963, Table 1A, p. 5.

Right-of-Way

It is even more hazardous to generalize about right-of-way costs than about construction costs. The reason is that right-of-way costs are entirely specific to a given locale, while fairly large segments of construction costs vary with the kind of construction and not too greatly with locale. Also, analysis of actual data on right-of-way costs is considerably more treacherous than the analysis of construction cost data because construction often uses varying proportions of existing rights-of-way or of land previously owned by governmental bodies. Still, analysis of right-of-way costs from data obtained from the Bureau of Public Roads, and information from other sources, provide strong evidence that right-of-way costs as a percentage of total costs or construction costs increase with net residential density from 5 per cent or less at very low density to 50 per cent or more at high densities. From this information the following expression for relating the right-of-way to construction costs for a k-lane facility was constructed:

(4) $$S_{\text{row}_i} = (0.005\,X_i)(y_k).$$

By substituting Eq. (3) into Eq. (4), the following equation for the yearly right-of-way cost (assuming an 8-lane mixed-traffic highway) is obtained:

(BC–8) $$SB_{\text{row}_i} = W_{\text{row}_i}(\$299.70\,X_i + \$21.27\,X_i^2),$$

where W_{row_i} applies to bus facilities, and

(RC–4b) $$SR_{\text{row}_i} = W_{\text{row}_i}(\$299.70\,X_i + \$21.27\,X_i^2),$$

where W_{row_i} now applies to rail facilities.

SR_{row_i} or SB_{row_i} is the yearly right-of-way cost for the *i*th mile of rail or bus facility using an infinite life and a 6 per cent interest rate, X_i is the corresponding net residential density in thousands of persons per square mile, and W_{row} is the average right-of-way width required by various highway and rail systems as a ratio of the right-of-way requirements for an 8-lane highway.[6] Relevant W_{row}'s are shown in Table 61. Because of the indexing, over- or underestimates of right-of-way costs impose about equal disadvantages on all systems, but the more right-of-way a system uses, the greater will be the error caused by a wrong estimate.

Right-of-way costs for the express bus type travel on mixed-traffic highways are obtained in the same way as construction costs for mixed-traf-

[6] Use of these equations (BC-8 and RC-4b) obviously is an oversimplification of the structural cost equation and overlooks cost differences resulting from pavement cost and lane relationships and from structural cost and exclusive use relationships.

fic use. Right-of-way costs for bus travel on a mixed-traffic 8-lane highway, and for automobile travel, are as follows:

$$\text{(BC–11)} \qquad SBE_{\text{row}_i} = \$0.156X_i\left(R + R_i - \sum_{x=1}^{i} R_x\right) + \$0.011X_i^2\left(R + R_i - \sum_{x=1}^{i} R_x\right),$$

where SBE_{row_i} is the yearly right-of-way cost for the ith mile, R_i or R_x is the number of bus trips per hour entering or leaving at the ith or xth line-haul station, and X_i is the corresponding net residential density in thousands of persons per square mile. Again, full utilization of the facility during peak hours is assumed.

Terminals

For both transit modes costs must be estimated for constructing station facilities every mile along the line-haul system and one underground, mezzanine-type stub terminal station at the downtown end of the route. Equivalent to these terminal costs for transit are the parking charges and the costs of constructing highway ramps for the automobile systems; however, because the on and off ramp costs have been included in the highway cost estimates, only the parking facility costs need be estimated separately.

Unit costs for constructing a rail transit mezzanine-type downtown terminal may be roughly estimated at $7200 per lineal foot for a 2-track terminal of about 50-foot width, including about $350 per foot of double track for trackage, electrification, and signaling costs.[7] These figures suggest a cost of about $144 per square foot of underground terminal construction.

In calculating the square footage for such a terminal, it is convenient to make the width of the terminal a function of the number of tracks. If there are two tracks, it would seem generally desirable to have a center loading platform about 25 feet wide in addition to the side platform; such a width seems reasonable in view of the high volume of rush-hour passenger loading and unloading required. Total station width would be about 50 feet. A 3-track terminal would require two center platforms, but since the passenger volume does not increase proportionally, an addi-

7 These unit costs are based primarily on data from the *Mass Transportation Survey, Civil Engineering Report,* Washington, D.C., 1959. The estimates are also in agreement with those indicated in: A. S. Lang and R. M. Soberman, *Urban Rail Transit,* MIT Press, Cambridge, Massachusetts, 1964; *Cleveland Subway-Operating and Engineering Feasibility,* Praeger-Cutting-DeLeuw, Board of County Commissioners, Cuyahoga County, Ohio, December 1955; and data obtained privately from the U.S. National Capital Transportation Agency.

tional center platform width allowance of 10 to 15 feet would probably be satisfactory, with another 12.5 feet for the third track. Thus, simple proportional expansion of the 50-foot total station width for two tracks to approximately 75 feet for three tracks would seem sufficient; therefore, 25 feet of width per incoming track is used to determine the width of the rail CBD terminals.

Terminal length can be conceived of as a function of the *maximum* number of cars in any arriving train and the car length, each car being 55.33 feet long in these analyses. Thus, with a capital recovery factor of 0.06344 (the one appropriate for a 50-year service life and a 6 per cent interest rate) and n cars in the longest train, the CBD terminal costs for 2-track systems would equal $0.06344 \times \$7200 \times 55.33n$, or $\$25{,}273n$; for a 3-track system the amount would simply be 50 per cent more, or $\$37{,}909n$.

Because of the close headways used in the rail systems analyzed, the crossovers between the incoming and outgoing or return tracks are provided beyond the station terminal, thus requiring an extension of the station tunnel by slightly over one train length. (For essentially the same reason, an underground extension loop for return trips is included as part of the underground bus terminal.) The cost of making the needed tunnel extensions can be placed at approximately $1811 per lineal foot of single-track subway; in addition $50,000 on a lump-sum basis should be allowed for each crossover. Since the length of the tunnel extension must be varied according to train length, 60 feet of tunneling extension have been required for every car in the train of maximum length. Finally, it was assumed that one single-track extension would be sufficient for a 2-track system, while two single-track extensions would be required for 3-track terminals. Thus, the total annual capital costs (for both station and extension) would be $\$3172 + \$32{,}166n$ for providing a 2-track CBD terminal, and $\$6344 + \$51{,}695n$ for a 3-track terminal.

For line-haul rail stations, only finishing costs are needed over and above the construction and track-structure costs estimated previously. Reasonable unit costs for finishing line-haul rail stations appear to be about $550 per lineal foot of track—that is, $1100 per lineal foot for 2-track stations and $1650 for 3-track stations. On an annual basis, and assuming a 50-year life, these costs are $\$3862n$ for each 2-track line-haul station and $\$5793n$ for each 3-track station. Total rail station costs can be found by adding these coefficients for line-haul stations, after multiplying by g (the number of line-haul stations for each route), to those previously reported for the CBD terminal, as appropriate.

Since the underground CBD terminal proposed for line-haul bus systems is novel in several ways, it is very difficult to cost; the unit cost of $6850 a lineal foot for a 50-foot-wide rail transit, mezzanine-type station (that is, the total unit cost for the rail terminal minus costs associated with track work, electrification, and so forth) is used here as a base figure upon which to compute CBD bus terminal costs. The bus terminal width and length requirements depend on a number of assumptions about safe headways and other circumstances. On the assumptions, however, that each diagonal bus slot in the terminal can handle 70 buses an hour, the terminal bus slots are constructed on a 45-degree angle to the main highway arterial, thus requiring about 140 feet of width, including the return lane, and about 28 feet of length for each slot (plus an allowance for acceleration and deceleration lanes); a 400-foot turnaround loop is provided at a cost of \$1636 per foot, and additional ventilation costs of \$1.5 million are required, both for each lane; it costs \$100,000 to construct each line-haul station (an estimate which is possibly low if every bus is stopped at every line-haul station); with a 50-year life and 6 per cent interest, the bus platform cost function can be summarized as:

$$\text{(BC–12)}\quad SB_p = \$34{,}100\left(\frac{R}{70}\right)^* + \$145{,}200\left(\frac{R}{480}\right)^* + \$6344g,$$

where SB_p = costs on an annual basis of constructing terminals and platforms;

R = the total number of vehicle round trips required every rush hour for the system;

g = the system's route length in miles (and thus the number of line-haul stations);

* indicates a value rounded upward to the next highest integer.

A more complete description of the derivation of this formula can be found in appendix B.

Parking

The downtown terminal charges for a line-haul automobile system are difficult to estimate with any degree of generality, since they vary according to population density and many other considerations.[8] For analytical purposes parking costs can be broken down into three basic components: right-of-way or site acquisition, construction, and operating and maintenance. The land costs per parking space can vary widely, between about \$500 or \$600 for parking lots in fringe or residential areas to well

[8] Sources for the parking cost estimates used are: C. E. DeLeuw, *Midtown Manhattan Parking Study,* prepared for the Department of Traffic, City of New York, November 1959; *Mass Transportation Survey, Civil Engineering Report,* Washington, D.C., 1959; and F. H. Wynn, "Downtown Off-street Parking: Economics and Techniques," in *The Dynamics of Urban Transportation,* a national symposium sponsored by Automobile Manufacturers Association, Inc., October 23–24, 1962, Detroit, Mich.

over $2000 for multistory garages in central locations. Similarly, construction costs per space can run as low as $400 for paved open lots in suburban locations to over $3000 for downtown garages. Annual maintenance and operating cost per space can run close to $150 for multistory garages and as low as $60 for parking lots; the exact level of operating costs will depend considerably on the design of the facility and how much automation is built into it. When these various costs are fused and discounted, middle-of-the-range figures for annual parking costs run between $150 for fringe parking lots and $400 for downtown garages. In the cost analyses that follow, the lower figure of $150 has been used for situations with medium population densities, and the higher figure of $400 with the high-density estimates. In reality, of course, corridor volume usually would be linked to density so that the mix of surface and multistory parking would vary with corridor volume.

Cost Parameters: Operating and Miscellaneous

Rail

Major difficulties are encountered in estimating operating and maintenance expenses for rail transit systems. The facilities employed have a long life-span, operating conditions vary, and suitable data are often lacking. To name only a few of the variables that influence operating expenses, one can identify station spacing, acceleration rates and running speeds, local labor rules, car weight and passenger loading, peak-hour scheduling and lengths of peaks, train lengths, roadbed structure, number of car-miles and passengers, route- and track-miles, and the fare collection system. Sufficient data are not available to permit the formulation of cost models that properly incorporate all these variables. Consequently, the estimates that follow are approximations based on the cost models (RC-5 through RC-9), which were derived on the basis of regression analyses and are given in appendix A.

To simplify computations, all rail costs other than those associated with investments in roadbeds, terminals, and related right-of-way are mainly expressed as functions of the number of train units required, U, or number of train cars required (U times n), and total annual car mileage, M. The annual capital charges (at 6 per cent interest and a 50-year life) for yards and shops needed in a rail system, including a 5 per cent allowance for downtime, is estimated at $533 per car.[9] Similarly, the

[9] This is the discounted value of an $8000 capital cost per car; this figure is based mainly on data furnished in a letter from E. L. Tennyson, dated September 13, 1962. Actually, these costs are variable with size of yard, but this aspect is ignored here for simplicity. The figure includes "engineering and contingency" fees.

capital charge for the cars themselves ($92,000 rail transit cars at 6 per cent interest and a 30-year life) is $7018 per car per year, again including a 5 per cent allowance for downtime. Some costs for maintenance of equipment also are best described on a per-car basis (see RC-5); for this study they are placed at $4119 per car annually, assuming an average age of 15 years and empty car weight of 48,500 pounds.[10] This latter charge, incidentally, includes a 15 per cent surcharge for overhead (as do all the operating and maintenance costs), as well as a 5 per cent allowance for downtime. When totaled, these annual car-associated costs are $11,670 per rail transit car.

Certain operating costs are obviously related to the number of trains and are essentially independent of the number of cars in a train. The most important are train crew or motormen and guard costs. These have been set at a basic cost of $16,200 annually for a 2-man crew for every scheduled peak-hour train, increased 10 per cent for crew relief, break time, sick leave and so forth. The 15 per cent surcharge for overhead must also be added, so that the total cost per train for crew labor is $20,495 annually. The over-all coefficient applicable to train units U for the rail cost analyses is thus equal to $\$11{,}670n + \$20{,}495$.

Charges placed on a per-car-mile basis or related to other factors for the rail analyses are those for power, portions of way and structure maintenance costs and conducting transportation costs exclusive of motormen and guards. These were determined by experimentation with a number of statistical regression functions.[11] Car-mile related costs are estimated to be 7.911 cents for power for the conditions of this study (see RC-6) and about 16.2 cents for both way and structure maintenance (approximated from RC-7) and conducting transportation costs exclusive of motormen and guards (approximated from RC-8); when marked up to include a 15 per cent allowance for overhead, these costs total approximately 27.7 cents per car-mile.

From the statistical regression analyses it was also determined that some of the way and structure maintenance and other conducting transportation costs were associated with total track mileage and passenger volume. Specifically, $3264 annually per track-mile plus $7384 annually per rush-hour passenger seemed reasonable for both way maintenance

[10] These car-related equipment maintenance charges and the other maintenance and operating expenses were developed from a statistical analysis of rail transit system data for New York, Chicago, Philadelphia, Toronto, and Cleveland; Boston data were excluded as their unit costs varied widely from those of the other five systems, generally running twice as high as those of the next most costly system (on a unit basis).

[11] Basic data on rail transit systems in New York, Chicago, Philadelphia, Toronto, and Cleveland, taken from Tables 6.1 through 6.5 of A. S. Lang and R. M. Soberman, *Urban Rail Transit*, MIT Press, Cambridge, Mass., 1964, served as the principal data sources for the cost models.

and other conducting transportation costs. These costs also were marked up by the usual 15 per cent for overhead to obtain an over-all cost coefficient for total track-miles of \$3760 and for rush-hour passengers of \$8.50. In sum, total operating and other nonstructural costs of rail transit, *TROC,* can be expressed as

$$\text{(RC–3)} \qquad TROC = (\$11{,}670n + \$20{,}495)U + \$0.277M + \$3760(2g + g') + \$8.50V,$$

where $(2g + g')$ equals total track-miles and g' is the route mileage of triple trackage (if any).

Bus

Costs associated with the number of bus units in any bus cost analysis will have three components: operator cost, capital cost for yards and shops, and the cost of amortizing the vehicle investment. As with rail line haul, the bus operator cost can be assumed to be approximately \$8100 per year per operator, and thus per bus scheduled in the peak hour; to this must be added a 10 per cent allowance for break time, sick leave, and so forth, so that the total annual operator cost per vehicle scheduled during the peak hour is \$8910. (Note that bus overhead costs are to be charged on a mileage basis, so this figure of \$8910 is *not* directly comparable to the train operator cost of \$10,247.50, which includes an allowance for overhead.) The investment in yards and shops can be assumed to be approximately \$4500 per vehicle; with a 50-year life and a 6 per cent interest rate, the total annual cost of these yards and shops per bus will be \$299. Similarly, the costs of amortizing the bus investment can be estimated at \$3910 a year on the basis of the vehicle cost of \$31,200, a 5 per cent allowance for downtime, the investment being written off over a 12-year service life and a 6 per cent interest rate. Excise taxes were included in the bus purchase price, even though these taxes are sometimes construed as user charges for highways and the full cost of constructing and maintaining the highway has been included elsewhere. The above vehicle unit-related costs total \$13,120 per bus per year.

The costs associated with annual bus-miles, *M*, are estimated to be: 10.7 cents per mile for maintenance and garage expenses; 2.5 cents per mile for fuel and oil; 3.1 cents for insurance and safety; 5.0 cents for administration; and 3.0 cents for conducting transportation charges other than operating labor.[12] It seems wise, moreover, to mark all of these costs up 20 per cent to cover contingencies and other unforeseen pos-

[12] The average unit operating and maintenance costs for some twenty "city-suburban" bus system operations (from ATA accounts and as reported by A. Mongini, "The Physical and Economic Characteristics of Express Bus Urban

sibilities. These figures imply a total charge of approximately 30 cents per bus-mile.[13] These average operating, overhead, and maintenance expenses per bus-mile have been deliberately set above those for ordinary bus systems because of the decentralized fare collection in the downtown terminal. This unit cost does not include any user charges (other than excise taxes) and thus is applicable only to bus operations where the highway charges for bus use are allocated separately. Since these line-haul operations include limited-stop service, and operations over high-grade facilities in contrast to stop-and-go service on local streets, it would probably be reasonable to expect some economies over present-day bus service with some of the above items.

In the bus cost estimates, a further allowance is included of $9000 per lane-mile for snow removal, deicing, sign repair, roadside maintenance, and similar costs.[14] This type of charge seems particularly necessary for exclusive bus highways since high-speed operation is so important, though it is likely that this unit cost estimate is somewhat high.

Putting all these different cost estimates together yields the following function for all bus costs, *TBOC,* other than structural costs:

$$\text{(BC–3)} \qquad TBOC = \$13{,}120U + \$0.30M + \$9000L,$$

where L equals total lane-miles of exclusive bus roadway.

Transit Systems," S. B. Thesis, MIT, Cambridge, Mass., June 1961, pp. 38–39) were as follows:

Bus vehicle maintenance and operating expense item	Average cost per bus-mile	Standard deviation (based on the 20 operations)
Maintenance and garage	$0.107	± $0.018
Fuel and oil	0.025	± 0.004
Insurance and safety	0.031	± 0.012
Administration	0.059	± 0.015
Conducting transportation (exclusive of bus operators)	0.030	± 0.015
Total	$0.252	

Note that the above figures do *not* include the annual costs for bus operators.

[13] This figure seems conservative when compared with the $0.26 per bus-mile estimate for the St. Louis express bus plan (excluding, of course, bus operator costs); see W. C. Gilman and Co., *St. Louis Metropolitan Area Transportation Study, 1957–'70–'80,* New York, 1959, p. 135. This $0.30-per-bus-mile figure—excluding operator costs—has also been corroborated by E. L. Tennyson, transit engineer, in a letter to the authors dated September 13, 1962, which said in part:

> Bus operating costs per mile seldom, if ever, fall below 50¢ per mile for any unionized large operator, of which 20¢ is for the driver on faster runs, leaving 30¢ for other costs . . . By using 9 1/2¢ for maintenance, 4¢ for operating garage (fueling buses), 4 1/2¢ for fuel, 5¢ for conducting transportation other than drivers (supervisors, dispatchers, etc.), 3¢ for insurance, and 4¢ for other, you will have an unassailable figure.

[14] This $9000 figure is stated on the high side to ensure good control, enforcement, and maintenance—and, thus, high capacity and service. See comparative data in *Freeway Operations,* Institute of Traffic Engineers.

These bus cost parameters are no more than rough approximations. Far too little information and analysis are available for properly estimating bus operating and maintenance expenses, particularly for an express bus operation of the sort described here. It is reasonable to expect, for example, that virtually all such expenses would be less for a congestion-free operation with limited stops than for present-day bus operations on city streets with frequent stops, upon whose maintenance and operating expenses the cost estimates presented here are nonetheless based.

Automobile

Operating, maintenance, and ownership charges used for the automobile line-haul analyses were based on the assumption that a reasonably economical or compact vehicle would be used; in other words, a specialized vehicle would be used for commuting rather than a heavy, all-purpose car. This assumption seemed wise since the bus and rail analyses also assume considerable optimality and specialization in basic commuter service.

Operating and maintenance charges for the automobile fleet were estimated on a vehicle-mile basis. The specific charges are:

Item	Cents per Vehicle-mile
Repairs and maintenance	1.70
Replacement tires and tubes	0.15
Gasoline (not including user taxes)	0.95
Oil	0.10
Total	2.90

These charges are somewhat lower than those typically incurred by today's American automobiles, but the differences are not large, mainly reflecting the substitution of a utilitarian vehicle for the more conventional family car which is put to all sorts of uses other than commuting. Also, gasoline taxes and similar excises were not included because they are usually regarded as payments for highway use, and highway costs have been separately assessed.

The ownership charges for the passenger car were also placed on a per-vehicle-mile basis. These costs are, to understate the matter, difficult to estimate. Automobile commuter operations often involve extremely short daily mileages and a low annual mileage, even though automobiles are presently designed to provide a much greater total annual mileage aside from amenities not usually found in public transportation. If economy and utility were his criteria, the commuter would generally choose among either new compact cars or used cars, perhaps old ones. His choice might seem to depend on the mileage he travels. If it is very low, perhaps 1000 or 2000 miles a year, he might find it most economical to buy an old used car; if he travels as much as 5000 miles, a new compact car is likely to be more economical. Experimentation with data on a number of used and compact cars (with different assumed mileage capabilities) indicates that the commuter should be able to buy and operate a satisfactory car at ownership costs of approximately 4 cents a vehicle-mile. If the interest rate were 6 per cent, he could achieve this figure, for example, if he bought a stripped-down compact for $1600 and drove it 5000 miles a year for twelve years, or if he bought a $600 used car and drove it about 4300 miles a year for four years, or if he bought a $200 used car and drove it about 1200 miles a year for three and a half years. In these three cases, the implied daily round trip distance would be 20, 17, and 5 miles, to be compared, for example, with the *average* daily line-haul round trip distance of 11 miles for the 10-mile line-haul route (and uniform distribution along this route).

For exclusive rush-hour travel by passenger car, an annual accident insurance cost of $100 per automobile is assumed, a cost roughly in line with insurance costs in large American cities.[15] Finally, as with bus operations, an additional $9000 per required lane-mile was included in the cost estimates for annual highway maintenance and administration to allow for the fact that the proposed line-haul automobile system must operate over a highway with high performance and maintenance standards.

Functional Relations

Rail

The basic relationships among the features of rail transit systems can be conveniently described by a set of equations. The full set is presented in appendix A. Two problems encountered in the analysis of rail transit costs merit special attention: determining the exact amount of track needed, in particular the extent to which it is desirable to provide third or fourth tracks in a route system, and determining the optimal train length.

With more than two tracks, or with intermediate crossovers, the operation of the rail system becomes analytically equivalent to the operation

[15] For the 10-mile route length, this accident charge results in an accident cost of about 3.6 cents per vehicle-mile, a seemingly high charge. Given the way in which insurance charges are now typically structured, however, such rates are probably not too far out of line with what must be paid by many who keep a car strictly for commuting purposes, and with the higher accident rates experienced during rush hours.

of two (or more) simultaneous and overlapping systems, and certain economies can sometimes be achieved by using this system duality to tailor the service offered more closely to actual needs. Moreover, under some of the high volumes and service standards stipulated as part of this study, it often becomes essential to provide an extra track in order to meet specified demand levels. The capacity of a 2-track rail transit system also can be expanded by means other than extra trackage—for example, by providing more intricate signaling or control devices or additional tracks and platforms at stations and downtown terminals, almost invariably a bottleneck in rail transit operations.[16]

For this study, a 2-track system with a 2-track downtown terminal is assumed to have an inbound capacity of thirty-seven or thirty-eight 10-car trains an hour, while the figure for a 2-track system with a 3-track downtown terminal is fifty-one or fifty-two 10-car trains. A 3-track system with a 3-track terminal is assumed to have an inbound capacity of about seventy-two 10-car trains an hour. These numbers increase if train length is shortened; with 4-car trains, for example, a 2-track system with a 2-track terminal could handle about sixty trains an hour.[17]

Capacity determinations are also needed for movements running counter to the direction of maximum flow (inbound in the morning, outbound in the afternoon). With no along-the-line stops in the minor flow direction, the maximum reverse direction capacity per track is about seventy-two 10-car trains an hour with an approximate 50-second headway and a 50 per cent braking safety factor.[18] This capacity would be slightly larger for shorter trains and smaller for longer ones. Actually, because these trains can usually be assumed to be traveling "light," that is, with few passengers, one or two cars might accommodate all the reverse direction passengers. If so, it is conceivable that 15- or even 20-car trains could be used. In this case, it is the number of occupied cars that basically determines train lengths, instead of the usual constraint of platform length. Reverse direction constraints are thus negligible enough to be ignored for the largely unidirectional, CBD-oriented systems analyzed.

It may sometimes be desirable to add a third track even when the 2-track system has not been strained beyond its capacity, if doing so will

[16] It has often been suggested, for example, that an expansion of platform space and trackage at New York's Grand Central Station would effect a very considerable expansion in total system capacity.

[17] References for these calculations are A. S. Lang and R. M. Soberman, *Urban Rail Transit,* MIT Press, Cambridge, Mass., 1964, appendix A, "Some Considerations of Minimum Headway," and W. H. T. Holden, "Notes on Rail Operation and Capacities."

[18] Apparently this is the usual safety factor for rail transit operation; however, since the average braking rate assumed here (about 4.2 mph/sec) is much higher than that normally used (about 3.0 to 3.5 mph/sec), this safety factor may be too conservative and the minimum headways somewhat low.

promote significant operating economies. The basic functional relationship for determining such desirability is:

$$\text{(R–5)} \qquad SR' = \frac{\partial TROC}{\partial g'},$$

where g' = miles of third track;

SR' = the incremental structural cost (on an annual basis) of adding a third track to a 2-track system;

$\partial TROC/\partial g'$ = the annual change (decrement) in nonstructural costs, $TROC$, associated with changes in g'.

The marginal cost, SR', of adding a track will depend on whether a 3-track downtown terminal already exists. If it does not, the function would be to a rough approximation

$$\text{(RC–4g)} \qquad SR' = \$3172 + \$21{,}461n + \$129{,}000g' + (0.05)\sum_{i=1}^{g'} (\$299.70X_i + \$21.27X_i^2),$$

where n is the number of cars in each train. If the 3-track terminal exists, the relevant function is

(RC–4h)

$$SR' = \$1931n + \$129{,}000g' + (0.05)\sum_{i=1}^{g'} (\$299.70X_i + \$21.27X_i^2).$$

(A functional expression for the partial derivative of total operating costs with respect to g', that is $\partial TROC/\partial g'$, is somewhat difficult to derive, but is derivable. Since g' is very much dependent on maximum and minimum headway constraints, it was determined by simply checking first against constraint values and then making the cost calculations for all cases that satisfied the constraints.)

It never pays to triple-track more than one-half of any system's route length for reasons of efficiency alone, since all potential operating economies are exhausted at the halfway point (assuming, of course, uniformly distributed volumes). This can be understood intuitively by observing the data in Table 64 pertaining to the basic performance of a rail line-haul system under different assumptions about route length, g, and additional third trackage, g'. Notes to Table 64 give the formulas for computing the basic performance data relating to distances, number of stops, and time required. These formulas and the data in the table quickly reveal that the basic rail performance data depend only on the assumed values of route length, g, and miles of third track, g', and that, in particular, they

TABLE 64

RAIL-HAUL SYSTEM: BASIC PERFORMANCE DATA

Route Variables				With 1-way service only						With complete 2-way service					
g	g'	d_1	d_2	f_1	f_2	t_1	t_2	r_1	r_2	f_1	f_2	t_1	t_2	r_1	r_2
6	0	12	—	7	—	1602	—	2.25	—	12	—	1816	—	1.97	—
6	2	12	4	6	2	1563	954	2.30	3.88	10	4	1741	992	2.10	3.59
6	3	12	6	5	3	1525	1123	2.36	3.29	8	6	1666	1198	2.20	2.98
10	0	20	—	12	—	2274	—	1.58	—	20	—	2640	—	1.36	—
10	2	20	4	10	2	2236	954	1.61	3.88	18	4	2565	992	1.42	3.59
10	3	20	6	9	3	2199	1123	1.64	3.29	16	6	2490	1198	1.46	2.98
10	4	20	8	8	4	2161	1291	1.67	2.85	14	8	2414	1404	1.51	2.55
10	5	20	10	7	5	2123	1400	1.70	2.51	12	10	2340	1610	1.56	2.22
15	0	30	—	16	—	3116	—	1.16	—	30	—	3670	—	.98	—
15	2	30	4	15	2	3078	954	1.17	3.88	28	4	3595	992	1.01	3.59
15	3	30	6	14	3	3041	1123	1.18	3.29	26	6	3520	1198	1.03	2.98
15	4	30	8	13	4	3003	1291	1.20	2.85	24	8	3445	1404	1.05	2.55
15	5	30	10	12	5	2966	1460	1.21	2.51	22	10	3370	1610	1.08	2.22
15	6	30	12	11	6	2928	1627	1.23	2.25	20	12	3294	1816	1.10	1.97
15	7	30	14	10	7	2890	1796	1.25	2.04	18	14	3219	2022	1.13	1.77
15	8	30	16	9	8	2853	1962	1.26	1.86	16	16	3144	2228	1.16	1.61

g = route length in miles.
g' = miles of third track.
$d_1 = 2g$ = round trip distance (miles) of long runs.
$d_2 = 2g'$ = round trip distance (miles) of short runs.
f_1 = number of stops needed on long or outer-loop runs.
f_2 = number of stops needed on short or inner-loop runs.
$t_1 = 93f_1 + 65.4(d_1 - f_1) + 10(f_1 - 2) + 600$ = time (seconds) required for outer-loop round trip.
$t_2 = 93f_2 + 65.4(d_2 - f_2) + 10(f_2 - 2) + 600$ = time (seconds) required for inner-loop round trip.
$r_1 = 3600/t_1$ = number of round trips per hour per train on long or outer-loop runs.
$r_2 = 3600/t_2$ = number of round trips per hour per train on short or inner-loop runs.

are independent of volume.[19] Table 64 also makes it evident that rail operations break down into two distinct subsystems when a third track is provided; the subscript 1 denotes runs over the longer or outer loop, while the subscript 2 denotes runs over the shorter or inner loop. In computing performance data for the 1-way express system, one overlapping station was assumed between the outer and inner loops so that along-the-line service could be provided, though such service would often require one transfer. For the costing exercises, this means that one 3-track terminal with related platforms must be provided at the overlapping line-haul station (as well as at the downtown terminal), and one extra stop is made on each trip in or out by trains operating over the outer loop. The *modus operandi* assumed is that morning trains making the outer loop stop to pick up passengers at all the outlying stations *not* served by a third track and stop at the first station they reach in the triple-tracked sector to discharge passengers with destinations at one of the stations on the inner loop; on the other hand, trains making the inner loop, over the third track, stop at every station they serve. With service provided in only one direction—that is, in the direction of maximum traffic flow—trains would be assumed to operate as empty nonstop expresses after discharging passengers and when they returned to the line-haul and "deadheaded" back to the first passenger pickup station. If a complete inbound and outbound service were provided, the only modification in the operating procedure would be that trains traveling over the longer or outer loop would operate without platform stops at the triple-tracked line-haul stations served by trains operating over the inner loop.

In 3-track systems, costs could be slightly reduced and service improved for CBD-bound travelers by eliminating the overlapping stop and thereby also eliminating along-the-line service. The economies to be achieved by this device are so slight, however, that they seemed not worth the effort to cost accurately. Table 65 lists the actual amounts of third-track and total track mileage that appeared approximately optimal under the circumstances hypothesized for the cost studies; these data define the route systems and most of the basic performance data for all of the subsequent rail cost analyses.[20]

[19] Actually, this result follows from the fact that no allowance is made in the time calculations for the slight differences that would occur in unloading and loading times at different volume levels. These differences are quite minute because the controlling factor on loading and unloading time is the ratio of doors in the cars to the number of passengers carried and this ratio is little altered by changes in volume because at the lower volume fewer cars are provided.

[20] As can be observed from Table 64, the addition of third trackage reduces the time required for each round trip made by a train and thereby improves the quality of the service rendered (and permits higher utilization of labor and equipment). In many circumstances a slight increment in total cost incurred by providing additional track might be deemed desirable for service reasons.

TABLE 65

REQUIRED AND APPROXIMATELY OPTIMAL TRACKAGE AT VARIOUS VOLUMES AND ROUTE LENGTHS

Route length (mi)	Volume 5,000		10,000		20,000		30,000		40,000		50,000	
	g'	$2g + g'$	g'	$2g + g'$	g'	$2g + g'$	g'	$2g + g'$	g'	$2g + g'$	g'	$2g + g'$
6	0	12	0	12	0	12	0	12	3	15	3	15
10	0	20	0	20	0	20	3	23	5	25	4	24
15	0	30	0	30	0	30	4	34	6	36	7	37

NOTE: g' = miles of third track; $2g + g'$ = total track-miles.

The most crucial performance data are those pertaining to the time, t, needed to complete a round trip by each train. The general function for t (for the particular rail car used) is

$$t = 93f + 65.4(d - f) + 10(f - 2) + 600, \qquad \text{(R–3)}$$

where t = round trip time in seconds;

f = the number of station stops (including that at the downtown terminal) made on each round trip;

d = the round trip travel distance in miles.

The first of these terms, $93f$, derives from the assumption that 93 seconds would be needed to accelerate, decelerate, and travel the 1-mile distance between stations wherever stops are required by a transit car with the operating characteristics assumed for the present analyses. The second term in the equation, $65.4(d - f)$, represents the time needed for completing a round trip over distances where no stops are needed. Since the stations are assumed to be 1 mile apart, this nonstop distance must equal $d - f$. The parameter 65.4 merely represents the number of seconds needed to complete 1 mile at the top operating speed of 55 mph. The third term, $10(f - 2)$, measures the time required for loading and unloading at all but the two terminal stations, both downtown and end-of-route.[21] Ten seconds was taken as a constant dwell time requirement per intermediate line-haul station stop. It would be more precise to formulate the loading and unloading time requirement in numbers of passengers loaded or unloaded at each particular station.[22] Such a requirement seemed unnecessarily detailed for the present analysis; furthermore, in actual situations, trains normally might be held longer than strictly required for loading and unloading at line-haul stations in order to balance the time spent at these stations with the longer times usually required at CBD or downtown stations. In this connection, it must be remembered that it is the maximum dwell time at any one station that determines minimum safe headways for a system.

The expression $10(f - 2)$ makes no allowance for loading or unloading times required at the two end stations in the line-haul system, that is, the CBD station and the last line-haul station. Loading and unloading

[21] This rate implies a loading or unloading station stop requirement of 1/4 second per passenger. With four load/unload doors per car, and two passengers using each door, this obviously is equivalent to saying that each passenger (on the average) needs two seconds to load or unload. This figure appears more than reasonable when compared with data for bus loading; see, for example, W. S. Rainville, Jr., *et al.*, "Preliminary Progress Report of Transit Subcommittee, Committee on Highway Capacity," *Highway Research Board Proceedings*, vol. 40, 1961, Table 6, p. 537.

[22] The loading rate is also in part a function of the time which is actually allowed, of the acceleration and deceleration rates, of the extent to which the cars and platforms are loaded or crowded, and of the extent to which passengers are all loading or unloading.

times for the end terminals have been incorporated into the turnaround constant; thus $(f - 2)$ rather than f alone is used as the multiplier of 10 in the third term of the time equation. The specific turnaround time has been set at 5 minutes for each end of the line so that the constant has been set at 600 seconds (total) in the equation.[23]

Once the route lengths are known and the basic performance data are defined, it is possible to determine optimum train lengths. This exercise involves balancing increased capital costs, mainly for the provision of additional length at station platforms, against decreases in operating labor costs achievable by running longer trains. The increment in costs incurred by increasing the maximum length of a train will depend on the particular track configuration and operating procedures employed. In the simplest of the present cases, where there is no triple trackage ($g' = 0$) and only a 2-track downtown terminal, the relevant function is

$$\text{(R–6c)} \qquad \frac{\partial SR_b}{\partial n} = \$3862g + \$32{,}166,$$

where n = the numbers of cars in each train,

SR_b = basic ROW and construction costs for a 2-track system (on an annual basis in dollars).

The first term in this equation, $\$3862g$, reflects the extra finishing costs at outlying line-haul stations, while the second term, \$32,166, represents extra downtown terminal costs. If a 3-track downtown terminal were used with a 2-track system, the function would be modified to

$$\text{(R–7c)} \qquad \frac{\partial(SR_b + SR'_T)}{\partial n} = \$3862g + \$51{,}696.$$

If a multiple-track system is employed ($g' > 0$), two marginal cost functions pertaining respectively to the inner and outer loops are needed:

$$\text{(R–8c)} \qquad \frac{\partial(SR_b + SR'_T + SR'_L)}{\partial n_1} = \$3862(g - g' + 1) + \$53{,}267$$

and

$$\text{(R–9c)} \qquad \frac{\partial(SR_{LS})}{\partial n_2} = \$3862(g' - 1),$$

where $SR' = SR'_L + SR'_T$ = additional annual ROW, construction, line-haul station (for outer loop) plus downtown terminal costs for a 3-track system over a 2-track system;

SR_{LS} = annual construction (finishing) costs for 2-track (inner-loop) line-haul stations;

n_1 = number of cars in trains operating on the outer loop;

n_2 = number of cars in trains operating on the inner loop.

[23] The turnaround time is based on data included in a letter memorandum from John S. Gallagher, dated June 1962.

In Eq. (R-8c), \$3862 pertains to costs associated with extending the double-track along-the-line stations (of which there are $g - g' + 1$), and \$53,277 designates costs associated with lengthening the 3-track end-of-the-line and CBD terminals. Because all the economies associated with triple track are exhausted when half the total route length is triple-tracked, it is assumed in deriving functions (R-8c) and (R-9c) that the optimal train length for the outer or longer loop will always be at least as great or greater than the optimal train length for the shorter or inner loops. Therefore, the length of the outer-loop trains, n_1, determines the costs of the overlapping 3-track line terminal and the triple-tracked CBD terminal.

These cost functions are to be balanced against the decreases in operating costs that could be achieved by increasing train length. When total costs for the train system exclusive of way and structure (but not equipment) capital costs, *TROC*, are differentiated with respect to n_1 and n_2, the following equations are obtained:

(R–8b)
$$\frac{\partial TROC_1}{\partial n_1} = \frac{\$20{,}495V(g - g')}{n_1^2 c_1 r_1 g}$$

and

(R–9b)
$$\frac{\partial TROC_2}{\partial n_2} = \frac{\$20{,}495Vg'}{n_2^2 c_2 r_2 g},$$

where $TROC$ = total nonstructural costs;

V = hourly passenger volume at maximum load point;

r_1 = number of round trips per hour made by each train on the outer loop or longer runs;

r_2 = number of round trips per hour made by each train on the inner loop or shorter runs;

c = passenger seat capacity of each rail car (assumed to be 79 in present case);

and the variables g, g', n_1, and n_2 are as defined before. Also, the ratio of $(g - g')/g$ or g'/g describes the portion of total volume on a particular loop. When there are no miles of triple-trackage ($g' = 0$), Eq. (R-8b) is applicable.

Once the optimal train length has been determined, the remainder of the rail cost calculations is straightforward. (The optimum train length will occur when the incremental structural and nonstructural annual costs are equal; analytically, this is developed in appendix A, in the section on functional relationships.) The only particular difficulties accrue when third trackage is used and two subsystems must be evaluated. The total number of required round trips for each subsystem, R_1 and R_2, can be found from

(R–11a) $$R_1 = \frac{V}{n_1 c_1}\left(\frac{g - g'}{g}\right)$$

and

(R–11b) $$R_2 = \frac{V}{n_2 c_2}\left(\frac{g'}{g}\right).$$

Again, if $g' = 0$, Eq. (R-11a), pertaining to the outer or longer loop, is applicable. These equations, moreover, define the schedule frequencies pertinent to evaluating whether minimal service standards are being met; specifically, if $g' = 0$, R_1 equals the schedule frequency, h, and must be greater than 30 to meet the minimal service standard (of a train at least every two minutes); also, R_1 must be less than 37 or 52, depending on whether a 2- or 3-track CBD terminal has been provided, in order to meet capacity constraints. In the same vein, if $g' > 0$, both R_1 and R_2 must be greater than 30 in order to meet the minimum frequency requirement, and less than 37 in order not to violate capacity or minimum allowable headways. These R's in turn can be used to immediately determine the total number of train units needed, U_1 and U_2, from

(R–12a) $$U_1 = R_1/r_1.$$

and

(R–12b) $$U_2 = R_2/r_2,$$

where r_1 and r_2 are the numbers of round trips per hour that outer- and inner-loop trains, respectively, can perform. Finally, the number of car-miles needed to meet the service requirements, M, is defined by

(R–10c) $$M = M_1 + M_2 = 1020(r_1 d_1 n_1 U_1 + r_2 d_2 n_2 U_2).$$

Again, only subscript 1 values need to be taken into account if $g' = 0$. Once computed, these U and M values can be inserted into the cost functions as described in the previous section to estimate total costs of the rail system; taken together with g and g', which are needed to define structure and some maintenance costs, they constitute the major information needed to estimate rail system costs.

Bus

The structure of bus transit operations can be described by a set of equations in much the same fashion as rail transit. A bus line-haul system, though, is generally describable by a much simpler set of functional relationships. This is particularly true whenever only express service is provided, and whenever passenger volume levels are above 10,000 hourly passengers (at the maximum load point). For example, when trip origination densities are high enough at every line-haul station to load every bus (with 50 seats) fully and to satisfy the schedule frequency constraint (assumed to be one bus trip every two minutes or 30 bus trips an hour), then buses can merely operate nonstop between the line-haul station pickup (or discharge) point and the downtown terminal. This implies, of course, that at least 1500 passengers an hour are picked up (or discharged) at each line-haul station. However, when volumes fall below this level, say to 1200 hourly passengers per line-haul station, it is evident that the operation of buses nonstop between each station and the downtown terminal at 2-minute intervals would result in underloading buses, specifically to an average of 40 passengers per bus trip. Rather than operate nonstop and thus provide unutilized bus capacity (in addition to other diseconomies), the bus operation could be altered and multistop trips introduced to the point at which all bus seats were occupied (in much the same fashion as a rail operation); such would be permissible so long as the trip speed and travel time restrictions set forth earlier were satisfied (in addition to schedule frequency constraints), and so long as over-all economies could be effected.

In those situations where along-the-line service is also to be provided, the type of operation and its analytical description is slightly complicated and involves important cost and service tradeoffs. Generally, there are two types of alternatives: independent operation of through service and along-the-line service (that is, nonstop or limited stop buses would provide service for those passengers moving directly to or from the downtown terminal, and separate shuttle-type buses would serve the intra-line-haul movement) and integrated express and along-the-line service with the buses moving between the *i*th line-haul station and downtown terminal, stopping at intermediate line-haul stations between the *i*th line-haul station and CBD terminal.

In the latter case, the use of transfers can improve the efficiency of bus operations at low volume levels much as they can for rail transit, largely by improving the average load factor in each vehicle; however, some offsetting diseconomies result because of reductions in speed and vehicle utilization (as well as introducing service disadvantages for through passengers). The procedure with transfers would be to operate with overlapping inner and outer loops. For example, consider a 10-mile system with 1-mile station spacing, 300 passengers an hour picked up at each station, and a schedule frequency of 30 buses an hour. In such circumstances, especially if it is also assumed that along-the-line service is desired at all points and in both directions on the system, it would seem best to operate with two overlapping loops: one would serve to pick up and discharge both downtown and along-the-line passengers at the outer five stations (at miles 6 through 10) and would stop at the 5-mile station to discharge or pick up passengers with along-the-line destinations or origins on the inner loop serving the inner five stations. As with multiple-loop rail transit, the *modus operandi* would be for buses serving the outer loop to operate express in both directions between the fifth station and the CBD terminal. As a whole, this scheme would lengthen the average distance traveled on each round trip but would reduce the number of stops required for a full along-the-line service and would avoid underutilization of bus capacity (that is, relative to an operation wherein each bus stops at each intermediate station). More importantly, the average time required for each round trip would usually decline, and the trip from a line-haul station to the CBD would be faster. On the other hand, passengers with intermediate destinations would suffer the inconvenience of having to transfer to reach some along-the-line stations. Transfers and loops in a bus transit system thus degrade service for some passengers and improve it for others.

A most important equation needed to describe any type of express-bus line-haul system is that pertaining to the time required for completing a round trip, t. As noted in the last chapter and reemphasized in the section on rail transit above, round trip time primarily depends on the distance traveled on each round trip, d, the number of stops required on each round trip, f, the total number of passengers carried or handled over the round trip, p, the bus performance capabilities, and the constant amount of time required for turnaround purposes on each trip. The specific equation for bus round trips between the ith line-haul station and the downtown terminal is (with the equipment analyzed here):

$$\text{(B–1)} \qquad t_i = 88f_i + 60.5(d_i - f_i) + 1.166p_i + 120 \quad \text{(in seconds)},$$

where t_i = total round trip time for a bus moving between the ith line-haul station and downtown terminal (in seconds);

d_i = total round trip distance (in miles);

f_i = total number of stops made on the round trip;

p_i = the number of passengers carried.

The first term, $88f_i$, derives from the assumption that 88 seconds would be required to move between stations spaced 1 mile apart (including acceleration and deceleration), and thus represents the travel time required for each mile of the round trip which includes stops. (The performance characteristics of the particular equipment used are noted in appendix B.) The second term, $60.5(d_i - f_i)$, represents the travel time needed for the portion of the round trip which is made without stops. (If, for example, a 6-mile round trip were being made, with stops at each inbound and outbound station, f_i and d_i would be equal to 6, and the second term would drop out.) The third term, $1.166p_i$, represents the total time required for loading and unloading passengers over the entire round trip, and thus the sum of both inbound and outbound passengers. The computation of loading and unloading time requirements assumes an average load or unload rate of one person per door every 1.75 seconds, the use of three doors, double-side loading-unloading, and centralized fare collection at the downtown terminal. The final term is a constant 120-second allowance for turnaround time. It should be noted that this turnaround time does *not* include any allowance for loading and unloading times, since these have been fully incorporated into the third term of the equation.

The round trip distance, d_i, the passenger load, p_i, and the number of bus stops per trip, f_i, will of course depend on the character of service offered, the volume level, and distribution of volume along the route. For example, where only through service is to be offered and where the volume level at each line-haul station is at least 1500 passengers per hour, the bus operation can be perfectly differentiated with buses operating express in loops between each line-haul station and the downtown terminal. In this case, there would be g bus loops or one for each mile of route length with each requiring $V \div gc$ hourly bus trips. Consequently, the significant features of this type of express bus system can be developed reasonably well simply by analyzing only the characteristics pertaining to the "average" line-haul station for the system. For the 6-, 10-, and 15-mile route length systems analyzed, the "average" line-haul station is one located 3.5, 5.5, and 8 miles, respectively, from the CBD terminal.[24] For other types of operations, fewer than g bus loops might be required, necessitating different computational procedures. This would occur, for example, in situations where volume levels were low and where multistop operation was used to increase load factors and reduce labor and equipment requirements. (See appendix B.)

Except in transfer and multistop situations, calculation of the distance traveled on an *average* round trip by bus is straightforward. Under the circumstances normally hypothesized in these analyses this distance will equal the route length plus 1; thus for the 6-, 10-, and 15-mile route lengths assumed for these cost analyses, the average round trip distances would be 7, 11, and 16 miles. The computation is more complex with multistop and transfer operations because it depends on the specific loops and type of operation hypothesized.

[24] Under the 1-mile station-spacing assumptions standard to these cost analyses, no station, of course, would be found at the 3.5 and 5.5 distances in the 6- and 10-mile systems; rather, the average station in that case is a composite or synthesis of the two middle stations in the systems, those located at distances of 3 and 4 miles in the 6-mile system, and those located at distances of 5 and 6 miles in the 10-mile system.

The load factor, p, is simply determined when no transfers are permitted and at high volume levels. If trip origination densities are high enough at every line-haul stop served so that the scheduled frequency constraint is automatically satisfied (one bus every two minutes or 30 buses an hour), then the 1-way load factor in each bus is generally the full capacity of the bus, 50 passengers. In other words, if 1500 passengers an hour are picked up at each line-haul station (30 buses an hour times 50 passengers per bus), 50 passengers will be carried in every bus (1-way) and the 2-minute headway requirement will be satisfied. For any volume lower than that, the number of passengers carried in each bus will depend on the total volume, number of stops, and the extent to which loads and capacity can be tailored.

The number of stops on each trip is almost as easily defined, but depends specifically on the type of service assumed. For example, if nonstop express service is to be rendered between each line-haul station and the CBD terminal (that is, with no along-the-line service in either direction), then obviously only two stops are made on each round trip—one at the line-haul station and one at the CBD terminal. If along-the-line service is provided, the number of stops depends on the distance traveled (and on requirements for multistop operation for through passengers). With the assumed 1-mile station spacing and along-the-line service in one direction only (nonstop on the return leg), and with no necessity for multistops for through service, the average number of stops would equal one-half the average round trip distance plus one, the additional one being for the CBD terminal. With along-the-line service in both directions, the stops required would be the same number as the average round trip distance (assuming no transfers are required).

Once the average trip time is known, the average number of round trips that each vehicle can make in an hour, r, can quickly be computed by dividing 3600 by the time required for one trip, t. When r is divided into the total number of round trips required per hour, R, then the total number of required or scheduled bus units, U, can be determined. For *other than* multistop or transfer operations,

(B–10a) $$R_i = \frac{V_i}{c} = \left(\frac{V}{gc}\right), \qquad \text{where} \quad \frac{V_i}{c} \geq h;$$

or

(B–10b) $$R_i = h, \qquad \text{where} \quad \frac{V_i}{c} < h;$$

and

(B–6) $$U = \sum_{i=1}^{g} \frac{R_i}{r} = \frac{gR_i}{r} = \left(\frac{gtR_i}{3600}\right)^* .$$

Similarly, the annual number of bus-miles required by the system, M, during the four rush hours can be computed by

(B–8) $$M = 1020\, drU.$$

The only additional computation needed for the analyses of buses operating on their own exclusive highways is that for the total number of lane-miles of highway required, L. This figure is needed in order to assess highway investment and maintenance costs. The specific expression for computing the lane-mile requirement is

(B–9) $$L = 2 \sum_{i=1}^{g} \left(\frac{R + R_i - \sum_{x=1}^{i} R_x}{H_B} \right)^{*},$$

where H_B is the lane capacity of exclusive bus highways (in bus trips per lane per hour). This expression simply represents a totaling of the lane-mile requirements for each mile of the route system, beginning with the mile closest to the CBD and systematically proceeding outward. For this analysis it is generally assumed that H_B equals 480, or that 480 buses an hour can safely and reasonably travel on one lane at the speeds specified. The totaling must take account of the fact that highway capacity can be provided only in discrete units, making it necessary to round upward to the next highest digit in each particular lane-mile calculation, as denoted by the use of the asterisk.

Automobile

The automobile line-haul analysis is quite simple compared with either rail or bus public transit. The automobile line-haul analysis, like that for bus, is greatly simplified by confining attention to the "average" line-haul station within each system. At uniform densities, each line-haul station originates a volume V_i, which equals the total hourly maximum load point volume for the entire system divided by g, the route length in miles. The only additional information needed to define U, the number of vehicular units (cars here) required per hour is the average load, c, that can be expected in each vehicle. The selection of this load is extremely important, both to the economics of automobile operation and to determination of the quality of service rendered. This load, in turn, is dependent on the amount of car-pooling practiced by commuters.

Car-pooling, on the one hand, represents a loss of privacy (though probably not so much as in public transit), an increase in waiting or delay time, and the loss of schedule flexibility, somewhat as a lower schedule frequency reduces the flexibility of transit operation. On the positive side, car-pooling means freedom from the driving burden for all but one member of the group; freedom to choose one's own company, read newspapers, smoke, and so on; and, finally, a reduction in travel cost as compared with driving alone in one's own automobile. A basic problem of the line-haul automobile analysis is to select a car occupancy figure that will establish a reasonable equivalence between the over-all service rendered by automobiles and by public transit modes. On this basis, and somewhat arbitrarily, 1.6 passengers per car have been assumed during the *rush* hours in the direction of major flow. This figure need not necessarily coincide with current data for urban areas, principally because the level of service assumed in this analysis, in both absolute and relative terms, with respect to all of the different modes is not necessarily comparable to that in the real world.[25]

On this basis, and with the assumed four rush hours a day, 255 days a year, the total number of automobiles needed is *twice* the number of automobiles needed for a single rush hour, U; this U can be estimated from the following expression:

$$U = \frac{V}{c} = \frac{gV_i}{c} = \left(\frac{gV_i}{1.6}\right). \tag{A–1}$$

Similarly, the mileage requirement (for four rush hours a day, 255 days a year) can be expressed by

$$M = 510\, dU, \tag{A–2}$$

where d is the average daily round trip distance (in miles).

The only other data required for completing the automobile line-haul analyses are estimates of the number of freeway lane-miles required. This calculation is made in essentially the same fashion as that for bus lane capacity requirements but is somewhat more complicated because automobile capacity per lane tends to be more dependent on the number of lanes in the highway.

Reasonably good estimates of lane capacity are available from freeway studies in California, Michigan, and Texas,[26] but are not exactly applicable to the present analyses because the supporting volume count data included mixed traffic, composed of both heavy and light vehicles. The present line-haul automobile cost analyses, by contrast, pertain strictly to automobiles, with no trucks or buses sharing the facilities.

[25] The 1.6 passengers per automobile per rush hour used in the present analyses compared with a 1.9 figure recorded in a 1955 Washington, D.C., O-D Study (see p. 29 of *Mass Transportation Survey, Civil Engineering Report*) and with some more recent (1961) data recorded on the Washington, D.C., Pentagon network ranging from 1.64 to 1.92 passengers per vehicle in the peak-hour major flow direction. Similarly, a figure of 1.8 passengers per vehicle was used in the *U.S. National Capital Transportation Agency Report,* November 1962.

[26] See, for example, *Freeway Operations,* Institute of Traffic Engineers, pp. 9–12.

Furthermore, measured demand as obtained from volume count data normally embodies some hourly counts pertaining to facilities used below actual capacity. It seemed reasonable or even necessary, moreover, to differentiate lane capacities according to number of lanes. Specifically, data from a California freeway capacity study[27] were used to estimate lane capacity and lane requirements for the line-haul automobile cost analyses. (See Table 66.) These lane capacities, when divided into the actual automobile volumes using each segment of the line-haul automobile system, rounded upward to the next integer, and summed over all segments, provide a total estimate of lane mile requirements.

TABLE 66

PASSENGER CAR EXPRESSWAY CAPACITIES AT VARIOUS HIGHWAY WIDTHS[a]

No. of lanes in one direction	Lane capacity (vehicles per lane per hour)[b]	Total roadway capacity (vehicles per hour)
1	1000	1000
2	1600	3200
3	1665	4995
4	1675	6700
5 or more	1650	

[a]All grade separated facilities with both medians and shoulders, etc.
[b]At average speeds of 35 mph or more.
SOURCE: G. M. Webb and K. Moskowitz, "California Freeway Capacity Study," *Highway Research Board Proceedings*, 36: 587–641 (1957).

COST COMPARISONS AND CONCLUSIONS

Many of the important essentials of the line-haul cost analyses are summarized in Figures 34 through 40. Shown in Figure 34 is a comparison of cost per trip incurred by the different transit modes for a complete inbound and outbound service at medium population densities and different maximum load point requirements; panel (A) in the figure pertains to 6-mile route systems, panel (B) to 10-mile systems, and panel (C) to 15-mile systems. Also shown are the costs for private automobile systems at different uniformly distributed and one-way, maximum load point volumes for the different route lengths. Figure 35 presents essentially the same data for high population densities. Figures 36 and 37 show similar comparisons, at medium and high population densities,

[27] G. M. Webb and K. Moskowitz, "California Freeway Capacity Study—1956" *Highway Research Board Proceedings,* vol. 36, 1957, pp. 587–641.

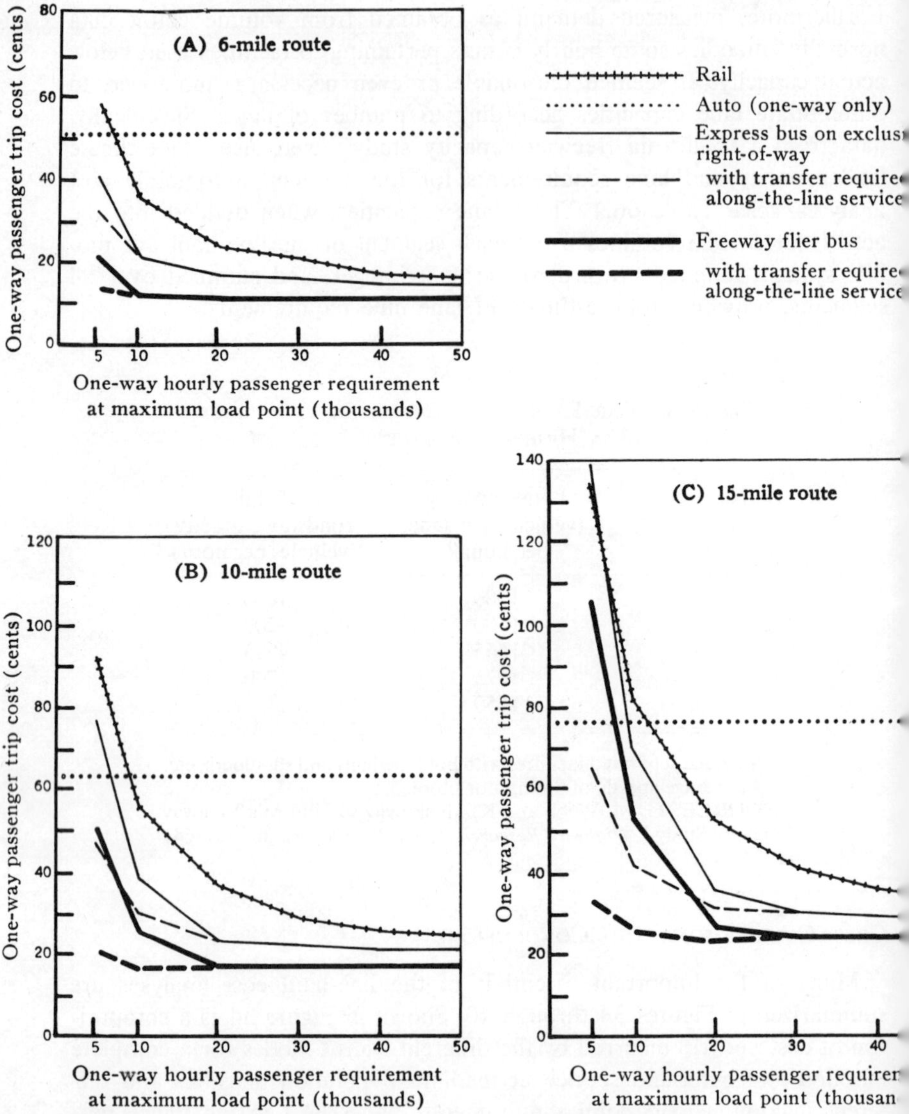

(A) 6-mile route

(B) 10-mile route

(C) 15-mile route

One-way passenger trip cost (cents)

One-way hourly passenger requirement at maximum load point (thousands)

Rail
Auto (one-way only)
Express bus on exclus
right-of-way
with transfer require
along-the-line service
Freeway flier bus
with transfer require
along-the-line service

Figure 34. Line-haul systems: medium population density (for example, Pittsburgh) with complete 2-way service.

respectively, but only with one-way service provided; that is, the costs are computed on the assumption that return trips in the low volume direction are made on a nonstop express basis. Figure 38 presents a special set of comparisons between two low-cost forms of line-haul transport, an existing or "sunk cost" rail system and freeway flier buses

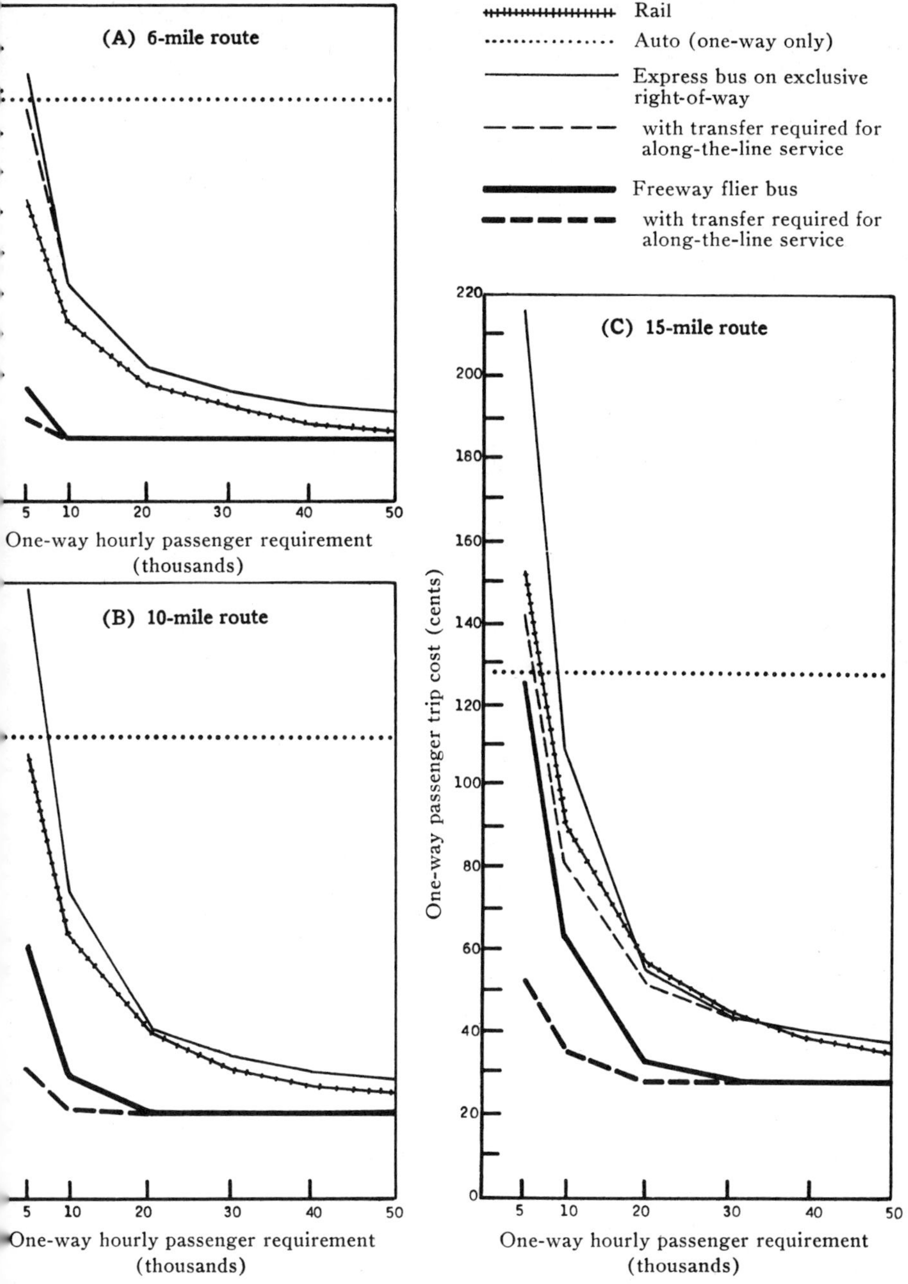

Figure 35. Line-haul systems: high population density (for example, Chicago) with complete 2-way service.

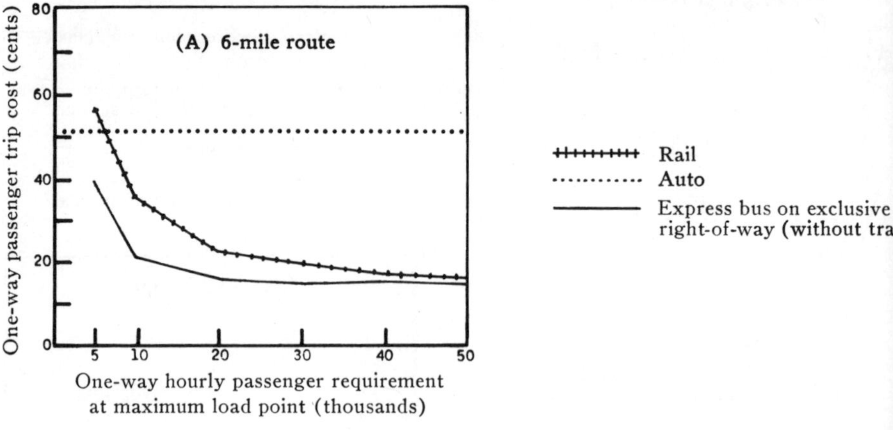

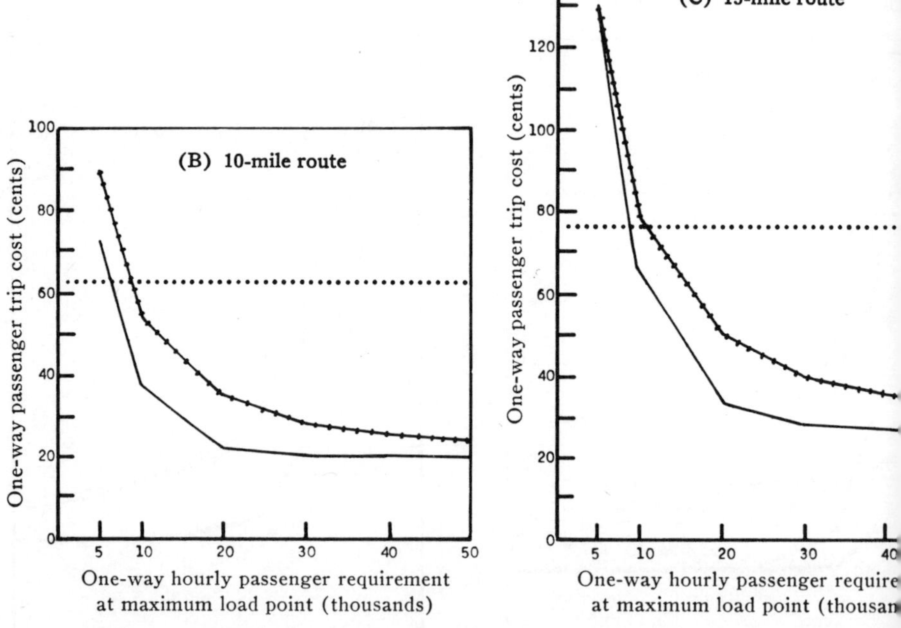

Figure 36. Line-haul systems: medium population density with 1-way (including along-the-line) service.

operating without congestion hindrances. Figures 39 and 40 compare costs for particular modes under different service specifications.

It should be noted that all of the volumes shown in the diagrams and used to compute the "average trip costs" pertain to the 1-way, maximum load point requirements on each system. In systems where 2-way and

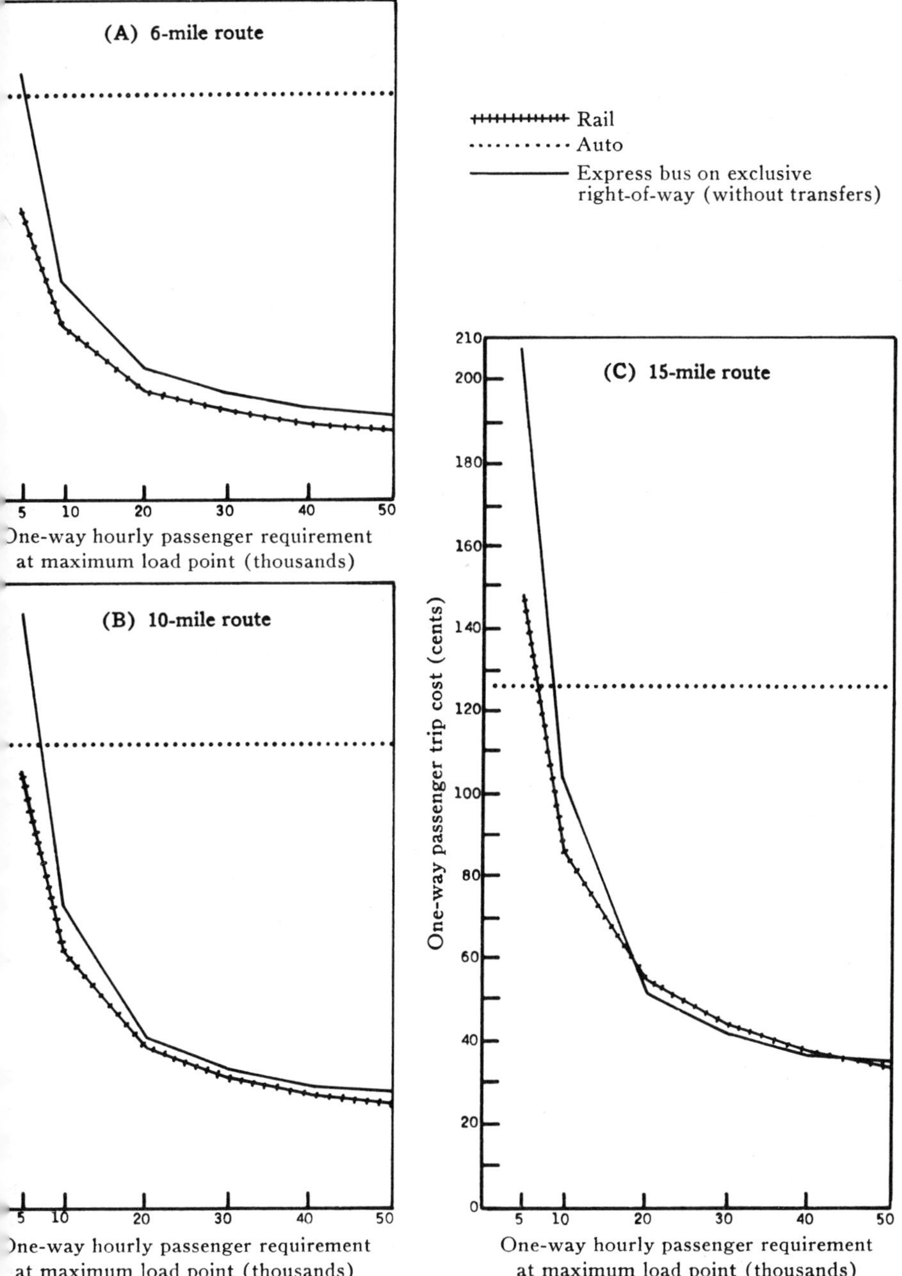

Figure 37. Line-haul systems: high population density with 1-way (including along-the-line) service.

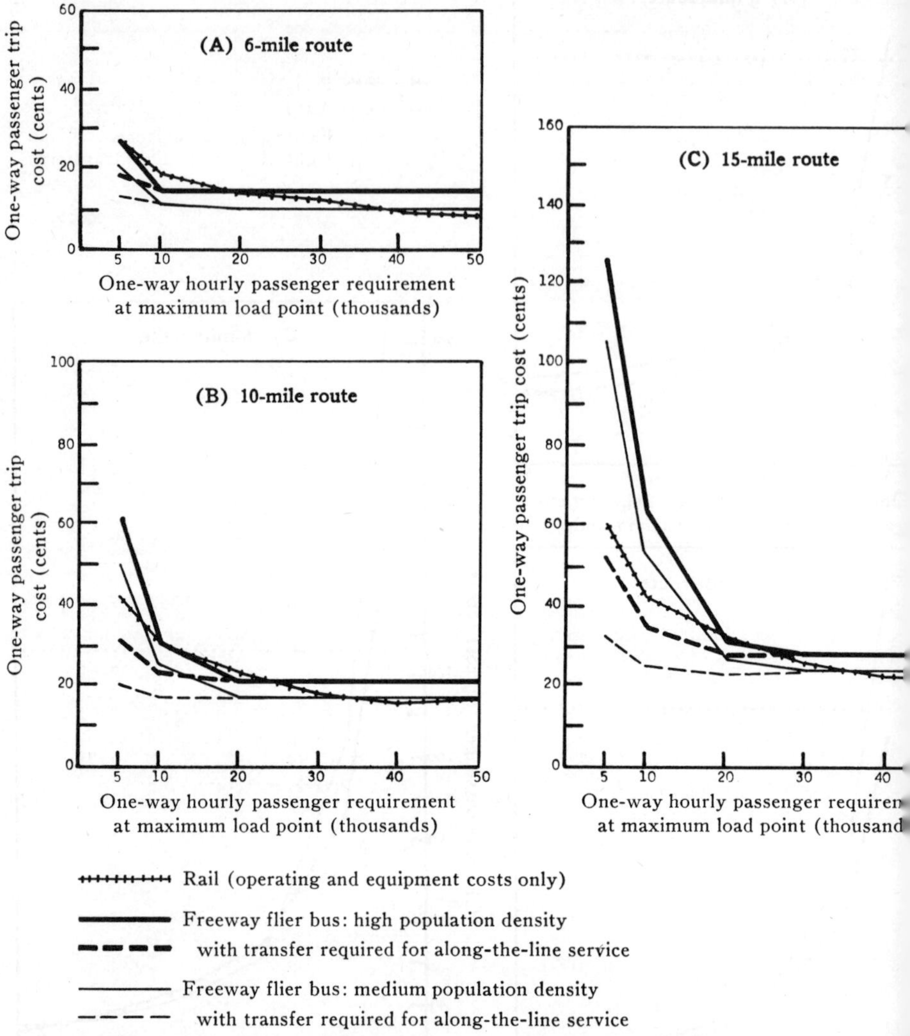

(A) 6-mile route

(B) 10-mile route

(C) 15-mile route

One-way passenger trip cost (cents)

One-way hourly passenger requirement at maximum load point (thousands)

Rail (operating and equipment costs only)

Freeway flier bus: high population density

with transfer required for along-the-line service

Freeway flier bus: medium population density

with transfer required for along-the-line service

Figure 38. Low-cost line-haul systems: complete 2-way service.

along-the-line services are provided, the actual average cost per trip normally would be lower than the costs shown because the total number of trips should exceed the 1-way maximum load point requirement; in other words, with multistop or minor direction services some trips should be completed without adding to capacity requirements at the peak load point. In such circumstances, an over-all average cost per trip could be calculated as follows:

(5) $$ACT_o = \frac{V_m}{V_t} ACT,$$

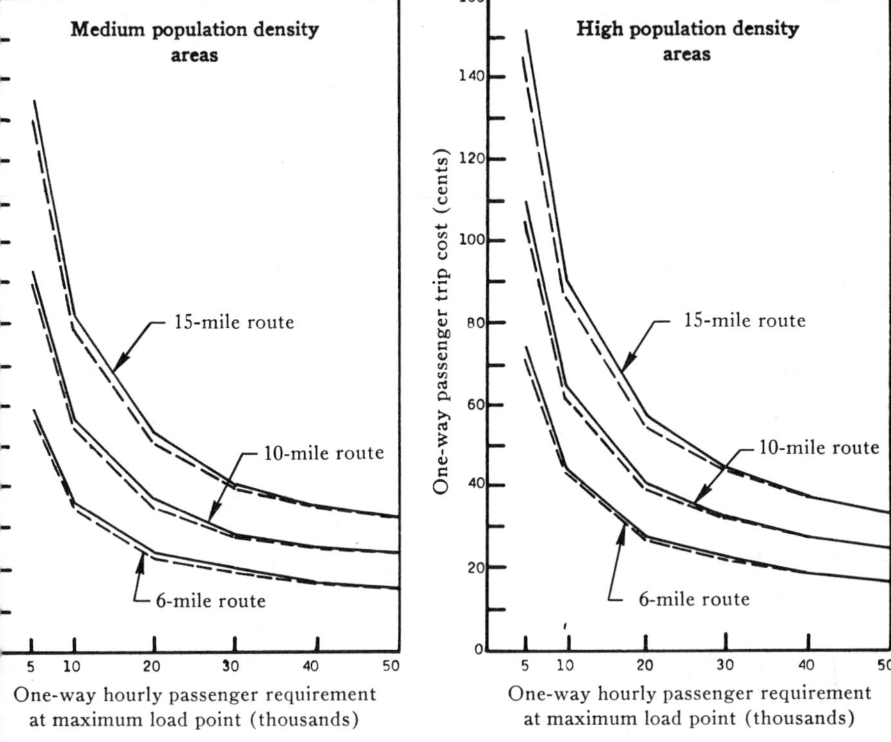

Figure 39. Comparison of rail costs under different service and operating conditions.

where ACT_o = the over-all average cost per trip for all trips;

V_m = the 1-way maximum load point volume (or maximum trip volume achieved at any one point as shown on the horizontal axis in the diagrams);

V_t = the total number of trips made;

ACT = the average cost per trip for maximum load point volume (as these costs are shown on the vertical axis in the diagrams) where complete 2-way service is provided.

The total number of trips made would depend, of course, on the demand for along-the-line and reverse commuter trips (as well as the through volume) and this obviously would vary widely from situation to situation, as suggested by the statistics previously reported.

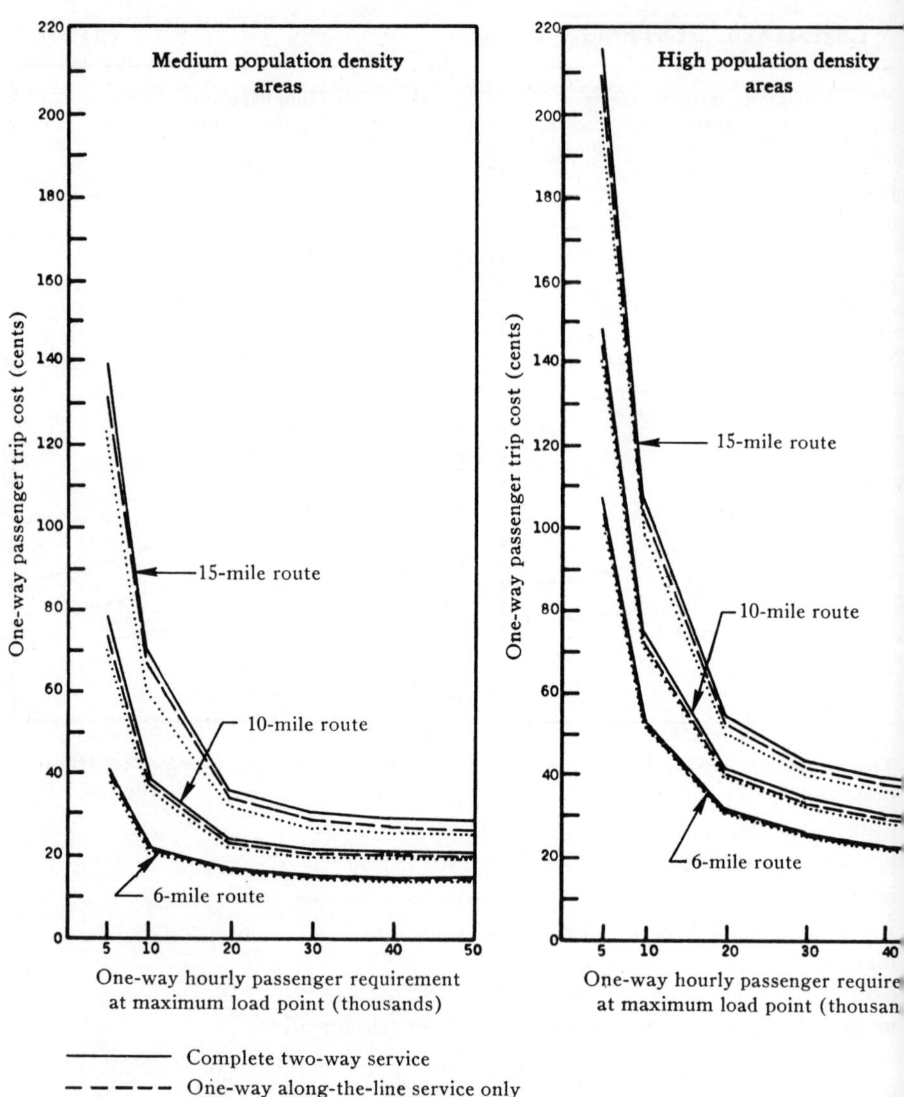

Figure 40. Comparison of bus costs under different service and operating conditions.

These over-all average costs per trip, however, would not be as generally useful for pricing decisions as the average incremental costs per additional trip generated by the addition of more service. On the usually justified assumption that maximum point loads control costs, these average incremental costs can be approximated by

$$ACT' = \frac{V_m ACT_c - aV_m ACT_s}{V_{t_c} - V_{t_s}}, \tag{6}$$

where ACT' = the average incremental cost per additional trip;
V_m = the maximum point load with the more complete service;
aV_m = the maximum point load that would use the system without the more complete service;
V_{t_c} = the total volume with the more complete service;
V_{t_s} = the total volume with the less complete service;
ACT_c = the average cost per maximum point load trip of the more complete service at its maximum point load, V_m;
ACT_s = the average cost per maximum point load trip of the simple or less complete service at its maximum point load volume, aV_m.

The costs defined by Eq. (6) provide an indication of the revenue level that must be met by the additional traffic to make it compensatory. While traffic normally would be expected to be greater for the more complex than the simpler service, it must be remembered that an improvement of service for some customers usually means a loss of service for others. If the loss is substantial enough, the total volume and maximum point load might decline after the initiation of the "additional" services, and over-all average costs could increase materially if the change occurred in a range where scale economies were pronounced.

The cost comparisons reveal that either bus or rail transit is considerably cheaper than the automobile for meeting peak hour line-haul transportation requirements when very high corridor volumes are encountered. The advantage of transit over private automobile also tends to be inversely related to route length. However, at low corridor volumes, an automobile system, even with only 1.6 passengers in each car, is often cheaper than either rail or bus transit if transfers are not permitted in the bus system; this is particularly true under medium to low population density assumptions. Costs can be reduced further for the automobile simply by increasing the number of passengers, which results in an almost proportional reduction in automobile costs. With five passengers per vehicle, automobile costs per trip drop close to and sometimes below those for public transit, even at the highest volumes. Of course, such a reduction must be "paid for" in reduced quality of service; and the low automobile occupancy rates observed in U.S. cities suggest that many commuters regard the drawbacks of car-pooling as not worth these cost savings.

The relatively favorable cost performance of the automobile system at low volumes is not too surprising. In our high labor cost economy, automobiles have the great virtue of being do-it-yourself vehicles. A private automobile system can "hire" its labor in exactly the amounts required. There are no problems of split shifts or finding off-peak employment for the driver. In general, there are no labor relations problems or costs of advertising, schedule printing, and administration. The private automobile also has no empty back-hauls. If parking space is available at both ends of the journey, a 1- or 2-person automobile trip will have very little waste motion—or, in the jargon, nonrevenue miles. In short, trip length will be tailored almost exactly to travel requirements. Exceptions occur mainly with car-pooling—which probably explains some of its unpopularity.

One particularly interesting set of figures emerging from the line-haul automobile cost analyses presented are the highway construction and related right-of-way costs for the automobile line-haul system when put on a per-vehicle-mile basis at medium population densities: 1.5 cents a vehicle mile for the 15-mile systems; 1.7 for 10 miles; and 1.8 for 6 miles. About 5 mills per mile should be added for maintenance to arrive at total "user cost" estimates. These figures correspond with the cost estimates for high-performance urban expressways developed in chapter 4, and can be compared with an estimated 1.1 cent per mile of user tax revenues yielded by automobile operations. It should be remembered, however, that the highway costs used in this chapter were constructed *de novo* and assumed only four hours of travel per workday, or twenty hours per week, of peak utilization; as noted in chapter 4 and shown in Table 30, expressways usually experience over two-thirds of their total use during off-peak hours and on weekends.

At high population densities, on the other hand, the construction and land acquisition costs per vehicle-mile for the high-performance automobile highway would be 6.1 cents at 15 miles, 7.5 at 10 miles, and 9.5 at 6 miles, including 5 mills for maintenance—again figured only on the basis of rush hour usage. It thus seems probable that the present structure of user taxes implies some subsidy of urban rush hour highway users in very high-density situations. Again, though, any such conclusion must be tempered by the consideration that the costs are computed on an extremely narrow estimate of the total number of hours of peak utilization.

A somewhat surprising result of the cost comparisons is that bus transit at low and medium densities is almost invariably cheaper than rail. Indeed, a freeway flier system, if afforded congestion-free travel, is always the cheapest form of high-performance line-haul transit, even at high population densities. This efficiency of the freeway flier is attributable, of course, to a line-haul structure that can be employed for other purposes, namely, the movement of private passenger vehicles and possibly trucks as well.

A bus system operating on its own reserved or exclusive highway (express bus on exclusive right-of-way) yields cost characteristics very much like those of freeway fliers, except that the absolute cost level is usually 15 to 20 per cent higher. The additional costs are enough, moreover, so that at high population densities an exclusive bus system almost invariably has a higher average cost per trip than does a rail system. Only at the very longest route length (15 miles) and at the highest volumes will an exclusive bus operation record lower costs than a rail transit operation at high population densities. At medium densities, on the other hand, the bus systems systematically record lower costs than rail. Even at medium densities, however, the bus systems do not have a pronounced cost advantage over rail transit at the higher volume levels, particularly on the shorter route lengths (6 and 10 miles).

It is also obvious that transfers are a tremendous aid to bus system economy at low volume levels, cutting costs sufficiently to allow the exclusive highway bus system to keep its advantage over automobile line-haul travel even at the low 5000 volume level. The use of transfers at low volume levels also improves service for CBD-bound bus travelers; this should at least partially compensate for the reduction in service afforded to along-the-line travelers when transfers are introduced. There is no particular point, however, in introducing transfers at volume levels of 20,000 or more per hour. When volume levels become high enough, in fact, there is little difference among the public transit modes in major cost or service characteristics.

Economies also can be achieved on bus systems at volume levels beneath 20,000 hourly by increasing the maximum allowable headway, an obvious alternative to transfers as a means of improving load factors at low volume levels. For example, at a 10,000 hourly volume and medium population density, buses will achieve an over-all cost reduction of approximately 18 per cent if maximum allowable headways are increased from two to five minutes; at the 5000 volume level the economies are even more significant, being approximately 30 per cent. As with transfers, the economies are achieved by reducing unused capacity. The importance of these findings about altering headways or introducing transfers should not be underestimated, since a considerable share of urban transit service meets peak hourly demands in these sensitive lower volume ranges.

Rail systems are clearly at their best when population densities are high, runs are short, and trip volumes are high. Such findings are hardly unexpected. They mainly reflect the well-known facts that rail systems require less right-of-way than do highway systems for handling high volume or density workloads, and that rail has a very heavy fixed-cost burden. Even the better cost performance of rail on shorter runs is basically a result of a shorter route length leading to increased volume density. Similarly, higher density of use yields most of the rail economies achievable by volume increases. In short, the rail system needs a very high traffic concentration in order to turn its special technological advantages to account.

Obviously, then, nothing is so conducive to the relative economy of rail transit as high volumes and population density. High population density increases the costs of all urban transportation systems, but substantially less for rail than for other modes. This phenomenon also suggests that caution is advisable in advancing the view that high-density cities are inherently more efficient for commuter transportation than are medium- or low-density cities. The crux of the issue is whether high density will sharply increase hourly corridor volumes in a given case. Generally speaking, it will, but the exact nature of this relationship is not obvious since it depends on many factors, not the least of which is the dispersion of workplaces.

Rail costs compare somewhat more favorably when the very heavy costs of rail structural investments are ignored. Ignoring such costs may be appropriate when structures already exist and there is no plan or necessity for replacing them in the future. In Figure 38 the average costs per trip, excluding all investment costs associated with rail structures, are compared with all costs for the freeway flier bus system. The rail costs do include investment costs associated with equipment, however, on the grounds that most rail systems are now operating with equipment that needs or shortly will need replacement (or has been replaced recently). Also, the rail operations hypothesized are probably somewhat more efficiently tailored to specific demand levels than could be expected in existing systems, especially where demand levels have undergone change.

With structural investment eliminated from the rail cost calculations, a freeway flier system is still somewhat cheaper in most cases at medium population densities, but not by a large margin. More obviously, an existing rail system for which structure costs might legitimately be considered sunk often would be a very attractive alternative when population and trip densities are high. The fact that an existing rail system is, by definition, already in operation and devoid of "starting-up" costs should increase this attractiveness. However, the comparisons in Figure 38 hardly constitute a *carte blanche* endorsement of efforts to maintain existing rail systems at any or all costs, particularly where hourly trip volumes have declined or were never high.

Offering additional along-the-line services seems to make little difference in the cost relationships of the different modes. At given volume and population density levels, doing so results at most in a 1- or 2-cent increase in the average cost per trip. In real situations, of course, most of this cost increase might be offset by spreading total costs over greater volumes with along-the-line service. In general, volume must increase about 10 to 15 per cent if average trip costs before and after the addition of along-the-line service are to remain equal. The possibility of such volume increases will depend on trip patterns and other circumstances in particular cases.

TABLE 67

COMPARATIVE AVERAGE TRIP TIMES TO CBD BY VARIOUS LINE-HAUL MODES (minutes)

Mode	Trip time when average distance to CBD is		
	3.5 mi	5.5 mi	8.0 mi
Rail[a]	4.2 to 6.2	6.5 to 9.5	9.4 to 13.8
Bus			
Complete service; no transfer required[b]	6.6	9.8	13.8
Complete service; transfers required for along-the-line service at low volume levels[c]	6.4 to 6.6	8.2 to 9.8	11.2 to 13.8
Express service only	5.2	7.2	9.6
Line-haul auto (at 45 mph)	4.7	7.3	10.7

[a]The lower value in each pair is the time achievable when a third track is added.

[b]Slightly faster times could be achieved at the lower volume levels of 5000 and 10,000; in these calculations, a maximum load is assumed.

[c]The faster times are achieved at the low volume levels with transfers required. Explicitly, they apply at the 5000 volume level for the 6-mile round trip route, at 10,000 for the 10-mile, and at 20,000 for the 15-mile route.

It is also certain, however, that adding along-the-line services in bus systems will slow service for CBD-bound travelers. This fact is brought out by the data in Table 67 on the average CBD trip times that might be expected on different line-haul systems under different service assumptions. (Actually, there is no impact upon service under the operating assumptions used for these analyses in the case of the rail systems; however, if the overlapping 3-track line-haul terminal had been eliminated from the 3-track rail systems, some slight improvement in rail CBD travel times could have been achieved by eliminating the one overlapping stop.) As noted previously, service sacrifices for CBD-destined bus commuters are considerably less when transfers are incorporated into the systems at low volume levels.

Table 67 also brings out some interesting intermodal comparisons in travel times. As might be expected, the automobile is generally the fastest line-haul mode, though admittedly the figures are somewhat oversimplified since no account is made of the delays incurred for car-pooling, parking the automobile and so forth. (However, these aspects are fully considered in the chapters on residential collection and downtown distribution.) Somewhat less expected, however, is the finding that bus systems are generally on a par with rail systems in the line haul. This is because buses have higher divisibility and thus the opportunity of making fewer stops under the service and operating conditions hypothesized (other than the complete service bus system with no transfers). It is irrelevant that today's bus operations (other than a few freeway fliers) do not presently record speeds as fast as rail rapid transit, since most buses operate over surface streets and almost never enjoy reserved rights-of-way or other congestion-free facilities; even freeway fliers are almost always slowed during rush hours by congestion on the freeways used. Fundamentally, however, an *express* bus operation on a congestion-free right-of-way should be an inherently faster form of travel than rail transit because the bus is a smaller unit of operation and therefore requires fewer stops to acquire a full load. In many ways this is also why the line-haul automobile system has a comparatively good time performance.

In general, an automobile system—through its operation, occupancy, and parking characteristics—offers flexibility and other advantages unmatched by virtually any other type of urban transport. For example, car-pooling can be viewed as a mode of low-cost transit available right now—a mode, moreover, with service characteristics perhaps as attractive as those of almost any conceivable rail or bus system.[28] Failure of car-pooling to attract more patronage therefore implies that many commuters place so high a value on convenience and service that public transit might have serious difficulty trying to win patronage back from the private automobile.

Above all else, private automobile travel lends itself to being "tailored" to meet the specific needs of users. If a traveler wants the maximum in comfort and convenience and can afford an automobile, he has the option *now* of driving alone and in comfort, with unexcelled schedule frequency, and can park close to his workplace (though at a cost of perhaps $1.50 a trip or more). Other automobile travelers can pool from two to five or

[28] The only service characteristics of car-pooling that are clearly inferior to public transit are schedule frequency and the fact that the driver must devote his full attention to driving—that is, he cannot read the newspaper or engage in other activities. But for workers keeping regular hours and with common residential areas and workplaces, the schedule-frequency differential should not be a too serious drawback.

six persons to a car, drive cheap used cars, park at cheaper, less centrally located parking lots (and have to walk farther), and reduce trip costs to as low as 10 or 15 cents a passenger. Automobile commuters thus have a variety of options, including that of changing their habits from day to day and year to year as their tastes and incomes permit. Transit systems afford fewer such freedoms, usually offering only a single level of service at one cost, on the basis of a long-term commitment.

Public transit modes are not completely devoid, however, of possibilities for diversifying service offerings. As already noted, many subtle tradeoffs are possible between improving line-haul express and along-the-line services, and between requiring and not requiring transfers for realizing some services. Similarly, reducing schedule frequency is often a simple way for bus operations to reduce costs, but at the expense of increasing average waiting time. The obvious question, therefore, is how many actual or potential users of transit find it worth while to wait extra time in order to save money. For example, at a 10,000 hourly volume level over a 10-mile route system at medium population densities, the consumer could be confronted with choices of the following type: going by automobile at an average 1-way trip cost of, say, 62 cents with virtually no waiting time or walking; going by rail at a cost of 54 cents per trip with 55 to 60 seconds of waiting time and a short walk;[29] going by bus with a waiting time of about 60 seconds, a short walk, and a cost of 39 or 25 cents per trip, depending on whether the bus operates on its own exclusive highway or shares a freeway; or going by bus with a waiting time of about 140 seconds and a cost of 28 cents or 15 cents, again depending on whether the bus operates on its own exclusive highway facility or shares a freeway. Without considerable knowledge of the demand structure for urban travel, it is, of course, impossible to say with assurance which alternative consumers would choose, and, more importantly, in what numbers. Such questions should be raised and answered, however, either implicitly or explicitly in planning urban transportation systems.

All of these cost calculations under different service and design assumptions point up the old truth that the consumer gets about what he pays for. Transit systems can be designed to provide cheaper travel than that of automobiles with one or two people in them, but with a loss of convenience, privacy, and other amenities travelers are likely to value. In sum, if quality of service is highly valued or volumes are low, the automobile is almost indisputably the cheapest or best mode of line-haul travel; if lower-quality service is required, or is all that can be afforded, the bus has advantages at moderate volumes, and either bus or rail will serve well at high volumes.

29 Rail transit with a 5-minute headway is not worth consideration; it reduces service without reducing costs materially.

Chapter 10 | Residential Collection and Distribution

All too commonly, past urban transportation analyses have either ignored or dealt casually with the costs of travel between the home and the line-haul system. The pattern has been to pass over any transit or nontransit costs that travelers incur and to neglect accurate costing of additional parking or feeder bus operations created to feed passengers to or away from the line-haul facility. For several reasons, this neglect is not defensible. Above all, it can hardly be overstressed that it is the cost and service characteristics of the entire trip between home and work that determine the typical commuter's urban transportation choices, rather than simply the circumstances of the line-haul portion of the over-all trip.

The commuter can travel between his home and the line-haul facility in many ways: (1) he may walk; (2) his wife may drive him there and drop him off (the so-called kiss-and-ride method); (3) he may drive his own automobile to the facility and leave it there (the so-called park-and-ride method); (4) he may ride a feeder bus; (5) he may ride a line-haul express bus that also operates as a feeder bus (here called an "incremental or integrated bus"); or (6) he may simply use an automobile for the entire trip—which of course would include the distance between the line-haul facility and his home (called an "incremental auto" system here).

A full-scale "real world" analysis should consider all alternatives, of course, and should stratify or split the population into groups walking, using kiss-and-ride, and so forth, according to differences in costs, quality of service, value scales, and consumer preferences. The present study, however, makes some simplifications in order to reduce the analysis to manageable size. In general, for the line-haul rail and express bus system, the residential collection service will not be stratified or split among all the above alternatives; instead, each alternative will be costed separately and on the assumption that it must individually meet a specified level of service. The single exception to this "one type of service" rule will be the assumption that all passengers living within two blocks of a line-haul station walk to it and therefore are deducted from the hypothesized hourly volume figures. All other passengers are handled by the particular type of collection service being considered.

Every method of getting people to and from the line-haul facility—even walking—entails some costs. If large numbers of people are to go on foot, they must live in high-density structures and the line-haul facility must run close by. In fact, there is a substantial positive correlation between residential density and the costs of constructing transportation facilities because when density is high, costly elevated or tunneled structures usually must be used. (Of course, it may not always be easy to disentangle cause and effect in this relationship.) Similarly, adding stations or stops will encourage walking, but only at a cost. Finally, it usually costs more per square foot to build high-rise apartment houses than to build single-family dwellings (although the higher cost is often offset by more intensive land use).

It would be interesting to estimate the costs of various methods for increasing foot travel to line-haul stations, but in the generalized context of these analyses any such exercise would probably be so artificial as not to be worth the effort. Accordingly, only the five vehicular modes of residential service—numbers (2) through (6) in the list above—will be specifically costed, with number (1), walking, being treated as a "no cost" service. The systems costed will subsequently be referred to as kiss-and-ride, park-and-ride, separate feeder bus, incremental feeder bus, and incremental automobile. The first three (and walking too, of course) conceivably could be used with virtually any kind of line-haul travel. The last two are integral parts of specific types of line haul, for both of which the cost and performance calculations are always placed on an incremental basis; that is, all cost, time, and performance characteristics reported for these two modes are regarded as increments created by the addition of residential service to the line-haul function and added to the equivalent line-haul-only figures of the preceding chapter.

Earlier assumptions regarding the maintenance of equivalent service will be altered slightly in the cost analyses. First, neither feeder buses nor automobiles will be provided with private rights-of-way, but will operate on the residential street system. *Under these conditions buses cannot match the average trip speed of automobiles on the residential collection portion of the trip and therefore cannot provide services of equal quality.* Bus quality is further lowered, in comparison with the automobile, by the fact that bus passengers usually have to do more walking.

Service variables considered especially important in the feeder bus operations are frequency of service, walking distance to bus stop, availability of seats, and necessity of transfer. Since all transit travelers using feeder buses will incur both waiting time and walking penalties, and will travel at lower speeds than automobile travelers, the following service conditions for bus transit will be honored in a crude effort to establish a modicum of service equivalence between feeder bus and automobile: seats will be provided for all passengers; bus stops will be located so that passengers have to walk no more than two blocks; and feeder bus headways shall be no more than 10 minutes.

No specific allowance is made in these service specifications for differences in travel times by the different modes. Travel times are calculated, however, under a number of different circumstances and compared subsequently. A major reason for not attempting to enforce a rigorous set of controls on travel time is that the effective travel time by bus transit is a function of a very large number of considerations. For example, with costs held constant, it is often possible to *improve* the effective time performance of a bus transit system by *reducing* scheduled frequency. Illustrative calculations indicating the nature of these and other tradeoffs are reported in Appendix C.

The foregoing remarks strongly suggest that it is difficult (within reasonable cost limits) to provide feeder bus service that is comparable in most respects to automobile travel for the entire commuter trip. It would follow, then, that if equivalent service were required, only the park-and-ride and kiss-and-ride[1] types of feeder service to transit line-haul systems should be included; even these two types of feeder service are not comparable, of course, to incremental automobile travel because of the required transfer from automobile to transit and waiting time at the line-haul station. Indeed, the very omission of any mention of transfers as among the service conditions to be controlled in the cost analyses is a confession of partial defeat in maintaining service equivalence.

All of the more essential features of the residential collection problem can be illustrated by confining attention to the collection and distribution problems encountered in serving just one stop on a line-haul system. Accordingly, all of the preliminary cost analyses of the basic residential travel modes will be developed exclusively in terms of differences in volume and trip origination densities and without regard to differences in the route length of the line-haul system. Specifically, four different hourly volume levels of passengers entering (or departing from) a line-haul station will be analyzed: 333, 1000, 3000, and 5000. Trip origination densities ranging upward from one per block will be considered.

[1] It should be evident that in this case the driver (for example a wife) suffers the "discomfort or inconvenience" penalty and time loss involved in providing such a "taxi service."

As in the last chapter, moreover, it will be assumed that the line-haul station being analyzed is equidistant between two other line-haul stations, each of which is 1 mile away; it follows, therefore, that the passenger origination volumes are assumed to originate roughly in a land area stretching a half-mile along the line-haul facility in either direction from the line-haul station.

Cost Parameters

Cost functions for residential feeder service are somewhat different from those required for line-haul analyses because no components are needed for structural costs associated with highways, roadbeds, and right-of-way. This occurs simply because all the services involved use the streets or sidewalks normally found in residential areas and assumed to be needed for other purposes. For vehicular use, the cost of these streets is usually recouped in the form of gasoline taxes, which essentially amount to a per-vehicle-mile levy on residential travel and, accordingly, can be directly incorporated into the β coefficient in the basic cost function. The general residential service cost function therefore is

$$TC = \alpha U + \beta M, \qquad (1)$$

where TC specifically refers to total annual costs for four hours of peak-period service. The mileage coefficient, β, incorporates street maintenance and ownership costs and vehicle fuel and maintenance costs to be applied to the annual vehicular mileage, M; the α coefficient represents vehicle ownership, operator, insurance, overhead, and similar costs to be applied to the number of vehicle units, U.

The α coefficient, or cost per bus unit, for any feeder bus operation essentially will have three components: operator costs, capital costs for yards and shops, and the debt service costs for the investment in the bus itself. As in the line-haul analyses, the bus operator costs are assumed to be \$8100 a year per bus plus a 10 per cent allowance for bus operator break time and sick leave, so that the total annual cost per scheduled peak-hour vehicle is \$8910. Again as in the line-haul analyses, the investment in yards and shops will be assumed to be \$4500 per vehicle, increased 5 per cent to allow for vehicle downtime, and it will be further assumed that these investments have a 50-year life and that a 6 per cent rate of interest prevails; under such circumstances the total annual costs of yards and shops per bus will be \$299. Bus ownership costs for the separate feeder bus service will be less than those encountered in the line-haul analyses, because a less expensive bus with lesser performance capability can be used on strictly residential feeder operations. This bus, including modification to incorporate three doors (the third door for use at the line-haul station), will cost an estimated \$29,100. With allowance for 5 per cent downtime, a 6 per cent interest rate, and a 12-year life, the annual capital recovery charge for this bus investment is \$3655. If the higher-performance line-haul vehicle costing \$31,200 is employed instead, these annual charges increase to \$3910, and this higher figure is used when costing integrated residential and line-haul service (that is, the incremental bus). Thus, total cost per unit, or α, is \$12,824 for a feeder bus service that is completely separated from any line-haul activity, and \$13,119 for a bus that is used in both residential and line-haul service. There are obviously situations where it would be more economical to use smaller capacity and lower cost buses than those assumed here. This aspect of optimality has been ignored for simplicity.

The β coefficient or cost per bus-mile for residential bus analyses must incorporate an allowance for the bus' share of residential street construction, maintenance, and administration, along with all the other bus operating and maintenance expenses usually incorporated into this coefficient. It is assumed that appropriate bus highway user charges per mile of bus operation on residential surface streets amount to 2.5 cents (about 130 per cent higher than that for passenger cars). Thus the β coefficient for analyzing such operations would be 32.5 cents—the 30 cents used for line-haul operations plus the additional 2.5 cents. Accordingly, the basic cost function for exclusively residential bus operations would be

(2) $$TC = \$12{,}824U + \$0.325M$$ (for separate feeder bus),

while the total incremental costs of adding a feeder operation to an existing line-haul service would be

(3) $$TC = \$13{,}119U_r + \$0.325M_r$$ (for integrated feeder bus),

where M_r designates miles of additional service on residential streets and U_r the extra units required to perform the residential service.[2]

Park-and-ride is the most complex of the automobile forms of residential service to cost because the cost per vehicle, or α, for this mode must include allowance for parking as well as accident (or insurance) costs. Estimates of parking costs were discussed in the last chapter in connection with analyzing line-haul automobile systems. It was concluded that

[2] The total costs of an integrated residential and line-haul service might not equal, however, the simple sum of these residential costs and previously estimated line-haul costs. For example, some reductions might be effected by elimination of terminals at line-haul stations, though such eliminations would raise problems in providing along-the-line and reverse direction services. Also, the volumes of travel on the line-haul facilities pertinent to estimating structural costs could be somewhat modified in the combined service, because with the combined service a basic alteration has been made in the service standard; specifically, ten-minute headways at residential street corners have been substituted for 2-minute headways at the line-haul stations. An interesting alternative for costing the integrated residential and line-haul service would be to take the line-haul service system as established and costed in the previous chapter and append to it a residential feeder operation with optimal characteristics, given the 2-minute headway and other basic service conditions hypothesized in chap. 9.

annual parking costs per space can range from $400 or a little more in downtown locations to as low as about $150 for paved lots in the suburbs. On the whole, estimates near the lower end of the spectrum should be more generally accurate for residential areas; accordingly, in the cost analyses that follow, parking costs per space have been assumed to be $150 a year.

Accident or insurance costs were placed on a per-vehicular-unit basis and estimated at $30 a year per automobile. It seems reasonable that the accident or insurance costs solely for residential collection service should be considerably lower than those for line-haul tripmaking because of speed and volume density differences, and since residential trip lengths are relatively short. Taken together with the $150 per vehicle already estimated for annual parking charges, the total α coefficient for the park-and-ride cost function can be placed at $180; moreover, since U is the number of automobile units needed per hour, this figure should be doubled in order to account fully for four rush hours a day.

The mileage cost for park-and-ride service has three basic constituents: vehicle operation and maintenance costs, user charges for residential surface streets, and ownership costs associated with the vehicle itself (depreciation, interest on investment, and so forth). As in the line-haul analyses, the operating and maintenance charges will be estimated on the basis of using a more economical "rush hour only" vehicle. The costs for repairs, replacement of tires and tubes, gasoline, and oil for such a car are estimated as before to be approximately 2.90 cents per vehicle-mile. The appropriate charge for using surface streets shared with other vehicular traffic will be estimated at 1.17 cents per vehicle-mile.[3] The ownership costs will be estimated at 6 cents per vehicle-mile.[4] Six cents a mile is used instead of the 4 cents a mile assumed for all-auto line-haul travel because park-and-ride trips are much shorter, thereby reducing the distance for spreading the ownership charges and increasing the unit costs.

Combining the 6-cent-per-vehicle-mile ownership cost with the 2.9 cents of operating and maintenance charges and 1.17 cents of user charges, a total β coefficient for park-and-ride of $0.1007 is estimated. Therefore, the park-and-ride cost function would be

$$(4) \qquad TC = \$360U + \$0.1007M \qquad \text{(for park-and-ride auto).}$$

The cost functions for kiss-and-ride and automobile residential feeder service incremental to an automobile line-haul service may be very

[3] E. W. Cope and L. L. Liston, *A Discussion of Gasoline Tax Rates and Consumption,* U.S. Department of Commerce, Bureau of Public Roads, U.S. Government Printing Office, Washington, D.C., January 1961.

[4] The assumption underlying use of this figure of 6 cents is that a car can always be found to yield this approximate charge for almost any average daily distance traveled.

quickly derived from the park-and-ride function. For both kiss-and-ride and the incremental automobile service the α coefficient can be placed at zero. For the kiss-and-ride service there would be no parking charges and the incremental insurance costs are assumed to be zero since the household normally uses and insures the automobile primarily for other purposes. As a first approximation, the β coefficient for kiss-and-ride would incorporate only allowances for vehicle operating and maintenance charges (2.90 cents) and for the use of residential surface streets (1.17 cents). It is somewhat arbitrary, however, to eliminate vehicle ownership charges from the kiss-and-ride cost calculations. It could be argued that the additional kiss-and-ride travel either shortens the life of the family automobile or requires it to be a more dependable vehicle than it would otherwise have to be. Similarly, it might be argued that ownership costs sometimes can be legitimately eliminated from park-and-ride charges since there may be no other use for the family automobile on weekdays; this might be true, for example, if the family did most of its shopping and recreational travel during evenings and weekends with the same park-and-ride vehicle. On the other hand, ownership costs of 4 cents per mile should be included when costing an incremental residential automobile service appended to an existing automobile line-haul facility, in order to maintain a consistent and symmetrical treatment of these costs, in addition to 4.07 cents a mile for vehicle operating charges and use of local streets. (Four rather than 6 cents per mile for ownership costs is appropriate here since the ownership costs for incremental automobile and park-and-ride automobile are spread over different trip lengths. For the incremental automobile service, however, there would be no additional parking or accident costs, since these are already incorporated into the line-haul cost estimates.)

The appropriate cost function for kiss-and-ride service would therefore be

$$TC = \$0.0407M \qquad \text{(for kiss-and-ride auto),} \tag{5}$$

while for the integrated auto service it would be

$$TC = \$0.0807M \qquad \text{(for integrated auto).} \tag{6}$$

In passing, it should be emphasized that the kiss-and-ride costs estimated in this fashion are not in a true sense directly comparable to the costs estimated for the other residential collection systems. The extremely dubious assumption is made that the chauffeur in the kiss-and-ride service (a housewife, typically) attaches no value to the time spent driving the commuter to and from the depot. In most other respects, however, the kiss-and-ride mode renders a high quality of service: a good time performance, considerable privacy, and virtually no waiting on the residential portion of the commuter trip. In the same vein, it should be noted that the incremental or integrated automobile mode not only has most of the service advantages of kiss-and-ride or park-and-ride, but also involves no transfer. But some inconvenience does accrue to the driver because of car-pooling arrangements and the driving task. These observations buttress the previous observation that it is virtually impossible to establish complete comparability of service among the different residential collection modes.

Functional Relationships

The procedures for estimating the number of vehicles required, U, and total mileage, M, are essentially the same as those previously employed in analyzing line-haul costs. A minor difference is that trip origination densities are more significant in the residential analyses.

In the present context, with the emphasis on CBD-oriented systems, the real question is the number of *trip originations destined for the downtown* per unit of geographic area that might be expected during the rush hours. Obviously, this number will vary widely depending on several considerations, not the least of which is population density in the residential area. In fact, data collected for the Chicago Area Transportation Study in 1956 show that in Chicago CBD trip origination rates per rush hour varied between less than one per block to as high as 75 or so per block.[5]

Trip origination information is essential in feeder bus analyses because it defines the number of passengers to be taken on or dropped off at each curbside transit stop in the residental area and sets the route lengths. A functional expression for this relationship is

$$v = \frac{2w^2 p}{h}, \tag{7}$$

where v = average number of passengers loading (or unloading) each bus at each feeder bus stop;

p = number of CBD-destined trips per rush hour originating (or terminating) in each block;

$2w^2$ = number of blocks covered by each transit stop location when people walk w blocks and bus stops are placed $2w$ blocks apart;[6]

h = the number of bus trips per hour (that is, schedule frequency) made to each feeder bus stop.

[5] These are the "standardized" blocks of this analysis set equal to 1/144 square mile including surrounding streets. However, it must be emphasized that these trip generation rates were based on data obtained from very large districts of land, the average of which covered 28 square miles of land use (four of which were residential land).

[6] This relationship was explained more fully in chapter 8.

In most of the analyses that follow, a uniform distribution of origination densities is assumed; that is, p is assumed to be the same within the entire geographic area specified for analysis. The only exception will be the assumption of somewhat higher densities within walking distance of the line-haul facility. Of course, Eq. (7) is not needed in automobile system analyses, since the average number of originations and of passengers per vehicle is usually between one and two and is determined by attitudes toward car-pooling rather than directly by the walking distances involved.

With uniform trip origination densities, the residential area (in standardized blocks equal to 1/144 square mile) to be served from a given line-haul station, A_i, can be defined as

(8a) $$A_i = \frac{V_i}{p},$$

again designating the volume served at any one line-haul station as V_i. However, Eq. (8a) must be modified if there are higher densities occurring within walking distance of a line-haul system, thus becoming

(8b) $$A_i = \frac{V_i - W}{p} + 2w^2,$$

where W = the number of persons walking directly to the line-haul system;[7]

$W/2w^2$ = the trip origination density within the walking radius, w, of the line-haul station.

Since the residential analyses generally can be performed in all basic essentials by simply confining attention to one station on a line-haul system, the subscript i will be omitted in subsequent discussion.

The area served, A, is essential in estimating the distance to be traveled on each transit round trip in residential service. Actually, extensive analysis would be necessary to estimate such distances precisely, especially if optimal characteristics were desired. Considerable experimentation with

[7] The number of persons walking directly to the line-haul system was rather arbitrarily estimated, specifically being set somewhere between 10 and 20 per cent of the total hourly volume entering the line-haul station during peak periods. The higher percentages were used with the lower hourly volumes and the lower percentages with the higher hourly volumes. These assumed percentages compare with the limited data available on commuters walking to transit facilities as follows. For example, 34 per cent of the commuters using the Highland Branch Rail Transit Line in Boston walk to the facility (Greater Boston Economic Study Committee, *Economic Base Reports,* No. 7, *A Survey of Commuters on the Highland Branch,* Boston, 1959, Part III, Table 12), while only 6 per cent of the commuters on the Cleveland Westside Line walk (Walter S. Rainville, Jr., *et al.,* "Preliminary Progress Report of Transit Subcommittee, Committee on Highway Capacity," *Highway Research Board Proceedings,* vol. 40, 1961, Fig. 5, p. 533), and both of these lines correspond roughly to the lowest volume levels employed in the present analysis. For the Congress Street–Douglas Park Rail Transit Line in

different possibilities has shown, however, that for uniform densities a reasonably good approximation to an optimal (that is, minimal d or round trip) distance, in blocks, for residential bus transit under a wide range of circumstances is provided by[8]

$$\text{(9a)}\qquad d = \frac{A}{24} + 6 + 2w(f - 1) = \frac{V}{24p} + 6 + 2w(f - 1)$$

(in blocks and for uniform densities for feeder bus),

where f designates the number of feeder bus stops (that is, not including the stop at the line-haul station) made per vehicle round trip and is equal to[9]

$$\text{(10)}\qquad f = \frac{c}{v} \qquad \text{(truncated)},$$

Chicago, with volumes generally in the lower-middle spectrum of hourly passenger volumes analyzed here, about 50 per cent of the commuters walk to the line. On the other hand, for the Toronto Yonge Street Line (basically a "downtown distribution" transit line), which is slightly above the middle spectrum of the volumes analyzed, about 15 to 20 per cent of the commuters walk to the line-haul facility.

[8] This expression takes advantage of certain specific characteristics assumed or built into the transportation systems under analysis. For example, because the line-haul stations are assumed to be placed 1 mile or twelve blocks apart, the residential area served by any one line-haul station has to extend outward from the line-haul station and has a total band width equal to $A/12$ (and running transverse to line-haul route); furthermore, it could normally be assumed in a geographically unconstrained and uniformly distributed population area like that hypothesized that the line-haul facility would be placed in the middle of the residential area to be served; thus it follows that one-half the total area served would be on each side of the line-haul facility, and the length or outward extension of the distance served on each side can be found by dividing A by 24. The actual distance that a bus or automobile would have to operate on the average to reach the line station or middle of such a residential area, on the other hand, would be only one-half the total length which the residential area extends on each side of the line-haul station; accordingly, $A/48$ would yield the average distance to reach the middle of the area. However, it must be remembered that a bus transit vehicle would have to make a round trip when performing residential services so that this expression would immediately have to be multiplied by 2 to obtain an estimate applicable to the typical or average trip, and thereby the expression would immediately revert to $A/24$. The constant of 6 included in the equation is obtained by rather similar reasoning; it would normally require three blocks to travel one-half of the distance from the line-haul station to the area served by the next line-haul station, and this, when doubled to obtain an estimate for the round trip, would be six. (Thus, the first term applies to transverse movement and the second term to longitudinal movement within the residential—relative to line-haul system alignment.) The final expression in the equation, $2w\ (f-1)$, represents an allowance for extra distances traveled on each round trip because of multistop bus operations.

[9] Where densities are very high, it could, of course, occur that Eq. (10) would yield a value less than 1. Obviously, in such circumstances no truncation is required since it would be ridiculous to suggest that each vehicle should have zero stops on its runs. In such cases the obvious solution is to increase h, the specified schedule frequency, until it is large enough to bring f up to 1 at the designated level of capacity.

where c, as before, is the capacity of the vehicle used. Truncation of Eq. (10) is necessary to ensure a seat for every passenger (for a given value of h). However, truncating f tends to provide some excess capacity in the feeder system, which in turn tends to reduce differences in service between public transit feeder systems and private automobile feeder systems. If it is necessary to truncate f, c should also be reduced so as to bring Eq. (10) into agreement. To take account of situations where there are higher densities within walking distances of the line-haul station, Eq. (9a) should be modified as follows:

(9b) $$d = \frac{V - W}{24p} + \frac{2w^2}{24} + 2w(f - 1) + 6$$ (in blocks and for nonuniform densities for feeder bus).

For the automobile modes, either Eq. (9a) or (9b) can be simplified by hypothesizing that f normally equals one;[10] furthermore, for the 1-way automobile modes, park-and-ride and integrated residential and line-haul service, the distance would only be one-half of Eqs. (9a) or (9b). For these 1-way automobile services, one distance estimation function therefore is

(9c) $$d = \frac{V - W}{48p} + \frac{2w^2}{48} + 3$$ (in blocks).

However, this function tends to overestimate distances for the *integrated auto mode* by underweighting originations in the high-density walking distance area near the line-haul station; therefore

(9d) $$d = \frac{V - W}{48p} + \frac{2w^2}{48} + 2$$ (in blocks for park-and-ride and integrated auto),

has been used to estimate distances for this mode. For kiss-and-ride, on the other hand, a round trip measure of the following type is required:

(9e) $$d = \frac{V - W}{24p} + \frac{2w^2}{24} + 6$$ (in blocks for kiss-and-ride auto).

As noted in chapter 8, d, f, and c make up the principal information needed to determine t, the time required per vehicular 1-way or round trip, whichever is appropriate. The specific expression used for determining t for separate feeder bus operations is as follows:

(11a) $$t = 11.8d + 12(f + 1) + 1.166c + 120$$ (in seconds).

[10] To a certain degree, such an assumption involves something of an oversimplification, since if there were considerable car-pooling it might be assumed that a bit of extra travel or distance might be incurred in order to pick up the additional riders; car-pooling, however, is not notably popular with American commuters and what little information is available suggests that car-pooling is done by neighbors or others living close to one another or at locations that involve little addition to the basic route distance.

The first term, $11.8d$, measures the time consumed in operations at full cruising speed in residential service and is equivalent to the t_1 component of the general time equation found in chapter 8. The 11.8 coefficient is merely the number of seconds required to move one standardized block at an operating speed of 25 mph. The second expression in the equation, $12(f + 1)$, derives from the fact that an additional time of approximately 12 seconds (over and above the running time in the first term) is needed to decelerate, accelerate, and open and close doors for each stop made; $f + 1$ is taken as the total number of stops, since f itself measures only the feeder stops made in the residential area and one stop must be added for discharging or taking on passengers at the line-haul station. The third expression, $1.166c$, simply expresses the time required for loading and unloading the vehicle; that is, it is assumed that with the type of vehicles hypothesized for the present analyses (in particular, buses with three doors) it would take 1.166 seconds to load and to unload one passenger. The final term, a constant of 120, represents the two minutes of turn-around time assumed to be required for bus operations. The last two terms in Eq. (11a) can be dropped for calculation of the increment of time required for performing the residential service by buses already on the line haul; that is, no additional time over and above that already included for the line-haul journey is required for loading or unloading or turning around because of the extra residential service. Also, the second term can be modified to $12f$ instead of $12(f + 1)$ since no stop is needed upon reaching the line haul for transfer purposes. (In actual operations, however, $f + 1$ stops normally would be made in order to serve those who are assumed to be within walking distance of the line-haul station; adding this stop would improve load factors and reduce costs for this already low-cost mode.) Thus, the integrated or incremental bus time function is

(11b) $$t = 11.8d + 12f \quad \text{(in seconds).}$$

The *passenger* travel time (or t') in residential areas for the travelers using automobile modes can be estimated by a simple modification of this equation; specifically, $11.8d$ would be the basic constituent for an automobile equation, when the same operating speed of 25 mph is assumed. Also, a constant allowance should be included for parking, walking, or discharge time at the line-haul station when park-and-ride or kiss-and-ride modes are employed; for want of any more specific information this constant will be assumed to be 60 seconds for both modes. In addition, for car-pooling modes an extra five minutes delay per rider will be included to allow for pickup and circuity delays. For kiss-and-ride residential service, the time equation is

(11c) $$t' = 11.8d/2 + 60 \quad \text{(in seconds).}$$

For park-and-ride service it is

(11d) $$t' = 11.8d + 60 + 30 \quad \text{(in seconds)},$$

where 30 is an allowance for car-pooling delays (5 minutes times 0.1 riders). For the integrated or incremental automobile service employing automobile in both the line-haul and residential operations the time equation is

(11e) $$t' = 11.8d + 20 + 180 \quad \text{(in seconds)},$$

where the constant of 20 is an allowance of extra time needed for entering and leaving the line-haul facility, and that of 180 is an allowance for car-pooling delays (5 minutes times 0.6 riders).

Once t has been determined, the remainder of the bus transit and other analyses are straightforward. The expression $3600/t$ yields r, the number of round trips that can be made in an hour by a specific transit vehicle. This number, r, in turn, when divided into the total number of round trips needed to provide the designated service, R, and rounded upward, yields the number of transit vehicular units needed per line-haul station, U. The total number of required hourly round trips per station, R, for separate feeder bus transit can be determined in the usual fashion by dividing total passenger volume (minus the number walking) by the resultant or modified capacity or load of the particular transit units being used, that is,

(12) $$R = \left(\frac{V - W}{c}\right)^*,$$

where c is the resultant passenger load determined from Eq. (10) after truncation. The total number of transit units required is

(13) $$U = \left(\frac{R}{r}\right)^*.$$

Determining U for the automotive modes is much the same, though simpler since U and R are equivalent. All that is necessary for park-and-ride and kiss-and-ride is to divide $(V - W)$ by the number of passengers carried per vehicular unit, or c. For kiss-and-ride service c will be assumed to be one passenger per unit, while for park-and-ride, for which a limited amount of car-pooling seems reasonable, 1.1 passengers per vehicle will be employed for c. For the integrated automobile service, however, U is simply equal to V divided by c; the figure of 1.6 passengers per vehicle previously employed in the line-haul analyses is used for c.

The remaining variable to be determined for use in the total annual cost equations (Eqs. (2) through (6)) is M, the annual vehicular mileage. For the transit modes, it is simply the number of hourly bus round trips times the round trip distance times the number of hours of service; thus, for four rush hours of service a day, 255 days a year, it is

$$M = 1020\, drU. \tag{14}$$

For the automobile modes, the annual vehicular mileage (for four hours of service a day, 255 days a year) can be computed using Eq. (14) except that r, the number of round trips per hour, is equal to one.

Comparison of the different residential feeder modes usually is best performed in terms of average additional costs per passenger-trip, or "AC/trip." For this purpose, the total annual costs, TC, can simply be divided by the total annual passengers using the residential service. However, because of the intricacies introduced by allowing some residential movements to be accomplished by walking, it seemed wiser to derive the unit costs, or costs per passenger-trip, on the basis of a more fundamental accounting method.[11] The functions for the average cost per passenger-trip (in cents) obtained by this procedure for each of the five vehicular modes of residential feeder service are

$$\text{(15a)} \qquad \textit{Separate feeder bus:} \quad AC/\text{trip} = 0.35\,\frac{t}{c} + 2.7\,\frac{d}{c},$$

where c is the resultant passenger load determined from Eq. (10) after truncation;

$$\text{(15b)} \qquad \textit{Integrated bus service:} \quad AC/trip = 0.36\,\frac{t}{c} + 2.7\,\frac{d}{c};$$

$$\text{(15c)} \qquad \textit{Park-and-ride:} \quad AC/\text{trip} = \frac{35.3}{c} + 0.84\,\frac{d}{c};$$

$$\text{(15d)} \qquad \textit{Kiss-and-ride:} \quad AC/\text{trip} = 0.34\,\frac{d}{c};$$

$$\text{(15e)} \qquad \textit{Integrated auto:} \quad AC/\text{trip} = 0.67\,\frac{d}{c}.$$

The costs are measured in cents in every case and the notation is as explained before. These functions, with occasional modification to take

[11] For this purpose it is first necessary to put the cost parameters on a per-vehicle-trip basis. To do this, the α's pertaining to annual costs per vehicle unit must be divided by the number of trips each vehicle makes in one year. (In the automobile cases, the number of vehicle units is equal to $2U$; thus use $\alpha/2$.) On the assumption of 255 workdays a year and four rush hours each workday, the annual number of trips for each bus unit will be $1020r$, and for each automobile unit will be 510. Mileage-related costs for each trip can be computed from the previously reported β's by simply dividing them by 12 (to convert from a block to a mileage basis) and multiplying by d. Finally, to find the costs per passenger-trip, these costs per vehicular-trip must be divided by c, vehicular passenger load.

account of alternative assumptions, are the basis for the cost comparisons reported in the next section.[12]

Cost Comparisons and Conclusions

Fundamental relationships for the costs of performing residential service by different modes can be inferred from the functional relationships just reported. Appendix C furnishes details on the evaluation of these relationships in specific circumstances and Figure 41 summarizes some of the more relevant or salient of these specific calculations. In that figure comparisons can be found of the average costs per passenger-trip incurred by using the different modes under different assumptions about peak-hour volumes per line-haul station served, V, and about trip originations per block, p. In every case the costs plotted in Figure 41 were calculated assuming that the maximum walking distance, w, was two blocks, and that the minimum frequency, h, for bus operations was six per hour. Calculations using other assumptions for w and h are shown in appendix C. The most relevant of the cost relationships presented in the figure are those pertaining to the three lowest peak hourly volumes. (The travel distances at low residential densities for the extremely high 5000 hourly volume, as shown in appendix C, are unrealistic for residential feeder situations since such distances are more suggestive of line-haul than of residential service.)

From the charted cost relationships and the appended calculations, it is clear that most of the basic modes for performing residential service have roughly comparable cost characteristics. The only major deviation is that park-and-ride is often several orders of magnitude more costly than the other modes. For all the modes, including park-and-ride, costs diminish as trip origination densities increase, and these costs tend to approach an asymptote quickly, usually at or near a density of ten trip originations per block. Furthermore, the estimated differences in cost for modes other than park-and-ride become small at the higher densities; and residential collection costs by all modes except park-and-ride become small in absolute terms as density increases, suggesting that at the higher densities residential service choices are not too critical.

The costliness of park-and-ride is primarily a result of the parking charges it must absorb, but also of accident or insurance charges, and

[12] It should be noted that these cost equations presume a considerable ability to adjust schedules to specified demands. Specifically, they make no effort to adjust for many indivisibilities that might occur. The net effect is perhaps to underestimate bus costs by about 10 per cent. This underestimate, however, is probably easily offset by the extreme conservatism used in estimating the specific cost parameters. Furthermore, recognition of these indivisibilities often would result in highly misleading discontinuities being incorporated into the final results.

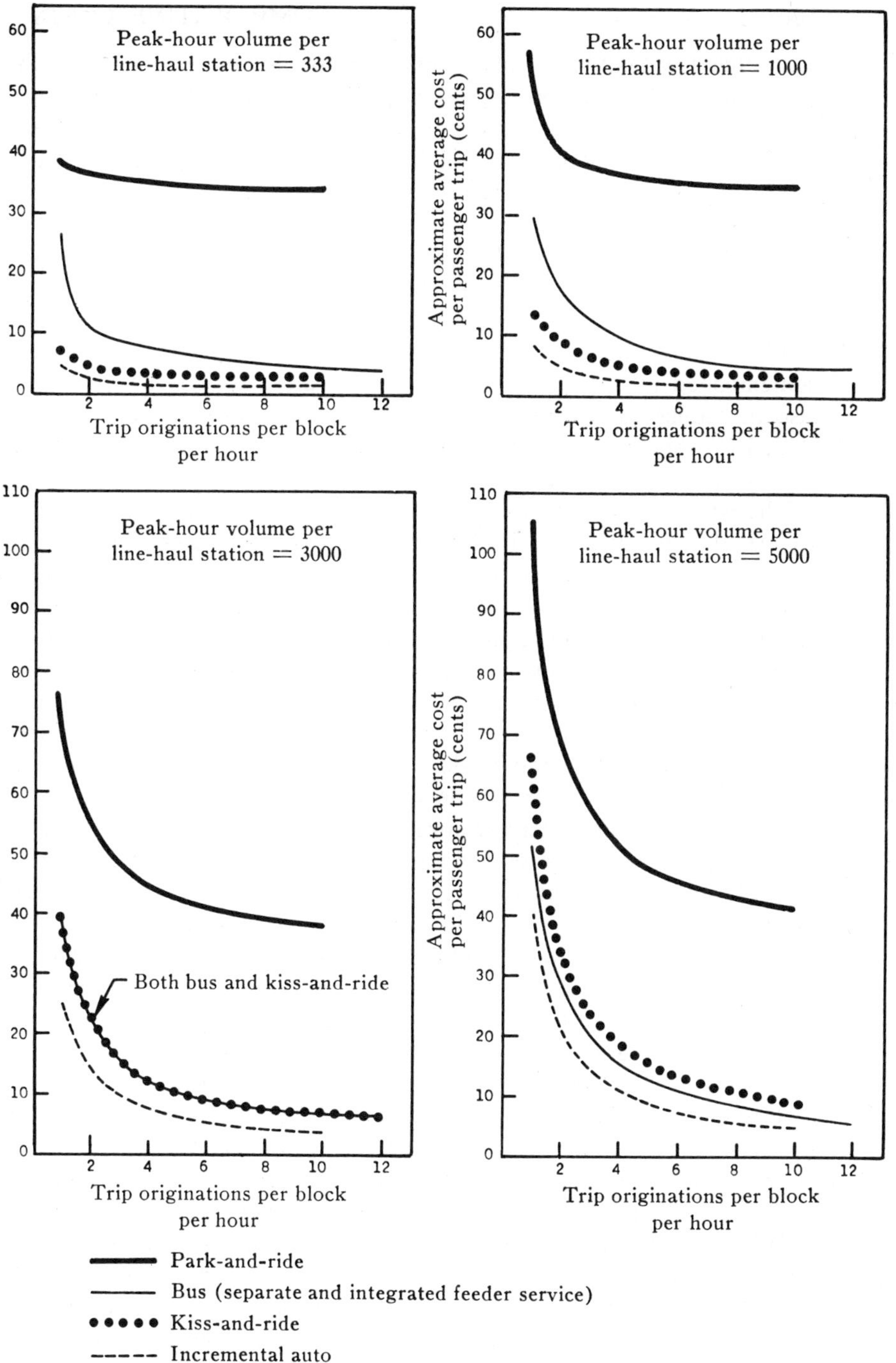

Figure 41. Approximate residential cost relationships under different trip origination densities and volumes.

the rather low load factor of 1.1 assumed for this mode. Increasing the factor to 2.0, for example, would generally cut the cost by almost one-half and make park-and-ride competitive with the bus at lower densities and with all other modes at the higher hourly volume levels and low trip origination densities. Furthermore, if parking charges could be greatly reduced by any means (for example, by the use of excess street capacity for on-street parking near a line-haul station), park-and-ride costs would become quite attractive, lying somewhere between the all-auto and kiss-and-ride costs in each case. One simple means to this end, obviously, would be any implicit or explicit subsidization of parking charges, as contemplated in some mass transit plans. Park-and-ride charges would also be reduced, of course, if automobile ownership costs were not included for this mode, an omission which would seem legitimate in some situations.

The two bus modes have essentially the same cost characteristics under almost all circumstances. The slightly higher capital costs incurred by using a vehicle with line-haul capability for performing residential collection are offset by some slight reduction in the number of units an integrated service would require. Those slight differences in the cost performances of the two bus modes that are observable tend to favor the integrated nontransfer service. And, given the fact that the integrated bus mode also has superior service characteristics (particularly, no transfer upon arrival at the line-haul station), there is strong reason for using the integrated mode wherever trip demands and densities are of a level to make a bus operation otherwise attractive.

Bus costs in residential service are sensitive to changes in the specifications of maximum walking distances, w, and headways, h. As can be seen by studying appendix C, a simple increase in the maximum walking distance from two blocks to three blocks, with headways kept at 6 per hour, generally reduces average costs per trip about 4 cents when trip origination densities are at the low level of two per block. Furthermore, the resultant deterioration in service (that is, extra walking distance) would be at least partially offset by a reduction in total vehicular travel time, under most conditions running about 20 to 25 per cent. Lesser, but still significant, economies would be achieved by similar increases in maximum walking distances at slightly higher trip origination densities.

Both of the automobile modes that do not incur parking charges—kiss-and-ride and incremental automobile—are extremely cheap methods of residential collection and distribution. The low costs recorded for kiss-and-ride are possibly misleading, however; as already noted, they do not allow for the driver's inconvenience and time. Furthermore, kiss-and-ride may have been given unfair advantage by eliminating automobile ownership charges in its case. Inclusion or exclusion of these costs is at least debatable; if included, the reported kiss-and-ride cost estimates would roughly double.

The cheapest residential feeder mode is extension of an automobile trip wherever the automobile performs the basic line-haul function, even aside from the service advantages it offers. The cost advantage over the bus is slight at very high volume levels, however. The integrated automobile mode also offers the most attractive service, particularly when compared with the separate feeder bus service.

It is also instructive to compare the average passenger travel times from home to the line-haul facility by all of the modes, as in Table 68. There is a sharper difference between private and public modes in this respect at the lower trip origination densities. The automobile modes, for example, considerably excel buses even at trip origination densities of ten per block. At the higher densities, however, the total travel time involved is so small that any relative advantage is of little absolute importance. Probably more important is the fact that, at all trip origination

TABLE 68

AVERAGE PASSENGER TRAVEL TIMES FROM HOME TO LINE-HAUL FACILITY BY DIFFERENT MODES OF RESIDENTIAL TRAVEL, INCLUDING WAITING DELAYS (minutes)

	Trip originations per residential block (p)							
	Hourly volume per line-haul station = 1000				Hourly volume per line-haul station = 3000			
Mode	p = 1	2	5	10	p = 1	2	5	10
Separate feeder bus[a]	16.94	11.75	8.45	7.28	20.83	13.67	9.23	7.68
Integrated feeder-express bus[b]	15.65	10.43	7.27	6.03	19.53	12.34	8.00	6.43
Park-and-ride[c]	6.43	4.67	3.68	3.48	14.10	8.63	5.45	4.27
Kiss-and-ride[d]	6.53	4.76	3.78	3.48	14.20	8.69	5.35	4.27
Integrated residential and line-haul auto[e]	7.27	5.30	4.32	4.12	14.93	9.23	6.08	4.90

[a]Calculated as $\frac{1}{4}$ the total round trip vehicle travel time, t, minus the turnaround time (2 minutes) and plus a 6-minute allowance for walking (2 minutes), waiting at both the residential stops (3 minutes), and line-haul stops (1 minute); see Eq. (11a).

[b]Calculated as $\frac{1}{4}$ the total round trip vehicle travel time plus a 5-minute allowance for walking (2 minutes), and waiting at the residential stop (3 minutes); see Eq. (11b).

[c]Calculated as the total 1-way vehicle travel time plus a 1-minute parking delay, 1 minute for waiting at the line-haul station, and $\frac{1}{2}$ minute for car-pooling to achieve a 1.1 load factor; see Eq. (11d).

[d]Calculated as $\frac{1}{2}$ the total vehicle round trip travel time plus 1 minute for waiting at the line-haul station, and 1 minute for discharge and walking after "delivery"; see Eq. (11c).

[e]Calculated as the total 1-way incremental vehicle travel time (which already includes a 20-second allowance for gaining access to the line-haul facility) plus 3 minutes for car-pooling. See Eq. (11e).

densities, the traveler on public modes has to spend some time walking or waiting while exposed to the elements. This could be a controlling factor in some climates, at least for those able to afford the luxury of avoiding inclement weather. Needless to say, with rising incomes, the size of this "privileged group" could be expected.

An important conclusion that emerges strongly from these cost and service comparisons is that the integrated systems, either bus or automobile, have certain inherent advantages as residential collectors. They not only have better performance times and lower costs than "separated" versions of the same technologies, but they also tend to eliminate transfers and other disagreeable service aspects.

From the viewpoint of both residential area cost and service, it would appear that the bus modes lose attractiveness at lower volume levels and as trip origination densities drop below five, particularly, relative to incremental auto and kiss-and-ride. The automobile's strength in residential collection and distribution at low densities and volume levels undoubtedly helps explain the attractiveness of automobile commutation in many cities; and this attractiveness will grow if residences and workplaces continue to disperse.

On the other hand, any trend in the opposite direction would work to the advantage of public transit in all the commutation functions. In this connection, and in light of the housing choice characteristics outlined in chapter 6, it is worth reemphasizing that residential densities can be affected by many factors other than purely economic ones, not the least of which are the age and family status composition of the population and work force. Cost and service differences among modes tend to be slight at high densities (but not volume levels) and residential services account for a relatively smaller proportion of the total urban transportation bill as density increases.

All of these conclusions are subject to considerable qualification when the complementarities and interchangeabilities of different modes are taken into account. For example, at least some of the cost disadvantages of park-and-ride would disappear (by eliminating automobile ownership costs) if the commuter used the family automobile only on days when it was not otherwise occupied. Similarly, kiss-and-ride would be less inconvenient if buses, even slow ones, were available on days when the "family chauffeur" is particularly pressed for time. In general, the "optimal" system for residential collection and distribution often may incorporate two or more options and be a complex synthesis of many technologies and modes.

Chapter 11 | Downtown Distribution

The cost, service, and operational characteristics of downtown distribution are normally important elements in any urban transportation system. Downtown distribution costs can be analyzed simply and with reasonable accuracy on an incremental basis, that is, as the additional costs that would be incurred for the local distribution of travelers within downtown areas while assuming the existence of line-haul facilities. Generally, it can be further assumed that operating costs increase or decrease proportionately with the incremental hours of vehicle use required for downtown distribution. This implies that no scheduling discontinuities exist which would cause less than or more than proportional increases or decreases in cost with changes in round trip time.

As in the line haul and residential collection analyses, the volume and service characteristics of the several alternative transport systems considered should be controlled to ensure reasonable comparability. Specifically, each alternative downtown distribution mode was costed at the same six volume levels as before, ranging from 5000 passengers per hour per corridor to be distributed within the downtown area up to 50,000. For each mode and volume level, the incremental costs were computed for four different downtown or CBD sizes: 144 blocks (1 square mile); 270 blocks (1.88 square miles); 378 blocks (2.63 square miles); and 648 blocks (4.51 square miles). It was assumed that these four CBD sizes would be served by four, six, six, and eight entering line-haul corridor facilities, respectively. Further, it was assumed that downtown distribution would be provided along lines or routes connecting pairs of line-haul routes (thus eliminating the stub terminal just at the edge or fringe of the downtown area previously assumed for each corridor). For the small 144-block CBD area, for example, with only four entering line-haul routes, downtown service would be provided along two downtown routes directly connecting pairs of line-haul facilities; for areas having six line-haul routes, service would be provided along three different downtown routes, and for eight line-haul routes, along four. Importantly, this analysis and costing pertains only to four hours of peak-period travel a day, 255 days a year.

There is an important interrelationship among the downtown area (and its configuration), the number of line-haul corridor routes serving it, the station or stop spacing (which is a function of the distance travelers are willing to walk), and the downtown route length. This is

$$f = \frac{A}{(2w^2)(m/2)}, \tag{1}$$

where f is the number of passenger stops or stations along *each* downtown route; A is the downtown area (in blocks) served by all routes; m is the number of entering line-haul corridors (so that $m/2$ is the number of downtown routes or pairs of line-haul facilities serving the CBD); $2w^2$ is the number of blocks of downtown area served by each passenger stop or station along each downtown route; and, as before, w is the maximum walking distance of passengers in blocks. Implicit in the above equation is the assumption that stations will be spaced so that no area will be served by more than one passenger station; it is further assumed that there are no common or transfer stations (though pairs of corridors could be connected at an additional expense). Also, f includes the downtown passenger stop made at the end of each line-haul route.

For all analyses, an arbitrary walking distance of three blocks is used; the resultant number of passenger stops and route lengths for the four CBD areas are as shown in Table 69. It might be noted that the use of a longer walking distance for downtown distribution than for residential collection does not appear to be inconsistent with existing practice or logic, the main reasons being the higher marginal costs of reduced station

TABLE 69

DOWNTOWN DISTRIBUTION SYSTEM CHARACTERISTICS

Downtown area (blocks) A	Number of line-haul routes serving area m	Number of passenger stops or stations on each downtown route[a] f	Length of each downtown route[b] (blocks) d
144	4	4	18
270	6	5	24
378	6	7	36
648	8	9	48

[a]For each case, w is three blocks.

[b]Where $2w$ is the station or stop spacing, d is equal to $(f - 1)(2w)$. Again, standardized blocks are used with twelve to the mile.

spacing in downtown areas (relative to those in residential areas) and the greater possibility of multiple purposes being served by walking in downtown areas.

Five different types of downtown distribution service were costed: (1) integrated rail transit subway, whereby pairs of line-haul rail transit routes were extended in subways through the downtown area and operations were connected; (2) integrated bus transit subway, whereby pairs of line-haul bus highways were extended in subways through the downtown area and operations were connected; (3) integrated bus transit on downtown streets, whereby operations on pairs of line-haul bus highways were interconnected by operating line-haul buses over downtown surface streets (on a continuous and nontransfer basis); (4) separate feeder bus transit on downtown streets, whereby local downtown buses shuttle or "loop" back and forth between the stub terminals or fringe parking spaces of each pair of line-haul routes; and (5) integrated automobile on surface streets, whereby the automobile travelers continue on to local downtown destinations (or leave origins), moving on surface streets directly from (or onto) the line-haul facilities.

Functional and Operational Relationships

In the line-haul analyses, it was noted that some of the so-called line-haul equipment requirements and costs could properly be allocated to downtown distribution, for example, a portion of the stub terminals for transit and fringe parking for automobile. In particular, the last station on the line-haul facilities (that is, the station located roughly at the fringe of the CBD) also serves as the first station on the downtown distribution route and provides downtown distribution service for those passengers having destinations within walking distance of that station. Requirements and costs for downtown distribution were computed while distributing the 1-way hourly maximum load point line-haul passenger volumes uniformly over all downtown distribution route stops, including the two made at the ends of line-haul facilities.

Essentially the same *modus operandi* is assumed for the three different types of integrated transit service. Buses or trains move back and forth between the ends of two line-haul facilities, passing over the downtown distribution link connecting them. On a complete train or bus round trip, for example, the unit would make four 1-way line-haul journeys and would move through the downtown area twice. On each 1-way trip through the downtown area, moreover, each train or bus unit would make f passenger stops, two at the in-town ends of the two line-haul routes and $(f - 2)$ at the intermediate downtown stations. For separate feeder buses, the operation is somewhat different in that buses merely shuttle back and forth between the downtown stub terminals of a pair of line-haul facilities, stopping at $(f - 2)$ intermediate downtown stations, and thus function independently of the line-haul operation. The integrated automobile system is even simpler in that the vehicles proceed directly between line-haul facilities and downtown parking garages without stops.

Only for separate feeder bus downtown distribution is it therefore necessary for passengers to transfer from one operation to another at the junction of the line-haul and downtown distribution service. Also, for each downtown distribution travel mode, the costs are computed for the same downtown routes and lengths and for the same number of passenger stops.

Integrated Bus on Downtown Surface Streets

The fundamental information necessary for computing additional equipment and labor requirements for integrated surface bus is the *additional* travel time required to make a 1-way journey along the downtown distribution route. This can be estimated from the following relationship:

(2) $$t_d = 22.5d + 5(f - 1) + 2.4c' - (120/2),$$

where t_d = additional travel time incurred by buses on a 1-way journey through downtown (in seconds);

$d = (2w)(f - 1)$ = downtown route length (in blocks);

f = number of passenger stops or stations along each downtown route (including the stops made at the ends of line-haul routes);

c' = total number of passengers per bus loading or unloading at the intermediate (or, $f - 2$) downtown stops (on a 1-way journey).

The first coefficient, 22.5, is the average number of seconds needed to travel each block on downtown streets where no passenger stops are made (amounting to an average speed of about 13 mph); it includes acceleration and deceleration delays and time delays at signalized intersections. The second coefficient, 5, represents the deceleration and acceleration delay incurred for each passenger stop; only $(f - 1)$ stops are included, since part of the deceleration or acceleration delay incurred by buses coming into or going out from the line-haul terminal is already included in the line-haul travel time equation. The third coefficient, 2.4, is the number of *additional* seconds needed to unload or load a passenger on a surface street, over and above that needed at a high-capacity bus terminal with centralized fare collection and triple-door operations; it is equal to (3.0 seconds − 1.166/2 seconds), where 3.0 is the average time to load or unload a passenger on surface streets (and collect the fare) and 1.166/2 is the average time to load or unload a passenger at a centralized terminal. The additional loading or unloading is time required (at intermediate downtown stations) because of downtown surface operation, where loading or unloading is limited to a single door (since the driver must collect the fare). Extra time for loading or unloading is incurred only for those passengers using the intermediate downtown stations, since the line-haul travel time equation includes both loading and unloading time for all maximum load point passengers. Thus

$$c' = \left(\frac{f-2}{f}\right)(c),$$

where c is the bus seating capacity (or load per bus at the maximum load point, whichever is less). The last term, 120/2, represents the time deduction or saving that results from integrating two line-haul operations and eliminating a turnaround allowance.

Once the 1-way downtown distribution travel time has been computed, the number of additional bus units, U_d, and number of additional annual bus-miles, M_d, required for downtown distribution service per corridor can be computed as follows:

$$U_d = \left(\frac{R}{r_d}\right) \quad \text{(per corridor)}, \tag{3}$$

where r_d = number of 1-way downtown trips each bus unit makes per hour = $(3600/t_d)$;

R = number of bus trips per hour coming into a single line-haul stub terminal (that is, per corridor);[1]

and

$$M_d = 1020(d/12)(R) \quad \text{(per corridor)}. \tag{4}$$

These equations have been formulated to determine the incremental costs for a single corridor, while assuming that the downtown distribution route connects a pair of line-haul facilities. For this integrated bus operation it was assumed necessary to retain the high-capacity line-haul terminal, rather than have the buses discharge passengers on surface streets at the in-town end of line-haul routes. For low volume levels, this assumption probably is unduly conservative and increases costs more than necessary; but in the higher volume cases, where 400 to 1000 buses an hour are massed at the end of the line-haul route, it hardly seems un-

[1] Values of R will thus come directly from the line-haul analysis; these are shown in Table 70, column (1).

reasonable to retain the stub terminals (since considerable confusion and congestion could result if the buses had to fan out from the line-haul facility and discharge passengers in a fairly tight area).

Separate Feeder Bus on Surface Streets

The separate feeder bus operation is a simple, local downtown distribution service whereby buses shuttle back and forth between the in-town ends or stub terminals for a pair of line-haul facilities. Obviously, the additional passenger-trip costs for this type of downtown service can be superimposed on the line-haul and residential collection costs for any mode.

The equipment and labor requirements for a separate bus service are determined in much the same way as for integrated bus, with a couple of exceptions. First, when picking up or discharging passengers at the stop located at the in-town end of the line-haul facilities, the feeder bus is assumed not to use the stub terminal but to remain on the street and utilize less elaborate slots and platforms adjacent to the terminal. Second, less expensive two-door buses will be used since the driver will collect fares and loading or unloading can only be done on one side of the bus.

The travel time equation for making a 1-way bus trip between the ends of two line-haul facilities is

$$(5) \qquad t_d = 22.5d + 5(f - 1) + 5c + 60,$$

where t_d is the travel time (in seconds) to make a 1-way bus trip over a downtown route length of d blocks with f passenger stops (including those at the stub terminals), and c is the full bus seating capacity. The first two terms are the same as those for the integrated bus equation. The third term represents the time needed for loading and unloading a full busload of passengers; it allows about 3 seconds for loading and 2 seconds for unloading. The fourth term, 60 seconds, is a constant allowance for turnaround per 1-way trip.

The number of 1-way separate feeder bus trips required for each corridor, R_d, can be stated as follows:

$$(6) \qquad R_d = \left[\left(\frac{f-1}{f}\right)(V) \div (c)\right],$$

where V is the 1-way hourly passenger requirement for each line-haul corridor at the maximum load point. The separate feeder buses need capacity only for $[(f - 1)/f](V)$ passengers per hour (in each direction) since some of the line-haul passengers walk directly to their downtown destinations from the in-town line-haul terminal or parking lot, thus needing no additional downtown service.

The equations for the number of bus units, U_d, and annual bus-miles, M_d, required for the separate downtown distribution operation are similar to those for integrated bus service. They are

(7) $$U_d = \left(\frac{R_d}{r_d}\right) \quad \text{(per corridor)},$$

where $$r_d = (3600/t_d);$$

and

(8) $$M_d = 1020(d/12)(R_d) \quad \text{(per corridor)},$$

where, as before,

(9) $$d = 2w(f - 1) \quad \text{(in blocks)}.$$

Integrated Automobile on Downtown Surface Streets

Downtown distribution by automobile differs from the all-automobile line-haul only in that some of the vehicles and passengers move to downtown parking locations which are closer to their downtown destinations, rather than terminate their journey at parking locations adjacent to the in-town end of the line-haul facility. Thus, for these travelers additional vehicular mileage and parking costs will be incurred (the latter on the assumption that parking space within the CBD will be more expensive than that located at the fringe or edge of downtown).

The number of vehicles per corridor which must be accommodated at central downtown garages will be

(10) $$U_p = 2\left(\frac{V}{c}\right)\left(\frac{f-2}{f}\right) \quad \text{(per corridor)},$$

where U_p = the total number of vehicles *per day* per corridor which will require central downtown parking garages;

c = the number of persons per automobile (or car occupancy);

and f is defined as in Eq. (1).

For the computation of the additional vehicular mileage performed for downtown distribution, the additional number of vehicles, U_m, to be used in computing additional annual vehicular miles for downtown distribution is

(11) $$U_m = 2\left(\frac{V}{c}\right)\left(\frac{f-1}{f}\right) \quad \text{(per corridor)}.$$

Equations (10) and (11) differ because those travelers who move from the end of the line-haul facility along the entire downtown route and then park adjacent to the end of another line-haul facility will not experience an increase of parking costs (over and above those charged for line-haul operation), but only an increase in vehicular mileage and mileage-associated costs. Also, a factor of 2 is used in both equations to account for vehicles which enter during a 2-hour rush period each morning.

The equation expressing the annual additional vehicular mileage for downtown distribution per corridor is

$$(12) \qquad M_d = 510\left(\frac{d+1}{24}\right)(U_m) \qquad \text{(per corridor)},$$

where the first factor, 510, indicates the total number of 1-way downtown trips each vehicle makes annually, and the second factor represents the distance (in miles) an "average" vehicle travels on a 1-way downtown distribution trip.

Integrated Rail Transit in Downtown Subway

For downtown distribution by integrated rail transit, the trackage of two line-haul facilities is extended along the downtown route and connected by subway. Since the line-haul facilities already include an underground station (at the in-town ends of routes), only $(f - 2)$ additional downtown subway stations must be added for complete downtown distribution services.

The basic travel time equation for 1-way train trips through the downtown area is

$$(13) \qquad t_d = 56(f-1) + 32.7[d/6 - (f-1)] + 10f - 300,$$

where t_d is the 1-way travel time (in seconds) for a trip over a route of d blocks and f passenger stops (including one at the in-town end of each line-haul facility). (It should be emphasized that these particular coefficients apply only for the walking distance of 3 blocks and the station spacing of 6 blocks or 1/2 mile used in these analyses.) The first term, $56(f - 1)$, expresses the travel time (in seconds) needed to move over the portion of the route length where stops are to be made at 1/2-mile (or 6-block) intervals; thus 56 seconds are needed to move 1/2 mile, stopping at both ends and including all acceleration and deceleration delays, but not station dwell. The second term represents the time needed to travel over any portion of the route length where no stops are made; therefore, only 32.7 seconds are needed to travel 1/2 mile at top speed. However, in these analyses no express services are considered, so all trains make f stops and this second term always reduces to zero. The third term expresses the time required to load and unload passengers, with a 10-second dwell or stopping time being allowed at each station. (All f stations are included because in the line-haul analysis the dwell time at the line-haul terminal was considered part of the turnaround time, which in the equation above is deleted.) The last term represents the elimination of turnaround time caused by the integration of two line-haul operations.

The number of additional train units required per corridor, U_d, will be

$$U_d = \left(\frac{R}{r_d}\right) \quad \text{(per corridor)}, \tag{14}$$

where R = hourly number of trains moving into a single line-haul stub terminal (that is, per corridor);[2]

$r_d = (3600/t_d)$.

The total number of additional train cars required is n times U_d where n is the number of cars per train. The additional annual car-miles per corridor can be found from

$$M_d = 1020(d/12)(nR) \quad \text{(per corridor)}. \tag{15}$$

For the above equations, and for those that follow, the general relationships will hold both for 2-track or multiple-trackage situations; however, for the latter case, where there are two incoming (or outgoing) tracks per corridor and thus inner and outer "loops," variables without primes (such as R and U_d) will be used for the outer "loop," and variables with "primes" (such as R' and U'_d) will be used for the inner loop with the "primed" and "unprimed" equations summed. When only two tracks are used, the equations without "primes" will suffice.

The only other data necessary as inputs to the costing analysis pertain to the length of connecting subway (that is, subway between but not including stations) and the length of subway stations required for the downtown distribution route. In calculating the connecting subway length, or D_s, it can be assumed that each underground (stub terminal) station at the in-town end of line-haul facilities extends one-half a station length (or, $nk/2$, where k is the car length in feet) into the downtown route length. Thus

$$D_s = (db) - (f - 1)(nk), \tag{16}$$

where D_s = downtown connecting subway length (in route feet);

d = downtown route length (in blocks);

b = downtown total center-to-center block length (in feet);

n = number of cars per train;

k = car length (in feet).

[2] R, the number of hourly train trips per corridor, stems directly from the line-haul analyses; values are shown in Table 70, column (2).

TABLE 70

TRAIN AND BUS REQUIREMENTS FOR INTEGRATED RAIL AND BUS TRANSIT OPERATIONS

1-way hourly passenger volume at maximum load-point of each corridor	1-way hourly bus or train units entering or leaving downtown area along each corridor or line haul: (1) Bus trips per hour (total) (R)	(2) Train trips per hour: Outer loop (R)	(2) Train trips per hour: Inner loop (R')	(3) Number of cars per train: Outer loop (n)	(3) Number of cars per train: Inner loop (n')
50,000	1,000	38	30	10	10
40,000	800	32	32	8	8
30,000	600	38	30	7	4
20,000	400	36	—	7	—
10,000	200	30	—	5	—
5,000	100	30	—	3	—

Twelve blocks are assumed to the mile (or a block length of 440 feet) and a rail transit car whose length is 55.33 feet. The values for n, the number of cars per train, are shown in column (3) of Table 70 as obtained from the line-haul analyses. Substituting these values, Eq. (16) becomes

$$D_s = 440d - (f - 1)(55.33n) \qquad \text{(in feet)}.$$

The total length of mezzanine subway station (per corridor) for all the intermediate (or, $f - 2$) downtown stations, D_m, is simply

$$\text{(17)} \qquad D_m = (f - 2)(nk) \qquad \text{(in feet)}$$
$$= (f - 2)(55.33n).$$

Some important aspects of the integrated rail transit subway analysis should be noted. First, if a downtown service is added to an existing line-haul operation, the system should be reoptimized and operations rescheduled. That is, the train lengths, train frequency, and extent of multiple trackage should be recomputed in light of the costs of underground connecting subway and mezzanine stations to ensure that the most economic combination is obtained. In order to simplify the calculations this reoptimization was not executed in the present analyses; the result almost certainly is some slight overstatement of rail system costs for downtown distribution. A reoptimization probably would produce slightly higher line-haul costs, perhaps with multiple trackage extending farther than indicated, but would lower downtown distribution costs. Also, a reoptimization should produce shorter train lengths than indicated for the optimum line-haul (to economize on high-cost CBD terminals) and higher train frequencies. *Finally, where double-loop line-haul systems are used, the relationships shown in Eqs. (14), (15), (16), and (17) must be applied separately for inner- and outer-loop rail transit operations and the requirements for the loops summed.*

Integrated Bus Transit in Downtown Subway

The downtown bus subway differs little from the rail. The basic travel time equation for 1-way bus trips along the downtown distribution subway would be

(18) $$t_d = 58(f - 1) + 30.2[d/6 - (f - 1)] - 60,$$

where t_d is the time (in seconds) necessary to make 1-way trips along the downtown route length of d blocks while making f passenger stops (including those at the in-town ends of the line-haul facilities being connected). Again, the particular coefficients for this equation hold only for the case of 1/2-mile station spacing, and for this analysis the middle term always reduces to zero because no skip-stop operations are analyzed. The last term, 60 seconds, represents the reduction in turnaround time which results from integrating two line-haul operations. No additional loading or unloading time is necessary, since the line-haul travel time equation includes sufficient loading and unloading time for all passengers, the only difference being that the intermediate downtown subway stations are also points at which passengers are discharged or picked up, as well as the stub terminals of similar design.

The number of additional bus units, U_d, and the annual bus-miles, M_d, required per corridor for downtown distribution are

(19) $$U_d = \left(\frac{R}{r_d}\right) \quad \text{(per corridor)},$$

where R is the hourly number of incoming bus trips per corridor at the maximum load point,[3] and

$$r_d = (3600/t_d).$$

Thus

(20) $$M_d = 1020(d/12)(R) \quad \text{(per corridor)},$$

where M_d is the additional annual bus-miles required for downtown distribution per corridor.

[3] R is determined directly from the line-haul analyses, the values of which are shown in Table 70, column (1).

As with the rail case, $(f-2)$ additional downtown mezzanine stations are required; similarly, the underground station at the in-town end of each line-haul facility is assumed to extend one-half a station length into the downtown route length.

Since the bus subways will often have multiple bus lanes (in each direction along the route length) and since there will not always be an equal number of bus slots in the lanes, it is helpful to place the total lengths of connecting subway and mezzanine stations (per corridor) on a total lineal rather than route footage basis. The total lineal footage required for the additional mezzanine stations in one direction, that is, per corridor for all lanes and slots, is

$$(21) \qquad D_m = (f-2)\left[28\left(\frac{R}{70}\right)^* + 7\left(\frac{R}{480}\right)^*\right] \qquad \text{(per corridor)},$$

where D_m is the total lineal feet of a 128-foot-wide mezzanine station required for each corridor; the first factor, $(f-2)$, is the number of additional stations required over the route length of d blocks; the second factor indicates the lineal feet of a 128-foot-wide station area required at each station, with the first term representing the footage needed for bus slots, and the second term the (equivalent) footage required for acceleration and deceleration lanes. The coefficients for the two terms in the second factor and the 128-foot width for mezzanine stations hold only for a station where the bus slots are placed roughly at a 45-degree angle to the general direction of through movement. In essence, the total station length needed is equal to 28 feet times the total number of bus slots required for all lanes. Since the capacity of a single bus slot (with triple-door buses, double-side loading-unloading, and centralized fare collection) is approximately 70 buses an hour, the total number of bus slots needed at each station is $(R/70)^*$, rounded upward since only an integral number can be provided. (Obviously, the lineal footage needed for each bus slot is 28 feet.) The equivalent amount of a 128-foot-wide station area added because of allowances for acceleration and deceleration lanes is equal to 7 lineal feet, and applies to each lane entering a station; the number of bus lanes entering each station area is $(R/480)^*$, rounded upward since lanes can only be provided in discrete units. The capacity of through lanes, or lanes entering the station area, is considered to be about 480 buses per lane per hour.

The total lineal footage of bus lanes provided for downtown distribution in each direction, or per corridor, is simply the route length (in feet) times the number of bus lanes in each direction minus the total lineal footage needed for all downtown stations (including the two stub terminal half-stations at the ends of the downtown route). Thus, the amount of connecting subway can be determined from

(22)

$$D_s = (d)(b)\left(\frac{R}{480}\right)^* - (f - 1)\left[28\left(\frac{R}{70}\right)^* + 7\left(\frac{R}{480}\right)^*\right] \quad \text{(per corridor)},$$

where D_s is the total lineal feet of single-lane connecting subway required for each corridor for a downtown route length of d blocks having f stations, and b is the total block length (in feet).

Cost Parameters

Proper costing of downtown distribution networks is in many respects an even more difficult proposition than that of line-haul and residential collection. Particularly difficult are the estimation of construction costs for subways, mezzanine stations, and downtown parking garages, all of them significant items in the makeup of total incremental costs for downtown distribution. Even so, an attempt to select "reasonable" values seems useful. Since the costing is handled in much the same way as that used for line-haul and discussed at some length in chapter 9, an abbreviated form of the analysis will be presented here.

Integrated Bus on Downtown Surface Streets

Costs for this type of service include three principal components: costs for constructing additional platforms in streets and for providing concrete "stopping pads" along the downtown route, in order to supplement the loading and unloading space provided at curbs and to prevent pavement "raveling"; costs associated with the additional bus units required for the downtown service (included will be charges for buses, yards and shops, and additional operators); and costs associated with additional bus mileage (included will be bus maintenance and operating expenses, other than operators, and highway user taxes which are made in payment for street "ownership" and maintenance expenses).

The additional street expenses were estimated to average about $50,000 a block for each bus lane, with a passenger stop spacing of six blocks. (This figure includes loading platforms and concrete stopping pads.) When placed on an annual basis (with a 50-year life and 6 per cent interest rate), this is about $3200 a block per bus lane. For exclusive lane bus operation on surface streets with signalized intersections, a capacity of 120 buses per lane per hour has been assumed.

The annual expenses per bus unit are identical to those shown for the line-haul service, and amount to $13,120 per additional bus unit; included are costs for operators, yards and shops, and equipment.

The mileage-associated expenses for the downtown distribution service were set at 32.5 cents per bus-mile, and include all maintenance, operating, and administration expenses and an allowance for highway user charges (amounting to 2.5 cents).

Thus, the total annual costs for each corridor for downtown distribution by buses using surface streets, *TBSC,* can be estimated from

(23)

$$TBSC = \$3200(d)\left(\frac{R}{120}\right)^{*} + \$13{,}210(U_d) + \$0.325(M_d) \quad \text{(per corridor).}$$

These annual costs can be distributed over the annual volume of passenger-trips served by dividing by $1020(V)$.

Separate Feeder Bus on Surface Streets

The cost parameters for separate feeder bus service are similar to those for integrated bus on surface streets. It is necessary, however, also to construct additional platforms and bus loading and unloading slots adjacent to the high volume stub terminals or parking areas at the in-town ends of line-haul facilities where passengers transfer to the downtown feeder buses; these requirements are over and above those for platforms and concrete stopping pads located along the downtown route length. For each terminal location these costs can be estimated to be slightly under $100,000 (for both right-of-way and construction) for each lane of feeder buses served; annually they amount to $6200 for each lane.

The annual expenses per required bus unit were slightly lower than those for an integrated bus service, since buses of lower performance standards and with only two loading and unloading doors are satisfactory; thus the purchase price per feeder bus can be placed at $28,300 as compared with $31,200 for the integrated service buses. (Both prices include excise taxes.) The resultant annual cost per additional bus unit, to include capital, operator, and yard and shop expenses, is $12,760 per bus.

The unit costs for platforms and stopping pads, $3200 a block per lane, and those for mileage-associated expenses, 32.5 cents per bus-mile, are identical to those for the integrated surface bus service. Including all cost items, the total annual costs per corridor for providing downtown distribution by separate feeder buses, *TBFC*, are

$$(24)\quad TBFC = \$6200\left(\frac{R_d}{120}\right)^{*} + \$3200(d)\left(\frac{R_d}{120}\right)^{*} + \$12{,}760(U_d) + \$0.325(M_d) \quad \text{(per corridor).}$$

Integrated Automobile on Downtown Surface Streets

There are two cost components for use of automobiles in downtown service, the first associated with vehicular mileage, and the second with the number of vehicular units. The mileage expenses include ownership charges (at 4 cents per vehicle-mile), vehicle operating and maintenance costs (2.9 cents), and an allowance of 1.17 cents for street ownership and maintenance, assessed in the form of user taxes; these total 8.07 cents per vehicle-mile.

Each commuter vehicle that continues into the downtown area, instead of parking at the fringe or edge of downtown, should experience increased parking costs; these result from the acquisition of higher valued land and from the construction and operation of more expensive multistory garages. Since every vehicle in the line-haul analysis was charged with the parking cost for downtown fringe parking, only those vehicles entering the central downtown area need be assessed the additional or increased unit parking costs; the increment of cost over the fringe parking garage was estimated to be $150 per vehicle per year.

The resultant total annual costs to provide complete downtown distribution by automobile for 1020(V) annual automobile commuter passengers for each corridor (that is, for four hours of peak-period travel a day, 255 days a year) are

$$(25) \qquad TAC = (\$0.0807)(M_d) + (\$150)(U_p) \qquad \text{(per corridor).}$$

Integrated Rail Transit in Downtown Subway

Costing downtown distribution by rail subway is somewhat more complex than for the other modes because of multiple trackage or "loop" considerations and certain design changes which must be made as trains are run through the downtown area rather than turned around at line-haul stub terminals.

The considerations are as follows: (1) Costs for the line-haul turnaround extension can be eliminated. As noted in chapter 9, these cost deductions, for each terminal or corridor, are a function of car and train length, and number of tracks; when placed on an annual basis they amount to $6893 per incoming track or "loop" times the number of cars in a train.[4] (2) Costs of additional downtown stations must be included; in chapter 9, the unit cost for each station was shown to be a function of the number of cars per train, with the annual cost for a 2-track, 2-directional station being $25,273 times the number of cars per train, assuming a 55.33-foot car length. Since the downtown distribution analysis is stated

[4] Thus, the number of cars will be n when g' is zero, and will be n plus n' when g' is greater than zero; values of n and n' are provided in Table 70.

in terms of single-corridor requirements, or what is essentially a 1-direction basis, the annual unit cost per station can be restated as \$12,636 per incoming track or "loop" times the number of cars in a train. (3) Costs for connecting subway construction must be included. For this purpose, the capital costs per 2-track mile were based on cut-and-cover construction and were assumed to be \$17.5 million, including all engineering and contingency fees; easement costs were assumed to be negligible. (See Table 63.) With a 50-year life and an interest rate of 6 per cent, the annual capital charges per incoming track or "loop" are \$105 per lineal foot. (4) Costs for operating, maintaining, and administering the downtown distribution portion of the rail transit system, including capital costs for rolling stocks and yards and shops, can be calculated using the cost models outlined in appendix A and chapter 9. The unit costs differ from those used in the line-haul analysis because one of the variables—station spacing—was changed. As before, some of these costs are car associated, some are train associated, some are car-mile associated, and some are single track-mile associated. They are on an annual basis: \$11,660 per car, \$20,495 per train, \$0.2815 per car-mile, and \$40,840 per track-mile.

Summarizing all the above costs, the following equation for total annual downtown distribution costs is derived when only 2-track systems are employed (that is, when $g' = 0$):

$$(26a)\quad TRC = (-\$6893)(n) + \$12{,}636(n)(f-2) + \$105(D_s) + [\$11{,}660(n) + \$20{,}495](U_d) + (\$0.2815)(M_d) + (\$40{,}840)(d/12) \quad \text{(per corridor)}.$$

The total annual downtown distribution costs when multiple trackage exists (that is, when $g' > 0$) are

$$(26b)\quad TRC = (-\$6893)(n+n') + \$12{,}636(n+n')(f-2) + \$105(D_s + D'_s) + [\$11{,}660(n) + \$20{,}495](U_d) + [\$11{,}660(n') + \$20{,}495](U'_d) + (\$0.2815)(M_d + M'_d) + (\$40{,}840)(2d/12) \quad \text{(per corridor)}.$$

Since in multiple-trackage cases (that is, when $g' > 0$) the inner and outer loops may have different train frequencies and train lengths, it is necessary to make a distinction in the cost computations. The appropriate values of D'_s, U'_d, and M'_d are computed with the same equations as used previously for those quantities without "primes," but with values of R' and n' replacing those for R and n. Again, the values for both sets of values—n, R, and n', R'—are included in Table 70.

The total annual costs in Eqs. (26a) and (26b) are those for providing downtown service for $1020(V)$ annual passengers or one corridor's annual volume, assuming four hours of peak-period service a day, 255 days a year.

Integrated Bus Transit in Downtown Subway

The bus transit downtown subway costing has six major components: elimination of costs for constructing line-haul terminal turnaround loops; costs for constructing additional downtown mezzanine stations; cost for constructing downtown connecting subway; costs for rolling stock, yards and shops; costs of operating, maintaining, and administering downtown distribution bus service; and costs for maintaining the downtown bus subway.

The cost deduction for the turnaround loop (whose length was 400 feet) for each corridor was set, as in chapter 9, at $41,400 a year for each lane coming into the line-haul terminal, where the number of entering lanes is $(R/480)^*$.

The downtown subway station construction costs, as noted before, were based on those for rail transit after excluding trackage and electrification costs, increased proportionally according to respective widths—128 feet for bus stations and 50 feet for rail stations. The resultant annual cost per lineal foot of an underground mezzanine-type bus station of 128-foot width was $1110. Additional ventilation costs over those included in the rail transit station base cost were assumed to be $95,000 annually for each incoming lane of each station.

Connecting subway construction costs (to include an allowance for proper ventilation equipment) were assumed to be $8.576 million per lane-mile; placed on an annual basis (50-year life and 6 per cent interest) this equals $103 per lineal foot of single-lane bus subway.

The annual costs for operators, buses, and yards and shops are set as before at $13,120 per additional bus unit. The mileage-associated costs are assumed to be 30 cents per bus-mile; user taxes are excluded since all roadway construction and maintenance costs are accounted for separately. The final cost item, subway maintenance, is established as $9000 annually per lane-mile of subway, where the total of lane-miles per corridor is the number of lanes in each direction times the miles of downtown route, or $(R/480)^*(d/12)$.

Summarizing all the above components, the total annual costs for providing downtown bus subway distribution to $1020(V)$ annual passengers is

$$(27)\quad TBD = (-\$41{,}400)\left(\frac{R}{480}\right)^* + (\$95{,}000)(f-2)\left(\frac{R}{480}\right)^* + (\$1110)(D_m) + (\$103)(D_s) + (\$13{,}120)(U_d) + (\$0.30)(M_d) + (\$9000)\left(\frac{R}{480}\right)^*(d/12) \quad \text{(per corridor).}$$

Cost Comparisons and Evaluations of Downtown Distribution Modes

Figures 42 through 46 display the results obtained in costing each of the five types of downtown distribution modes on the basis of the cost relationships reported in the previous section. The three surface systems—integrated bus, separate feeder bus, and integrated automobile—exhibit near-perfect divisibility for all downtown route lengths, and the two types of surface bus service (integrated bus and separate feeder bus) have unit costs which are identical for all practical purposes. By contrast, the rail and bus subway modes are both highly indivisible, thus produc-

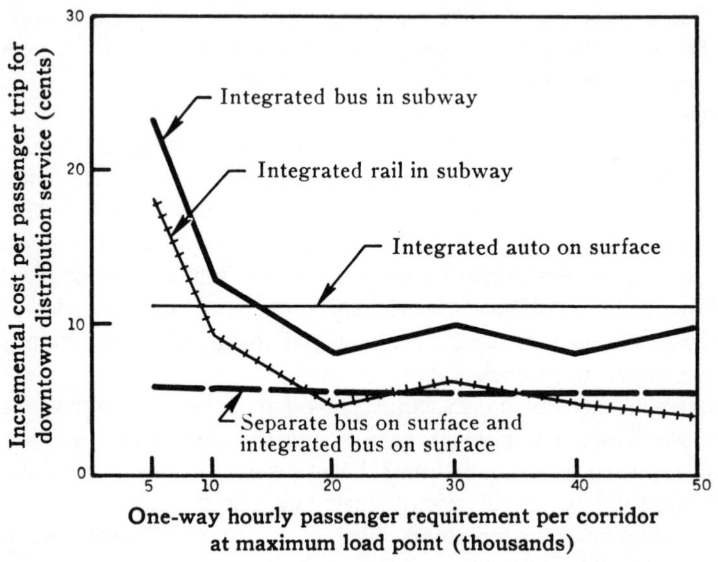

Figure 42. Comparative costs of downtown distribution modes, 1½-mile downtown route length.

ing high unit costs at the lowest volume levels, but a leveling-off in costs as volumes approach a 1-way hourly maximum load point volume of 20,000. It should be noted that some of the rail subway cost undulations indicated in Figures 42 through 45 undoubtedly result from the failure to reoptimize the over-all system operation, and some result from inherent indivisibilities. They can be ignored for most comparisons.

For all travel modes an almost linear relationship exists between unit costs and downtown route length—with cost increases being more or less directly proportional to route length increases for all modes except automobile on surface streets. (See Figure 46 in particular.) For automobile on surface streets, the increases are somewhat less than proportional,

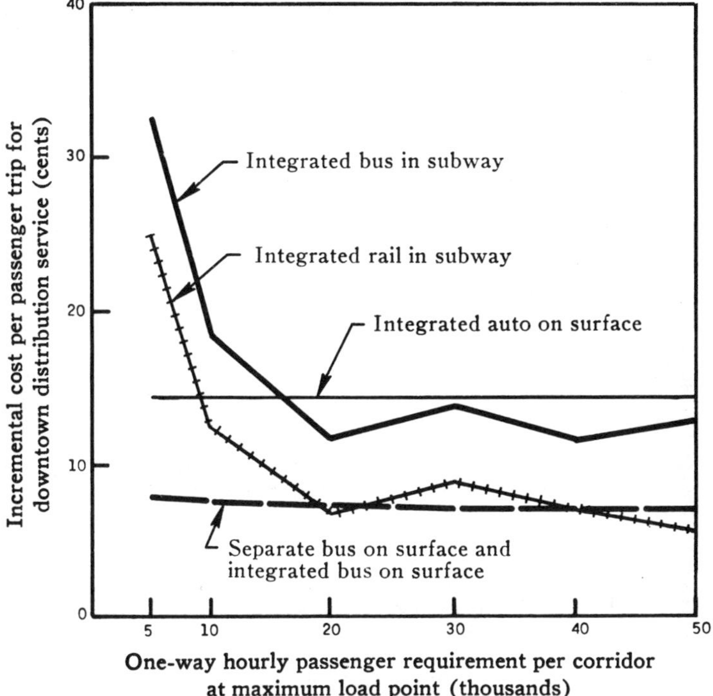

Figure 43. Comparative costs of downtown distribution modes, 2-mile downtown route length.

since fixed parking costs are spread over longer trip distances with route length increases. These relationships seemingly hold for all volume levels.

A clear distinction can be made between the cost relationships applicable above and below 20,000 passengers per corridor per hour. At corridor volumes below 20,000 an hour, the surface bus modes are the cheapest in downtown operations, particularly when compared with either bus or rail transit in subway on the longer downtown route lengths. Of the two surface bus modes, the integrated bus service generally would be the more desirable since passenger transfers would be avoided, less travel time would be involved, and no important cost differentials exist. Furthermore, even at the lowest volume ranges, the integrated automobile downtown service runs about 6 cents a trip higher than integrated bus for a 1½-mile downtown route, and about 8 cents a trip higher for a 4-mile route; in relative terms, the integrated bus service is generally 50 to 60 per cent less costly than integrated automobile for downtown service on surface streets.

Estimates of the travel times for the various modes are shown in Figure 47. (Bus passenger trip times were assessed as one-half of the one-

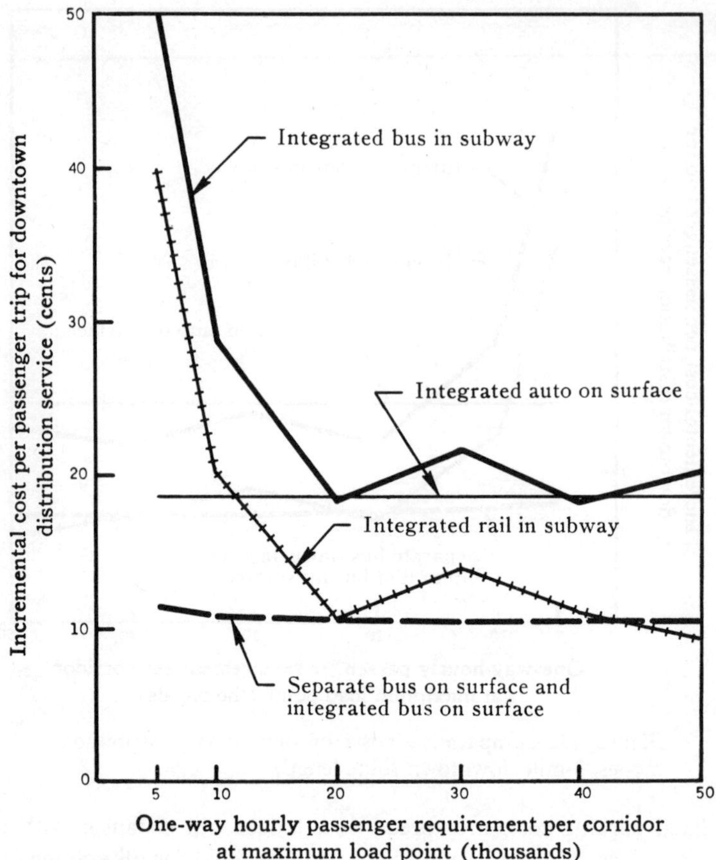

Figure 44. Comparative costs of downtown distribution modes, 3-mile downtown route length.

way bus trip time, plus one-half the headway for waiting, plus 3 minutes walking [for one and a half blocks]; automobile passenger trip times for surface travel were based on a 15-mph average speed plus 2 minutes for parking [or leaving] plus 3 minutes for walking.) For surface travel, the automobile mode shows only a slight time advantage over both integrated and separate bus service in downtown distribution. If less conservative speed figures for automobile travel were assumed, the advantage for automobile passengers might increase to something in the range of 2 to 4 minutes per trip; even so, the time differentials do not appear large enough to justify much greater cost.

Viewing the downtown distribution service alone, at volumes on the order of 20,000 1-way passengers an hour or more per corridor, rail transit subways would appear cost competitive even with low-cost surface bus modes at high volume levels. However, both the bus and automobile's

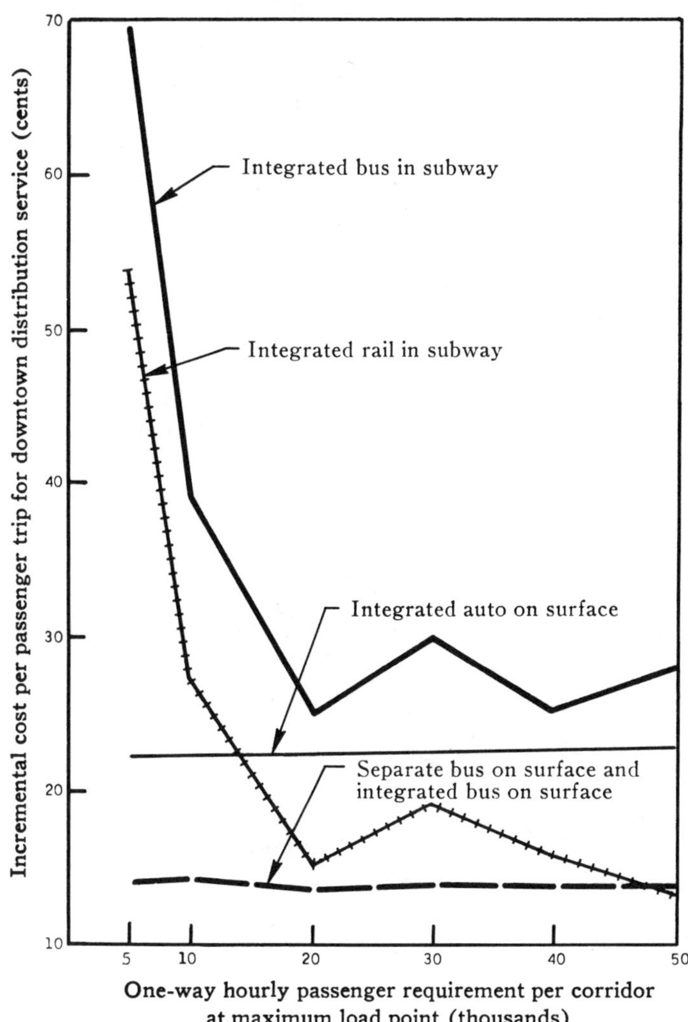

Figure 45. Comparative costs of downtown distribution modes, 4-mile downtown route length.

relative and absolute cost position improve both as route length increases and volumes decrease. An obvious and important advantage of subways for downtown distribution over surface modes, particularly at high volumes, lies in travel time differentials, as indicated in Figure 47; for example, the subway modes show trip time savings over surface modes ranging from about 3 to 7 minutes per passenger trip.

In any discussion of downtown distribution modes, attention must also be paid to such questions as the availability and use of downtown street and parking space. Where substantial volumes of downtown commuter

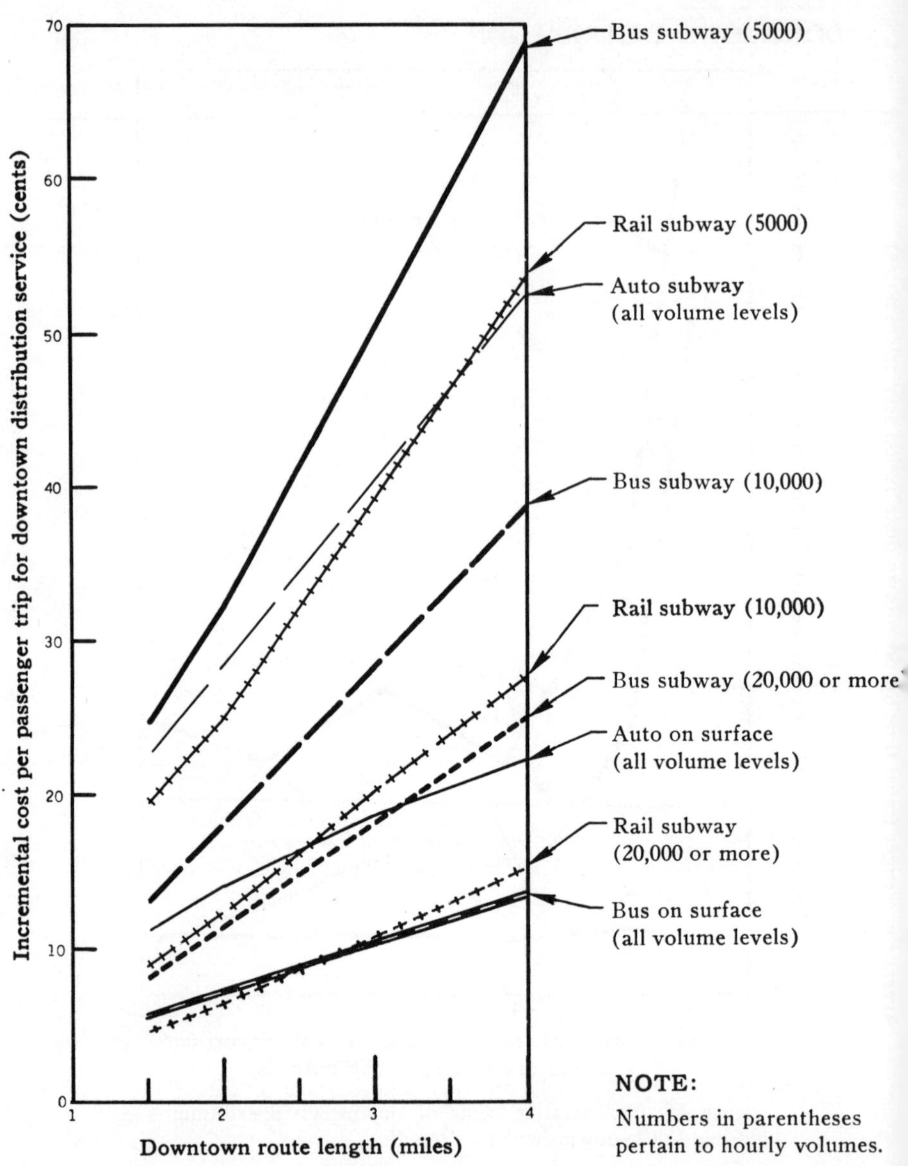

Figure 46. Relationship between route length and passenger-trip cost for downtown distribution service, by mode, type of downtown facility, and volume level in number of 1-way passengers per hour at maximum load point per corridor.

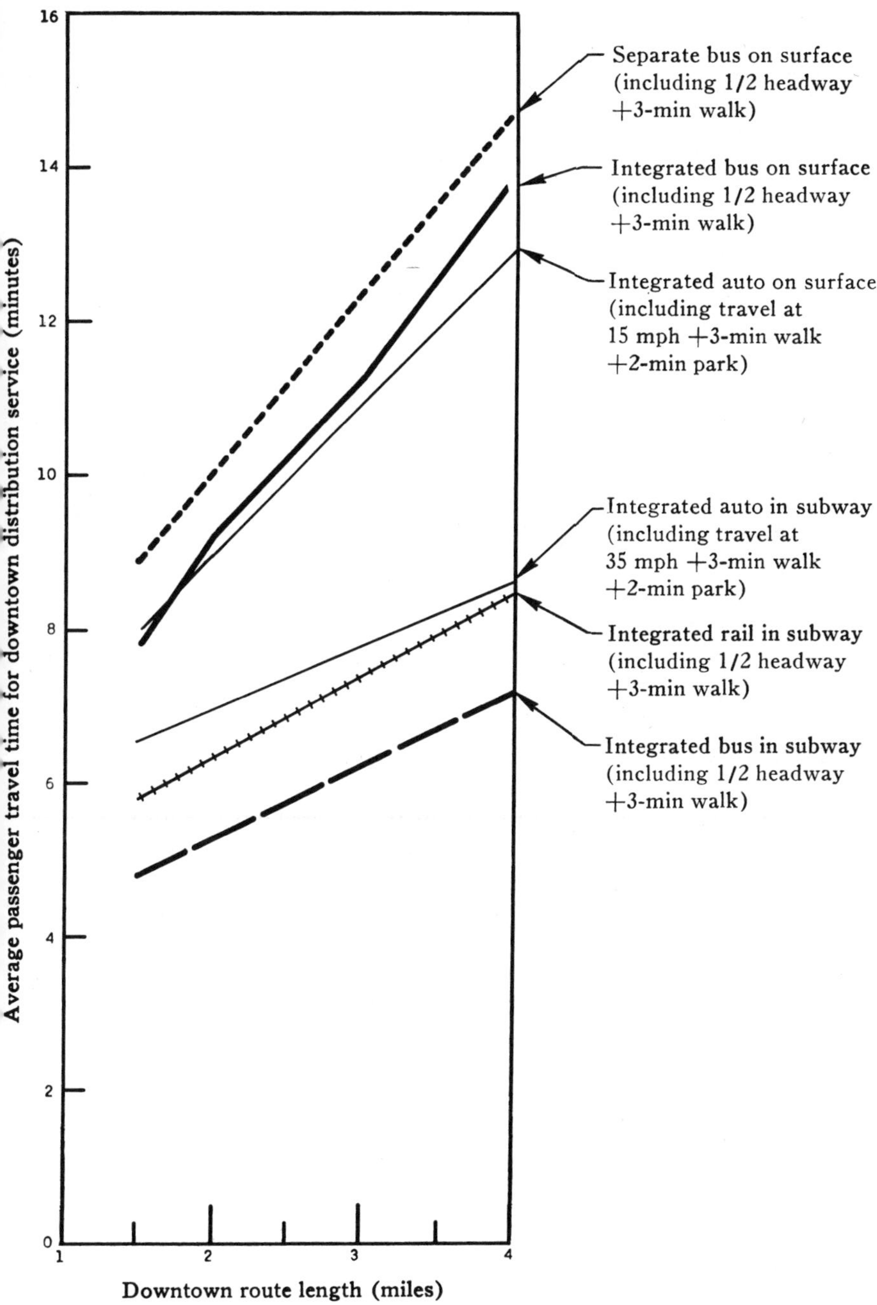

Figure 47. Downtown travel time by mode and downtown route length.

automobile traffic (or through traffic using downtown streets) are anticipated, there is the simple question of whether enough street space is available to handle them, not to mention other demands on streets for peak-hour trips. For the four downtown-area sizes considered, the maximum capacities available for handling vehicular and passenger volumes can be approximated and compared with requirements at various volume levels. These data are plotted in Figure 48. The assumptions with regard to number of downtown blocks and number of corridors generating passengers are noted on the figure. Streets were assumed to be 1 way and 40 feet wide (curb-to-curb), with hourly (1-way) approach or entrance capacities of about 1780 vehicles an hour.[5] Car occupancy was assumed, as before, to be 1.6 persons per automobile. Under these conditions, the entire downtown street capacity would be required just for downtown automobile commuters at hourly corridor passenger volume levels of about 20,000, leaving no street space for alternative uses, modes, or trips. At higher volumes the downtown street space would have to be supplemented by elevated or subsurface facilities. In a situation where 20,000 or so hourly passengers per corridor desired to travel to (or from) the downtown area, and additional travelers desired to travel into and then out of the downtown area—that is, through the CBD to some outlying destination—it would be possible, of course, to meet the problem by providing belt or bypass highways, or by supplementing street capacity with through elevated or subsurface facilities.

To provide a rough cost estimate for these possibilities, both bypass or belt highways and subways can be costed for passenger car use under certain specified conditions. Annual belt highway costs can be estimated using the construction cost formula indicated earlier, Eq. (3) in chapter 9, and with right-of-way costs equal to $0.005X_i$ times the construction costs, where X_i is the net residential density for the ith mile of highway in thousands of persons per square mile. The density figures selected for the cost computations were 250,000 persons per square mile for high-density situations and 70,000 for medium-density; from Figure 33 it can be seen that these assumed densities are, respectively, higher than those for areas of Chicago and Pittsburgh located 1 mile from the center of the CBD, and thus imply a very central belt highway location. A *passenger car* subway would have capital costs of approximately \$6 million per lane-mile, a figure which seems reasonable in view of the fact that subway dimensions and costs could be substantially reduced if use is restricted to passenger cars; with a 50-year life at 6 per cent interest, the annual costs of an automobile subway per lane-mile would be \$380,000.

[5] Assumes a 50–50 directional split of green time at intersections, an amber time allowance, and no commercial vehicles or curb parking.

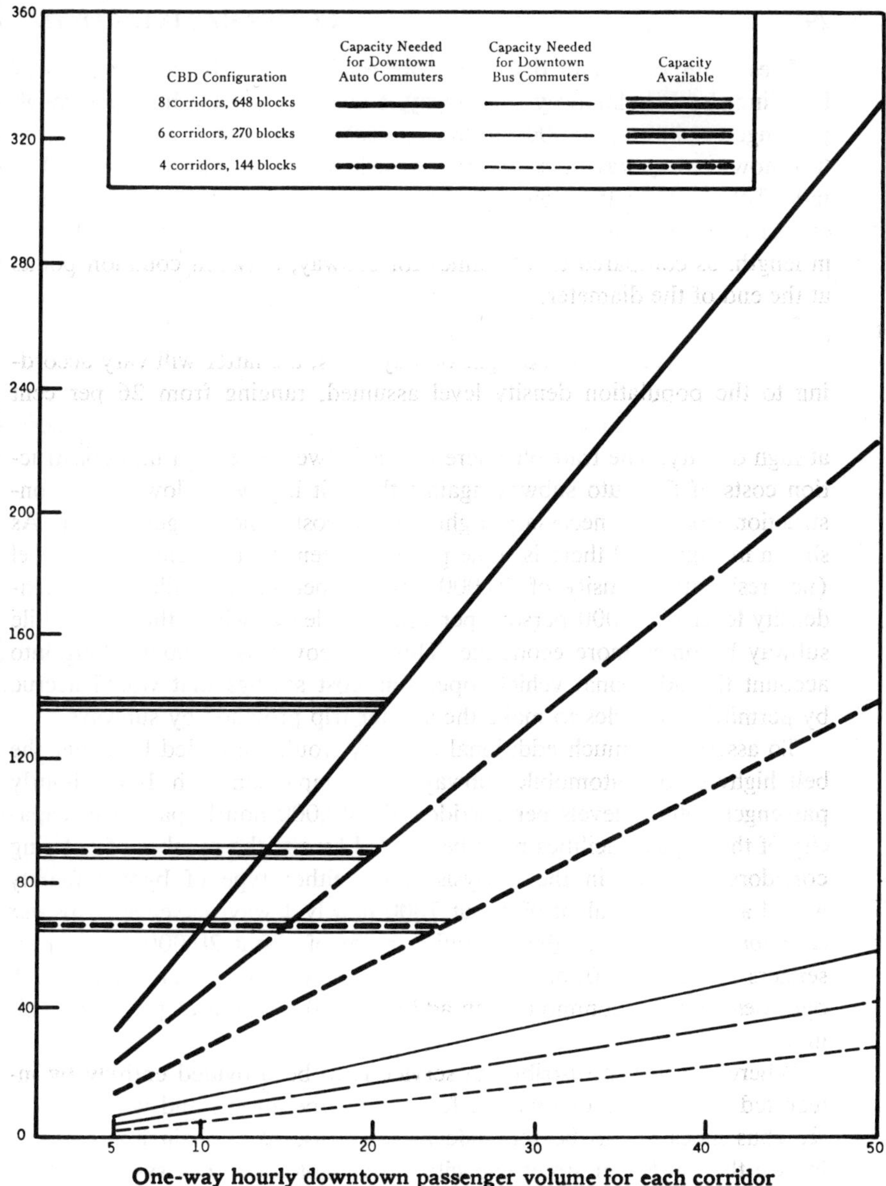

Figure 48. Street capacity and requirements for downtown automobile and bus commuters, by passenger volume level, CBD configuration, and number of corridors.

These unit costs and densities were applied to estimate the costs of handling, by belt highway or subway, a total of 40,000 hourly through passengers (that is, 40,000 one-way passenger trips an hour through the downtown area) having a straight-line trip length of approximately 1½ miles.[6] With the belt following a fairly circular route and having a diameter of about 1½ miles, each lane of belt highway will measure 2½ miles in length, as compared to 1½ miles for subway, between common points at the end of the diameter.

Subway costs are entirely for construction. The belt highway must include both construction and right-of-way costs; the latter will vary according to the population density level assumed, ranging from 26 per cent of the total costs at medium density, up to 55 per cent or so of total costs at high density. The tradeoff, therefore, is between the high unit construction costs of the auto subway against the belt highway's lower unit construction cost but necessary right-of-way costs and longer length. As shown in Figure 49 there is some point between the medium-density level (net residential density of 70,000 persons per square mile) and high-density level (250,000 persons per square mile) at which the automobile subway becomes more economic. This, moreover, is without taking into account the additional vehicle operating cost savings that would accrue by permitting vehicles to make the shorter trip provided by subways.

To assess how much additional capacity would be added by either the belt highway or automobile subway, for comparison with 1-way hourly passenger volume levels per corridor, the 40,000 hourly passenger capacity of the bypass facilities must be divided by six, the number of entering corridors assumed in the analysis. Thus either type of bypass facility would add an equivalent of about 7000 hourly 1-way passenger trips *per corridor*. Therefore, at the saturation point of about 20,000 1-way passengers going to or from the downtown area (see Fig. 48), adding such bypasses would accommodate an additional 30 per cent of passenger volume.

Where downtown distribution service is to be provided entirely by integrated surface bus or separate feeder bus operations, and where exclusive bus lanes are to be set aside for their use, it is again important to ensure that sufficient street capacity is available. The bus system's street capacity requirements, computed for the six hourly volume levels per corridor and three corridor configurations, are shown in Figure 48, along with those for automobile commuting. For these calculations it was assumed that 40-foot-wide streets could provide only three full lanes of

[6] An implicit assumption has been made that an 8-lane, full circle belt highway would provide sufficient capacity to handle 40,000 passenger-trips an hour, with each trip traveling only halfway around the circumference; each lane could handle 1675 vehicles an hour and would have a car occupancy of 1.6 persons.

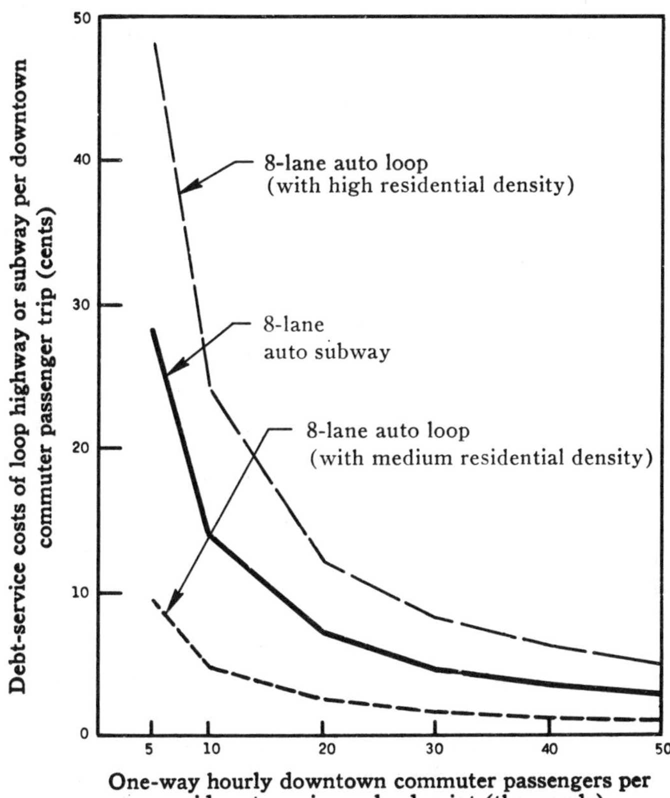

Figure 49. Comparison of debt-service charges for 8-lane loop highway of 2½-mile diameter and 16-lane through automobile subway with 1½-mile route length. (Highway or subway annual costs are distributed over annual *downtown commuter* passengers using six corridors.)

exclusive bus traffic, and that each lane would handle 120 buses an hour.

It is obvious that at any volume level, and even for as many as eight corridors, the amount of street space required for bus use is far less than that which is normally available. In fact, at the maximum condition—with a 144-block downtown area and four corridors of arriving passenger volumes at a level of 50,000 passengers per hour—only 45 per cent of the total street-carrying capacity is needed for buses. This leaves sufficient street space to handle up to 40,000 additional hourly automobile passenger trips (going to or through the downtown area). Stated another way, heavy reliance on surface bus for downtown distribution would at worst still permit at least 10,000 hourly passengers *per corridor* to enter or leave or go through the downtown area by automobile—not an insignificant figure for most urban areas.

At the other end of the spectrum, rail or bus transit subways would leave full use of the available street capacity for other purposes and types of trips. Generally, street capacity for downtown-area configurations would be sufficient under the conditions hypothesized to provide service to approximately 15,000 or 20,000 hourly automobile passenger trips per corridor. It is evident that with downtown rail or bus subways the total downtown system capacity—including both street capacity and subway capacity—would be *extremely* high. It is important, of course, not to confuse "supply" (or capacity) with "demand." Specifically, the total downtown system capacity with a transit subway would permit hourly passenger volumes per corridor of 20,000 automobile commuters plus whatever volume capacity would be provided by the transit subway—presumably at least 20,000 hourly. In all probability, a total downtown system capacity at or above 40,000 hourly passengers per corridor would be more than ample for all but one or two American cities.

Another aspect of downtown distribution worth consideration is the land-use commitments implied by the various modes. As suggested earlier, local street space would generally be provided to the extent assumed (40-foot-wide streets with 12 blocks to the mile), regardless of the nature of the downtown distribution system, simply because of general welfare service requirements and local access needs, not to speak of aesthetic reasons, such as light, air, view, and so forth. Such street space allowances, not including alleys and sidewalks, would amount to approximately 18 per cent of total CBD land area. Additional land would be needed, of course, for downtown parking if automobiles were to be used and if there were a ban on curb parking. The number of ground blocks required for offstreet parking for three different area configurations at different volume levels are shown in Figure 50. For these estimates it is assumed that the average garage has four levels. Also, only the ground blocks required within the downtown area itself are included and not those needed at the fringe. For the small area and four-corridor case, maximum parking needs amount to about 38 per cent of the total land available; with a 270-block downtown and six corridors, the maximum needed for parking is 36 per cent, and with 648 blocks and eight corridors the figure is about 26 per cent. The most stringent of these three cases—four corridors coming into a 144-block downtown—is examined in more detail in Figure 51, where the parking requirements are computed for three cases: 2-level parking structures; parking lots (or 1-level parking); and 4-level parking. Most cities now devote more than 40 per cent of CBD land area to streets, alleys, and parking, and this figure can be compared with the data in Figure 51. Clearly, very substantial auto-

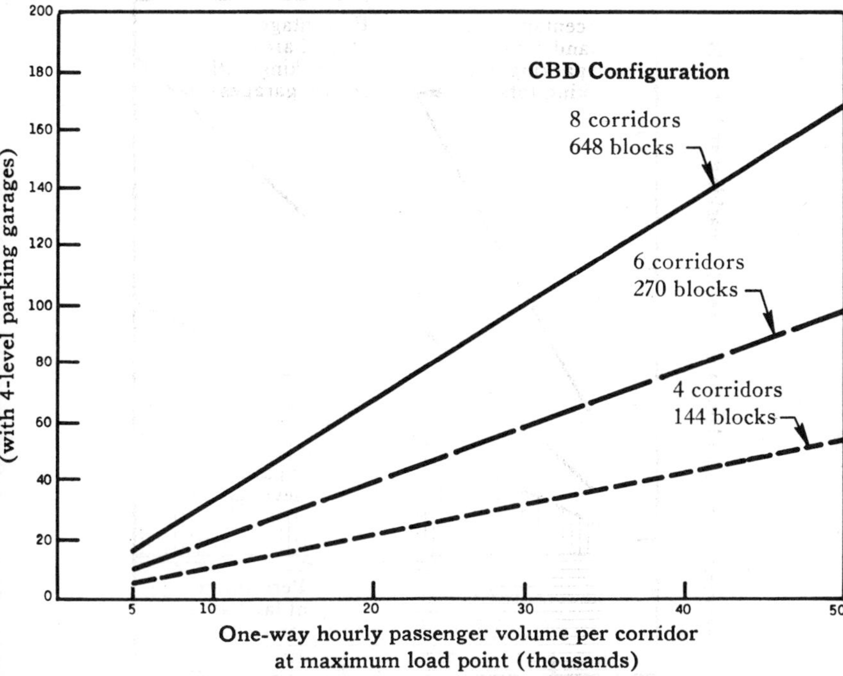

Figure 50. Ground blocks required for CBD automobile commuter parking (with four-level parking garages).

mobile commuter volumes, in the range of 30,000 hourly passengers per corridor, could be handled without violating this 40 per cent (though nonmagical) figure if 4-level parking garages were used. With 2-level garages, corridor passenger volumes of 15,000 to 20,000 still could be managed without increasing the amount of area normally devoted to traffic flow and parking.[7]

Of course, if downtown curb parking is permitted, and if additional highway capacity is needed, it may be added either by prohibiting curb parking and substituting offstreet parking, or by constructing additional roadways, for example, either belt highways or subways. Some of the relevant data to be considered in choosing between these alternatives are: (1) approximately 18 curb parking spaces can be made available on each side of each block; thus, by prohibiting curb parking some 430 spaces would be lost for each mile of street; (2) with 40-foot-wide streets, the elimination of curb parking (from both sides of the street) would increase the total street capacity by approximately 1100 vehicles

[7] Note the extent to which high volume flows can be handled if one uses 60 per cent, the figure commonly attributed to downtown Los Angeles.

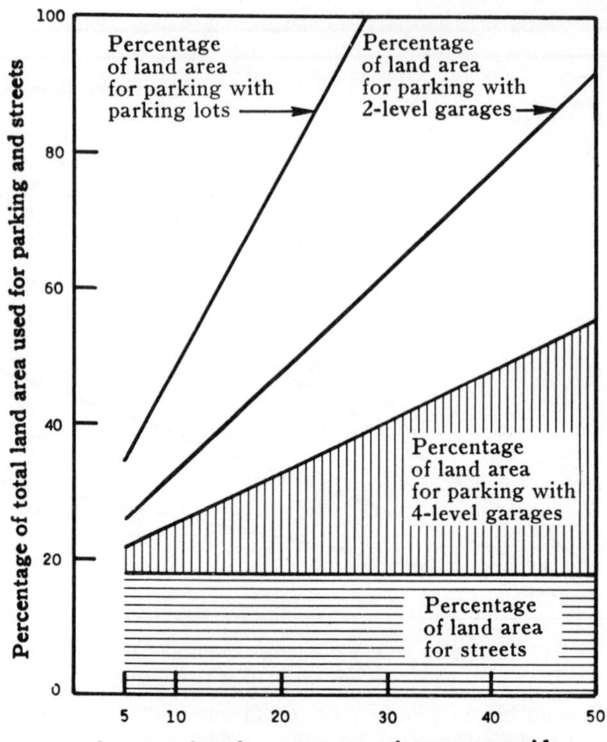

Figure 51. Percentage of CBD land required for streets and parking, by passenger volume level; four corridors, 144 blocks, 1-, 2-, and 4-level parking. (Chicago devotes about 41 per cent of CBD land area to streets, alleys, and parking, for example.)

per hour, as compared with the capacity of a lane of grade separated subway or belt highway of about 1675 vehicles per hour per lane.

With curb spaces removed and replaced by offstreet parking garages, and assuming unit offstreet parking costs of $300 a year per space for medium density and $550 for high density an extra cost of $130,000 a year at medium population densities and $238,000 at high density would be incurred to replace a mile of curb parking with offstreet space and thus increase street capacity by 1100 additional vehicles an hour. Under these circumstances the alternative of adding automobile subway capacity, assuming a 50-year life and 6 per cent interest, will be more attractive than offstreet parking whenever the subway capital costs fall below $3 million per lane-mile at medium density, or $5.5 million per lane-mile at high density.[8] Similarly, a belt highway will be a cheaper means of providing additional capacity whenever the total construction and right-of-way capital cost falls below $1.9 million *per lane-mile* for medium-density situations, or $3.7 million per lane-mile for high density.[9]

Evaluation of Travel Modes for Over-all Transport Between Home and Downtown

To synthesize properly all the cost and service data and the implications recorded thus far is no mean task. Yet there can be no doubt that it is of paramount importance, both from the standpoint of system decisionmaking and of understanding travelers' modal choice patterns. To summarize and combine results for all levels of maximum load point volumes, for all line-haul route lengths, for all downtown distribution route lengths, for all levels of residential density, or trip origination values, and for all residential, line-haul, and downtown distribution travel mode combinations clearly would be a major undertaking. While recognizing the desirability of a more complete accounting—an obvious necessity when facing any specific situation—it still seems helpful and relevant to provide an abbreviated picture of *over-all system* costs and service and to summarize the more obvious implications of the line-haul, residential collection, and downtown distribution analyses just reported.

Residential collection, line-haul, and downtown distribution cost and travel time data are summarized in Figures 52 through 55 for the following five systems: (1) line-haul rail transit with downtown subway and separate feeder bus service for residential collection; (2) line-haul rail transit with downtown subway and park-and-ride service for residential collection; (3) line-haul bus transit on exclusive rights-of-way (that is, not shared with other highway traffic), with integrated, continuous-service residential collection and downtown distribution on surface streets; (4) line-haul bus transit on exclusive rights-of-way, with integrated, continuous service on surface streets in residential collection and in exclusive bus subways in downtown distribution; and (5) auto-

[8] A simple proportional correction was made to account for capacity differentials between a lane of subway and removing curb parking from both sides of a 40-foot street.

[9] These figures have been corrected for the extra length required for belt highways and for the capacity differentials noted earlier. Also, in computing these costs, the right-of-way cost model provided in chapter 9 was used. Further, it should be pointed out that these are not low costs; for example, placed on an 8-lane basis, the lower limits for belt highways would be $15.4 million per mile for medium-density conditions, and $29.4 million per mile for high-density situations. Seldom do American inner belt highways cost so much. See, for example, Wilfred Owen, *The Metropolitan Transportation Problem,* Brookings Institution, Washington, D.C., 1956, p. 49.

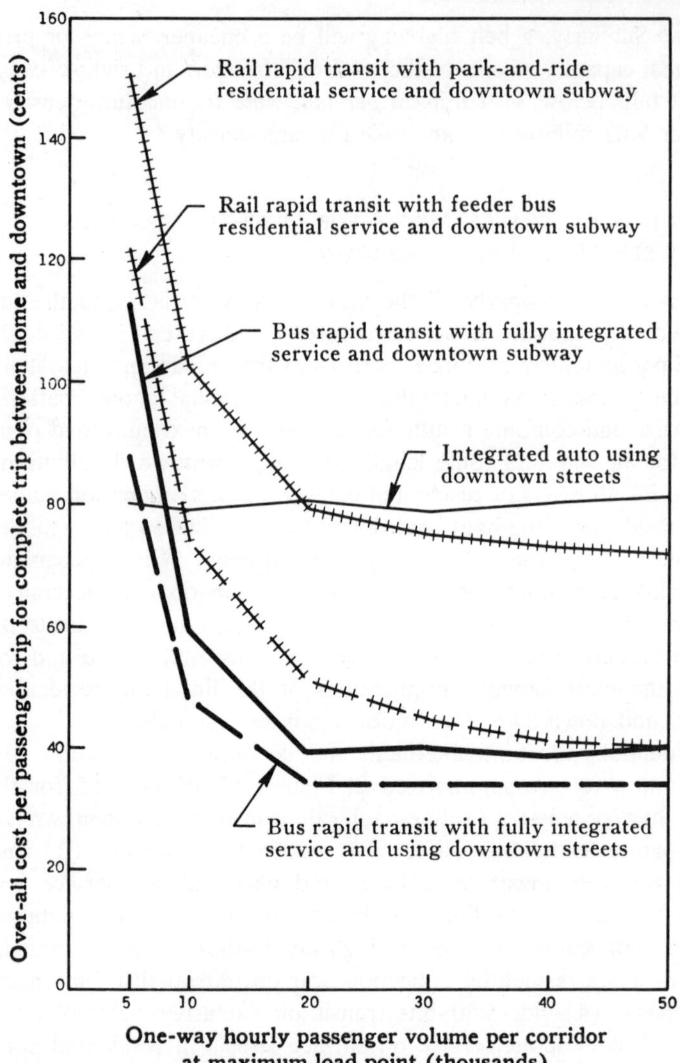

Figure 52. Over-all home-downtown passenger-trip costs for medium residential density along corridor, hourly downtown passenger-trip originations of ten per block at the home end, 10-mile line-haul facility, and 2-mile downtown distribution system route length.

mobile service on exclusive rights-of-way for the line haul and on surface streets within residential and downtown areas.

Some reasonably definite conclusions are evident. To begin, once hourly maximum load point volumes per corridor (with six corridors being assumed for the 2-mile downtown route length, and eight for the

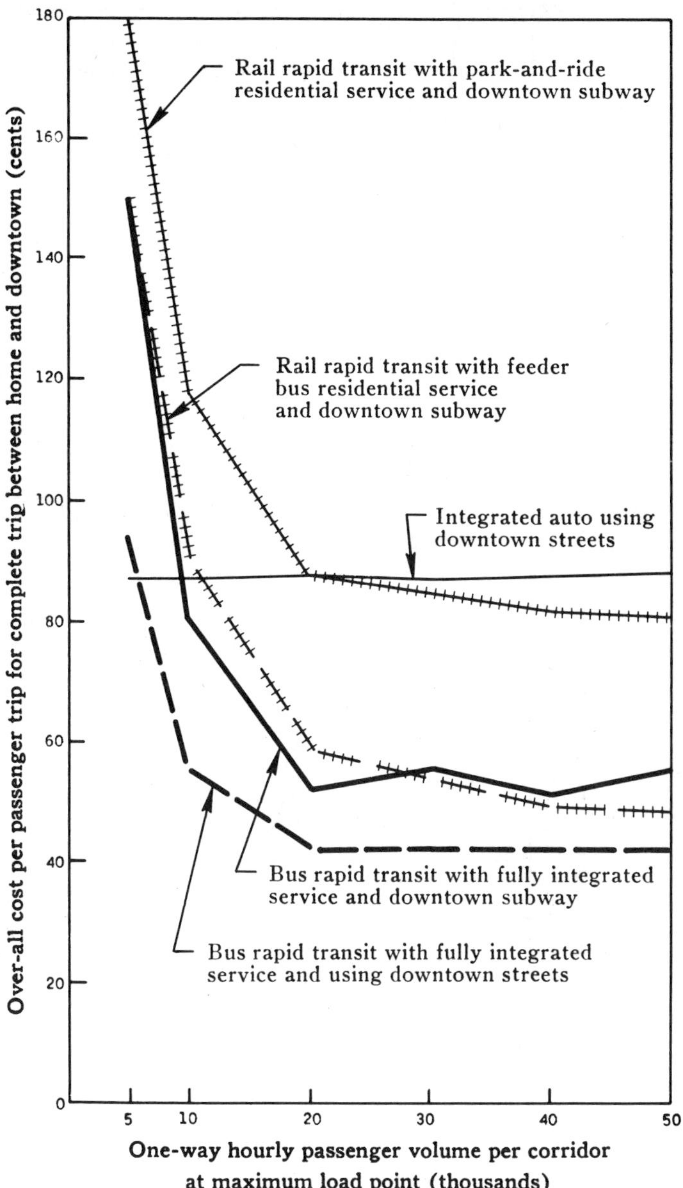

Figure 53. Over-all home-downtown passenger-trip costs for medium residential density along corridor, hourly downtown passenger-trip originations of ten per block at the home end, 10-mile line-haul facility, and 4-mile downtown distribution system route length.

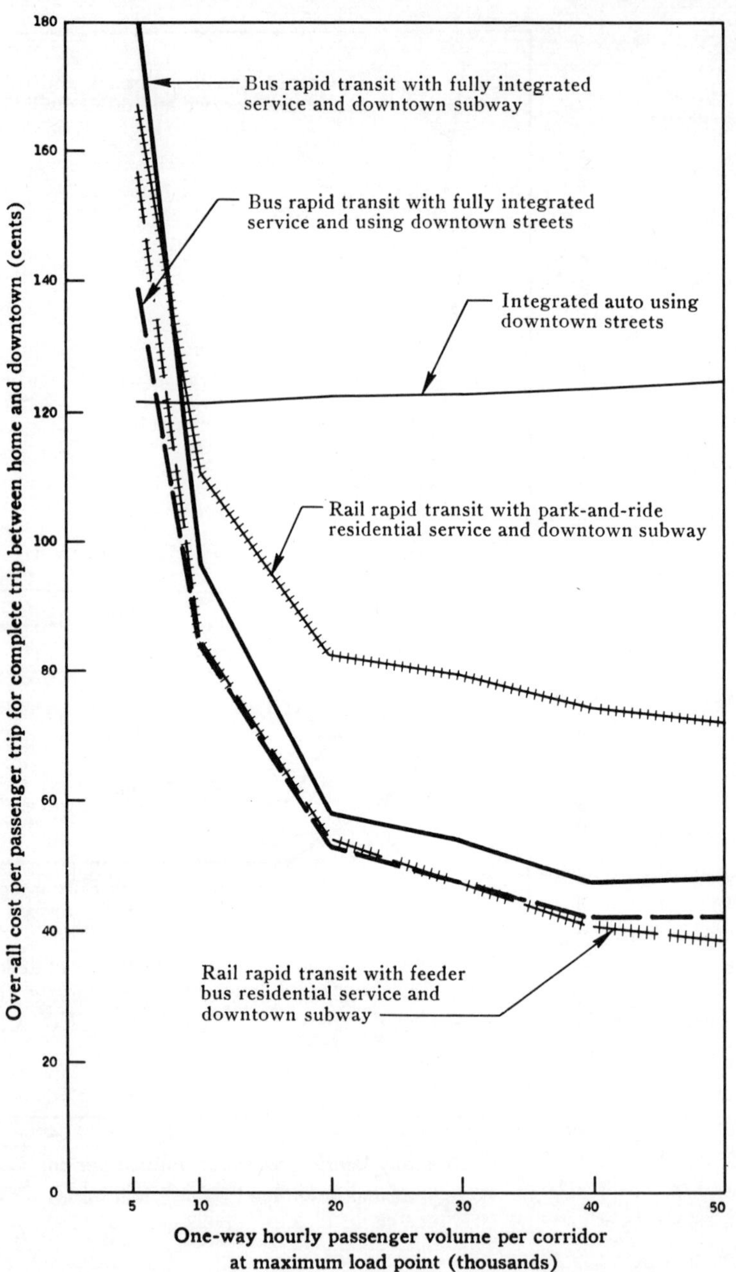

Figure 54. Over-all home-downtown passenger-trip costs for high residential density along corridor, hourly downtown passenger-trip originations of ten per block at the home end, 10-mile line-haul facility, and 2-mile downtown distribution system route length.

4-mile case) reach a level of about 10,000 passengers per hour or higher, an integrated bus service appears to be competitive with or cheaper than other urban transport within a wide range of circumstances. Also, this particular form of "mass transportation," if well organized, will enable passengers to travel between homes and downtown destinations, and vice versa, without transferring at intermediate stations or junctions.[10] Bus system costs, moreover, have probably been overstated in these analyses, particularly where subways are involved, because of the use of a conservative design capacity figure of 480 buses per lane per hour. As noted in chapter 9, footnote 4, this figure falls far below the 720 to 1100 range suggested by others, even for the high speeds desired.

Circumstances under which rail transit can become attractive or less costly are, however, several: whenever residential densities are high; whenever the passenger ridership is distributed over the route so that passenger volume tends to be more or less equal over all parts of the route (instead of being distributed along the route with uniformly decreasing volume levels); whenever downtown distribution increases as a proportion of the over-all trip length; and whenever rail facilities already exist and do not need much replacement. Of course, whenever passenger-trip distances increase to the point where the driving burden is no longer considered a "free" service, both rail and bus transit become more attractive relative to private automobile.

The circumstances of very high densities and substantial hourly corridor volumes necessary to support grade separated transit modes, whether bus or rail, are most likely to be encountered in the larger and older cities of the Eastern Seaboard and Middle West. Since these cities very often have rail rapid transit systems in existence, whose capital costs in large measure may be regarded as sunk, the least expensive solution to the transportation problem in such cases almost invariably involves keeping these rail systems in operation. Occasionally some expansion or contraction of existing systems also may be justifiable. Large Eastern Seaboard cities, because of age or difficult geographic barriers, also commonly confront serious limitations on their surface street space and available land; in such circumstances transit subways and grade separated line-haul facilities again appear to offer advantages. (Of course, aesthetic or other considerations might induce use of subways for noneconomic reasons as well.)

Automobile commutation is about as inexpensive as any urban transport mode available when hourly maximum load point volumes per corridor are in the range of 5000 to 10,000 or below. In addition, the

[10] These remarks apply to bus transit wherein the line-haul is performed over exclusive rights-of-way; a stronger economic case can be made for bus transit using mixed-traffic expressways for the line-haul function—an aspect to be discussed later.

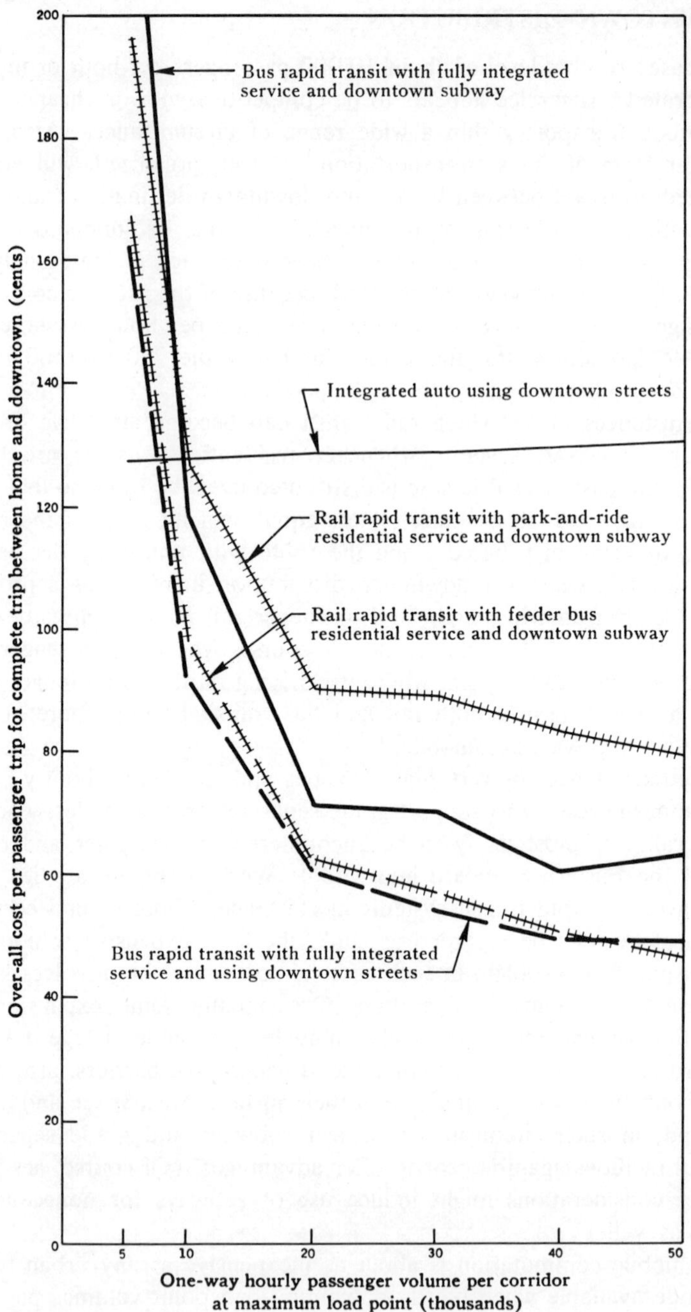

Figure 55. Over-all home-downtown passenger-trip costs for high residential density along corridor, hourly downtown passenger-trip originations of ten per block at the home end, 10-mile line-haul facility, and 4-mile downtown distribution system route length.

automobile usually has service advantages. This suggests that the automobile will be the dominant consumer choice in those cities characterized by low-density residential development.[11] Bus transit operating over the same highways as the automobiles should be the most economic public transit to supplement the automobiles in such cases.

In between the high and low volume cases occur situations common to many moderately large cities of medium to low residential and work-place densities. These cities are often newer, more rapidly growing, and located outside of the industrial Northeast. For these cities some blend of the previous solutions is probably needed if urban transportation costs are to be kept moderate. The particular synthesis will depend on the special circumstances of each city. However, in most such cases a highway-oriented solution usually will be cheaper with integrated express feeder bus services playing an important role. In the larger of these middle-sized cities, limited amounts of private rights-of-way for rail transit or buses may even be justified, though a more satisfactory solution in most instances might be to discipline use of high-performance urban highways during commuter hours and give the public transit vehicles priority access. (Such possibilities are discussed more fully in chapter 12.) If these cities have reasonably broad downtown streets and large and dispersed single-family residential suburbs, the appeal of integrated express bus services will be heightened. A major drawback, it must be emphasized, of attempting to meet the needs of such cities by rail transit is that rail must be supplemented in the suburbs by separate feeder buses, kiss-and-ride or park-and-ride residential feeder operations that either are costly or have very serious service disadvantages.

The reported costs of specific travel modes were computed while observing certain service constraints which, it was hypothesized, put all modes at about the same advantage or disadvantage and therefore permitted a determination of the "best" mode on the basis of cost considerations alone. This analytic approach is sound enough so long as we can assume that all travelers attach about the same values to travel time savings, avoidance of transfers, schedule frequency, and the like, and that the service standards established accord with these values. It is more realistic, however, to take human differences into account. Some travelers would pay dearly to save time on the work-trip; others would not. Some travelers highly value privacy, personal comfort, and convenience; others are relatively unconcerned. Some positively enjoy walking considerable

[11] From Figures 52 and 53, those illustrating costs with medium density along corridors, it is evident that at the three lower corridor volume levels the rail transit system combined with park-and-ride residential service is the most expensive of all transport modes—and is even considerably costlier than integrated automobile travel. For that matter, even at the three highest volume levels, travel by rail transit plus park-and-ride is only a few cents a trip cheaper than automobile travel.

distances while others would pay money to avoid walking even half a block to a bus stop. Some probably feel that the effort of driving in rush hour traffic is trivial, while some would pay heavily to avoid it. In sum, aspects of cost, price, service, and the specific demand characteristics of the traveling public are all vitally important and must be integrated and synthesized to arrive at the most effective and economic choice or combination of choices in any particular application.

PART III | SOLUTIONS AND PUBLIC POLICY

Chapter 12 | The Role of Technology

Technological solutions to urban transportation problems appeal strongly to the popular imagination. Many of them are picturesque; futuristic devices especially, such as monorail and the recently publicized hydrofoil boats, are great favorites with Sunday supplement editors and their readers, if not with those making use of them at amusement parks and in other limited situations. Their enthusiasm, even if mistaken, is certainly understandable. A sudden solution to the urban transportation problem through machinery would have the virtues of drama and simplicity. Perhaps at a single stroke it could minimize or banish the headaches of having to deal with politically vocal groups, at odds over all sorts of legitimate but discouragingly labyrinthine issues.

The sober truth is that most improvements in urban transport technology, whether proposed or actual, are not dramatic but marginal. For the most part, designers, engineers, and manufacturers apparently do not even regard far-reaching functional changes or technological breakthroughs as a major objective. This comparative lack of drama, of course, should not be allowed to detract from the steady marginal improvements and adaptations that have typified urban transportation developments since the end of World War I.

Still, virtually no major functional change has been achieved in urban transport in recent years. The bus of today, for example, differs little from that of 1930, particularly in the way it functions. Passengers still have to step up into the bus, even in large terminal operations where convertible high- and low-level platform steps might be used (such as those used on railroad cars for many, many decades); loading and unloading is restricted to two doors; express service is offered only in very limited circumstances; and, other than for terminals and their connecting ramps, operation on exclusive rights-of-way is nonexistent. In short, the bus operates more or less as it always has, though operating economies have resulted from diesel engines, automatic transmissions have promoted smoother rides, exterior appearance has possibly been improved by moving the motor to the rear, and so forth. Similarly, in rail transit, higher power and better bogies have resulted in higher speeds, greater comfort, and some operating economies; also, better signaling and communication equipment have improved rail safety. But the subway train basically operates as it did when it was instituted in the nineteenth century (except for the introduction of skip-stop and express operations which, in effect, represent a tradeoff among lower schedule frequency, higher speed, and better economy of operation). Finally, the private automobile and taxi also function more or less as they did many decades ago, with the more notable recent improvements being associated more with highways than with the vehicles themselves.

In short, today as in past years, mass transit passengers must undergo multiple stops for their journeys, usually must transfer, and often must do considerable walking to complete their trips. Automobile users must still put up with the driving burden, and normally must allow their high-cost vehicles to stand idle all day when used for work-trips. There has been very little effort to develop operational procedures and equipment that would permit origin-to-destination travel by public transit without transfers and intermediate stops, or that would free private automobile users from the driving burden and from idling capital equipment. This neglect continues in spite of growing evidence that the public highly prizes service and seems to strive unceasingly for private, nonstop, nontransfer, and comfortable travel, almost regardless of cost.

The few technological *innovations* that have been proposed are thus all the more noteworthy—automated highways (electronic or mechanical), integrated highway-rail vehicle systems, and continuous operation express rail systems.[1] Each bears promise of distinct improvements. Automated highways could eliminate the driving task, heighten the use of highway capacity, increase speed and safety, and lower land requirements and land costs. Integrated highway-rail vehicle systems might be extended to either private or public transport and incorporate at least some of the inherent technical and operational features of each type of support or guidance subsystem. For example, a transit vehicle that could operate both on rails and on uncontrolled highways could provide direct service between low-and high-density areas, without requiring passenger transfer and its resulting operational and service inefficiencies. Comparable advantages could accrue to a passenger automobile able to operate both on highways and on controlled rail facilities.

This chapter assesses some of the more promising adaptations and changes in urban transport. Though thc application of technology is

[1] This discussion excludes such proposals as monorail and a suggested "transit expressway" since they represent not functional innovation but merely different or slightly improved vehicle, support, or control/guidance forms.

generally construed in the narrow sense of *physical* change, the outlook here will extend over a broader and more meaningful range; that is, there will be no hesitation to point out that some physical changes may necessitate political or social changes as well, and that operational or functional modifications may be highly desirable.

The Urban Environment and Technological Change

Certain long-standing facts of the urban environment automatically limit the feasible scope of technological innovation. Regardless of any new types of downtown rush hour transport systems or devices that are likely to be developed in the foreseeable future, for example, it seems undeniable that local streets and arterial highways will continue to be needed for a variety of public and private activities. These local access requirements account for nearly all transportation land uses in urban areas and for about 20 to 24 per cent of total urban land use. To augment this basic highway system with arterials at half-mile intervals would require only 1 per cent more land; and to superimpose expressways on the arterial system at 4-mile intervals would require only another 3 per cent, for a total land commitment of 24 to 28 per cent.[2] (Interestingly enough, the well-advanced freeway system in Los Angeles in 1960 occupied only 1.6 per cent of the total land area.[3]) With newly developing urban areas, proper and timely provision of expressways and arterial highways might further reduce that need since high-performance highways usually move urban traffic more efficiently than ordinary access streets. It should be evident, at least, that no significant *over-all* reduction in land-use requirements would result from the large-scale development of mass transit systems for downtown-oriented travel movement except to the extent that such systems eliminate substantial quantities of parking requirements.

Also important is the apparent fact that public mass transit is less than a fully popular travel mode for social, recreational, and shopping activities. The superior convenience, mobility, and privacy (and oftentimes lower cost) of the automobile seem to give it an almost insurmountable advantage for noncommuter trips. The implication is that high-speed highways will have to penetrate to the very center of the city if people are to be attracted into cities for social, recreational, and shopping activities. But if such highways are constructed, the economical solution to the urban transportation problem almost certainly consists of finding some

[2] D. S. Berry *et al., The Technology of Urban Transportation* (Northwestern University Press, Evanston, Ill., 1963), pp. 8*ff*.

[3] Karl Moskowitz, "Living and Travel Patterns in Auto-oriented Cities," *California Highways and Public Works,* 43:51 (July-August 1964).

way to use them as much as possible as the basis of a commuter system.

Changing urban travel patterns also have profound implications for potential improvements to be had through technology. Formerly, most urban travel was confined to the dense, central-city core and to heavily built-up radial corridors which were served at various stages by streetcar, trolley car, elevated rapid transit, subway, or commuter railroad lines. In bygone years when private automobiles were beyond almost everyone's means, residential growth and urban travel were limited by the coverage of transit systems and by what was then reasonable walking distance. Crosstown travel was rare because of the expense, time, discomfort, and inconvenience involved. Over the past fifteen years, by contrast, downtown-oriented travel generally has remained stable or decreased; the growth in urban tripmaking has been mainly in crosstown and intrasuburban movement. These trip patterns do not share the high intensity of downtown-oriented travel, if for no other reason than that the areas involved are of very different geographic size. All of this reflects, simply, the sharp increase in urban mobility, with the clear implication that high-capacity systems and vehicles are increasingly less necessary.

The ubiquity of highway systems additionally provides a superior capability to adjust to sociological and economic changes—that is, to changes in living patterns, industrial location, and market structure. The past fifteen years have seen dramatic shifts in North American residential and industrial location and in employment and retailing centers. Bus transit systems and highway and automobile systems have demonstrated at least some ability to adapt to these changes. By contrast, extremely inflexible and long-lived rail transit systems have not been able to bend to these changes without considerable cost and sacrifices in service.

Accordingly, even if exclusive reliance is not placed on highway facilities, it is still wise to promote better highway transport in urban areas. At a minimum, such a policy would help ease the existing transportation problem by *all* modes and would lead to an improved performance of urban transport functions.

An obvious first step would be to promote more effective use of highways during rush hours, perhaps through rationing accomplished by differentiated tolls or special licensing. Such recourses would run up against a number of obstacles, however, including the fact that they would be politically difficult to implement. The question therefore arises, what alternative policies might be more acceptable to the public; and it is here that technological changes might be particularly effective.

In assessing the potential benefits of technological improvements, it is helpful to know the present cost structure. Figure 56 presents, in crude bar chart form, cost breakdowns for bus transit, rail transit, and auto-

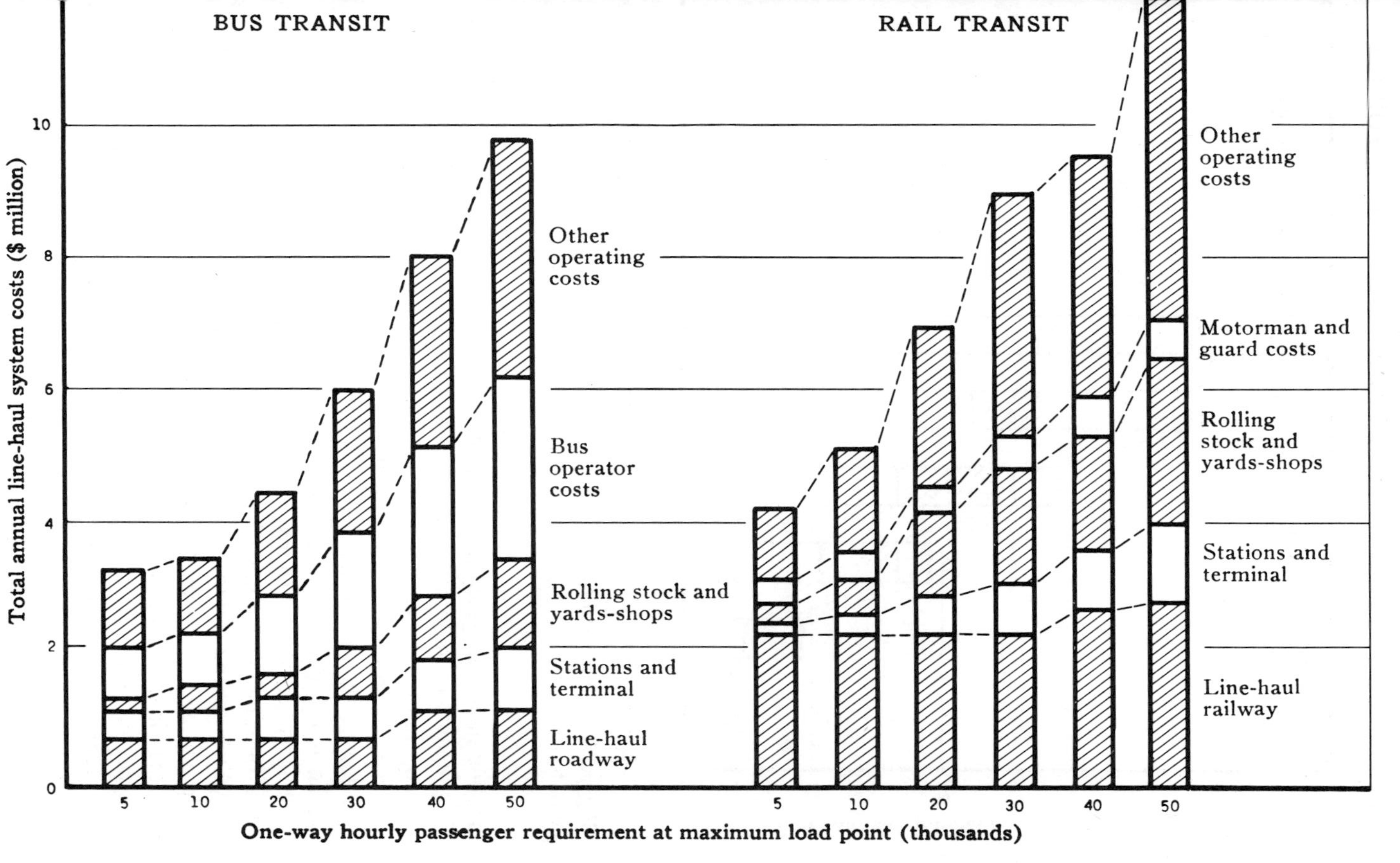

Figure 56. Costs of line-haul system with downtown stub terminal or parking by category and mode (10-mile route length). *continued on p. 314*

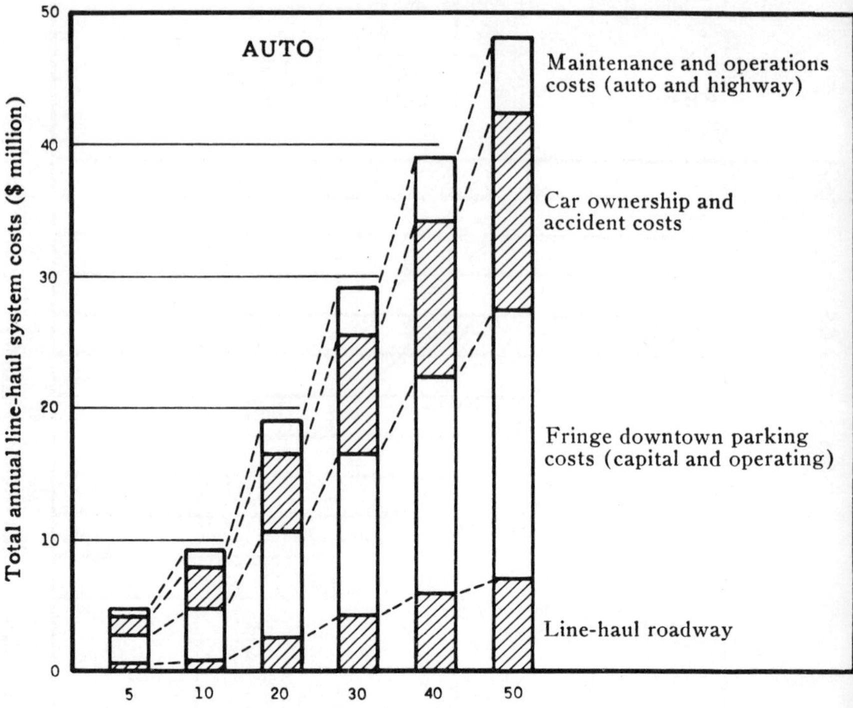

Figure 56 (Continued from p. 313). Costs of line-haul system with downtown stub terminal or parking, by category and mode (10-mile route length).

mobile line-haul systems. Such cost breakdowns can be extremely useful in pinpointing the most promising areas for cost reduction. For example, bus operator costs are much higher than rail motorman and guard costs, strongly suggesting that automation of bus operations might be more productive than automation of rail transit. Potential rail economies seem to lie more in reducing the capital and operating costs associated with rolling stock, yards, shops, stations, terminals, and the roadbed itself. The outstanding feature of automobile costs, by contrast, is the extent to which parking charges are dominant, and to a lesser extent car ownership and accident costs. Surprisingly, highway construction expenses (including land acquisition) and automobile operating costs—popular sources of major concern—together generally account for less than 30 per cent of total automobile line-haul system costs. These cost data constitute much of the essential background against which possible changes in automobile, bus, and rail technologies are evaluated (in the designated order) in the next three sections.

Possible Automobile System Innovations

Given the cost structure of urban automobile transport and the expected income projections, three promising possibilities for significant cost reduction or service improvement in automobile systems appear to be the large-scale use or development of small cars, leasing or rental arrangements, and electronic highways or other automated (or mechanized) line-haul facilities.

Small specialized commuting automobiles (with, say, two or three seats, small efficient powerplants, no special trunk compartment, and low weight) could effect major economies. By far the most important and easiest cost reduction could stem from reduced parking space requirements; however, lower ownership and operating costs also should result. It is at least possible, moreover, but considerably less likely, that smaller cars could reduce line-haul roadway costs. For example, if enough of the commuting automobile fleet consisted of small automobiles, reductions might be made in lane-widths and thus in highway requirements. At present, urban interstate highways have 12-foot lanes (in large part, of course, to accommodate buses and trucks). If a highway were restricted to use by smaller cars, 8- or 9-foot lanes would be feasible,[4] which alone could increase highway capacity and reduce highway costs by some 30 to 40 per cent.[5] Indeed, it might well prove cheaper to promote or subsidize small car use than to build elaborate subsidized public transit systems. A small car system has the further advantages of being specialized mainly in its rolling stock and of greater consistency with apparent trends in consumer preferences.

It must be recognized, however, that considerable uncertainty surrounds the extent and feasibility of the immediate economies that small cars might promote in highway investments. For one thing, too little is known about how small cars would affect peak-hour highway use; most available estimates are deductively based, usually on the assumption that *all* rush hour vehicles would be small (on the particular facility being analyzed). To make such an assumption a reality, some sort of rationing or controls seemingly would be required, over and above the economic incentives for owning smaller and cheaper cars. Again, one rationing

[4] To appreciate the fact that a 12-foot lane width is liberal, one need only remember that Boston's 2-lane Sumner Tunnel operated with 2-way traffic for some 30 years with high volumes (over 1500 vehicles an hour per lane) and with low accident experience, even though its lanes were (and still are) only 10 1/2 feet wide, were not divided, and were not restricted to passenger cars.

[5] Aside from the obvious reductions in pavement width and construction cost, the lightweight vehicles would also permit reductions in pavement thickness and roadway strength.

scheme might be simply to charge larger cars the full costs of the additional highway facilities they require, in order to discourage their peak-hour use, although it is not clear that the differential costs would be large enough to affect the market seriously. Another scheme might be to set aside some highway lanes, or even certain highways, for small cars during the rush hours.

Many difficulties obviously beset such schemes. One is the seemingly well-established preference for the large car as *the* family car. The small car may never be anything more than a second car except for very young or very old or childless families. The likelihood of widespread adoption of small cars for commuting thus may hinge on greatly enlarging the number of 2-car families in the society which is at least a possibility with increasing affluence. (Already over 20 per cent of American households own two or more cars.) Also, roadway costs account for a relatively small proportion of total automobile system costs. Taken together, all these considerations suggest that the major, and certainly the quickest, economies from small vehicles lie in reduction of parking and ownership costs, which are largely independent of universal or even widespread adoption of small cars for commuting.

Economies in automobile parking and ownership costs also might be achieved by more widespread leasing of automobiles. Leasing provides an urban transportation service that has most of the service attractions of private automobiles, such as privacy, schedule flexibility, and ubiquity; avoids high labor costs by having people do their own driving; potentially reduces parking space requirements in high-cost urban locations by increasing the average daily hours of utilization of urban vehicles; and spreads the high overhead or capital costs associated with ownership of commuting automobiles. It can at least be argued that present arrangements for vehicle leasing have not explored the full range of possibilities. For example, it may be worth while to explore further special overnight leasing schemes, weekend leasings, and other special marketing devices.

Interesting proposals have also been made for integrating expanded leasing schemes for specialized urban automobiles with new line-haul technologies, by which automobiles would be moved automatically or mechanically without guidance or control by the individual driver. Under such schemes, a single system could exploit the inherent physical and operating efficiencies of both rail and automobile. Within residential areas drivers would continue to manage their own automobiles, thus keeping labor costs within bounds. They would enter electronic or mechanized highway or fixed rail systems at circumferential or radial line-haul facilities, and from there be carried on a controlled right-of-way. Such systems would probably improve performance speed, eliminate the driving burden, and improve safety. Perhaps they could be extended into downtown areas and incorporate automated or mechanized downtown distribution and parking. It is even conceivable that the vehicles could be used for more than one peak-hour trip and could be removed "automatically" from the downtown area in the daytime, thus further reducing downtown congestion and demands for parking space.

It is easy to become enthusiastic about such proposals. They provide individual transportation, permit high flexibility, reduce discomfort and inconvenience, need not inhibit the privacy of travelers, and take advantage of the high-capacity features of rail transit—all without requiring passenger transfers and without the severely restricted flexibility and immobility of present-day and proposed rail transit systems. For any such system to be effective, however, the automotive industry would have to manufacture vehicles capable of operating both on city streets and on automated or mechanized highways or rail facilities, and possibly with lower probabilities of breakdown. Government agencies responsible for funding, building, and operating highway and transit facilities would have to pursue more integrated planning and, more importantly, would have to maintain close liaison with the private industry that would build, sell, and maintain the vehicles. In short, some formidable institutional roadblocks stand in the way.

Furthermore, the savings achievable from the installation of electronic or mechanical control and guidance systems for passenger cars probably would be marginal compared to those achievable by the simpler innovations of smaller cars or leasing arrangements. Line-haul automation or mechanization further involves a number of technological uncertainties which make it difficult to assess its potential savings. Seemingly, its main technological advantage is that it would permit closer headway spacing and higher speeds, thus increasing highway capacity and reducing travel times. But for short trips—typical of urban travel—the time savings would not be large. At present, for example, a 6-mile trip may take a little over 10 minutes at 35 mph; increasing this speed to 60 mph would save only 4⅓ minutes. Moreover, since roadway costs represent only 12 to 14 per cent of total system costs in most cases, automation or mechanization of urban highways needs some justification other than cost reduction—perhaps its ability to reduce whatever discomfort or inconvenience is associated with the driving task,[6] or to reduce accident costs. Cost estimates for automating automobile travel are only rough approximations, but it appears that an annual cost of $150 or less per automobile would suffice (and thus about 30 cents a trip for work-trip

[6] Many of these advantages can be achieved with more modest use of electronics through use of flow control devices on limited-access highways. See, for example, R. H. Haase, *Decreasing Travel Time for Freeway Users,* The RAND Corporation, RM-3099-FF, October 1962.

commuting). It is difficult to say whether improved service alone would induce the motoring public to support this charge.

Many other types of technological improvements applicable to highway vehicles merit attention. For example, improvements in the gas turbine engine may be in the offing; it appears that fuel consumption in such engines can be measurably improved, that even the lowest-quality oils would be suitable fuels, and that the exhaust would be virtually clear.[7] Only for buses, however, would turbines probably be more economical than internal combustion engines, and particularly for nonstop express bus services in which acceleration performance is not particularly crucial.

Of somewhat more general interest and probably greater potential is the battery-operated electric automobile—not at all an innovation since it was a major predecessor of the more flexible and economical gasoline-driven automobile over four decades ago. Now, however, with the likely advent of cheaper and higher voltage batteries that can operate longer before needing to be recharged, with rising public concern over air pollution and noise, with the increase of multicar families, and with the price of gasoline increasing faster than that of electricity, the electric automobile may come into its own again.[8] It could bring other economies in its wake, quite possibly, by adding to the feasibility of developing a small car fleet with all its attendant savings.

Possible Bus System Innovations

Almost any analysis of the economics of bus systems or improvements in bus technology must begin with the fact that bus operator costs range from 22 to 29 per cent of total system costs, compared with 5 to 10 per cent for rail. Accordingly, substantial economies lie in reducing the number of bus operators.

Electronic or other automatic guidance and control on highways used for bus line hauls would permit buses to operate with closer headways and at higher speeds. This would increase highway capacity and reduce line-haul construction and right-of-way costs, which run from 13 to 20 per cent of total bus costs. In turn, higher speeds would permit higher utilization of the buses, thereby permitting economies with respect to operators and buses. Buses might also be operated in trains, with virtually the same advantages as rail transit, while retaining much of the flexibility that allows buses to operate on city streets and in residential areas with-

[7] See discussion of pulse-jet generators used with impulse-type turbines in an unpublished report to the Institute of Public Administration by A. R. Cripe, "National Urban Transportation Study."

[8] George A. Hoffman, *Battery-operated Electric Automobiles,* The RAND Corporation, P-2712, March 1963.

out passenger transfer. The latter scheme, however, would require complete automation either by electronic or mechanical control and guidance, for example, using "troughs" or rails in conjunction with steel-and-rubber double-wheel bogies.

Even without automation, highway passenger capacity could be raised by allocating more highway space to buses during peak hours. Conservatively estimated, a lane of limited-access highway reserved for buses *can* handle upward of 25,000 or 30,000 seated passengers an hour at 35 to 40 mph with fully loaded buses, while private automobiles, even with full loads of 5 or 6 people, would do well to handle about 10,000 people at the same speed in a single lane. (Since the average commuter hour load is 1.5 to 1.9 persons per automobile, this automotive capacity figure is normally around 3000 or so.) One immediate impact of setting aside more highway space for buses might be a reduction in congestion and travel time and thus in bus operating costs.

Other bus economies, almost immediately available, are expressed implicitly in the operation methods assumed for the earlier cost analyses. Four items in those analyses are of particular note: operation of more buses on nonstop express schedules between line-haul entry points and downtown areas; centralized bus fare collection systems like those common to rail systems, in conjunction with nonstop express service; design of buses to include a third door and double-side loading and unloading; and use of diagonal, multislot, high-speed, high-capacity bus stations and terminals. All four of these items are aimed at reducing travel time and cost by reducing loading and unloading delays and their attendant acceleration-deceleration time losses. At present, loading and unloading time accounts for 10 to 30 per cent of total bus trip time; further, loading time alone accounts for close to 60 per cent of trip delays.[9] Consequently, bus terminal redesign along lines shown in appendix B, Figure 61 (so that successive buses do not interfere with one another following loading or unloading and while decelerating or accelerating, and so that fare collection can be centralized within a mezzanine-type terminal) can effect considerable time and cost economies and ensure effective use of high-capacity through-lanes. Multiple doors, double-side loading, and frequent limited-stop service would also reduce delays and permit present and future buses to operate more in accordance with their power capabilities (50 to 70 mph, depending on the particular vehicle and transmission).[10]

The main cost and service disadvantages of present bus systems derive from a relatively poor speed performance during peak hours, even for

[9] See, for example, W. C. Gilman and Co., *St. Louis Metropolitan Area Transportation Study, 1957–'70–'80,* New York, 1959, Tables 35–37.

[10] Full extension of these principles, as done in the cost analyses, will permit high operating speeds and utilization rates, so that bus operator costs should run only as high as 25 per cent and rolling stock another 10 per cent of total system costs.

express service. This is due partly to entanglement in traffic congestion. Various rationing devices (as an alternative to the politically difficult one of differential pricing—where such would be appropriate) have been suggested or actually put into practice on urban highways to "solve" this problem. For example, a few cities have allotted exclusive lanes to buses on surface streets, and the same scheme has been proposed for freeways during rush hours. These schemes are tantamount to assigning a prohibitively high price to private automobile use of these lanes during rush hours (at least if the police fines for violation are high and enforcement is strict). A closely related proposal is to provide special busways in high-density, high-congestion areas, but otherwise to have the buses operate as they normally do on streets and expressways where congestion is lower. An interesting example of such a proposal is the St. Louis express bus plan.[11] Others have suggested that buses might best be accommodated by an expressway design that incorporates an express bus roadway within the median island. They add that such a roadway could be used wholly or partly for "unbalanced" traffic operations as well, and could gradually be devoted to exclusive transit use as volumes require. As they further point out:

> Exclusive bus lanes or rights-of-way could possibly be used by highway traffic during weekends and holiday periods, thus providing additional highway capacity to serve recreational peaks since few of these trips would be accommodated by public carriers. The special busways would, therefore, serve the dual purpose of accommodating home-to-work and weekend peaks.[12]

Unfortunately, while all these schemes are promising, they share a major disadvantage: they usually necessitate at least some underutilization of highway capacity. With any reasonable frequency of buses there would be a substantial increase in the number of persons that could be carried by the highway, although it is likely that the bus lanes would still be used far below their maximum capacity except in situations of very high demand.

There is another possibility which could avoid these losses and also improve the performance of express bus systems. The procedure would be to control the entry of vehicles onto limited-access facilities, and thus keep the express facilities operating at designed capacity and speed.

Figure 57 illustrates in a general way the relationship between travel time or delay and traffic volume on uncontrolled facilities (but not, for example, at signalized intersections); this functional relationship holds roughly for the indicated volume and capacity scales, and where the

[11] *St. Louis Metropolitan Area Transportation Study.*

[12] Wilbur Smith and Associates, *Future Highways and Urban Growth* (New Haven, Conn., 1961), pp. 154–155.

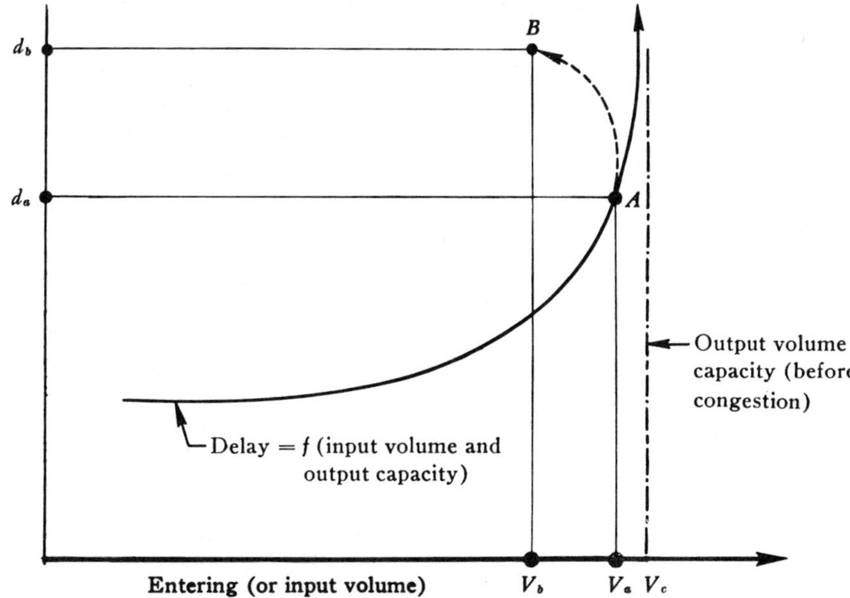

Figure 57. Relationship between travel time or delay and traffic volume on uncontrolled facilities. (Above point *A*, the broken-line curve also roughly describes output volume capacity.)

volumes may be thought of as rates of flow for specified time periods (say one hour).[13] Under most circumstances, as the entering volume on facilities approaches the maximum capacity, "wave" or "shock action" commonly develops and results in reducing effective capacity. As the input volume reaches V_a in Figure 57 and congestion develops, the delay-volume curve follows the broken line (in approximate terms); in essence, this means that the broken-line curve becomes the output-volume or capacity curve which expresses the (modified) delay function for input volumes in the region roughly between V_b and V_a once congestion has developed. Further, if input volumes are *sustained* at or above volume V_a it should be evident that not only may the output-volume capacity drop to V_b, for example, but the average delay becomes indefinitely large for entering or arriving vehicles.

Such situations are of course to be avoided. It is apparent that controlling input volumes so that they cannot approach output capacity too closely will result in over-all net benefits to travelers; such control usually will permit both higher output volumes and lower over-all delay or travel time. Obviously, however, the costs of installing a suitable communica-

[13] The resultant travel time or delay would obviously be smaller for equivalent volume rates over shorter periods.

tion and control system must be taken into account when assessing the over-all economic feasibility of input control.

Reasonably simple control systems could be designed to handle most highway input problems. For example, each entrance ramp onto an expressway could have a detector which would signal a master control station of the arrival of vehicles. The master control mechanism would integrate the total flow and compute expected rates of flow at potential bottleneck points along the expressway, and thus anticipate "backward-bending" delay-volume situations. When advantageous to do so, selected ramps could be closed to prevent capacity reduction[14] or, if more complicated devices were used, the inflow could be reduced proportionately at each point of entry. Of course, it would be necessary to erect controls, informational signs, and feedback mechanisms for actually adjusting flow at the various entry points, and to design and install suitable programming equipment.

Another control principle that might be instituted is the so-called head-of-the-line or priority merge.[15] Its principal application would be directed to transit vehicles or other high-priority emergency service vehicles. Where entrance ramps onto expressways frequently develop long queues and consequent delays (that is, when the input volume approaches or exceeds the output-volume capacity along lines noted before), it might be advantageous under some circumstances to permit buses to go around the queue to the head of the line. Such a practice is illustrated in Figure 58. It should be evident that at least two ramp lanes would be required for priority merge;[16] where 2-lane ramps are already provided (or where the incoming expressway lanes plus ramp input lanes to the merging area exceed the outgoing expressway lanes by two or more), one of the ramp lanes can merely be striped off for bus use (or for *no* use) with no loss in operating efficiencies.

Three things must be considered in permitting buses to use the extra ramp lane for a priority or head-of-the-line merge. First, where two ramp lanes are in existence and are used by waiting vehicles for storage, one

[14] The programming for such a system would hardly be simple. For example, it should take into account potential backward-bending situations on alternate routes that travelers might be forced to take. It would be especially difficult to establish which ramps would be closed in the process of maximizing flow (and reducing delay), and whether the long or the short trips would be diverted.

[15] This scheme was originally suggested by Henry M. Bain, Jr., and has been analyzed in detail in an unpublished report to Metro Consultants by Martin Wohl, "Improvement of Bus Service between Washington and Portions of Northern Virginia," May 1962.

[16] In Fig. 58 the bus ramp lane is shown on the left-hand side to facilitate moving around the queue; however, whenever a bus stop is located at near proximity to the ramp on the minor road, it would be desirable to place the bus ramp lane on the right-hand side. Or, a one-lane ramp would be suitable if closed to private vehicles.

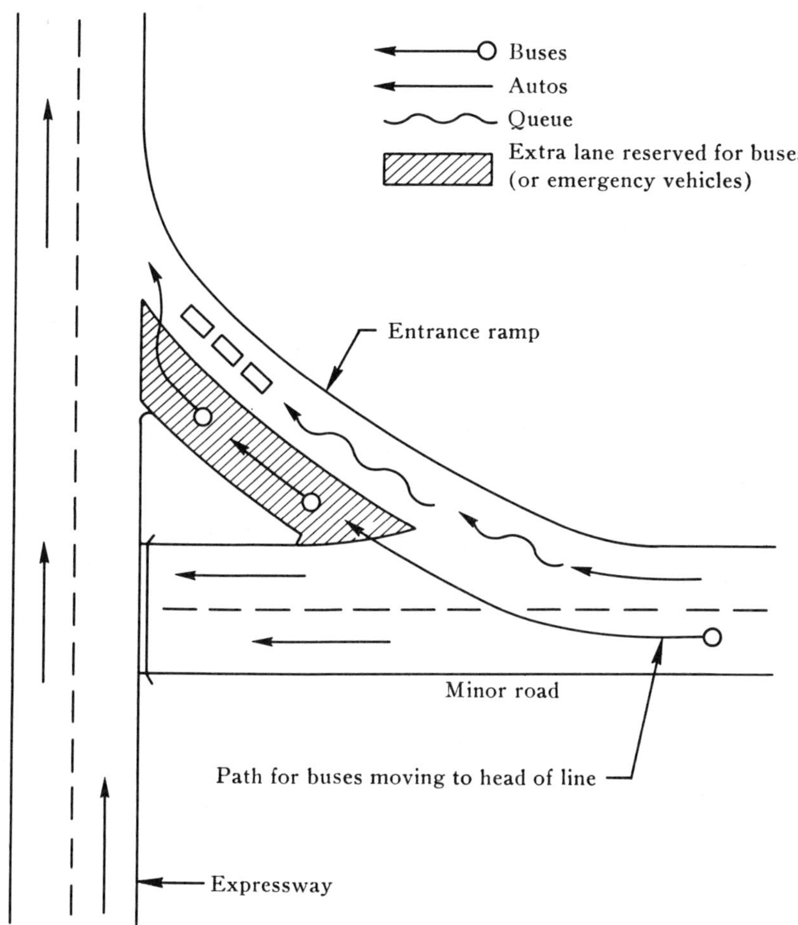

Figure 58. A priority-merge scheme for buses entering expressways (fig. is not to scale).

must be assured that reduction of the storage space for vehicles in queue will not cause a more serious problem at some other point on the minor road or at an adjacent intersection. Second, questions must be raised regarding allocation of the costs of the extra ramp lane. Third, the time savings accruing to bus patrons (by their moving directly to the head of the line) must be balanced against the time losses to automobile travelers (who lose time when the buses move ahead) to assure that a net over-all gain in passenger travel time does in fact result.

Regarding the latter point, it should be evident that no single automobile will be "unduly" delayed, although their aggregate delays may become large if queues are long. In Figure 58, for example, if ramp arrivals were 1300 vehicles an hour and if there were a constant 2-mile queue[17] moving about 10 mph, a bus (and thus each of its passengers) could reduce its travel time from about 12 to 4 minutes by moving around the queue and to the head of the line at 30 mph. In so doing, however, the bus would move ahead of about 1⅓ miles of automobiles —about 173 autos—delaying each of them an additional amount equal to the time it would take the bus to merge into the traffic stream. If the merge took the bus an average of 10 seconds, the automobiles would be delayed a total of 1730 seconds; with 1.7 passengers per automobile, the total automobile passenger delay would be about 2940 seconds each time a bus moved ahead. Under these circumstances, then, with the bus saving 480 seconds, a net over-all time saving would result from the priority merge scheme so long as a bus has at least seven passengers.

Again, it should be pointed out that such a priority system would have little if any effect on the ramp or merging capacity. Furthermore, priority merge without access control would require striping of the extra ramp lane (or paving of the shoulder area if no extra lane exists) and the installation of signs noting the proper use of the striped lane combined with proper enforcement. No special electronic controls or detectors would be necessary and new highways could be so designed at very little additional cost. Obviously, though, once onto the expressway, the buses would be subjected to the same travel conditions and delays as passenger cars—at least until input control devices were instituted on entry ramps as well.

Some General Highway Innovations and Possibilities

Other types of highway improvements are possible, but since many of them have been explored at some length in the literature they will be passed over briefly here. Pertinent examples would be: use of synchronized and interconnected volume density or actuated traffic controls on downtown streets and radial arterials so as to maximize over-all system capacity or reduce over-all travel times; use of analogue detector and control devices so that backup from one intersection can be prevented from blocking adjacent cross-streets and intersections; and use of reversible or imbalanced highway lanes on expressways, arterials, and other city streets.

These techniques have sometimes been subjected to field experimentation and have yielded improvements when accompanied by sufficiently comprehensive analysis and planning.

[17] Obviously this assumes that output capacity at the merging point is restricted relative to the input volume.

Toll collection is another possibility for highway operational control. As pointed out earlier, differential pricing of highway services may be desirable since higher costs may be incurred for peak-hour users than for off-peak. A toll collection system for achieving differential pricing might also be used to control the inflow of traffic and thus prevent backward-bending or capacity-reduction. While most toll facilities now operate with barriers and collect the tolls manually or by automatic coin machines or by the presence of a sticker or plate permitting passage, some authors have recently suggested electronic toll detection and assessment systems for differential pricing.[18]

Clearly, toll systems could be used for better adjustment of highway prices or charges to costs where peak and off-peak differentials exist. It must be decided, however, whether the social and economic gains from better pricing mechanisms (and in some cases from preventing capacity reduction) actually do offset the costs of building and operating the toll collection system. These costs are not negligible, presently running at about two cents and up per vehicle-trip; and the low, 2-cent costs are achieved only where volumes are extremely high or where automatic coin machines are used. From the few data available, it appears that the total annual costs of an electronic toll assessment system (with monthly toll bills) would offer little cost advantage (if any) over a toll barrier system with automatic coin collectors;[19] the electronic system would have the distinct advantage, however, of permitting travelers to avoid stops (and possible queues) at toll barriers.

As for opportunities to institute input or access control systems, additional control equipment and information devices would be needed for both the toll barrier and electronic assessment systems, and neither seems to offer any *distinct* advantage. A crude sort of input control could be offered with a toll barrier operation, however, at no additional expense, by carefully selecting the number of toll gates to operate at various times. A 1-lane entrance ramp, for example, might accommodate about 1600 vehicles an hour,[20] and a toll booth at the head of the ramp might handle about 400 an hour. Thus if a ramp volume of over 800 vehicles an hour would result in backward-bending or capacity reduction on the expressway, the use of only two toll booths would provide both differential

[18] See, for example, statements of William Vickrey at the Hearings before the Joint Committee on Washington Metropolitan Problems, *Transportation Plan for National Capital Region,* 86th Congress, 1st Session, on report of Washington Mass Transportation Survey, November 1959, pp. 454*ff*.

[19] Based partially on data from William Vickrey at the Hearings before the Joint Committee on Washington Metropolitan Problems, *Transportation Plan for National Capital Region,* 86th Congress, 1st Session, on report of Washington Mass Transportation Survey, November 1959, pp. 454*ff*., and on data from Garden State Parkway and Port of New York Authority.

[20] Assuming little or no capacity restrictions at the merging point.

pricing and proper metering of input flow. In general, toll gates or plazas can be low-cost locations for metering flow and for developing priority access for more efficient use of expensive peak-hour capacity.

All schemes for improving highway and bus performance also have the incidental but special virtue of permitting experiments with high-speed transit without subjecting a community to large capital expenditures or fixed commitments. If high-speed transit systems actually will attract large numbers of people away from automobile commutation, it should at least be possible to investigate the possibilities with a high-speed express bus system. More capital intensive, high-capacity systems then could be built if the number of people attracted justified the higher capital costs. In other words, valuable information could be gathered in this way on the time elasticity of demand for transit service, without any great capital expenditure.

Possible Rail System Innovations

The monorail deserves a prominent place in the discussion of technological changes in rail transit, not so much for its high potential but because it has captured so much public attention.[21] This attention persists even though thorough examination and analysis by engineers and economists have indicated little if any promise for monorail systems.[22] The underlying reasons for the appeal appear to be the submission of exceedingly low cost proposals for monorail designs, and the attention to modern-day, sleek exterior design. In truth, the monorail offers little hope of providing comparable rapid transit at lower cost than conventional 2-rail systems, nor is monorail inherently superior from the viewpoint of aesthetics and right-of-way requirements. Tomorrow's 2-rail transit cars can be made as attractive as monorail, even to including attractive noise-reducing "skirts" for the bogies, and the support structure for 2-rail cars could also achieve the trim modern design so often pictured for monorail (though the structure would be a couple of feet wider but not so deep). Moreover, the right-of-way requirements for monorail and bi-rail are identical.

Monorail entails serious stability and switching problems which place it at a considerable disadvantage in most conventional applications. Furthermore, while sufficient data are not yet available, it seems reason-

[21] Discussion of monorails was not included in a previous section on innovative systems since they have been operated continuously for well over fifty years, and thus are hardly new.

[22] See, for example, D. S. Berry, *et al., The Technology of Urban Transportation* (Northwestern University Press, Evanston, Ill.,) pp. 81–88, and A. R. Cripe, "National Urban Transportation Study" (an unpublished report to the Institute of Public Administration).

able to expect that the operating and maintenance costs of a monorail system would be as high as or higher than those for a comparable quality of 2-rail systems. In short, monorail bestows no apparent special advantages and suffers a number of disadvantages.

As for rail transit in general, there is a common belief that rail operations are technologically easy to automate and therefore offer substantial reductions in labor costs. It should be evident from Figure 56, however, that a reduction in motormen and guard costs would have relatively little effect on total rail costs; more important savings from automation seem possible through schemes for reducing train headway, shortlining trains, reducing turnaround time, and the like. At the same time, any economies reaped through automation must be balanced against the additional capital outlays and maintenance and operating expenses directly associated with automation equipment.[23]

Automated control and guidance, though, would enable trains to run at closer headways (with at least comparable safety), thus permitting an increase in track capacity as well as elimination of motormen and guards.[24] Ignoring the institutional and psychological constraints, automation probably would produce over-all economies, especially if capacity is reasonably fully utilized;[25] however, capacity increases often do not loom important in the short or long run since only rarely (as in New York, Toronto, and Chicago) does passenger demand even approach present-day track capacity with manual control. Better equipment utilization and therefore capital cost savings on rolling stock also might be brought about by automation.

Considerably greater benefits for rail systems might be achieved more simply through continuous operation of more express-type trains. A system of this type was proposed recently[26] and seems to offer considerable promise for improving transit service, possibly reducing costs, and allevi-

[23] The development of electronic control and guidance mechanisms also is about as technologically feasible for private automobiles and buses as for rail. For all modes, in fact, automation may be mainly a matter of time. It is no longer doubted that transit vehicles, or even private automobiles, can be automated with reasonable safety, but problems remain with institutional constraints and with some technical matters. Obviously, though, one social question—that of substituting automation equipment for labor—is nonexistent for automated passenger car systems, but troublesome for transit systems.

[24] Any speed effects would be negligible since the controlling factors are permissible acceleration and deceleration rates (from the standpoint of passenger comfort and safety), station spacing, station stop length, and vehicle power.

[25] Other operating economies would be possible if trains were scheduled so that power requirements of trains were offset, thus reducing peak loads. For a more detailed discussion, see A. S. Lang and R. M. Soberman, *Urban Rail Transit,* MIT Press, Cambridge, Mass., 1964, pp. 56*ff*.

[26] L. Fogel, "Personal Express: A New Concept for Intra-Urban Transportation," report on behalf of General Dynamics, dated January 23, 1963.

ating rush hour congestion, particularly for metropolitan communities with existing rail transit systems of some magnitude. The layout and method of operation of this system can be described by referring to Figure 59.[27] A continuous-operation through track is provided with sidings at each station. The main body of the train (or trains, if more than one trip length or higher frequency is to be provided) operates at essentially constant speed on the through track without stopping at the station. As the train passes by a station, such as point A in Figure 59, the rear car is decoupled and is automatically decelerated so that it comes to rest at the station platform. In the meantime, the car that was loaded in the station (and was dropped off by the previous train) is automatically accelerated on the siding and may be automatically coupled to the head of the through train. Thus, each passenger can board at any station and be transported to any other desired station without loss of time as a result

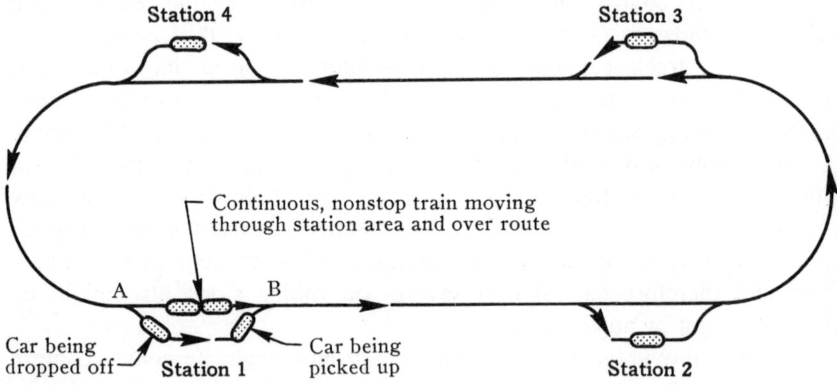

Figure 59. Layout and method of operation for a continuous-operation express rail system. (For layout shown, the passenger-trip length will depend on the train length as follows: with two cars [at station], trip length is three stations; with one car [at station], trip length is two stations; with one car [at station], trip length is one station.)

of stopping and starting at intermediate stations. For particular track layouts it might be necessary to use separate trains which serve alternate stations or, say, every third station. For the case shown in Figure 59 the train length (of two cars) is such that each car will travel to the third station ahead before stopping again.

Of course, passengers need not be limited to a trip distance of one, two, or three stations' lengths as shown in the figure. Other possibilities or combinations exist. One possibility would be, for the example shown, to

[27] It can be seen that continuous system operation can be applied to multiple-trackage layouts which have been used for years with only slight modification and the introduction of new control equipments.

run two or more continuous trains on the same track. One train might have two cars as shown, and the other just one. Passengers could then select between the two trains serving their station according to their trip length. A second possibility, which could be used in conjunction with the first, would be to allow the passengers to walk through the cars until they reached the car destined for their intended stop. Having continuous movement on the track system allows much higher train density of transportation, thus making it easier to ensure that all passengers may be seated if they so desire. Walking between cars while in transit would then be unobstructed. The extent of benefit which such a system would provide is dependent upon a number of factors, including the volume of traffic, the nature of customer preference, walking speed, track layout, speed of the continuously moving train, distance between stations, number of stations, train length, safety requirements, and so forth.

Such continuous-operation systems probably have their greatest utility as downtown distribution systems, where the track capability and volume level are most critical. Such operation would greatly decrease individual travel time, increase the utilization rate of the capital equipment, and decrease the expenditure required for system operation. At the same time there are some diseconomies in terms of siding rquirements, possible additional cars, and the necessary control equipment.[28]

Some Miscellaneous Possibilities

A number of suggested or potential technological innovations for urban transport are not specifically related to any one mode. Some have received so much popular attention that they warrant some consideration for this fact alone; others have not, but nevertheless have some importance and potential.

Hydrofoils and ground effect machines (GEM's) have been widely popularized, but their large-scale development for urban transport seems highly unlikely. GEM's basically differ from present automobiles and buses in that wheels are replaced by "air cushions," and the vehicles allegedly can operate over any smooth surface, or rail, or even water. Their higher speed capabilities would be offset, however, by difficulties of acceleration and deceleration, not to mention the usual right-of-way problems confronting land transport vehicles.

Hydrofoils are specialized in much the same way, but offer some potential in specific situations. The hydrofoil differs from the usual boat in that it is supported not only by buoyancy but also by hydrodynamic

[28] Many of the required modifications already exist in certain urban transportation systems; further, the control equipment appears to be well within the present state of the art.

forces, in much the same fashion as an airplane is by aerodynamic forces; these forces permit the hull to clear the water and total friction resistance is thereby reduced, since friction is considerably less from air than from water. Hydrofoils can thus move substantially faster than surface ships—at speeds from 40 to 100 knots. This speed capability has been exploited for some years off the coast of Italy, and seems to have promise for short-distance, medium-density, interisland or offshore runs in such places as New York City, San Francisco, Miami, the Hawaiian Islands, and Seattle.[29] While high waves, fog, and floating debris can be problems for the hydrofoil, it should also have considerable intrinsic appeal in areas where overland trips are either circuitous or impossible.

GEM's do not appear competitive with hydrofoils for interisland and offshore passenger transport, particularly for shorter runs, where hydrofoils have the speed advantage. Since GEM's would be amphibious, however, they could eliminate transfers at shorelines. In any case, GEM research and development is somewhat behind that of hydrofoils, so that a reliable comparison of performance and cost is not now possible.[30]

Certain important marginal improvements in existing urban transport systems can be expected to emerge from time to time, depending on income levels, consumer preference patterns, and institutional constraints.[31] Two examples might be the introduction of automatic fare collection and billing procedures for transit systems, and fully air-conditioned automobiles, transit vehicles, and stations. Automatic fare collection seems to present no serious technical problems, though it is evident that the labor displacement question presents a considerable barrier to implementation. As for air conditioning, there is little doubt about its eventual widespread implementation. Air-conditioning costs for transit vehicles generally run somewhere around five cents a passenger-trip (with full seated loads) and in time may be justifiable to most consumers, at least in those places with hot and humid summers. These costs would rise sharply if there were many standees and exceptionally heavy loads. Air conditioning for private automobiles, with a cost of around fifteen cents a trip even if the

[29] D. G. Haney and S. R. Smith, "The Economic Feasibility of Passenger Hydrofoil in U.S. Domestic and Foreign Commerce," prepared for Maritime Administration, U.S. Department of Commerce, August 1961.

[30] Philip Mandel, "A Comparative Evaluation of Novel Ship Types," presented to the Society of Naval Architects and Marine Engineers, June 1962, and R. Hammer, "The New Lift for Transport: Earth Skimmers," *Fortune,* December 1962, pp. 122*ff*.

[31] Some changes in consumer preference patterns could bring about some significant shifts in the market. For example, if people suddenly or gradually decided that rush hour driving is unendurable, then in the absence of highway improvement (either the addition of capacity or automation of highway travel) they might shift over to public transit.

automobile is used exclusively for work-trip commuting, does not seem out of the question over the next generation, particularly in the face of expected real income increases.[32]

Technology may also affect urban transportation in other general ways.[33] For one thing, it is reasonable to expect advancements and improvements in construction techniques over the years, many of which will doubtless alter comparative cost patterns. Construction techniques for transport facilities, being labor intensive, have become increasingly costly and have always required a great deal of time, particularly for tunnels and elevated structures in downtown or other heavily built-up areas. Potential for improvement rests with better boring equipment, improved equipment for earth and rock excavation, and the use of precast and prefabricated slabs and other structural items.[34] If these or other improvements materialize, reductions in construction cost and time may be expected; these in turn *may* change such things as the relative attractiveness of tunneling within high-density areas, and thus the layout, nature, and extent of transport systems.

Special importance attaches to some of these developments in construction techniques, particularly in tunneling equipment, because at the moment there is no available transportation technology that seems to be inherently very efficient in serving the secondary distribution needs of CBD's as they are now constructed. Almost all the suggested systems for handling downtown distribution and collection, such as a proposed "backbone" rail subway system in Los Angeles and elevated bus highways in St. Louis, are inherently very costly, simply because existing urban transportation technologies are not very well adapted to the present designs or plans of most cities. This fact suggests a further innovation (but one beyond the scope of this book) often advanced by city planners and architects: that perhaps the most sensible procedure economically is to adapt cities and CBD's to transportation technology. Indeed, such adaptation may be the only satisfactory solution, especially when aesthetic as well as economic criteria are taken into account. To a large degree this type of adaptation has been happening in the United States in recent years, although somewhat haphazardly. The rise of the suburban shopping center is certainly a most important example. Similarly, the Gruen Plan for redesigning Fort Worth's downtown area represents a very ambitious

[32] The percentage of new automobiles with air-conditioning equipment has increased gradually from 3 per cent in 1955–1956 to 10 per cent in 1961–1962; for the 1963 model year, the figure was 13.7 per cent (Automobile Manufacturers Association, *Automobile Facts and Figures,* 1963 ed., p. 14, and 1964 ed., p. 14).

[33] Herein it is vital to view technology as including both "hardware" and "software."

[34] George A. Hoffman, *Urban Underground Highways and Parking Facilities,* The RAND Corporation, RM-3680-RC, August 1963.

scheme of this type. The development and proposal of multilevel streets and sidewalks in limited areas of Chicago's downtown make up yet another example. Finally, the Buchanan Report on handling the traffic problems of British cities also emphasizes such adaptations and provides some very imaginative suggestions on how to implement such changes.[35]

One thing is immediately clear: It is likely to be very costly to make existing CBD's more suitable for modern transportation and material-handling technologies, perhaps as costly as building more downtown rail and highway systems or continuing the present strategy of adapting cities to the available technology through decentralization. Also, the challenges of reorganizing CBD's in this way may be as much legal and institutional (to achieve "appropriate" urban land use) as technological. For example, imaginative innovations in legal contracts, leases, and cooperative associations might greatly simplify or reduce the economic and technological requirements for making the needed adaptations. Certainly it is worth stressing, as city planners often point out, that these adaptations call for a great deal more than flowerbeds and random patches of grass, or pedestrian malls created out of context and without relation to other downtown needs.

Predictive capabilities for planning and designing transport systems should also improve greatly in the future. While planning and design do not directly represent a large portion of system costs (they generally run from 5 to 10 per cent of the total capital costs), they importantly influence both the capital and operating costs of the facilities over their entire life, and affect the costs and service to travelers as well. Considerable effort has already been expended on developing techniques for predicting consequences—economic and social costs, performance, and demand—of alternative system designs and operations, (as in the Chicago and Penn-Jersey studies[36]), and for "searching" for reasonable design alternatives and translating them into actual plans (as in recent studies conducted at MIT[37]). Economies and other benefits are certain to result as work continues in these important study areas, but how extensive they will be it is impossible to say.

[35] Great Britain, Ministry of Transport, *Traffic in Towns: A Study of the Long Term Problems of Traffic in Urban Areas,* Reports of the Steering Group and Working Group Appointed by the Minister of Transport, Her Majesty's Stationery Office, London, 1963. Highly interesting commentaries on this report are M. E. Beesley and J. F. Kain, "Urban Form, Car Ownership, and Public Policy: An Appraisal of *Traffic in Towns*," *Urban Studies*, November 1964; J. F. Kain and M. E. Beesley, "Forecasting Car Ownership and Use," *Urban Studies*, November 1965; and a review by Peter Self in *The London Economist*, April 10, 1964.

[36] See, for example, *Chicago Area Transportation Study, Final Report,* 1959–1962.

[37] See, for example, P. O. Roberts and A. Villaveces, "DTM Design System," Research Report R62–6, MIT, Department of Civil Engineering, December 1961, and C. Alexander and M. L. Manheim, "The Design of Highway Interchanges: An Example of a General Method for Analyzing Engineering Design Problems," Research Report R62–1, MIT, Department of Civil Engineering, March 1962.

SUMMARY

Imaginative use of new technologies and facilities might bring about substantial economies in urban transportation. One immediate possibility is to use major highways to meet effectively both peak-hour commuter needs and off-peak demands for social, recreational, and shopping trips. If price rationing of peak-hour capacity is ruled out as infeasible, politically or otherwise, technological solutions can be tried. Some of the more promising and immediate are reserved lanes for buses and small cars, special bus highways, input flow control for expressways, and priority access for public transit vehicles moving onto controlled-access highways.

It is possible, of course, that drastic and expensive policies may become necessary if these relatively simple technological solutions prove insufficient. If it is undesirable to abandon older CBD's, the promising alternatives appear to be guidance systems for private automobiles and drastic redesign and rebuilding of downtown areas. Since knowledge of both alternatives is still rudimentary, a good deal of preliminary research would be necessary; and since large innovative efforts of this kind are likely to be expensive and risky, there are compelling incentives for proceeding sequentially, trying the cheapest and simplest procedures first.

For various reasons, this chapter has emphasized the possibilities of improving the line-haul capabilities of efficient secondary distribution vehicles—automobiles and buses. Because it is impossible to anticipate all promising technological configurations, however, the possibility of improving the efficiency of rail line-haul vehicles for secondary distribution in low-density residential areas should not be summarily dismissed. In this regard, it has often been proposed that rail vehicles be equipped with rubber tires and steering mechanisms so they can run on both highways and rails.

Even more radical vehicles have been proposed, the most notable being ground effect machines and hydrofoils. Useful as these devices may be in some areas, however, the available cost and demand evidence makes them appear less promising, and certainly of less general applicability, than marginal improvements in automobile, bus and rail operations.

It is noteworthy that the more immediately promising innovations usually share a common trait: each combines the best features of two or more modes into one transportation system. There is nothing very new about this concept in transportation; it underlies, for example, most of the current thinking and experimentation with piggybacking and containerization in intercity freight shipping.

Chapter 13 | Pricing, Subsidies, Market Structure, and Regulatory Institutions

Discussions of urban transportation policy almost invariably branch off into the complications of pricing, economic efficiency, and social welfare. These problems can be conveniently arranged under the headings of pricing principles, the possibility and justification of subsidy, and market structure and regulatory institutions. An almost inherent characteristic of these problems, when they touch on urban transportation policy, is the extent to which their resolution hinges on empirical evidence or value judgments. A few of the more important of these empirical questions have been partially answered in preceding chapters. This chapter reevaluates some of these findings in the context of an analytical discussion, not so much to arrive at final conclusions as to clarify and define the relevant issues.

Pricing Principles

The economist usually starts with one basic precept concerning prices: let everyone consume any good or service whose incremental cost of producing he is willing to pay. This "incremental cost pricing principle," however, is almost immediately modified in actual practice by consideration of another and often apparently conflicting principle: to the greatest extent possible, the total costs of producing a specific good or service should be paid by those actually consuming it. Still another important and occasionally complicating dictum is that only one price usually should be charged for any single homogeneous commodity; markets for such a commodity are cleared by the price that equates demand and supply, and this price provides a simple, unmistakable indicator for evaluating investments in such activities.

Despite difficulties, the incremental rule almost always receives primary emphasis in the search for optimal pricing policies. In the somewhat idealized world of economic theory (e.g., perfect competition, a specified income distribution,[1] and no scale economies[2]) charging each consumer according to the incremental resource cost of providing the services he consumes should lead to an optimal use of resources.

The real world, of course, does not always reflect the idealized conditions of economic theory. For one thing, market imperfections do exist in the real economy—and much can be made of this fact by those who wish to criticize or reject the implications of the incremental cost pricing principle and its related economic theory. The most sophisticated of the market imperfection arguments against marginal cost pricing is that of the so-called general theory of second best.[3]

The central point of this theory is that with market imperfections a rationalization of prices in one sector of the economy might lead to an over-all deterioration rather than improvement in resource allocation and efficiency. Specifically, limited rationalization might induce the public to overconsume goods produced in the rationalized sector. A classic illustration of this principle is to be found in the relationships between international customs unions or common markets and other trading partners left out of the union. For example, the English have insisted that the European Common Market's laudable improvement of resource allocation among its members must be weighed against the fact that the same process of rationalization may lead these countries *as a group* to buy less from outside producers who might still be their cheapest sources of supply (at least in terms of comparative advantage). That is, by reducing the market imperfection represented by tariffs only for member countries, a common market induces people in the member countries to buy too much from each other and too little from the outside. In the context of urban transportation, the analogous argument would be that a rationalization of urban transportation markets in a world of market imperfections (created, say, through "monopolistic markups" or special excise taxes existing elsewhere) could lead to excessive consumption of urban transportation services at the expense of other consumer goods.

The importance and validity of the "second best" argument for urban transportation depends largely on the extent to which the rest of the econ-

[1] Since economic theory abstracts from value judgments on the optimality of existing income distributions, the question of whether an income distribution should or could be improved by modifications in the pricing structure is avoided.

[2] Scale economies are the savings possible when, at a given point in time and space, larger amounts of a commodity can be produced at a unit cost lower than smaller amounts can.

[3] R. K. Lancaster and R. G. Lipsey, "The General Theory of Second Best," *Review of Economic Studies,* 24:11–32 (December 1956); Paul A. David and Albert Fishlow, "Optimal Resource Allocation in an Imperfect Market Setting," *Journal of Political Economy,* 69:529–546 (December 1961); M. McManus, "Comments on the General Theory of Second Best," *Review of Economic Studies,* 26:209–223 (June 1959).

omy approximates the competitive norm, and the cross-elasticities of demand between urban transportation and other sectors in the economy —specifically, to what extent expenditures on urban transportation are close alternatives or complements for those on other goods or services. On the whole, it seems improbable that expenditures on urban transportation are closely competitive with other expenditures, although the available evidence is more heuristic than definitive. The main direct competitive impact from rationalization of urban transportation pricing would probably be a reallocation of activity among different modes, which seemingly are highly interdependent in their demand patterns and are at least to some degree substitutes for one another.

When we shift attention from competitive to complementary goods, however, a major qualification to this argument is needed. As noted in chapters 6 and 7, the demand for urban transportation apparently is complementary to the demand for suburban residential land. Thus, if urban transportation markets are rationalized, and in the process the average price of urban transportation goes sharply up or down, it would be reasonable to expect sharp drops or rises in the demand for suburban residences. Of course, an increase or decrease in the consumption of this land would in turn involve at least a short-run increase or decrease in the consumption of urban transportation resources as well.

Even taking into account the complementarity between suburban residential land and urban transportation, it might be easy to exaggerate the possible extent of any resource misallocation induced by rationalization of urban transportation market prices. First of all, it is not at all clear that other sectors of the American economy, when closely scrutinized, depart markedly from competitive pricing conditions. While important pockets of "administered" oligopolistic or monopolistic price positions may exist, there is considerable evidence that such positions are extremely difficult to sustain in the long run, being continually challenged by new technologies and shifts in consumer preferences. Furthermore, even within areas of so-called administered prices, there is often a very strong tendency for competition in quality or service to supplant the inhibited competition in price, the result being that costs rise toward the administered price level. The net result is usually a much closer approximation of prices to costs than initially was intended by those attempting to control the market relationships. As a secondary consequence, some reduction in the range of consumer choice also may occur; a not uncommon result is that consumers are more or less required to consume a higher quality of a product than they really desire. However, even these enforced quality markups are usually difficult to sustain if consumers are really insistent, the recent revival of smaller American-made cars being a suggestive case in point.

Another important factor qualifying the empirical importance of the "second best" argument in urban transportation is the considerable evidence that, within relevant historical ranges, the consumption of urban transportation services and residential land has been much more sensitive to income changes than to price changes; that is, these commodities appear to be more income elastic than price elastic in their demand characteristics. It must be emphasized, however, that this conclusion is based on analyses of historical data in which the price fluctuations, especially in urban transportation services, have not been extensive.

Taking all these arguments together, it seems likely, though far from certain, that the adverse effects attributable to second-best influences can easily be exaggerated. The corollary is that a move toward a more rational pricing structure in urban transportation, as embodied in wider adoption of incremental cost pricing principles, would probably improve the general economic welfare.[4]

The problems of implementing this principle in a service industry like transportation should not be underestimated, however. Since it is usually difficult or impossible to carry an inventory of outputs for a service, fluctuations in demand must be met mainly by directly varying output. Thus, if it becomes necessary to provide sufficient capacity to meet the peak demand or load, under the incremental cost pricing principle the capacity costs associated with peak loads should be charged to peak-period users.

In urban transportation, peak demands normally occur during the morning and evening rush hours—at least if peak demand is measured exclusively in numbers of people and vehicles demanding transport space. As noted in chapter 4, however, transport capacity is usually a function of several dimensions, including the speed with which people or vehicles are carried. Accordingly, the differences between peak- and off-peak-hour demands on transport capacity in urban areas can be easily magnified by looking at flow figures alone because performance speed is usually higher in non-rush-hour periods. This phenomenon is particularly observable on limited-access radial express highways, which are often designed to carry about 1500 to 1600 cars an hour per lane at an average speed of 40 to 50 mph (when they do not have ramp entry controls). During rush hours, the volume per lane may range from 1600 to 1800 vehicles an hour (and in a few isolated instances, over 2000),

[4] A broader defense of the principle of economic rationality as a guide to public policymaking can be found in J. V. Krutilla, "Welfare Aspects of Benefit-Cost Analysis," *Journal of Political Economy,* 69:226–235 (June 1961); O. Eckstein, *Water Resource Development: The Economics of Project Evaluation* (Harvard University Press, Cambridge, Mass., 1958); and Roland N. McKean, *Efficiency in Government through Systems Analysis: With Emphasis on Water Resource Development* (John Wiley & Sons, New York, 1958).

but speed will drop to an average of 30 to 35 mph or below. During midday off-peak hours, by contrast, the traffic flow will usually be well below design capacity but performance speed may average 45 or 50 mph or more; the net result in terms of capacity-performance utilization is thus much closer than is often realized. In short, while the incremental principle clearly indicates that any extra capital or capacity costs should be charged to peak-period users, it does not resolve the difficult question of how to measure the exact extent of the peak period and certainly does not preclude the possibility that off-peak users should be charged for some costs of the extra capacity that enables them to enjoy a superior service.

This tradeoff between performance characteristics and capacity as measured by total flow creates another difficulty in applying incremental cost pricing principles to highways. The incremental costs of highway use are usually described as comprising two components: a physical resource component, pertaining to the actual cost of constructing and maintaining the facility under use, and a congestion or service component associated with the costs created when additional users employ the same facility. Normally there is an important interrelationship or tradeoff between these two types of cost; congestion costs can usually be reduced by spending more money for additional facilities.[5] Thus, to reduce congestion under the incremental principle, highway investments should be increased until the incremental cost of creating additional capacity (appropriately discounted) is equal to the incremental reduction in congestion costs. However, because the long-run equilibrium implied by this rather thorough adjustment of investment outlays to requirements is rarely achieved today, short-run congestion costs can be a relevant consideration in many immediate highway pricing problems.

It should be stressed, however, that a persistence of congestion costs does not economically justify the permanent application of short-run pricing solutions to the highway rationing problem. As long as there are no important scale economies, it can easily be shown that under conditions of so-called perfect competition in the economy at large an optimum highway user charge or toll scheme would in the long run impose tolls just sufficient to cover the incremental costs of providing the facilities used by each consumer, as measured in terms of the actual resources employed. If there are increasing returns in the provision of additional facilities, as seems likely in many cases, then the argument for perpetuat-

[5] A more complete discussion of these matters can be found in H. Mohring, "Relation between Optimum Congestion Tolls and Present Highway User Charges," *Traffic Congestion as a Factor in Road Users Taxation,* Highway Research Record no. 47, Washington, D.C., 1964.

ing underinvestment through high congestion cost tolls is even further weakened.

Finally, even if urban transportation is operated in an environment of decreasing returns to scale, the case for congestion cost tolls still may be less than fully compelling. For example, under deceasing returns a marginal cost pricing scheme should lead to revenues in excess of total cost. Unless physical or other reasons exist that prevent expansion, that is, for some reason or another a monopoly exists in the provision of the service, the normal economic reaction would be an expansion of supply until the monopolistic returns were eliminated. If continued exploitation of the monopoly position were undertaken instead, an income transfer usually would occur. The question therefore arises of whether this income transfer is considered to be in the best interests of society, as defined, say, by the political process. In this connection, it might be observed that it is usually presumed that public enterprises will not attempt to exploit a monopoly position in the long run without a very well-defined social or other reason for doing so.

In essence, to adhere to marginal cost pricing in circumstances where marginal costs exceed average costs because of congestion amounts to imposing user charges on the basis of some elusive social cost concept rather than the cost of the physical resources consumed or used. Specifically, price discrimination based upon social or congestion cost concepts is quite different from price discrimination based upon differential resource costs created, say, by use of the facility during a peak period when extra and expensive capacity is needed to meet additional demands. Differential peak period charges to cover these additional capacity costs have a much sounder basis in economic theory and perhaps also in common equity as well.[6]

Higher charges for peak-hour uses also could provide useful information for evaluating investments in urban highways. As suggested at several points in the preceding analysis, much of the increased capacity recently made available has mainly allowed more people to move in and out of the congested part of the city simultaneously. A very interesting question is whether this "simultaneity" is worth the cost of the extra capacity. That is, do people really want to pay this price simply for the privilege of moving in and out of the city all at once? At a minimum,

[6] For an excellent summary discussion of these questions see Richard M. Zettel and Richard R. Carll, "The Basic Theory of Efficiency Tolls: The Tolled, the Tolled-off, and the Untolled," *Traffic Congestion as a Factor in Road Users Taxation,* Highway Research Record no. 47, Washington, D.C., 1964. Another good review of the same problems, stated more from the standpoint of the engineer than of an economist, is contained in the same volume: G. P. St. Clair, "Congestion Tolls—An Engineer's Viewpoint."

data on changes in peak-period demand that occur because of the introduction of new facilities would permit more rational inferences about what such installations really achieve.[7]

Technological infeasibility is another often-cited obstacle to a rationalization of highway tolls. As noted in chapter 12, however, this problem may have been exaggerated. The real obstacle to better pricing of urban highways would appear to be public opposition. For reasons left to political pundits to define and explain, the American public seems to feel that highways should be "free"—that is, have "tolls" extracted in the form of fuel and other excise taxes. A large number of practicing politicians are fully convinced that it would be political suicide to support direct tolls on urban expressways, and it is hard to dispute their first-hand knowledge of these matters. One sensible explanation of their views might be that under existing circumstances—that is, without tolls—the rush hour use of urban highway facilities is essentially rationed by congestion. If it is argued that lower-income groups have much more leisure time at their disposal and therefore value it less than higher-income groups, it follows that the use of congestion to ration highway facilities may amount to a more progressive scheme of taxation than the use of monetary tolls. It also seems probable that higher-income groups are more likely than lower-income groups to follow professions in which they have some discretionary control over the exact hours they work; accordingly, higher-income groups should be more able to devise ways of escaping highway congestion costs. In short, the present scheme of rationing urban highway facilities by congestion may promote a more progressive taxation scheme than would direct price rationing and places the major incidence of congestion costs on those groups most able to take corrective action.

It is not clear whether the same argument would apply with equal force to the pricing of public transit facilities. Where a large cross section of the public actually uses the transit facilities, the highway and transit cases seem reasonably similar. On the other hand, commuter facilities

[7] One aspect of urban transportation pricing might appear susceptible to useful reform, however, even without detailed knowledge of demand patterns: parking fees, at least for all-day or peak period parkers. It is incongruous, to say the least, to charge only five or ten cents an hour for metered curbside parking, specifically during rush hours or when street capacity is otherwise fully utilized or needed, and twenty to fifty cents, or even more, an hour for offstreet facilities. Under the circumstances, including the usual scarcity of downtown street parking, the rate discrepancy implies public encouragement of curbside parking. The only defense offered is that it acts as an inducement to shoppers; but the scarce information available suggests that shoppers seldom get to park on the street, and what little access they do have depends on rigorous enforcement of peak-hour parking bans and maximum time limits. By eliminating what often amounts to an implicitly subsidized form of competition, higher prices for curbside parking might also encourage private parking enterprises to provide new capacity.

largely patronized by high-income groups are likely candidates for a revision of transit charges, by which higher tariffs would be charged to peak-hour users and lower ones to off-peak users. In fact, wherever the existing single tariff structure results in charges for off-peak users exceeding the marginal costs of providing such services, an argument might be made for at least cutting the fees to off-peak users. This would be particularly true if it could be established that the elasticity of demand for off-peak uses was such that net revenue would be greater after a fare reduction.

Subsidies in Urban Transportation

The subsidy question in urban transportation centers mainly on the propriety of using government money to bolster or sustain public transit facilities. Proponents of subsidy generally champion it as a means of effecting "desirable" income redistributions, inducing desirable economies or efficiencies in urban transportation, countervailing other and reputedly undesirable subsidies, creating superior aesthetic values, or providing a 1-shot stimulant needed to place public transit on a sound economic or financial footing.

From a purely economic standpoint, the most solidly justifiable argument for subsidies is that urban transportation is characterized by increasing returns as scale increases, and that only by subsidization can the consuming public fully reap the benefits of these increasing returns. The empirical validity of increasing returns seems undeniable on the basis of the cost analyses presented in previous chapters, particularly for the public transit modes. With scale economies, the cost of providing a unit of service declines as the volume or density of services consumed increases, and the result is that revenues will not cover total costs if incremental cost pricing is adopted. Under such circumstances the average cost per unit will always be greater than the incremental cost. In short, under increasing returns to scale (or declining marginal costs) the incremental pricing principle conflicts with the proposition that a facility should be created and operated only if those employing the facility pay the total costs.

When increasing returns exist there are three major alternatives, each with certain undesirable aspects. First, there could be a complete or partial abandonment of the incremental cost pricing principle in favor of average costs as the basis for establishing a market price. The most acceptable form of "average cost pricing" would probably be one that placed the major burden of the additional charges on those who used the facilities during "heavy-use" periods, and who therefore might be considered the most legitimate subjects for extra charges on the basis of cost considerations.[8] This alternative, however, would mean that some people would be unable to consume a commodity even though willing and able to pay the additional incremental costs of producing it. In essence, an average cost pricing solution implies that the principle of equality between total cost and total revenue takes precedence over the incremental cost principle.

A second alternative would be to abandon the principle of equality between total cost and total revenue in favor of the incremental cost pricing principle, using subsidies to make up the revenue loss impelled by the incremental cost price. Assuming that the subsidy would come from general governmental tax revenues, or similar broadly based tax sources, the objection to this approach is that it tends to provide a service to certain consumers without their having to pay the full costs of producing it. Such a procedure in most cases would create an income transfer between the general taxpaying public and the users of the service—in this case, subsidized public transport. Whether or not such a transfer is desirable depends in large measure on individual preferences and attitudes, which are mainly subjects for political evaluation and do not lend themselves to objective treatment by conventional economic theory. The same, incidentally, applies to most secondary or nonuser benefits imputed to transport improvements (for example, increases in value of adjacent land) which, on close inspection, usually reduce to transfers from one group in society to another.

The third solution to the increasing-returns quandary is a compromise between the previous two solutions; the form it usually takes is price discrimination—in essence, charging different consumers different prices for the same service according, roughly, to the degree of satisfaction they derive from it.[9] By charging different prices, it is often possible to extract enough revenue from users to pay total costs, while still making the lowest of the prices charged equal to incremental cost, thus preserving many of the advantages of incremental cost pricing. While this procedure does not suffer from exactly the same objections as the subsidy procedure just discussed, it still involves an implicit income transfer un-

[8] Such a compromise between long-run marginal cost pricing and average cost pricing is to be found in the practices of Electricite de France. Descriptions of these procedures can be found in M. Boiteux, "Peak-Load Pricing," *The Journal of Business of the University of Chicago,* 33:157–179 (April 1960); T. Marschak, "Capital Budgeting and Pricing in the French Nationalized Industries," *The Journal of Business of the University of Chicago,* 33:133–156 (April 1960); and J. R. Nelson, "Practical Applications of Marginal Cost Pricing in the Public Utility Field," *American Economic Review,* 53:474–481 (March 1963).

[9] This type of price discrimination—charging different prices for exactly the same service—should not be confused with differential pricing of on- and off-peak use of highways or railways where the service and costs are differentiated (by the time dimension).

der most circumstances. Again the question arises of whether this transfer is socially to be preferred—and again, the answer is a matter for political settlement. Indeed, it should be emphasized that value judgments conventionally enter into all three solutions, and that in the final analysis choosing a solution is really a matter of subjective preferences. It should be noted, at least in passing, that price discrimination also encounters administrative problems.

The increasing-returns-to-scale quandary will be particularly acute if there are sharp differences in the time horizons required for making different cost adjustments in the production of the service under analysis. That is, if many costs are essentially fixed in the short run, there probably will be increasing returns to scale over the relevant range of operation, and an accompanying divergence between the short-run marginal cost pricing solution and adherence to the principle of total cost being equal to total revenue. Accordingly, the importance of the returns-to-scale quandary is likely to depend on the length of the time horizon adopted for the analysis. The longer it is, the more likely will marginal and average costs tend to equality, thus minimizing the practical relevance of the problem. Technological change in the long run however, can, complicate the issue by placing the incremental costs of additional capacity in the future below historical levels. In the same connection, another important consideration is how long the demand for the particular service is expected to continue beyond the life of the capital investment used in producing the service. Specifically, if demand is not expected greatly to outlive the capital facilities, there is a stronger case for adhering to incremental cost pricing since capital renewal is not a relevant problem.

This at least suggests that incremental cost pricing might be in order wherever excess rail transit capacity is in being and no renewal of that capacity is contemplated when its economic life is exhausted. Indeed, if demand elasticities are substantial, self-interest might induce such an outcome in cases of private ownership. Without such favorable demand conditions, a subsidy to induce incremental cost pricing might seem warranted.

Such arguments, though, overlook a number of important considerations and are at least partial oversimplifications. Above all, subsidizing lower prices on rail facilities may induce other, nontransportation investments, and these in turn may create strongly vested interests with a desire, perhaps justified in equity, to perpetuate the lower fees even after the rail assets have been exhausted. The high degree of complementarity between urban transportation costs and urban residential choices fortifies this counterargument. In short, it is entirely possible that subsidizing commutation could (or even already has!) induce people to adopt a suburban life which might not otherwise be economically justified or possible. These people, when later confronted with higher charges —and after having put their residential investments in place—might feel quite unfairly treated.

A second argument for subsidy (often closely related to and confused with the increasing-returns problem) is that some needed service can be instituted only by employing subsidies or price discrimination. This circumstance can arise when the entire demand curve for a service lies below its supply or cost curve. Vickrey cites a case in point to sum up such situations:

> If a bus, for example, can be run to a given area for seven dollars a trip, and if there are ten passengers willing to pay thirty cents a trip, and ten more passengers willing to pay fifty cents a trip, then providing the service to all twenty passengers would be worth eight dollars, and thus the service would be well justified; but if there is no means of discriminating between the two groups of passengers at the leveling of charges then there is no fare that will make the service pay its own way. In this case the alternatives are worthwhile subsidized service, or no service at all.[10]

Several difficulties beset this contention. The first is simply that abandonment of the single price principle jeopardizes much of the justification for incremental cost pricing created by economic analysis. Nor is this a trivial matter: one major effect would be a drastic alteration in the income and other assumptions employed in defining the conventional demand curve which economists use in so-called partial equilibrium analyses. To put the matter in fairly simple terms: if price discrimination were allowed for all commodities now being produced, almost all might "justify" an expansion in their output and sales. If all attempted such expansion simultaneously, however, it is probable they would immediately violate certain constraints pertaining to the availability of both consumer income and productive resources. At any rate, explicit in the definition of most demand curve or output-to-price relationships used to specify circumstances like those in Vickrey's example is the assumption that a certain amount of real income is available at each point on the demand curve. Furthermore, this available income is usually defined in terms of a single price for the commodity under analysis; that is, the price at the point being defined is relevant only if no sales have been made at any of the prices higher up on the demand relationship. Even more importantly from a quantitative standpoint, the definition of available income also depends on similar single price policies having been adhered to in defining other demand relationships within the economy. In general, abandonment of the single price principle used for defining the conventional demand curve would precipitate a downward shift in demand relationships for most commodities and services in the economy. Thus,

[10] William Vickrey, "Transit Finance: A Review," paper delivered before the National Tax Association, Philadelphia, Pa., October 30, 1958.

it would be entirely possible that if the privilege of price discrimination were uniformly extended to all, services and products theretofore unjustifiable without price discrimination would still be unjustifiable after the revision.

The question is, then, whether a selective abandonment of the single price principle can be justified. While it is clear that price discrimination has often made goods or services available which would not have been otherwise, such cases are usually not officially sanctioned by government; in fact, there are laws against extreme versions of such practices. The general official feeling, as reflected in legislation, seems to be that price discrimination is justifiable only when there is some underlying cost justification. The only notable exception is the strong governmental sanction of price discrimination in certain educational, artistic, and cultural activities and services provided by nonprofit organizations. Also, some sanction seems to exist for price discrimination on a limited scale in certain professional services such as medicine and law. At any rate, philharmonic orchestras and many art museums, to select obvious examples, are financed by fairly direct price discrimination since some patrons make large voluntary contributions and usually receive only the modest reward of preferential seating or other arrangements. The notable aspect of this price discrimination, however, is that those who make the additional contributions do so voluntarily.

Income redistribution through urban transportation price discrimination and subsidies is also widely advocated and practiced—for example, through discount prices accorded to "especially worthy" groups in society who, it is argued, have very little access to other forms of transportation and, in particular, cannot use private transportation. Such groups include school children, older people, and people with special infirmities. It is noteworthy that a reasonably well-defined political concensus seems to have been established on the desirability of such practices.

Still, there are two useful questions to be raised about these and similar subsidy schemes. First, who is to define "worthy" or "needy"? Second, are there better ways to promote the desired income transfers? The first is generally and appropriately decided by political authorities. With the second, however, the economist can often rightly question whether present practices for effecting income transfers are really efficient and achieve the desired objectives. He may, for example, question "cross-subsidization"; this technique, commonly practiced in transportation, forces some users of an activity to pay a higher markup over the cost of the services they consume in order to provide services to other consumers at a price below costs. Clearly, this practice is merely another version of price discrimination. It might be more equitable, and as a rule yield a somewhat better resource utilization pattern, if the government directly subsidized the agency performing the service, perhaps by direct grant or contract or, better still, directly transferred income.

Another argument used to justify subsidy as a means of bringing an economically justified but market impeded service into being is that of the "one-shot stimulant." One version of this argument is based upon the dual hypotheses that demand for transit service is extremely elastic at low prices and that the costs of providing transit service decline very sharply with increases in output. Under such circumstances historical evidence of low output, high prices, and high unit costs creating insufficient revenues to cover transit cost are said to be irrelevant; rather, the proper policy in such circumstances, it is argued, is to cut prices, expand output, and thereby reduce costs until a point is eventually found at which total revenues exceed total cost. In the economist's jargon, the demand curve lies above the average cost curve only at very large volumes of output and relatively low prices. Of course, if such circumstances existed and were fully perceived by the private owners or public authorities rendering transit services, self-interest should suffice to bring about the needed expansion of output and lower prices. Subsidy thus can be justified only because these facts are not understood; that is, subsidy acts as a catalyst that stimulates operators to discover the facts of their own situation. The subsidy is mainly a guarantee against the risks involved in exploring unknown regions of output and demand.

Obviously, the validity of such an argument depends on certain empirical considerations. On costs, the crucial question is the extent of realizable economies of scale. These appear reasonably substantial for rail transit but not so much for most bus operations, particularly if the bus is organized reasonably efficiently with regard to transfers and schedule frequencies. Subsidized expansion of rail transit therefore *might*—if population density is extremely high—reduce rail transit costs to where they would be "competitive."

Far more doubtful is the presumption of extremely high elasticities of demand for public transit. While less than full information exists on these elasticities,[11] that information which is available suggests that the demand for public transit is not very price elastic; rather, commuter choices seem to be far more sensitive to income levels and service considerations. It apparently will take more than a mere cut in transit rates to induce a considerable shift from automobile commutation to transit use; the specific requirement would seem to be a great improvement in

[11] The program of experimentation with different fares and service offerings sponsored by the Housing and Home Finance Agency should do a great deal to clear up these uncertainties. In fact, this HHFA program has done quite a bit already to improve knowledge of these elasticities and suggests how even small information-gathering subsidy programs can be rewarding.

the quality of transit services and an even greater subsidy of fares than has been commonly practiced for commuter railroads and most rail transit systems.

In recognition of precisely this, some people have championed transit subsidies as a means of improving the quality of public transit and enabling it to compete more effectively with the private automobile. The more optimistic even argue that, once improved, the public transit mode would generate so great a demand for its services that it would be self-sustaining. Obviously, this is a variation of the contention that subsidy can be regarded as a one-shot stimulant that will encourage transit authorities to discover their own self-interest. Such arguments are puzzling, in a way; one wonders why it is that those who have the most intimate knowledge of an operation are supposed to be so unaware of its potentialities. Furthermore, in the particular case of service competition, some skepticism on the part of transit operators about the beneficial effects of improvements may be well founded. It would be very costly to endow public transit with a service of "private auto quality," particularly at low population densities. In fact, if workplaces and residences continue to disperse, it may be difficult to design a transit system that is even cost competitive, let alone service competitive, with the automobile.

Another, more novel version of these latent demand justifications for subsidies is what might be termed the "unexercised option" proposition.[12] This pertains to a reputed inability of the market to reflect that some people may enjoy the anticipation of purchasing urban transit services even if they never actually so purchase. Such individuals, it is argued, would quite rationally be willing to pay something for an option to consume the transit service in the future. In short, subsidy is justified because it extracts contributions from individuals who never use transit but still value its availability.

While a highly intriguing proposal, many of the usual arguments against subsidy apply to the unrealized option proposition. First, as recognized even by an advocate,[13] the real problem in such circumstances may well be designing a proper structure of user charges to capture option values from infrequent users.[14] The practical effect of such a proposal

[12] Burton A. Weisbrod, "Collective-Consumption Services of Individual-Consumption Goods," *The Quarterly Journal of Economics,* 78:471–477 (August 1964).

[13] *Ibid.*, p. 475.

[14] Weisbrod's contention, *ibid.,* that no such structure of user charges has ever been successfully implemented is not entirely relevant. For reasons explained subsequently in this chapter, the structure of user charges for public transit services in most cities in the United States has been more a function of regulatory institutions and political convenience than of economic rationality. However, rather complex schemes for differentiating between different classes of users have been developed and successfully implemented in a few specific cases in this country and abroad, as for example in London where a very highly structured system of zone charges is successfully implemented.

would be to allow transit operators to levy exceptionally high charges on irregular users in, for example, rush hour or other circumstances that occasion particularly heavy use of transit systems.

The fact that these surcharges would not necessarily capture a payment from all the persons who value transit availability is not, moreover, an inevitably fatal flaw. Indeed, if a really strong latent demand for unrealized options of this type existed, it might be expected that these options could be sold in the market. There would be some extra costs associated with administering such a program but there are usually some costs attached to direct government subsidization as well. Furthermore, sale of specific options in this fashion would tend to limit payments to persons who really *do* derive satisfaction from the availability of the option to ride transit, even though they never exercise it. By contrast, subsidization from general tax funds would mean that *every* taxpayer would pay for the availability of such options whether he valued them or not. Even a cursory inspection of basic urban travel patterns would suggest that there are many individuals traveling to workplaces not served or inconveniently served by transit; there are also people entirely removed from the work force who would likely find such options of very little or no value. It is not at all clear, in short, that the public welfare would be better served by using general tax funds to subsidize such options rather than organizing a market in which to sell them.

Also, it must be recognized[15] that all commodities might have a latent demand that could be effectuated through sale of such options. The question therefore again arises: if such options were made available on all commodities and services, would there be any distinct change in society's decisions to produce particular commodities or services? In this connection, the fact that a commodity is already under production because it is profitable is no guarantee that some expansion of its production might not take place with the options; specifically, even if a commodity is already produced it could well experience a significant expansion at marginal locations or for marginal product lines. Despite these offsetting possibilities, it does seem probable that there would be at least some modification in society's decisions to produce or not produce particular commodities and services occasioned by taking "unexercised options" into account. However, these options probably would be much more important in expanding recreational, park, and similar services (often cited as other areas where such latent option demands exist) than public transit. Subsidies may also be easier to justify for parks than transit because of somewhat greater difficulty in constructing a reasonable structure of user charges to capture option benefits for parks; for transit, those who

[15] That option demand exists for all commodities is recognized by Weisbrod, *ibid.*, p. 476.

really do value the option to ride are far more likely to appear as consumers at some point in time.

Another argument for subsidies is that greater transport efficiency can be achieved by granting "countervailing subsidies." The essence of this argument is that if certain modes of urban transportation are subsidized, then a better resource utilization pattern can be achieved by granting similar subsidies to the other, competing modes. For this reason, many observers complain against what they regard as subsidies for people commuting by automobile to the CBD's of our large cities, arguing that automobile user taxes are considerably less than the cost of the highway facilities consumed. As noted earlier, it is difficult to verify this argument, although there probably is a degree of truth in it for very high cost urban expressways (though not for the over-all urban highway system).

Even if substantial highway subsidies exist, however, it is not obvious that counterbalancing subsidies would improve the over-all performance of the economy. In general, extending more subsidies to urban transportation would almost certainly increase, at least slightly, the total consumption of urban transportation and of its complementary good—urban residential land—which in turn could lead to further decentralization of cities. From the purely economic standpoint a preferable solution to putting subsidies on an equal level would be to reduce the inequality by bringing user charges more closely into line with user costs on the facilities now subsidized (unless market conditions prevail that make the general theory of second best strongly applicable).

A less sophisticated but politically persuasive version of the countervailing subsidy argument is that government largesse falls mainly to rural areas, and that this imbalance should be redressed by greater expenditures for urban needs—including urban transportation. Of course, if sheer imbalance is the essence of the problem, an obvious alternative would be to cut down on rural expenditures.

A critic might also raise the possibility that there are more urgent urban needs than expansion of urban transportation facilities and, even more pertinently, subsidization of inefficient ones. Indeed, the specific direction usually suggested for urban transportation subsidies seems questionable, particularly any emphasis placed on long-distance commuter facilities. If central cities are, in fact, as interested as they profess to be in retaining or attracting as residents high- and middle-income families employed in their CBD's, and in redeveloping central areas, a consistent transportation policy might be to improve local circulation in central areas to the maximum while permitting systematic deterioration of transit serving outlying areas. Specifically, it might be more promising for the city to provide frequent and high-quality local transit services within central areas, and between actual or planned renewal areas and employment centers where large numbers of high- and middle-income people work. For much the same reasons, subsidies to long-distance commuter systems might far better be spent on capital improvements for the older parts of central cities—for example, on improved schools, parks, and other social services, which would help central areas compete with the suburbs as desirable places to live.

It is ironic, in fact, to discover that financially hard-pressed central cities which have waged a postwar feud with competitive suburbs and central-city commuters residing there, which have accused the outlying communities of not paying their fair share of urban social services and have proclaimed their intention of making them do so, and which continually devise schemes for attracting high- and middle-income commuters back to the central city, will nonetheless support transport programs whose effects are to provide significant income redistributions to these same commuters and to make suburban communities even more attractive to live in.

Still another argument for subsidies, justified ostensibly on economic grounds, is that subsidization of particular types of urban transportation would engender social benefits that cannot be achieved by private market mechanisms. Probably the commonest instance of this argument is that subsidies to public transit, particularly electrified rail transit, are justified because people would be attracted away from automobiles and the health dangers and hazards created by automobile-induced smog would consequently diminish. The obvious question, though, is whether there are not other means, possibly cheaper and more direct, of meeting the same problem. Automobiles might be equipped with special exhaust inhibitors, for example, at a cost variously estimated between $50 and $150 per car. At that cost, it may well be cheaper to equip all the automobiles in an area than to build an electrified rail transit system; and even if the cost were higher, consumers might still prefer to use automobiles with exhaust inhibitors. Such devices are not the only alternative, of course; in the next ten years or so, for example, it may become possible to store electrical energy so efficiently that electrical propulsion systems can be used on specialized commuter automobiles. At any rate, the relevant problems are determining the true patterns of consumer preferences and the relative costs of achieving the same ends by different means.

Another variation of the social benefit argument for subsidies is that mass transportation must be provided so that people with various kinds of special training and talent can assemble in central urban areas and interact and stimulate one another. The argument is that these people, when they are in groups, create ideas which cannot be marketed by the individuals themselves but nevertheless are valuable to society. Obviously, an argument of this kind is very difficult to assess empirically; but whether or not it is true, it seems irrelevant to the evaluation of mass transit subsidies. Only a few people seem to have the special talents usually mentioned, and even making allowances for the secretarial and other technical and logistics support they might require, it is difficult to see how a large-scale demand for transportation would be generated, except possibly in New York City which is already well-provided with public transit. If there really is a social benefit attributable to such intellectual interaction, the real need would appear to be a specialized transportation scheme to get these superior individuals into and out of downtown areas, or the creation of small close-in residential neighborhoods to house them.

It is also argued that the support of highly specialized artistic, musical, and dramatic activities requires easy access to a large market, since only a small percentage of people consume or participate in these activities. Again, this is not an easy proposition to assess empirically, but the central question once more seems to be whether there are good alternatives. With modern communications technology, for example, it is less certain that the support of cultural activities requires collecting people in face-to-face situations. In particular, pay television and high-quality sound reproduction hold promise that these activities can be financed and adequately broadcast from a central production center.

There might be, of course, an undeniable demand for urban rapid transit for recreational-cultural purposes if there were a prolonged and successful drive to improve the general level of education which, in turn, increased the numbers of people interested in cultural activities. For the present, however, the same comments made earlier about limited scale and high specialization seem to apply to these transportation demands as well. Further, the fact that most demands associated with cultural activities would occur during off-peak or noncommuter hours suggests that these demands would be met easily within almost any conceivable organization of an urban transportation system, with or without subsidization. There is also, finally, the undeniable fact that people seem to have a strong preference for private automobile when traveling for recreational purposes.

Another argument for urban transit subsidies involves the urban planning process. It is the contention that subsidization of particular types of urban transportation will lead to the creation of more aesthetically desirable or appealing land-use patterns in urban areas. The validity of this argument is questionable because the available evidence does not strongly support the view that American urban growth patterns differ substantially according to whether a city does or does not have a rapid transit system. A large number of forces operate on urban land-use decisions; the form of an urban transportation system is only one of them. Another obvious question is what person or group is to decide that one land-use pattern is more desirable than another. Apparently some "expert" views are to be substituted for those that result from consumer choices—at least consumer choices as exercised within present market relationships. Of course, it can be argued that these market relationships badly distort consumer choice patterns and lead consumers to select items they would not normally or conventionally want. Put in this form, the argument reduces to the basic question of whether or not it is desirable to move to a better organization of the market by, say, bringing charges and costs more closely into balance, as discussed previously.

The consumer choice question, with its related emphasis on consumer sovereignty, also enters crucially into evaluating another popular argument for special forms of urban transportation subsidy: to wit, subsidy of particular forms of transportation will lead people to select urban transportation patterns that are cheaper or lower in total costs than presently existing patterns. The usual suggestion is that subsidized bus or rail transit would induce enough people to give up private automobile commutation to reduce the total costs of transportation to society. This argument, which has a large superficial appeal, is subject to several objections.

First of all, as demonstrated previously, bus or rail transit is not always cheaper than automobile commutation, and in fact is seldom cheaper for other than the largest cities. It is not sufficient, for example, to point out that a public transit system *can* carry 40,000 people an hour much more cheaply than a private automobile system can; it is also necessary to establish that enough demand exists to sustain a large-volume operation.

A second objection is that cost is by no means the only or most important criterion to be used. Many people prefer the automobile because of its privacy, convenience, freedom of movement, and the like. It is possible that not even a considerable subsidy would make these people give up automobile travel. As noted previously, it has been seriously estimated that public transit riders would have to be paid fifty cents or more to induce a solid majority of automobile commuters to give up automobile commutation in Chicago's circumstances.[16]

A final argument is that urban transportation subsidies are required to maintain the tax revenue base of cities. That is, superior transportation access to downtown areas helps maintain downtown real estate values. This desideratum in and of itself, incidentally, is often argued as a justifiable rationale for urban transportation subsidies, since it is considered objectionable by some to see these values written down "prematurely." Of course, if urban transportation really accomplished this goal, and did so at a reasonable cost, it would seem appropriate for downtown property

[16] Leon N. Moses and Harold F. Williamson, Jr., "Value of Time, Choice of Mode, and the Subsidy Issue in Urban Transportation," *Journal of Political Economy,* 71:247–264 (June 1963).

owners to maintain their property values by instituting urban transportation systems on their own initiative.

From a purely economic standpoint, the task of maintaining real estate values is essentially the old question of whether and how to rehabilitate an investment in outmoded facilities. Pressures for doing so come from numerous sources. Owners of depressed properties, for example, have an understandable proclivity for seeking government aid to protect them from financial loss—particularly because the needed adaptations can be costly.

Arguments in favor of government aid and subsidies for urban transportation often are buttressed by the assertion that it is in the public interest to preservc real estate values in order to maintain many desirable urban services. Again, most of the usual counterarguments are applicable. It is not clear, for example, that mass transit or other highly specialized transportation facilities will greatly modify urban development patterns or maintain downtown property values. And there seem to be more direct and feasible alternatives. For example, if the maintenance of city finances is the essential question, a better solution might be to redefine city boundaries or reform state legislatures to make them more responsive to urban constituencies and their wishes. Furthermore, rapid deterioration of city property tax bases and increased costs of social services are associated with larger proportions of city residents being at lower socioeconomic status, which, in turn, is related to many influences, including housing segregation practiced within urban areas and the general level of economic prosperity in the society.

Market Structure and Regulatory Institutions

Pricing practices and subsidies obviously must take effect in a context of market institutions. With urban public transit, as with most common-carrier transportation, the most important fact for market organization is that these activities have ordinarily been considered matters of public interest and consequently proper objects for government regulation. A knowledge of regulatory institutions is therefore essential to understanding market performance, pricing patterns, and the role of subsidies in urban transportation. An evaluation—or better, a reappraisal—of regulatory institutions is all the more pertinent at the moment because the performance of any regulatory framework largely depends on its compatibility with underlying technological and consumer preference patterns. In urban transportation, as in the economy at large, these have been obviously undergoing extensive and rapid change.

In the United States at least two types of government regulation are distinguishable. The first is that pioneered and practiced by the Interstate Commerce Commission in its regulation of the railroad industry. It involves extensive sharing of the managerial function between private business and the public regulatory agencies and is aptly described as "joint public-private management." Under this form of regulation, competitive forces are little used to protect the public interest, and the agency usually sees as its function the "promotion" of the industry being regulated, by suppression of competition if necessary. This type of regulation also emphasizes "cross-subsidies," by which economically unsupportable but publicly desirable transportation activities are sustained by profits made by the private carrier in economically advantageous markets, often monopolized under government protection. An outstanding example is the use of profits on rail freight traffic to subsidize losses incurred on many rail passenger services. In urban public transit, low-density operations in the late evening and early morning hours, and feeder bus services in the more remote suburbs, are usually loss operations being cross-subsidized by more profitable runs.

A different approach to regulation is found in practices of the Civil Aeronautics Board and also in some urban transit regulation. While often similar in legal aspects, the second approach to regulation can develop extremely important economic differences; under it an attempt is usually made to create, through appropriate franchising, an environment of limited but workable competition. This competition is largely relied upon to protect consumer interests, especially in determining the offerings of different qualities and frequencies of services. In aviation, this policy has been greatly facilitated by the availability of government funds to subsidize unprofitable but "socially desirable" services, thus eliminating much of the need for granting monopoly protection in other markets. This type of regulation might be called "franchised competition."

These two types of regulation are not necessarily mutually exclusive. When private rather than public enterprise has been relied on to provide urban transit in the United States, the accompanying regulation has usually involved both the joint-management and franchised competition approaches (at least recently), with the joint-management approach tending to dominate. Each system has its advantages and disadvantages, and the appropriateness of each depends not only on the objectives of the regulation but also on basic technological and economic considerations. If workable competition is to be fostered, for example, entry into the industry must not be too difficult; and there should be no markedly increasing returns to scale.

At present, a franchise scheme in urban transit would appear operable only where the bus is the major source of line-haul transportation. With rail, it would be extremely difficult to organize and coordinate numerous users of the same tracks at the same time. A feasible system might be to have the government own the roadbed and terminal facilities and lease them to private owners. The administrative complexities of operating such a system would be burdensome, however, and in any case it seems inconceivable that any but the very largest cities would ever have enough need for rail transit facilities to enable more than one rail line to operate efficiently. Consequently, if the need for urban transportation develops to the point where it can be efficiently served by rail, the regulation, if one is needed or deemed desirable, probably will be of the detailed joint-management type. Government ownership would be the only major alternative if competition were deemed insufficient to protect the public interest. Government-owned transit facilities, incidentally, generally operate with about the same pricing and marketing rules as in joint-management regulation.

Special problems would arise, of course, if urban development proceeded in such a way that an existing bus service operating under a system of franchised competition were to be replaced by a rail system.[17] If it is assumed that the rail service has a cost or other advantage that fully justifies its installation, the capital investment in the bus service would have to be systematically withdrawn without severely interrupting public transportation as the bus service phased out and rail operations phased in. One way to ease the transition would be to grant the holders of existing bus franchises preference in obtaining new franchises, either in new bus services or, if the rail facilities are to be privately owned, in the new rail system. In other circumstances, no formal action would be necessary by the regulatory agency at the time of changing from a bus to a rail system. For example, there would be no need to terminate the bus franchises if the rail facility really had a substantial cost advantage, since the rail system would not need protection from bus competition. On the other hand, if the rail facility were not fully efficient, potential or actual bus competition should give it an incentive to adopt more economic practices.

The kind of regulatory scheme adopted can affect the structure and quality of an urban transportation system. In this connection, it is striking to note the polar extremes of service qualities now to be found in American cities. Urban travel tends to be dominated by relatively high-quality private automobile or by bus or rail transit of fairly low quality. There are few in between, such as taxis, jitneys, or limousines. At present, only private automobile commutation with car-pooling offers much opportunity to achieve intermediate levels of service in the United States. This situation contrasts sharply with that in many other countries, particularly in Latin America and to a lesser extent in Europe and Japan.

[17] In effect, the National Capital Transportation Agency has proposed such a transition for Washington, D.C.

High labor cost at least partly accounts for this difference. Private automobiles are free of operating labor charges, while mass transit uses more capital and less labor than do the intermediate technologies, almost by definition. In general, high wages in the United States encourage do-it-yourself and capital intensive production techniques, and urban transportation is no exception.

However, franchise and license limitations imposed by local governments on bus and taxi operations also have contributed to the bifurcation in service offerings. The common practice of limiting taxi licenses (and bidding up the price of cab medallions) has kept taxi fares higher and utilization rates lower than they might otherwise be.[18] The greater number, heavier use, and lower fares of taxis in Washington, D.C., a city which imposes no serious limitations on entry into taxicab operations, illustrate what can be achieved under less rigid regulations. In fact, for group riding and short distances, Washington taxi fares are almost cost competitive with transit charges, service differences notwithstanding.

Taxi service apparently involves no great economies of scale or safety problems that would require public regulation. Control by the private market in competition seems quite feasible. Taxi operations also tend to be very intensive users of relatively unskilled labor and therefore should have desirable employment effects if expanded. Yet, for reasons that are again best explained by the mores of American local politics and the fears of excessive competition generated by the Great Depression, most American cities employ fairly restrictive limitations on entry into the taxi business. Limitations on entry into specialized bus and jitney services, moreover, may be quantitatively more harmful to urban transportation efficiency than are the limitations on taxis, since taxis are more of a service to off-peak travelers and out-of-town visitors than to workday commuters. The failure of taxis to meet more commuter needs, though, is also a result of regulation in many cases, specifically the failure to allow taxi rates to rise in rush hours when taxi costs can increase because of street congestion.

A traditional justification for restricting transit franchises is that private operators must be protected if they are to be induced to make large capital outlays on transit equipment. Such outlays, it is argued, would otherwise be jeopardized by the threat of competitive obsolescence. Needless to say, political institutions that protect against economic obsolescence can retard technological innovation at the same time. Still, the argument may have had some force when transit was predominantly rail-oriented

[18] Current medallion prices are hardly insignificant; in New York and Boston, for example, they presently range from $20,000 up.

and much of the capital was therefore immobile; but it is of dubious validity when transit is dominated by buses using public highways. The major private transit investment is now in rolling stock—buses—which is mobile and thus transferable to new operating areas, and therefore has high salvage value.

Time has also eroded several other arguments for franchise restriction. In fact, about the only major justification for it that remains is that monopoly privileges are needed in some markets to cross-subsidize losses incurred on "needed" social services elsewhere in the system; but many difficulties also beset the defense of cross-subsidy schemes. Among the more important are a tendency for uneconomic services to be perpetuated even when there is no longer any real public demand and people's natural unwillingness, when asked to pay the higher prices of monopoly services, to accept their fates ungrudgingly; that is, they try to escape, often using socially less efficient modes if they can improve their own private welfare by so doing. On the whole, transportation activities can usually be organized more rationally by abandoning cross-subsidies and having any socially required but unprofitable public services sustained by direct government subsidy. Direct subsidy makes it feasible, moreover, to consider using competitive market pressures to regulate the remaining, economically remunerative portions of the market. In urban transportation this would set the stage for removing entry controls and permitting free market experiments with new technologies and specialized services. At a minimum, if urban transit must be subsidized, it seems desirable to employ at least some of the funds in the direct support of socially desirable but uneconomic services, thus lifting any cross-subsidy justification, rather than confining attention to simple across-the-board subsidies to grandiose and questionable expansion schemes.

Almost certainly, though, the major consequence of urban transportation regulation today is to keep transit and commuter rail fares lower than they would otherwise be. This in turn motivates those providing these services to lower their quality standards in an effort to keep costs within the bounds established by regulation. Lower schedule frequency, antiquated equipment, and abandonment of less-patronized lines are all methods of effecting service and cost reductions. These, of course, in turn improve the competitive attraction of alternative transport by private automobile and lead to demands for public subsidies to correct the deterioration of service. Accordingly, less regulation of urban transportation at least deserves consideration in many cases as an alternative to subsidization. In short, the justification for transit subsidy based on "breaking out of a vicious circle" could also be an argument in some instances for less regulation as well.

Summary

Pricing policies, subsidies, and regulation are obviously controversial matters. Economic theory provides some loose guidelines in the selection of policies for achieving stipulated objectives, but offers little direct help in defining what those objectives should be; these are largely matters for political settlement. In a negative sense, however, economic theory is helpful in identifying policies that are inconsistent with stated objectives, and in defining the implied or explicit value judgments required to justify certain policies.

For example, it is difficult to defend any one simple rule for pricing urban transportation services on the grounds of pure efficiency, especially since the efficiency objective itself is often very ambiguous. In general, economists believe that incremental cost pricing has the best efficiency properties, particularly if the time horizon on which the increment is defined is fairly distant. Average cost pricing is a common and close second choice, and one which essentially eliminates the time horizon problem. Both rules, however, derive their efficiency properties only under rather strict assumptions that are rarely duplicated in the real world. Consequently, picking an appropriate pricing rule is partly an empirical as well as a conceptual problem. The final choice of a pricing policy also is likely to involve a considerable element of art, since empirical data are commonly lacking and judgments often of necessity enter into the choice of an efficiency criterion.

Subsidy questions are even less amenable to decision on pure efficiency grounds. Subsidy operations almost invariably embody an element of income transfer, and evaluating the desirability of such transfers is normally considered beyond the province of objective economic analysis. An economic analysis of many subsidy proposals often does suggest, however, that the desired results may not be achievable, particularly by the methods of subsidy commonly suggested, and that it is very easy to oversimplify and be misled by first appearances in subsidy proposals. Under the usual specification of objectives for urban transit subsidies, moreover, simpler and more effective methods of achieving the same ends can usually be found. The objective here, however, is not to establish that urban transportation subsidies are necessarily wrong, but merely that in the final analysis almost every argument for subsidy must rest upon noneconomic grounds. Like most other subsidies in our economy, transit subsidy is likely to be more justifiable on political, aesthetic, or other purely subjective arguments than on economic considerations.

A final question that almost invariably arises, implicitly or explicitly when considering urban transportation subsidies and government regulation, is whether the general social welfare can really be improved by supplanting the preferences recorded in the marketplace with the announced views of various groups. Possibly it can, but the evidence is by no means decisive. It may be true that urban transportation and urban land markets as now organized are so imperfect that the consumer, who is also the voter, is thwarted from the objectives he seeks; it is not clear, however, that subsidization or enforcement of specific pricing rules are the best ways to rectify these imperfections. A preferable solution might simply be to improve these markets, perhaps granting them more rather than less freedom and allowing prices and costs to come into closer alignment regardless of the political implications.

A particularly promising source of quick improvement in urban transport would appear to be the elimination of archaic regulations on the granting of public transit and taxi franchises in most cities. These regulations either serve no useful purpose under present conditions, or create artifical property values at the expense of consumers. The market for urban public transit is in large measure a creation of government regulations, most of which seem designed to meet outdated objectives under outmoded technological assumptions. At the moment their role is almost certainly more negative than positive, since they obstruct many needed innovations and experiments in the marketing of more specialized and varied transit services.

Chapter 14 | Urban Transportation in Summary and Perspective

An array of technological, economic, and social forces has altered the structure and character of American cities in recent decades. The particular form, mode, or even presence or absence of public transit facilities in a city is only one of these forces, and apparently one of limited importance. In fact, the patterns of land use, population growth, employment locations, and residential choices recorded in recent years by the most transit-oriented American cities have essentially mirrored those of other cities with very strong highway orientation. At least the broad outlines, though probably not the details, of land use in urban areas seem to be independent of the availability of public transit. With or without mass transit, American cities have been decentralizing.

This trend implies that the urban transportation problem in most American cities will change in character. Continued decentralization could ameliorate the single most difficult aspect of urban transportation: moving people during the morning and evening rush hours into and away from areas of high population and workplace density. In fact, even now, with *both* public and private transportation taken into account, it is not at all clear that the quality of urban transportation has been declining in most major cities. On the contrary, it seems to have improved in the last five years, if such quantitative measures as the number of transit route miles or the time required to complete commuter trips of a certain length or to clear a central city of people going home in the evening rush hours are applied.

Public transport and private transport are, of course, highly interdependent. Better highways into a city, especially limited-access facilities, not only speed up the movement of a specific number of people out of central areas by private automobile, but also usually reduce demands on public transport by diverting people to private modes. If service offerings on the public facilities are not reduced correspondingly, their quality of service will improve by reducing numbers of standees and thus congestion inside transit vehicles. Even if some service is curtailed, quality can still improve because higher performance speeds may be possible. This improvement can ensue, moreover, even if public transit vehicles do not operate over new express highways, since limited-access highways usually improve performance on parallel neighboring streets by reducing their congestion. In fact, new expressways are sometimes called inadequate because they speed up rush hour traffic from 25 to only about 35 mph on *both* the expressways and neighboring streets, rather than achieving the maximum expressway design speeds of 55 to 60 mph. Grumbling about the "failure" of new urban expressways is often traceable to this gap between expectation and reality.

In some important senses urban transportation did deteriorate, though, immediately after World War II. During the immediate postwar years, the stock of private automobiles expanded much more rapidly than did urban highway facilities. Throughout the postwar period, moreover, the quality of public transit has declined, at least as measured by frequency of service. This decline is heavily attributable to the negative interaction between public transit and private transportation. As more and more people used private transport, transit services were curtailed for economy reasons. This was particularly true for non-rush-hour periods, because the abandonment of public transportation for noncommuter purposes was much greater than for trips to or from work. The increased specialization of public transit in commuter work-trips mainly reflects its disadvantage for shopping, social, and recreational trips in comparison with the private automobile. In fact, an outstanding feature of urban passenger travel demands is a strong preference for the private automobile for virtually all noncommuter trips.

The private automobile is also increasingly used for commuter trips. Private automobile commutation, by eliminating transfers and supplying greater privacy and schedule flexibility (where car-pooling is limited), is unquestionably a superior economic good in the minds of many urban commuters. Therefore, as income levels have increased, it is hardly surprising that more and more commuters have taken to the automobile. In short, there is considerable evidence that consumers may prefer an "automobile" solution to their urban transportation needs, even if it is a costly solution.

Another important postwar phenomenon is the increasing prevalence of cross-haul and reverse commuter trip patterns in urban areas to the point where non-CBD trips are now more than twice as numerous as those to and from the CBD. In the past, it was common to find a high concentration of urban travel demands along a few corridors originating in the CBD and radiating outward to residential neighborhoods. The cross-haul pattern results from an increase in the number and geographic dispersion of trip origins and destinations, which in turn are a function not only of lower residential densities but of decentralization in manufacturing, transportation, shopping, and recreational facilities. The CBD-oriented, corridor pattern remains important only in a few of the largest cities, notably New York, and even then accounts for far less than a majority of regional trips.

One especially important problem has been intensified by the increase in cross-haul trips. This is the long-standing phenomenon of rush hour traffic which is not bound for the CBD area but is merely passing through. Ironically, this kind of traffic, which becomes entangled with CBD rush hour congestion against its will, often accounts for a remarkably high percentage of the rush hour demand pressure on downtown highways and streets. The solution advocated by highway engineers is to bypass this through traffic by creating "inner" or intermediate belt highways at the outer edges of downtown districts or slightly beyond.

In a different vein, the development of lower-density residential neighborhoods in American cities and suburbs is hardly attributable solely or even strongly to the automobile. Rising incomes have enabled households to consume more space; and at the same time, dispersion of workplaces has made it easier and cheaper for families to find desirable housing within commuting range of their workplaces. Tax concessions favorable to home ownership, and Federal programs to make housing credit cheaper and more available to low-income families, have also contributed. In general, commuter transportation and suburban land, particularly for new housing with private yards, are highly complementary economic goods; any policy or undertaking that promotes the demand for one is likely to do the same for the other. In the postwar period there has been a remarkable convergence of public policy and economic and demographic developments which has increased the attractiveness of both suburban housing and private transportation.

There is also limited evidence that transit facilities are suffering from a failure to adapt to a peculiar bifurcation apparently emerging in the demand for urban public transit. Specifically, the relative increase in the importance of office and control functions as a source of downtown employment has apparently resulted in relatively more demands for trips to downtown areas originating from professional groups and other office workers; these are superimposed on the trip demands of low-income employees in the service and retail industries that have remained in the central area. The future demands for transportation into downtown areas, therefore, may come from opposite poles in the spectrum of social and economic classes, and past experience suggests that it may be difficult to get these contrasting groups to accept the same quality of transportation service, or in some cases to travel together.

Little is known about how extensively opposition to social or racial integration causes declines in transit patronage, but there is at least some suggestive evidence that desegregation in parts of the South has caused transit patronage to decline. In the same vein, public transit has recorded some of its strongest recent performances in certain Northern areas where social and racial segregation is a function of geography. The Shaker Heights Line in Cleveland and the Chicago and Northwestern Railroad's North Shore operation in Chicago continue to enjoy considerable popularity, and it seems possible that some of this popularity is a result of a geographically built-in selection process that guarantees unusual social and economic homogeneity in the clientele. More information with which to test the validity of these and related hypotheses would at least contribute to a more realistic discussion of the basic problems involved in trying to develop mass public transit as an alternative to private automobile commutation. Furthermore, the problems created by this cleavage in the urban transportation market are intensified by racial segregation in housing. This restricts both the opportunity and the willingness of some people to reside closer to their workplaces and forces others to live closer than they might otherwise desire. As a consequence, the demand characteristics for urban transportation services are altered.

More explicitly, reverse-hauls running against the direction of major commuter flow in the morning and evening and long commuter trips are mostly made by three groups: multiple-wage-earner families; minority groups with restricted housing opportunities; and high-income families. Multiple-wage-earner families obviously find it difficult to select a residential location that minimizes transportation time and cost for their two or more wage-earners, while still meeting other family requirements. Minority groups commonly are limited to housing in older residential areas near the CBD, thus experiencing shorter trips for central-area jobs, but longer ones where suburban employment is involved. As suburban employment becomes increasingly important, minority groups could experience increasingly longer work-trips—assuming a continuance of geographical segregation as it now exists. High-income groups, on the other hand, commute to the CBD from outlying residential areas where they can satisfy high space demands and more easily find other housing amenities they desire.

These few observations on urban transportation demand patterns, while useful, are still notably incomplete. Much more needs to be known about patterns of demand, particularly demand elasticities and cross-elasticities for the different urban transit modes.

By contrast, considerable information is available on the costs of providing urban transportation. In fact, by making a few simplifying assumptions, reasonable estimates can be made of the relative costs of performing urban transportation by various modes. In making these cost analyses it is useful to differentiate among the three basic urban transportation functions: the line-haul, residential collection and distribution, and downtown collection and distribution.

The line-haul to the CBD is usually the most costly (and longest) part of the over-all urban transportation operation, though its relative importance diminishes as workplaces and residences disperse. A striking feature of line-haul cost comparisons is that a highway-oriented system is almost always as cheap as or cheaper than rail alternatives. Rail transit remains economically attractive for the line-haul only where population densities are extremely high, facilities are to be constructed underground, or rail roadbed structures are already on hand and can be regarded as sunk costs. It is therefore significant that most American cities with enough population density to support a rail transit operation, or even with prospects of having enough, usually possess rail transit already.

A surprising aspect of the line-haul cost comparisons is that a private automobile system even with a car occupancy of only 1.6 persons will usually be cheaper than either bus or rail transit when specific channel or corridor demands fall much below 10,000 persons per hour—a level well within the range of maximum channel or corridor demands in many American cities.

Highway vehicles are particularly well suited for residential collection and distribution. To be most efficient, residential collection requires flexible and preferably continuous (or nontransfer) transportation—more easily supplied by the bus and automobile than by rail transit. In recognition of this fact, all pending proposals for new rail transit incorporate a heavy reliance on feeder buses and private automobiles to bring passengers to suburban rail stations, and contain plans for large numbers of parking spaces at outlying points along the rail facility. Park-and-ride, however, is a very costly mode for residential collection and distribution. The least expensive approach to residential distribution is to incorporate residential operations into the line haul by extending line-haul express bus or automobile trips whenever feasible. In fact, where trip origination densities and line-haul volume levels are low, extension of the automobile trip is about the only inexpensive recourse—unless the housewife can be pressed into chauffeur duty in a kiss-and-ride operation. Bus operations, either as extensions of line-haul express runs or restricted to residential collection and distribution, become attractive, though, when trip origination densities reach a moderate level.

Collection and distribution in downtown or other high-density employment districts is much more complicated. Designing an efficient system for this particular function is made difficult by the fact that no available technology is well suited to the existing structures and plans of many older American cities. This is particularly true where streets are narrow and little offstreet parking is provided. Every city, moreover, is likely to have a number of special geographic and other traits that will offer obstacles.

Some general principles can be laid down, however. First, extending rapid transit facilities into downtown areas by tunnel or elevated structure is costly. This expense is likely to be justified only if corridor volumes are very high or street capacity is very limited, or if passenger travel time or convenience is highly valued. Generally, the cheapest solution (except at very high corridor volumes) to the downtown distribution problem is simply to extend via surface streets line-haul trips made by automobile or bus. Also, it rarely becomes attractive to think of having virtually *all* line-haul express facilities terminate at the edge of the CBD, with travelers transferring to specialized surface vehicles for the last part of their journeys. A special CBD secondary distribution system may be helpful on a limited basis, though, as a means of tying peripheral parking to the CBD and facilitating shopper and other short-hop movement during the day.

Frequently the key to choosing an efficient CBD distribution system is whether downtown street capacity will be sufficient to handle collection and distribution by surface modes. This, in turn, can depend on the availability of a belt highway around the CBD since such highways reduce congestion by diverting through traffic. Available street space can be further expanded by providing more offstreet or peripheral parking facilities, especially for all-day parkers. A good downtown collection and distribution system also can make peripheral parking more attractive.

In very-high-density employment districts, especially with little surface street area, the simplest and most economical solution for downtown collection and distribution usually will be rail or bus transit operating either in subways or on elevated structures. The choice between elevated and subway is largely an aesthetic question, the answer depending on whether burying the facility is worth in beauty the extra cost. If long tunnels are required or deemed desirable, rail transit has a substantial cost advantage for the downtown distribution function in being able to carry much larger volumes in a small bore than other modes. It is in this quality more than any other that rail has a particular or special advantage.

Obviously, the optimum over-all transportation system for a city will depend on a large number of factors: the age of the city, the existing supply of wide avenues and rail transit rights-of-way, the geographic density of its workplaces and residences, the income level and tastes of its population, and its future prospects and patterns of population and employment growth. At present, only a handful of American metropolitan areas seem to have enough rush hour CBD cordon crossings or sufficiently optimistic prospects for the future to justify even serious consideration of elaborate grade separated transit system investments, whether bus or rail. For American cities of moderate size, efficient urban transportation seems most readily obtainable by using private automobiles, complemented by various amounts and types of bus transit using common rights-of-way. In many ways the most crucial transportation question facing these cities is whether they can achieve the self-discipline required for coordinated, efficient use of their highway facilities, particularly during rush hours.

This coordination might be achieved in several ways. One would be to levy tolls on the use of important urban highway facilities and to charge substantially more for use during the peak commuter hours where differential costs are common; the same objective also might be achieved by special licensing or related schemes. A number of political and technical obstacles complicate the implementation of such price rationing schemes; they do, though, have appeal on the basis of economic considerations alone, particularly if the marginal costs of additional peak-hour costs are very high.

A more strictly technical solution to the highway coordination problem—one without so many obvious difficulties—would be to monitor flows and limit expressway access to levels that could be expeditiously accommodated, that is, that made full use of the highway capacity and did not overtax and thereby coagulate the traffic flow. The technical means exist for such schemes and actually have been applied in a few experimental cases. If monitoring and controlled access of major urban expressways were coupled with priority access for public transit buses, a simple and quite inexpensive form of rapid transit would be quickly available in most American cities. At a minimum, it would be sensible to experiment with these priority access schemes for buses before committing large sums to rail rapid transit installations. The fact that priority access for buses might be put into effect almost immediately, rather than in the five or more years often required to build a rail transit system, only heightens the appeal. Indeed, a good argument might be made for giving buses priority access to urban expressways as an interim measure even if a rail system is to be constructed.

Useful changes also could be made in transit operating and scheduling practices that would both cut costs and improve service in many instances. Very often today's operating practices represent a slavish adherence to meeting past needs rather than a rational assessment of how best to serve present needs. For example, simple modifications in door, seating, and terminal arrangements in many cases could do much to improve the quality and cut the costs of transit operations.

Several institutional changes, some of them quite minor in character, could also contribute to improving urban transportation. If differential pricing of highways for use at different times of the day and by different vehicles is ruled out as impractical, it still seems conceivable that much could be done to rationalize urban transportation by making parking charges more reflective of costs. In particular, the present trend toward offering cost-justified rate concessions for parking smaller cars in crowded downtown areas could encourage greater use of small cars as commuter vehicles. Any step in this direction is likely to be beneficial, not only in terms of reducing parking costs but also by permitting somewhat more intensive use of highway and street capacity, cutting operating costs, and even alleviating smog problems by reducing gas consumption in urban areas.

A general reduction in market controls and government regulations on urban transit and taxi operations also seems in order. Free entry into the taxi business and the availability of private or rented automobiles would provide a more than sufficient competitive check on any "monopolistic tendencies" in which modern transit companies might be tempted to indulge. As a promotion of public transit, less regulation and more flexibility in pricing and service offerings, including the possibility of earning a positive return on invested capital, might be just as salutary as direct government subsidy.

It is difficult, in fact, to build many strong justifications for subsidizing urban transit on economic grounds alone. In general, economic theory offers little direct help in defining policy objectives for urban transportation. The theory provides only some loose guidelines in the selection of policies for achieving objectives stipulated by the political process. For example, alternative pricing and subsidy policies can be evaluated for their technical feasibility, their probable effects on efficiency, their applicability to urban transportation markets, and probable implications for income redistribution. Many times, it seems, currently proposed urban transit subsidies, when subjected to careful economic evaluation, appear to be internally inconsistent, ill-conceived, and often in conflict with other goals of government policies in urban areas.

APPENDIXES | INDEX

Appendix A | Summary Description of Rail Line-Haul Systems

NOTATION

TRC = total costs in dollars on an annual basis (in this analysis, for four rush hours during 255 days a year).

$TROC$ = total annual costs in dollars, excluding costs of building structures and terminals and acquiring related right-of-way (ROW).

SR = total annual costs in dollars of building structures and terminals and acquiring related right-of-way.

SR_b = basic annual ROW and construction costs for a 2-track system, including all line-haul and terminal costs.

SR'_T = additional annual costs for providing a 3-track instead of a 2-track CBD terminal.

SR'_L = additional annual line-haul ROW and construction costs for a 3-track system (instead of just two tracks), including extra costs at line-haul station serving inner and outer loops.

SR' = additional annual costs for a 3-track instead of a 2-track system = $SR'_T + SR'_L$.

SR_{LS} = annual (finishing) construction costs for 2-track line-haul stations.

U = number of trains required.

n = number of cars per train.

M = annual car-miles required.

g = route-miles (assumed to be 6, 10, or 15).

g' = miles of triple or third track.

T = total track-miles required = $2g + g'$.

V = total system passenger volume per rush hour at maximum load point.

R = total number of round trips required per hour for the system.

r = number of round trips per hour each train can make.

c = seating capacity of each car (assumed to be 79, using bus seating space standards).

d = distance in miles traveled by a train on a round trip.

$\mathrm{CRF}_{n,i}$ = capital recovery factor, assuming service life of n years and interest rate of i.

t = time required to complete a round trip.

f = number of station stops make per round trip, including that at the downtown terminal.

k = car length (in feet).

h = minimum schedule frequency, that is, number of trains passing a given point per hour (so that the headway in seconds is 3600/h).

X_i = net residential density at ith route-mile (in thousands of persons per square mile).

^{1} as a subscript denotes values relevant to operations over the longer or outer loop in triple-track systems.

^{2} as a subscript denotes values relevant to operations over the shorter or inner loop in triple-track systems.

∂ designates a derivative.

* indicates a value to be rounded upward to next highest integer.

Characteristics of Rail Transit Vehicle Used in Costing

Empty car weight	48,500 lb
Average gross car weight	54,000 lb
Length	55.33 ft
Width	9 ft
Maximum running speed	55 mph (or 80.5 ft/sec)
Cost	$92,000
Power/weight (HP/avg load tonnage) ratio	14.8 to 1.0
Estimated effective floor space	400 sq ft
Seats	79 (using bus seating space standards)
Average deceleration rate	4.2 mph/sec
Average acceleration performance	0 to 20 mph in 8 sec
	0 to 30 mph in 14 sec
	0 to 40 mph in 27 sec
	0 to 46 mph in 40 sec
	0 to 52 mph in 60 sec
	0 to 55 mph in 80 sec

Cost Relationships

(RC–1) $$TRC = TROC + SR,$$

(RC–2) $$SR = SR_b + SR'_T + SR'_L = SR_b + SR',$$

(RC–3) $$TROC = \alpha U + \beta M + \gamma T + \mu V,$$

where

α = ($11,670$n$ + $20,495);

$11,670 = annual cost per car for debt service of rolling stock ($CRF_{30,6\%} \times$ $92,000 + 5 per cent allowance for standby cars), and of yards and shops ($CRF_{50,6\%} \times$ $8000 + 5 per cent allowance for standby cars), plus annual costs for direct equipment maintenance (assuming an average car life of 15 years, and empty car weight of 24.25 tons, using Eq. (RC–5) plus 15 per cent for overhead items) = $7018 + $533 + $4119;

$20,495 = annual cost per train scheduled during peak hour for crew (using 2-man crew cost per train of $16,200, plus 10 per cent allowance for sick leave, and so forth, plus 15 per cent allowance for overhead items);

β = \$0.277;

\$0.277 = car-mile associated maintenance and operating charges; includes power costs (using Eq. (RC–6) and assuming gross car weight of 27 tons, a cost per kwh of 1.456 cents, 1-mile station spacing, a power-weight ratio of 14.8 to 1.0) and a portion of maintenance of way and structure costs (using part of Eq. (RC–7), both plus 15 per cent allowance for overhead items = 1.15(\$0.07911 + \$0.162);

γ = \$3760;

\$3760 = annual track-associated maintenance costs, including a portion of way and structure maintenance costs (using part of Eq. (RC–7), and a gross car weight of 27 tons), and a portion of conducting transportation costs (using part of Eq. (RC–8), and average station spacing of 1 mile), both items plus 15 per cent allowance for overhead items = 1.15(\$14,440 − \$35,766 + \$89,130 − \$64,500);

μ = \$8.50;

\$8.50 = annual passenger-volume associated costs, including a portion of conducting transportation costs (using part of Eq. (RC–8), plus 15 per cent allowance for overhead items = 1.15(\$7.384).

(RC–4a) $$SR_b = \sum_{i=1}^{g} SR_{c_i} + \sum_{i=1}^{g} SR_{\text{row}_i} + (\delta)n + \epsilon,$$

where

SR_{c_i} = annual construction cost for ith mile of double-track line-haul facility, which is equal to the $\text{CRF}_{50,6\%}$ times the capital construction cost of \$3.960 million per 2-track mile for $X_i \geq 40$ or \$3.300 million for $X_i < 40$;

SR_{row_i} = annual right-of-way cost for ith mile of double-track line-haul facility, which is equal to the $\text{CRF}_{\infty,6\%}$ times the capital construction cost for an 8-lane mixed-traffic facility ($0.999 + 0.0708X_i$, in \$ million) times 2-track right-of-way width cost index (W_{row_2}; see Table 61) times the ratio of right-of-way to construction capital costs ($0.005X_i$)
= $(0.06)(0.999 + 0.0709X_i)(W_{\text{row}_2})(0.005X_i)$, in \$ million;

(RC–4b) $SR_{\text{row}_i} = (W_{\text{row}_2})(\$299.70X_i + \$21.27X_i^2)$, in dollars;

δ = annual (finishing) construction costs for 2-track line-haul stations per train car plus annual construction costs for 2-track (50-foot-wide) underground terminal station and turnaround extension per train car; or, $\text{CRF}_{50,6\%}$ times the line-haul station finishing capital costs per 2-track lineal foot (of \$1100) times k (car length of 55.33 feet) times the number of line-haul stations (g) plus $\text{CRF}_{50,6\%}$ times the 2-track subway station construction costs per lineal foot (of \$7200) times k plus $\text{CRF}_{50,6\%}$ times extension construction cost per lineal foot (of \$1811) times 60 feet per car
= (\$3862g) + (\$25,273) + (\$6893)
= (\$3862g) + \$32,166;

(RC–4c) $(\delta)n = (\$3862g)n + \$32{,}166n;$

ϵ = annual construction costs for crossover at downtown subway extension, which is $CRF_{50,6\%}$ times lump sum cost of crossover (of \$50,000)
= \$3172.

(RC–4d) $$SR'_T = (\delta'_T)n + \epsilon'_T,$$

where

δ'_T = difference in annual construction costs per train car between a 3-track and 2-track underground terminal station and extension, or $CRF_{50,6\%}$ times one-half the 2-track subway station construction costs per lineal foot times k plus $CRF_{50,6\%}$ times extension construction cost per lineal foot times 60 feet per car (that is, a 2-track extension replaces a single-track extension)
= (\$12,636) + (\$6893) = \$19,530;

ϵ'_T = difference in annual construction costs for crossovers required for a 3-track instead of a 2-track terminal, or $CRF_{50,6\%}$ times cost per crossover
= \$3172;

$SR'_T = (\$19{,}530)n + \$3172.$

(RC–4e) SR'_L = difference in annual line-haul construction and right-of-way costs between a 3-track and basic 2-track facility, including extra costs for one 3-track line-haul station (at juncture of inner and outer loops)

$$= \sum_{i=1}^{g'} SR'_{c_i} + \sum_{i=1}^{g'} SR'_{\text{row}_i} + \Theta(n),$$

where

SR'_{c_i} = difference in annual construction costs per ith route-mile between a 3-track and 2-track line-haul facility, which is equal to $CRF_{50,6\%}$ times the difference between \$5.980 million per 3-track route-mile and \$3.960 million per 2-track mile = \$129,000 (if it is assumed that a 3-track facility will be considered only when $X_i \geq 40$);

SR'_{row_i} = difference in annual right-of-way costs per ith route-mile between a 3-track and 2-track line-haul facility; it is merely equal to SR_{row_i} for three tracks minus SR_{row_i} for two tracks, or $(W_{\text{row}_3} - W_{\text{row}_2})(\$299.70X_i + \$21.27X_i^2)$
= $(0.05)(\$299.70X_i + \$21.27X_i^2)$; (see Table 61);

Θ = difference in annual line-haul station costs (at one station) between 3-track and 2-track facility; it is equal to $CRF_{50,6\%}$ times one-half the 2-track line-haul station finishing costs per lineal foot (or \$550) times k (of 55.33 ft.) = \$1931;

$$SR'_L = \$129{,}000(g') + 0.05 \sum_{i=1}^{g'} (\$299.70X_i + \$21{,}27X_i^2) + \$1931(n).$$

(RC–4f) $$SR_{LS} = \lambda n,$$

where

SR_{LS} = annual (finishing) construction costs for 2-track line-haul stations on inner loop (just one portion of the $(\delta)n$ term in Eq. (RC–4a));

λ = annual costs for inner-loop line-haul stations per train car = $3862(g' − 1);

SR_{LS} = $3862(n)(g' − 1).

(RC–4g) SR' = incremental annual cost of adding a third track to a 2-track system *when there is a 2-track downtown terminal*

$$= SR'_T + SR'_L$$

$$= (\$19{,}530)n + \$3172 + \$129{,}000g' + (0.05)\sum_{i=1}^{g'}(\$299.70X_i + \$21.27X_i^2) + \$1931n.$$

(RC–4h) SR' = SR'_L *when there is a 3-track downtown terminal*

$$= \$1931n + \$129{,}000g' + (0.05)\sum_{i=1}^{g'}(\$299.70X_i + \$21.27X_i^2).$$

Equations (RC–5) through (RC–9) do not account for administrative and other overhead items.

(RC–5) $$EC = (\$1022 + \$69.45a + \$55.58w_e)(n)(U),$$

where

EC = annual maintenance of equipment costs (in dollars);
a = average car age (in years);
w_e = empty car weight (in tons).

(In this analysis, a was 15 years, and w_e was 24.25 tons; n times U is the number of cars required for the system including standby allowance.)

(RC–6) $$PC = (\$0.05916 + \$0.01102p_w - \$0.02127s)(c_p)(w_g)(M),$$

where

PC = annual power costs (in dollars);
p_w = ratio of horsepower per car to gross car weight (in tons);
w_g = gross car weight (in tons);
s = average station spacing (in miles);
c_p = power cost per kwh (in dollars);
M = annual car mileage.

(In this analysis, p_w was 14.8, W_g was 27 tons, s was 1 mile, and c_p was $0.01456.

(RC–7) $$MWC = \$0.1617(M) + \$533.40(w_g)(T) - \$35{,}766(T),$$

where

MWC = annual maintenance of way and structure costs (in dollars);
T = total miles of single track = $(2g + g')$.

(RC–8) $$CTC = \$89{,}130(T) - \$64{,}500(s)(T) + \$7.384(V),$$

where

CTC = annual conducting transportation costs, not including motormen and guards (in dollars);
V = peak-hour passenger volume.

(RC–9) $AOC = (0.1598 - 0.00669P_T)(EC + PC + MWC + CTC),$

where

AOC = annual overhead costs (in dollars);
P_T = annual passengers per track-mile.

In this analysis overhead costs were set equal to 15 per cent for all cases (to ease computations), rather than derived from Eq. (RC–9).

Functional Relationships

	1-way service		2-way service	
(R–1a)	$f_1 = g + 1$	or	$f_1 = 2g$	for $g' = 0$.
(R–1b)	$f_1 = g - g' + 2$	or	$f_1 = 2(g - g' + 1)$	for $g' > 0$.
(R–1c)	$f_2 = g' + 1$	or	$f_2 = 2g'$	

(R–2a) $d_1 = 2g.$

(R–2b) $d_2 = 2g'.$

(R–3a) $t_1 = 93f_1 + 65.4(d_1 - f_1) + 10(f_1 - 2) + 600$ (in sec).

(R–3b) $t_2 = 93f_2 + 65.4(d_2 - f_2) + 10(f_2 - 2) + 600$ (in sec).

(R–4a) $$r_1 = \frac{3600}{t_1}.$$

(R–4b) $$r_2 = \frac{3600}{t_2}.$$

(R–5) For optimum length of triple trackage, $SR' = \frac{\partial TROC}{\partial g'}$.

For optimum train length (that is, number of cars per train, n):

(R–6a) $$\frac{\partial TROC}{\partial n} = \frac{\partial SR_b}{\partial n}, \text{ for } g' = 0 \text{ with 2-track terminal,}$$

where

(R–6b) $$\frac{\partial TROC}{\partial n} = \frac{\$20{,}495V}{rcn^2},$$

(R–6c) $$\frac{\partial SR_b}{\partial n} = \$3862g + \$32{,}166,$$

$$\frac{\$20{,}495V}{rcn^2} = \$3862g + \$32{,}166.$$

(R–7a) $$\frac{\partial TROC}{\partial n} = \frac{\partial(SR_b + SR'_T)}{\partial n}, \text{ for } g' = 0 \text{ with 3-track terminal,}$$

where

(R–7b) $$\frac{\partial TROC}{\partial n} = \frac{\$20{,}495V}{rcn^2},$$

(R–7c) $$\frac{\partial(SR_b + SR'_T)}{\partial n} = \$3862g + \$51{,}696,$$

$$\frac{\$20{,}495V}{rcn^2} = \$3862g + \$51{,}696.$$

(R–8a) $$\frac{\partial TROC_1}{\partial n_1} = \frac{\partial(SR_b + SR'_T + SR'_L)}{\partial n_1},$$ for outer loop of 3-track system (not including costs for inner-loop line-haul stations, other than stations at juncture of loops),

where

(R–8b) $$\frac{\partial TROC_1}{\partial n_1} = \frac{\$20{,}495V(g - g')}{r_1 c_1 n_1^2(g)},$$

(R–8c) $$\frac{\partial(SR_b + SR'_T + SR'_L)}{\partial n_1} = \$3862(g - g' + 1) + \$53{,}627,$$

$$\frac{\$20{,}495V(g - g')}{r_1 c_1 n_1^2(g)} = \$3862(g - g' + 1) + \$53{,}627.$$

(R–9a) $$\frac{\partial TROC_2}{\partial n_2} = \frac{\partial(SR_{LS})}{\partial n_2},$$ for inner loop of 3-track system,

where

(R–9b) $$\frac{\partial TROC_2}{\partial n_2} = \frac{\$20{,}495V(g')}{r_2 c_2 n_2^2(g)}.$$

(R–9c) $$\frac{\partial(SR_{LS})}{\partial n_2} = \$3862(g' - 1),$$

$$\frac{\$20{,}495V(g')}{r_2 c_2 n_2^2(g)} = \$3862(g' - 1).$$

(R–10a) $M_1 = 1020(d_1)(r_1)(n_1)(U_1).$

(R–10b) $M_2 = 1020(d_2)(r_2)(n_2)(U_2)$, for inner loop when $g' > 0$.

(R–10c) $M = M_1 + M_2$; $M_2 = 0$ when $g' = 0$.

(R–11a) $$R_1 = \frac{V}{n_1 c_1}\left(\frac{g - g'}{g}\right) = h_1.$$

(R–11b) $$R_2 = \frac{V}{n_2 c_2}\left(\frac{g'}{g}\right) = h_2.$$

(R–12a) $$U_1 = \frac{R_1}{r_1}.$$

(R–12b) $$U_2 = \frac{R_2}{r_2}.$$

CONSTRAINTS AND SYSTEM SPECIFICATIONS USED FOR COSTING

(R–13a) $$(30) \leq h \leq (57 - 2n),$$

for 2-track operations with 2-track CBD terminal or 3-track systems.

(R–13b) $$(30) \leq h \leq (72 - 2n),$$

for 2-track operations with 3-track CBD terminal.

(R–14) $$n \leq 10.$$

(R–15) $$c \leq 79.$$

(R–16) $$s = 1 \text{ mile}.$$

(R–17) $$w_e = 24.25 \text{ tons}.$$

(R–18) $$w_g = 27.0 \text{ tons}.$$

(R–19) $$a = 15 \text{ years}.$$

(R–20) $$p_w = 14.8.$$

Appendix B | Summary Description of Bus Line-Haul Systems

NOTATION

- TBC = total costs in dollars on an annual basis (in this analysis, for four rush hours during 255 days a year).
- $TBOC$ = total annual costs in dollars, excluding costs of building structures and terminals and acquiring related right-of-way (ROW).
- SB = total annual costs in dollars of building structures and terminals and acquiring related right-of-way.
- SB_c = annual costs for constructing line-haul roadway.
- SB_{row} = annual cost for acquiring line-haul facility right-of-way.
- SB_p = annual cost for constructing building structures and terminals.
- U = number of bus units required.
- M = annual bus-miles required for system.
- L = total lane-miles of highway required for system.
- g = route-miles of line-haul facility.
- V = total system passenger volume per rush hour at maximum load point.
- k = number of highway lanes (both directions).
- R = number of bus round trips required.
- r = number of round trips per hour each bus unit can make.
- c = bus seating capacity.
- d = distance traveled by a bus on a round trip.
- f = number of bus stops made on a round trip.
- t = time required to complete a round trip.
- p = passengers carried per bus round trip.
- h = minimum schedule frequency at each line-haul station.
- q = number of bus-loop operations for system.
- m = number of intermediate line-haul stations served by each bus-loop operation.
- $\text{CRF}_{n,i}$ = capital recovery factor, assuming service life of n years and interest rate of i.

^{i} as a subscript denotes the numbering of line-haul stations (in ascending order from the CBD terminal), and distance (in miles) from the CBD terminal for a station spacing of 1 mile; $i = 1, 2, \ldots, g$.

^{j} as a subscript denotes the numbering of bus loops between line-haul stations and CBD terminal; $j = 1, 2, \ldots, q$.

* indicates a value to be rounded upward to next highest integer.

Physical Characteristics and Specifications

Vehicle

Modified GMC-TDH 5303 bus, equipped with three doors and SDM 5303 power and transmission units:

Length	40 ft
Top speed	$59\frac{1}{2}$ mph
Seats	50
Effective floor space	254 sq ft
Floor space/seat	5.08 sq ft/seat
Gross weight (including passengers)	28,200 lb
Average deceleration rate	4.2 mph/sec
Estimated cost (including tax)	\$31,200 (with modifications)
Average acceleration performance	0 to 20 mph in 7 sec
	0 to 40 mph in 25 sec
	0 to 48 mph in 40 sec
	0 to 56 mph in 60 sec
	0 to 59 mph in 70 sec

Highway Interchange and Line-Haul Station Design

Mixed-traffic urban interstate systems incorporate interchanges capable of handling traffic movement in four, six, or eight directions—by use of diamond-type, cloverleaf, or more complicated interchanges. Exclusive express bus highways, however, need not have such intricate interchanges, nor ramps for all the directions "required" (or at least provided) for interstate, mixed-traffic highways. Simple slip-ramps—with an underpass or overpass loop for turnaround at line-haul stations—will usually suffice for line-haul bus system service; for an express bus service which also performs residential collection, only a simple modification is required. The design for an express bus highway line-haul interchange might look somewhat as shown in Figure 60.

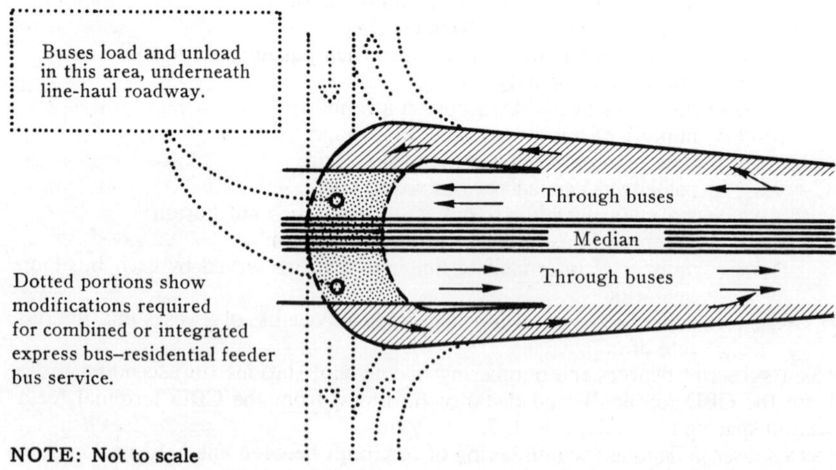

Figure 60. Bus ramps and design at each station on line-haul system.

With this design no elaborate line-haul station buildings are required since simple curb platforms would be ample, except for comfort, and since in most cases only two or three buses would be loading or unloading simultaneously at the line-haul stations. Furthermore, some protection from weather is automatically provided if the bus passengers load and unload underneath the line-haul roadway. However, to be conservative and to provide station comfort somewhat more directly comparable to that of the rail transit system, a station shelter cost of $100,000 per line-haul station is incorporated in subsequent cost estimates.

CBD Terminal Design

A suggested configuration for downtown bus terminals or stations is shown in Figure 61. It is designed for double-side passenger loading or unloading, with diagonal slots, and with circulation as shown in order to eliminate "crossing" or "weaving" conflicts, both between buses and passengers. The bus slots are long enough for only one bus. The number of slots will depend on the bus headway of incoming buses and the time required for bus deceleration, loading and unloading, and acceleration. In general,

$$\text{Number of bus slots (for each incoming lane)} = \frac{\text{Time required for deceleration/acceleration and loading/unloading}}{\text{Bus headway per lane}}.$$

It is important to note that the number of bus slots—and thus terminal length and cost—partially depends on the loading and unloading times. Since the buses in low volume cases are not fully loaded, this fact should be taken into account. Furthermore, if downtown distribution is provided, the passengers normally will be loaded or unloaded at more than one station; terminal length requirements are thereby reduced (since the loading and unloading time per station and thus the required number of slots will be reduced). In the line-haul cost analyses, however, it is assumed that all passengers unload at one point and that each bus slot can safely handle only 70 buses an hour.

The total lineal feet of terminal required for bus slots (for each incoming lane) depends on both the "angle" of the bus slots (relative to the general direction of travel) and the number of slots. The design shown in Figure 61 is for a 45-degree angle layout for which a 140-foot width is needed (to include a return lane) and 28 feet of length are required for each bus slot. In addition, approximately 7 extra lineal feet of terminal are needed to account for acceleration and decleleration lanes and for platforms at sides of outside bus slots. In general, a 30-degree or lesser-angle terminal would be more expensive than a 45-degree; however, in certain cases, because of utility relocation or underpinning problems, the reverse may be true. The 45-degree angle slots are used in the cost analyses.

Cost Parameters and Functions

(BC–1) $$TBC = TBOC + SB.$$

(BC–2) $$SB = SB_c + SB_{\text{row}} + SB_p.$$

Operating Costs, Including Equipment

(BC–3) $$TBOC = \alpha U + \beta M + \gamma L,$$

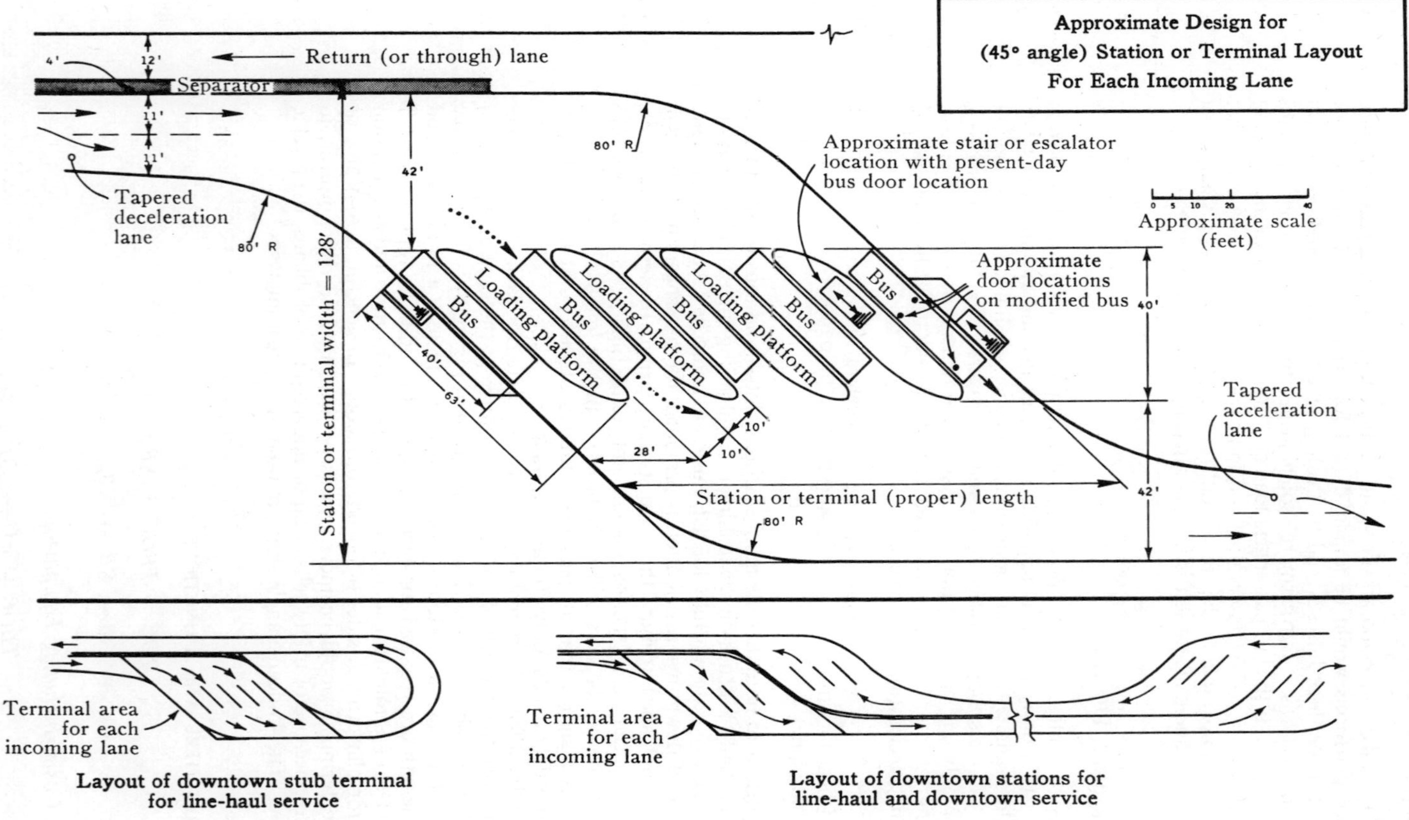

Figure 61. Downtown bus terminal or station design. (Number of bus slots varies according to incoming bus headway and passenger loads.)

where

α = \$13,120 = annual costs per bus unit for rolling stock, yards and shops, and operators; or, $CRF_{12,6\%}$ times purchase cost per bus (of \$31,200) plus $CRF_{50,6\%}$ times yards and shops investment per bus (of \$4500), both items plus an additional 5 per cent to allow for downtime, plus annual bus operator costs per (peak-hour) scheduled bus unit (of \$8100)[1] increased 10 per cent to allow for breaks, vacations, and so forth = \$3910 + \$300 + \$8910;

β = \$0.30 = cost per bus-mile, to cover bus fuel and oil, maintenance, administration, insurance and safety, and conducting transportation items (other than for operators), plus 20 per cent for contingencies[2] = 1.20(\$0.025 + \$0.107 + \$0.059 + \$0.031 + \$0.03);

γ = \$9000 = annual highway maintenance and administration costs per lane-mile.

Construction and Right-of-Way Costs (Exclusive of CBD Terminal)

All construction and right-of-way costs for exclusive bus highways were based on the following capital construction costs per mile for mixed-traffic highways:

(BC–4) $$Y_{i,k} = W_{c_i}(\$311{,}000 + \$70{,}800X_i) + \$86{,}000k_i,$$

where

$Y_{i,k}$ = capital construction costs for the ith mile of mixed-traffic highway of k lanes, and net residential density of X_i (in thousands);

W_{c_i} = ratio of nonpavement highway construction costs for k lane highway to those for 8-lane highway [in this analysis it was assumed that they were proportional to the traveled-way widths (as shown in Table 61)].

Thus, for an 8-lane mixed-traffic highway,

$$Y_{i,8} = (\$311{,}000 + \$70{,}800X_i) + \$688{,}000.$$

(*a*) *Bus Operation on Exclusive Bus Highways*

(BC–5) $$SB_c = \sum_i^g SB_{c_i},$$

(BC–6) $$SB_{c_i} = W_{c_i}(\$19{,}864 + \$4522X_i) + \$5800k_i,$$

where

SB_{c_i} = the cost per mile on an annual basis of constructing the ith mile of roadway;

W_{c_i} = the ratio between the nonpavement construction costs of a facility of k_i lanes and those of an 8-lane highway [in this analysis it was assumed that they were proportional to the traveled-way widths (as shown in Table 61)];

X_i = net residential density at the ith mile from the CBD in thousands per square mile and is assumed to be as in Chicago for high-density and as in Pittsburgh for medium-density calculations (see Fig. 33);

[1] This unit cost includes allowances for operators required during all four morning and evening rush hours, for swing shift rules, and so forth.

[2] Taxes were excluded since all highway construction, maintenance, and interest items were fully costed.

k_i = the number of lanes for the ith mile of highway;

\$19,864 = the annual construction costs (exclusive of paving) for an 8-lane "bus-only" highway which are not associated with population density. These costs are assumed to be 93 per cent of the same capital costs (of \$311,000) for a conventional mixed-traffic highway times $\text{CRF}_{35,6\%}$;

\$4522 = the annual construction costs for an 8-lane "bus-only" highway associated with population density; again assumed to be 93 per cent of the same capital costs (of \$70,800) for a conventional highway times $\text{CRF}_{35,6\%}$;

\$5800 = the paving costs per lane-mile on an annual basis for a "bus-only" highway, assumed to be 98 per cent of those capital costs (of \$86,000) for a conventional highway times $\text{CRF}_{35,6\%}$.

(BC–7) $$SB_{\text{row}} = \sum_{i=1}^{g} SB_{\text{row}_i},$$

(BC–8) $$SB_{\text{row}_i} = \lambda(W_{\text{row}_i})(CRF_{\infty,6\%})(Y_{i,8})$$

where

λ = $(0.005X_i)$, determined empirically;

$Y_{i,8}$ = $(\$999{,}000 + \$70{,}800X_i)$, from Eq. BC–4;

W_{row} = ratio of k lane highway ROW costs to those of an 8-lane highway, assumed to be proportional to total average right-of-way widths (see Table 61);

$\text{CRF}_{\infty,6\%}$ = 0.06.

Thus

$$SB_{\text{row}_i} = W_{\text{row}_i}(\$299.70X_i + \$21.27X_i^2).$$

(b) Bus Operation on 8-lane Mixed-traffic Highways

The portion of construction and right-of-way costs to be borne by bus passengers was determined in proportion to the amount of total 8-lane mixed-traffic highway capacity utilized by buses. In this analysis it was assumed that each highway lane can accommodate 1675 passenger cars an hour or 480 buses an hour (that is, each bus takes up the same amount of highway space as 3.49 automobiles).

Let

H_A = highway auto-lane capacity for a k lane highway (in automobiles per lane per hour);

$HA_{i,k}$ = capacity of ith route-mile of a k lane passenger car highway = $(H_A) \times (k)$ (in automobiles per hour);

H_B = highway bus-lane capacity for a k lane highway (in buses per lane per hour).

Since

R_i = number of bus round trips originating at ith line-haul station

and

$$2\left(R + R_i - \sum_{x=1}^{i} R_x\right) = \text{number of bus trips (in both directions) being made on } i\text{th route-mile of highway),}$$

therefore

(BC–9) $$\frac{(H_A/H_B)\,2\left(R + R_i - \sum_{x=1}^{i} R_x\right)}{(HA_{i,k})} = \text{portion of total } k \text{ lane mixed-traffic highway capacity utilized by buses}$$

$$= \frac{(1675/480)\,2\left(R + R_i - \sum_{x=1}^{i} R_x\right)}{(1675 \times 8)}, \text{ for an 8-lane highway,}$$

$$= \frac{\left(R + R_i - \sum_{x=1}^{i} R_x\right)}{1920}.$$

Both the construction and ROW costs of 8-lane mixed-traffic highways were allocated to buses by using Eq. (BC–9). Combining Eqs. (BC–9) and (BC–4), the latter of which provides construction costs for 8-lane mixed-traffic highways, and using a W_{c_i} value of 1.0 and a $\text{CRF}_{35,6\%}$ equal to 0.06897,

(BC–10)

$$SBE_{c_i} = \$35.90\left(R + R_i - \sum_{x=1}^{i} R_x\right) + \$2.54X_i\left(R + R_i - \sum_{x=1}^{i} R_x\right).$$

Using Eqs. (BC–9) and (BC–8), with W_{row_i} equal to 1.0:

(BC–11) $$SBE_{\text{row}_i} = \$0.156X_i\left(R + R_i - \sum_{x=1}^{i} R_x\right) + \$0.011X_i^2\left(R + R_i - \sum_{x=1}^{i} R_x\right).$$

(For some line-haul stations (or, i's), the value of R_i may be zero; this would be the case where the number of bus loops, q, is less than g.)

CBD Terminal Costs (Sp)

(BC–12) $$SB_p = \alpha(P) + \beta(N) + \gamma(S),$$

where

- P = total number of bus platforms needed for all incoming bus lanes at CBD terminal = $(R/70)^*$;
- N = number of incoming bus lanes = $(R/480)^*$;
- S = number of line-haul stations = g, for 1-mile station spacing;
- α = annual cost per bus platform; for a 45-degree angle, with each platform requiring 28 lineal feet of 140-foot-wide terminal area, with a capital cost of \$6850 per lineal foot of 50-foot-wide terminal, and with a 50-year-life and 6 per cent interest, the annual cost = $(28)(140/50)(\$6850)(\text{CRF}_{50,6\%})$ = \$34,100;
- β = annual cost per incoming bus lane, to include a \$1.5 million capital cost for ventilation, and an allowance for acceleration and deceleration tapers

(figured as equivalent to 7 extra lineal feet of 140-foot-wide terminal area), and including a 400-foot turnaround loop at a cost of \$1636 per foot, all amortized over 50 years; annual cost = $(\text{CRF}_{50,6\%})$(\$1,500,000 + 7 × 140/50 × \$6850 + 400 × \$1636) = \$145,200;

γ = annual cost per line-haul station; with a \$100,000 capital cost, a 50-year life and 6 per cent interest, annual cost = (\$100,000) × $(\text{CRF}_{50,6\%})$ = \$6344.

Thus

$$SB_p = \$34{,}100\left(\frac{R}{70}\right)^* + \$145{,}200\left(\frac{R}{480}\right)^* + \$6344(g).$$

Functional Relationships

Functional relationships for determining equipment, operation, and roadway requirements depend, of course, on the nature of the operation and service. Generally, we will consider the following types of operations:
nonstop, through express bus service between individual line-haul stations and downtown CBD terminal (that is, express service with no along-the-line service); through bus service between originating line-haul station and downtown CBD terminal, with multipickup (or discharge) line-haul stops but no along-the-line service (that is, multistop bus service with no along-the-line service); integrated through and along-the-line bus service between originating line-haul stations and downtown CBD terminal, with stops at all intermediate line-haul stations for pickup (or discharge) of downtown or along-the-line passengers (that is, integrated through and along-the-line bus service with *no* transfer); integrated through and along-the-line bus service whereby outer-loop buses provide along-the-line service only up to or out from the middle line-haul station, at which point along-the-line passengers moving to or from inner-loop line-haul stations must transfer (that is, integrated through and along-the-line bus service with transfer); and separate along-the-line bus service.

For all types of operations, the following relationships apply. (All cases assume 1-mile station spacing and a uniform distribution of passenger originations or terminations.)

(B–1) t_i = total round trip time for a bus moving between the ith line-haul station and the CBD terminal;

$t_i = 88f + 60.5(d_i - f_i) + 1.166p_i + 120$, in seconds,

where

d_i = round trip distance (in miles) = $2i$;

f_i = number of bus stops made on the round trip (including CBD terminal stop);

p_i = total number of passengers carried on a bus round trip.

(Equation (B–1) applies only for the particular bus performance specifications assumed and for 1-mile station spacing. Also, q is the number of separate bus runs or loops; at a maximum, q is equal to g.)

(B–2) $$r_i = \frac{3600}{t_i}.$$

(B–3) V_i = hourly passenger volume to or from the ith line-haul station

$$= \left(\frac{V}{g}\right).$$

(B–4) $$R = \sum_{j=1}^{q} R_j.$$

(B–5) $$U_j = \left(\frac{R_j}{r_j}\right)^*.$$

(B–6) $$U = \sum_{j=1}^{q} U_j.$$

(B–7) $$p = \left(\frac{V}{R}\right).$$

(B–8) $$M = 1020 \sum_{j=1}^{q} (R_j)(d_j).$$

(B–9) $$L = 2\sum_{i=1}^{g} \left(\frac{R + R_i - \sum_{x=1}^{i} R_x}{H_B}\right)^*,$$

where x is the number of the line-haul station.

(*a*) *Express Nonstop Service with No Along-the-Line Service*

For this type of operation, $j = i$, $q = g$, and $f = 2$.

(B–10a) $$R_i = \frac{V_i}{c}, \quad \text{if} \quad \left(\frac{V_i}{c}\right) \geq (h).$$

(B–10b) $$R_i = h, \quad \text{if} \quad \left(\frac{V_i}{c}\right) < (h).$$

(*b*) *Multistop Bus Service with No Along-the-Line Service*

For this type of operation, there would be q bus loop operations.

m_j = number of line-haul stations served by jth bus loop in major flow direction;

(B–11a) $$m_j = \left[\frac{(h) \times (c)}{(V_i)}\right]^*, \quad \text{for } j = 1, 2, \ldots, (q-1);$$

(B–11b) $m_q = g - (q - 1)(m_j)$, for the qth (or last) bus loop.

(B–12) $$q = \left(\frac{g}{m_j}\right)^*,$$

where q is the number of bus loops.

(B–13a) $f_j = m_j + 1$, for 1-directional service;

(B–13b) $f_j = 2m_j$, for 2-directional service.

(B–14) $$R_j = \left(\frac{m_j \times V_i}{c}\right)^*, \quad \text{or}$$

$R_j = h$, whichever is greater.

(B–15a) $i = (j)(m_j),$ for $j = 1, 2, \ldots, (q - 1);$

(B–15b) $i = (g),$ for $j = q.$

(*c*) *Integrated Through and Along-the-Line Bus Service with No Transfer*

Case 1

When $(V_i/c) \geq h,$

(B–16)
$$R_i = \frac{V_i}{c},$$
$$j = i,$$
$$q = g.$$

(B–17) $f_i = (i + 1),$ for 1-directional service,

$f_i = 2i,$ for 2-directional service.

Case 2

When $(V_i/c) < h$, there would be q bus loops.

(B–18)
$$m_j = \left[\frac{(h) \times (c)}{(V_i)}\right]^*, \quad \text{for} \quad j = 1, 2, \ldots, (q - 1);$$

$$m_q = g - (q - 1)m_j, \text{ for the } q\text{th bus loop.}$$

(B–19)
$$q = \left(\frac{g}{m_j}\right)^*.$$

(B–20) $f_j = (j)m_j + 1$, and $f_q = g + 1$, for 1-directional service;

$f_j = 2(j)m_j,$ and $f_q = 2g,$ for 2-directional service.

(B–21)
$$R_j = \left(\frac{m_j \times V_i}{c}\right)^*, \quad \text{or}$$

$$R_j = h, \text{ whichever is greater.}$$

B–22) $i = (j)(m_j),$ for $j = 1, 2, \ldots, (q - 1);$

$i = (g),$ for $j = q.$

(*d*) *Integrated Through and Along-the-Line Service with Transfer*

This type of service is an extension of that described in (c) above, though with more special circumstances and conditions. However, because of the lengthy details involved in setting up an analytical procedure, and the probability that with details such would be more complicated than revealing, the procedure will not be included.

(*e*) *Separate Along-the-Line Bus Service*

This type of operation would serve as a supplement to either type (a) or type (b) through bus service.

Thus for computing L, the highway lane requirements (see Eq. B–9), the values of R, R_i, and R_x should represent the combined totals for both the through and separate along-the-line bus operations.

(B–23) $f = g,$ for 1-directional service;

$f = 2(g - 1),$ for 2-directional service.

(B–24) $d = 2(g - 1)$, for either 1- or 2-directional service and for 1-mile station spacing.

(B–25) $$R = \left(\frac{V_{AMA}}{c}\right)^*, \quad \text{or}$$

$$R = h_A, \text{ whichever is greater,}$$

where

V_{AMA} = hourly along-the-line passenger volume in major flow direction;
h_A = minimum schedule frequency for along-the-line service.

(In this operation, R bus trips an hour are made between the first and last line-haul station.)

(B–26) $$p = \left(\frac{V_{AMA}}{R}\right).$$

(B–27) $$t = 88f + 60.5(d - f) + 1.166p + 120.$$

(B–28) $$U = \left(\frac{R}{r}\right)^* = \left(\frac{R \times t}{3600}\right)^*.$$

(B–29) $$M = 1020(d)(R).$$

Appendix C | Evaluation of Residential Service Costs under Different Hypothesized Conditions

NOTATION

V_i = volume of passengers originating at each line-haul station every peak hour; $V_i = V/g$, where V is hourly passenger volume for line-haul facility of g route-miles and 1-mile station spacing;

W = the hourly number of persons walking directly to a line-haul system station;

w = the maximum distance in blocks that any person must walk to reach a transit service stop;

p = hourly trip originations per residential block destined for the line-haul facility;

h = schedule frequency, or the number of buses per hour that pass each feeder bus stop within the residential area;

d = the average distance (in blocks) that a vehicle must travel to complete a trip in residential service; for transit and kiss-and-ride these distances are on a roundtrip basis, and for park-and-ride and integrated automobile they are the simple 1-way distances;

t = the vehicle time required (in seconds) to complete a trip of distance d;

f = the number of stops made by each vehicle on each trip;

c = the number of passengers carried by each vehicle on each trip;

AC/trip = average cost (in cents) per 1-way passenger trip for residential service.

BASIC RELATIONSHIPS FOR RESIDENTIAL COLLECTION MODES

(a) Separate Feeder Bus

$$d = \frac{V_i - W}{24p} + \frac{2w^2}{24} + 2w(f - 1) + 6;$$

$$t = 11.8d + 12(f + 1) + 1.166c + 120;$$

$$AC/\text{trip} = \frac{0.35t + 2.7d}{c}.$$

(*b*) *Integrated Bus*

$$d = \frac{V_i - W}{24p} + \frac{2w^2}{24} + 2w(f - 1) + 6;$$

$$t = 11.8d + 12(f + 1);$$

$$AC/\text{trip} = \frac{0.36t + 2.7d}{c}.$$

(*c*) *Park-and-ride Automobile*

$$d = \frac{V_i - W}{48p} + \frac{2w^2}{48} + 2.$$

$$AC/\text{trip} = \frac{35.3 + 0.84d}{c}.$$

(*d*) *Kiss-and-ride Automobile*

$$d = \frac{V_i - W}{24p} + \frac{2w^2}{24} + 6;$$

$$AC/\text{trip} = \frac{0.34d}{c}.$$

(*e*) *Integrated Automobile*

$$d = \frac{V_i - W}{48p} + \frac{2w^2}{48} + 2;$$

$$AC/\text{trip} = \frac{0.67d}{c}.$$

Specific Residential Collection Cases

Case No. 1 Mode: Separate feeder bus
Basic data: $w = 2, p = 1, h = 6, f = 37, c = 49.$

V_i	W	d	t	AC/trip (cents)
333	50	158	2498	26.6
1000	200	179	2746	29.5
3000	300	258	3678	40.5
5000	500	334	4575	51.1

Basic equations:

$$d = \frac{V_i - W}{24} + 146.4,$$

$$t = 11.8d + 634,$$

$$AC/\text{trip} = \frac{0.35t + 2.7d}{49}.$$

Case No. 2 Mode: Separate feeder bus
Basic Data: $w = 2, p = 2, h = 6, f = 18, c = 48.$

V_i	W	d	t	AC/trip (cents)
333	50	81	1370	10.4
1000	200	92	1500	16.1
3000	300	131	1960	21.7
5000	500	169	2409	27.1

Basic equations: $$d = \frac{V_i - W}{48} + 74.4,$$

$$t = 11.8d + 414,$$

$$AC/\text{trip} = \frac{0.35t + 2.7d}{48}.$$

Case No. 3 Mode: Separate feeder bus
Basic data: $w = 2, p = 5, h = 6, f = 7, c = 47.$

V_i	W	d	t	AC/trip (cents)
333	50	31	637	6.5
1000	200	37	708	7.4
3000	300	53	896	9.7
5000	500	68	1073	11.9

Basic equations: $$d = \frac{V_i - W}{120} + 30.4,$$

$$t = 11.8d + 271,$$

$$AC/\text{trip} = \frac{0.35t + 2.7d}{47}.$$

Case No. 4 Mode: Separate feeder bus
Basic data: $w = 2, p = 10, h = 6, f = 3, c = 40.$

V_i	W	d	t	AC/trip (cents)
333	50	16	403.8	4.6
1000	200	18	427.4	5.0
3000	300	26	521.8	6.3
5000	500	33	604.4	7.5

Basic equations: $$d = \frac{V_i - W}{240} + 14.4,$$

$$t = 11.8d + 215,$$

$$AC/\text{trip} = \frac{0.35t + 2.7d}{40}.$$

Case No. 5 Mode: Separate feeder bus
Basic Data: $w = 2, p = 12, h = 6, f = 3, c = 48.$

V_i	W	d	t	AC/trip (cents)
333	50	16.5	419	4.0
1000	200	17	425	4.1
3000	300	24	507	5.0
5000	500	30	578	5.9

Basic equations:
$$d = \frac{V_i - W}{288} + 14.4,$$
$$t = 11.8d + 224,$$
$$AC/\text{trip} = \frac{0.35t + 2.7d}{48}.$$

Case No. 6 Mode: Separate feeder bus
Basic data: $w = 2, p = 37.5, h = 6, f = 1.0, c = 50.$

V_i	W	d	t	AC/trip (cents)
333	50	6.7	281	2.3
1000	200	7.3	288	2.4
3000	300	9.4	313	2.7
5000	500	11.4	336	3.0

Basic equations:
$$d = \frac{V_i - W}{895} + 6.4,$$
$$t = 11.8d + 202,$$
$$AC/\text{trip} = \frac{0.35t + 2.7d}{50}.$$

Case No. 7 Mode: Separate feeder bus
Basic data: $w = 3, p = 1, h = 6, f = 16, c = 48.$

V_i	W	d	t	AC/trip (cents)
333	50	109	1666	18.3
1000	200	130	1914	21.3
3000	300	210	2858	32.7
5000	500	285	3743.0	43.3

Basic equations:
$$d = \frac{V_i - W}{24} + 97,$$
$$t = 11.8d + 380,$$
$$AC/\text{trip} = \frac{0.35t + 2.7d}{48}.$$

Case No. 8 Mode: Separate feeder bus
Basic data: $w = 3, p = 2, h = 6, f = 8, c = 48.$

V_i	W	d	t	AC/trip (cents)
333	50	55	933.0	9.9
1000	200	66	1062.8	11.5
3000	300	105	1523.0	17.0
5000	500	143	1971.4	22.4

Basic equations:
$$d = \frac{V_i - W}{48} + 48.4,$$
$$t = 11.8d + 284,$$
$$AC/\text{trip} = \frac{0.35t + 2.7d}{48}.$$

Case No. 9 Mode: Separate feeder bus
Basic data: $w = 4, p = 1, h = 6, f = 9, c = 48.$

V_i	W	d	t	AC/trip (cents)
333	50	83	1275	14.0
1000	200	105	1535	17.1
3000	300	184	2467	28.3
5000	500	259	3352	39.0

Basic equations:
$$d = \frac{V_i - W}{24} + 71.4;$$
$$t = 11.8d + 296;$$
$$AC/\text{trip} = \frac{0.35t + 2.7d}{48}.$$

Case No. 10 Mode: Separate feeder bus
Basic data: $w = 4, p = 1, h = 4, f = 6, c = 48.$

V_i	W	d	t	AC/trip (cents)
333	50	59	956	10.3
1000	200	81	1216	13.4
3000	300	160	2148	24.7
5000	500	235	3033	35.3

Basic equations:
$$d = \frac{V_i - W}{24} + 47.4;$$
$$t = 11.8d + 260;$$
$$AC/\text{trip} = \frac{0.35t + 2.7d}{48}.$$

Case No. 11 Mode: Integrated bus
Basic data: $w = 2, p = 1, h = 6, f = 37, c = 49.$

V_i	W	d	t	AC/trip (cents)
333	50	162	2350	27
1000	200	183	2614	30
3000	300	262	3534	41
5000	500	338	4430	52

Basic equations:

$$d = \frac{V_i - W}{24} + 150.3,$$

$$t = 11.8d + 444,$$

$$AC/\text{trip} = \frac{0.36t + 2.7d}{49}.$$

Case No. 12 Mode: Integrated bus
Basic data: $w = 2, p = 2, h = 6, f = 18, c = 48.$

V_i	W	d	t	AC/trip (cents)
333	50	81	1172	13
1000	200	92	1302	15
3000	300	131	1762	21
5000	500	169	2210	26

Basic equations:

$$d = \frac{V_i - W}{48} + 74.4,$$

$$t = 11.8d + 216,$$

$$AC/\text{trip} = \frac{0.36t + 2.7d}{48}.$$

Case No. 13 Mode: Integrated bus
Basic data: $w = 2, p = 5, h = 6, f = 7, c = 47.$

V_i	W	d	t	AC/trip (cents)
333	50	34	485	6
1000	200	39	544	6
3000	300	54	721	9
5000	500	68	886	11

Basic equations:

$$d = \frac{V_i - W}{240} + 14.4,$$

$$t = 11.8d + 84,$$

$$AC/\text{trip} = \frac{0.36t + 2.7d}{47}.$$

Case No. 14 Mode: Integrated bus
Basic data: $w = 2, p = 10, h = 6, f = 3, c = 40$.

V_i	W	d	t	AC/trip (cents)
333	50	16	225	3
1000	200	18	248	3
3000	300	26	343	5
5000	500	33	425	6

Basic equations:

$$d = \frac{V_i - W}{120} + 30.4,$$

$$t = 11.8d + 36,$$

$$AC/\text{trip} = \frac{0.36t + 2.7d}{40}.$$

Case No. 15 Mode: Integrated bus
Basic data: $w = 3, p = 1, h = 6, f = 16, c = 48$.

V_i	W	d	t	AC/trip (cents)
333	50	109	1478	17
1000	200	130	1726	20
3000	300	210	2670	32
5000	500	285	3555	43

Basic equations:

$$d = \frac{V_i - W}{24} + 97,$$

$$t = 11.8d + 192,$$

$$AC/\text{trip} = \frac{0.36t + 2.7d}{48}.$$

Case No. 16 Mode: Integrated bus
Basic data: $w = 3, p = 2, h = 6, f = 8, c = 48$.

V_i	W	d	t	AC/trip (cents)
333	50	55	745	9
1000	200	66	875	10
3000	300	105	1335	16
5000	500	143	1783	21

Basic equations:

$$d = \frac{V_i - W}{48} + 48.4,$$

$$t = 11.8d + 96,$$

$$AC/\text{trip} = \frac{0.36t + 2.7d}{48}.$$

Case No. 17 Mode: Park-and-ride automobile
Basic data: $w = 2, p = 1, c = 1.1.$

V_i	W	d	AC/trip (cents)
333	50	9	38
1000	200	20	47
3000	300	59	76
5000	500	97	105

Basic equations: $$d = \frac{V_i - W}{48} + 2.2,$$

$$AC/\text{trip} = \frac{35.3 + 0.84d}{1.1}$$

Case No. 18 Mode: Park-and-ride automobile
Basic data: $w = 2, p = 2, c = 1.1.$

V_i	W	d	AC/trip (cents)
333	50	6	36
1000	200	11	40
3000	300	31	55
5000	500	50	69

Basic equations: $$d = \frac{V_i - W}{96} + 2.2,$$

$$AC/\text{trip} = \frac{35.3 + 0.84d}{1.1}.$$

Case No. 19 Mode: Park-and-ride automobile
Basic data: $w = 2, p = 5, c = 1.1$

V_i	W	d	AC/trip (cents)
333	50	4	35
1000	200	66	36
3000	300	15	42
5000	500	22	48

Basic equations: $$d = \frac{V_i - W}{240} + 2.2,$$

$$AC/\text{trip} = \frac{35.3 + 0.84d}{1.1}.$$

Case No. 20 Mode: Park-and-ride automobile
Basic data: $w = 2, p = 10, c = 1.1.$

V_i	W	d	AC/trip (cents)
333	50	4	34
1000	200	5	35
3000	300	9	38
5000	500	13	41

Basic equations: $$d = \frac{V_i - W}{480} + 2.2,$$

$$AC/\text{trip} = \frac{35.3 + 0.84d}{1.1}.$$

Case No. 21 Mode: Kiss-and-ride automobile
Basic data: $w = 2, p = 1, c = 1.0.$

V_i	W	d	AC/trip (cents)
333	50	18	6
1000	200	40	14
3000	300	119	40
5000	500	194	66

Basic equations: $$d = \frac{V_i - W}{24} + 6.4,$$

$$AC/\text{trip} = 0.34d.$$

Case No. 22 Mode: Kiss-and-ride automobile
Basic data: $w = 2, p = 2, c = 1.0.$

V_i	W	d	AC/trip (cents)
333	50	12	4
1000	200	23	8
3000	300	63	21
5000	500	100	34

Basic equations: $$d = \frac{V_i - W}{48} + 6.4,$$

$$AC/\text{trip} = 0.34d.$$

Case No. 23 Mode: Kiss-and-ride automobile
Basic data: $w = 2, p = 5, c = 1.0.$

V_i	W	d	AC/trip (cents)
333	50	9	3
1000	200	13	4
3000	300	29	10
5000	500	44	15

Basic equations: $$d = \frac{V_i - W}{120} + 6.4,$$

$$AC/\text{trip} = 0.34d.$$

Case No. 24 Mode: Kiss-and-ride automobile
Basic data: $w = 2, p = 10, c = 1.0.$

V_i	W	d	AC/trip (cents)
333	50	8	3
1000	200	10	3
3000	300	18	6
5000	500	25	8

Basic equations: $$d = \frac{V_i - W}{240} + 6.4,$$

$$AC/\text{trip} = 0.34d.$$

Case No. 25 Mode: Integrated automobile
Basic data: $w = 2, p = 1, c = 1.6.$

V_i	W	d	AC/trip (cents)
333	50	9	3.8
1000	200	20	8.4
3000	300	59	24.7
5000	500	96	40.1

Basic equations: $$d = \frac{V_i - W}{48} + 2.2,$$

$$AC/\text{trip} = \frac{0.67d}{1.6}.$$

Case No. 26 Mode: Integrated automobile
Basic data: $w = 2, p = 2, c = 1.6.$

V_i	W	d	AC/trip (cents)
333	50	5	2
1000	200	10	4
3000	300	30	13
5000	500	49	20

Basic equations: $$d = \frac{V_i - W}{96} + 2.2,$$

$$AC/\text{trip} = \frac{0.67d}{1.6}.$$

Case No. 27 Mode: Integrated automobile
Basic Data: $w = 2, p = 5, c = 1.6.$

V_i	W	d	AC/trip (cents)
333	50	3	1
1000	200	5	2
3000	300	14	6
5000	500	21	9

Basic equations: $$d = \frac{V_i - W}{240} + 2.2,$$

$$AC/\text{trip} = \frac{0.67d}{1.6}.$$

Case No. 28 Mode: Integrated automobile
Basic data: $w = 2, p = 10, c = 1.6.$

V_i	W	d	AC/trip (cents)
333	50	3	1
1000	200	4	2
3000	300	8	3
5000	500	12	5

Basic equations: $$d = \frac{V_i - W}{480} + 2.2$$

$$AC/\text{trip} = \frac{0.67d}{1.6}.$$

Index

Selected RAND Books

Bagdikian, Ben, *The Information Machines: Their Impact on Men and the Media,* New York, Harper & Row, 1971.

Bretz, Rudy, *A Taxonomy of Communication Media,* Englewood Cliffs, N.J., Educational Technology Publications, 1971.

Dorfman, Robert, Paul A. Samuelson, and Robert M. Solow, *Linear Programming and Economic Analysis,* New York, McGraw-Hill Book Company, Inc., 1958.

Downs, Anthony, *Inside Bureaucracy,* Boston, Mass., Little, Brown and Company, 1967.

Fisher, Gene H., *Cost Considerations in Systems Analysis,* New York, American Elsevier Publishing Company, 1971.

Fishman, George S., *Spectral Methods in Econometrics,* Cambridge, Mass., Harvard University Press, 1969.

Harman, Alvin, *The International Computer Industry: Innovation and Comparative Advantage,* Cambridge, Mass., Harvard University Press, 1971.

Hirshleifer, Jack, James C. DeHaven, and Jerome W. Milliman, *Water Supply: Economics, Technology, and Policy,* Chicago, The University of Chicago Press, 1960.

Hitch, Charles J., and Roland McKean, *The Economics of Defense in the Nuclear Age,* Cambridge, Mass., Harvard University Press, 1960.

Johnson, William A., *The Steel Industry of India,* Cambridge, Mass., Harvard University Press, 1966.

Johnstone, William C., *Burma's Foreign Policy: A Study in Neutralism,* Cambridge, Mass., Harvard University Press, 1963.

Langer, Paul, and Joseph J. Zasloff, *North Vietnam and the Pathet Lao: Partners in the Struggle for Laos,* Cambridge, Mass., Harvard University Press, 1970.

McKean, Roland N., *Efficiency in Government Through Systems Analysis: With Emphasis on Water Resource Development,* New York, John Wiley & Sons, Inc., 1958.

Novick, David (ed.), *Program Budgeting: Program Analysis and the Federal Budget,* Cambridge, Mass., Harvard University Press, 1965.

Pascal, Anthony, *Thinking About Cities: New Perspectives on Urban Problems,* Belmont, Calif., Dickenson Publishing Company, 1970.

Phillips, Almarin, *Technology and Market Structure: A Study of the Aircraft Industry,* Lexington, Mass., D. C. Heath & Company, 1971.

Quade, Edward S. (ed.), *Analysis for Military Decisions,* Chicago, Rand McNally & Company; Amsterdam, North-Holland Publishing Company, 1964.

Quade, Edward S., and Wayne I. Boucher, *Systems Analysis and Policy Planning: Applications in Defense,* New York, American Elsevier Publishing Company, 1968.

Sharpe, William F., *The Economics of Computers,* New York, Columbia University Press, 1969.

Williams, John D., *The Compleat Strategyst: Being a Primer on the Theory of Games of Strategy,* New York, McGraw-Hill Book Company, Inc., 1954.

Wolfe, Thomas, *Soviet Strategy at the Crossroads,* Cambridge, Mass., Harvard University Press, 1964.